MOST COMMON BOAT MAINTENANCE PROBLEMS

Bob Whittier

ARCO PUBLISHING, INC.
NEW YORK

To my wife Helen, in appreciation for over a quarter of a century of help with typing, telephoning, errand-running and all the other chores that go into writing articles and books.

Published by Arco Publishing, Inc.
219 Park Avenue South, New York, N.Y. 10003

Copyright © 1981 by Robert J. Whittier

Library of Congress Cataloging in Publication Data

Whittier, Robert J   1922–
    Most common boat maintenance problems.

    Includes index.
    1. Boats and boating—Maintenance and repair.
I. Title
VM322.W46   623.8′208   80-27408

ISBN 0-668-04877-8

Printed in the United States of America

Contents

Introduction

Over the years, numerous books on boat maintenance have been published. Some have been excellent, others were superficial, a few have been full of misinformation. Some of the good ones are still in print but others, including some that contained information of great value to anyone doing certain types of boat work, are out of print.

This book was written to try to give boat owners a volume that will be of real help on a usefully wide range of maintenance problems. We do not presume to call it a "complete" book on the subject. Boats are made in so many types and sizes of so many materials that a truly complete text on the subject would amount to a multi-volume work selling for a formidable price.

We adopted the question-and-answer format because it makes for easy and interesting reading. You can skim pages and look for headings on subjects of direct interest when actually working on a boat. There is no need to plod through pages of text hoping to stumble on pertinent information. And also, it was a good way to cover the subject. We've been writing about boats and boating since the 1940s and over the years have received letters from thousands of boat owners seeking information. The questions we have chosen to answer in this book are the ones most commonly asked about a wide range of boat problems.

On the one hand, you can make your way through this book by reading a few of the questions at a time in odd moments. On the other hand, you can read page after page without falling asleep! If you read this book carefully you will emerge from it with a very broad and practical insight on the nuts-and-bolts of boat maintenance and within a short time find yourself saving substantial amounts of time and money!

One of the things we have learned in all our years of working on boats is that the waterfront abounds with people who will leap at an opportunity to show others how much they know about boats. Sadly, much of what they say is just so much misinformation. And we have found that people behind counters in marine stores are not always the reliable sources of information they're supposed to be. After all, they were hired to mind the counter, and few have actually used all the products they sell! Here and there in this book we have been quite frank about problems that arise in getting needed supplies and information. Some public relations people might not care for this. So be it. Our view is that a boat owner who "knows the score" is in a better position to ferret out hard-to-get parts, materials and information. And that puts you that much closer to solving your problem and getting back to enjoying your boat!

Another thing we have learned from reader mail is that a large number of people who live far from boating centers find themselves adrift when it comes to coping with maintenance problems—they simply have no place to go for help. And the rising cost of gasoline is becoming a problem even for those who live relatively close to boating centers, for it is possible to fritter away gallons of gas touring boatyards in search of specific items or knowledge. If that's your problem, this book should help.

We wish to point out that boat maintenance is not a static subject. Materials, tools and methods change as time passes. Firms and their products appear and disappear from the marketplace. Different manufacturers and boatyards develop different ways of doing things. So we would like to make a few points:

If our way of doing a certain job differs from the way your local boatyard would do it, remember there are usually more ways than one of doing a job.

We have found from reader mail that people today often want pat answers to questions. Around boats, there are no pat answers to many things! One has to learn to be flexible and to use one's horse sense and ingenuity.

A major problem in many maintenance jobs is locating obscure parts and special information. In this book we have taken something of a chance by printing the names and addresses of sources for many items. This information was as up-to-date as we could make it when this book was being produced in 1980. If you read this book some time after that year, you will have to assume that not all firms named will still be in business. For this reason, we have gone into some detail about how to trace companies that have moved about.

Because wooden boats are becoming a steadily smaller percentage of the total number in the pleasure boating fleet, we have not gone into vast detail on the subject. We have told enough to give a fair idea of what it's all about, and where to go for more detailed information.

To keep the size and price of this book within reason we have not gone into engines and electrical systems. There are a number of books now in print on these subjects and as you read through our book you will learn how to locate them. We would appreciate suggestions for changes and additions to a second edition of this book, should one be printed.

Bob Whittier

Chapter 1

Locating Parts and Information

Locating a Manufacturer

Q. I need parts and service information for my boat. There are no dealers for this make in my locality. Using the names of the state and city printed on the boat's nameplate, I wrote to the manufacturer and my letter was returned stamped "Addressee Unknown." How can I locate the company?

A. There are various ways. First try an annual publication called *Boat Owners Buyers Guide*. It is on sale at many large marine stores, or you can order it from the publisher. Write to *Boat Owners Buyers Guide*, c/o Ziff-Davis Publishing Company, One Park Avenue, New York, N.Y. 10016, and ask the price of the current issue. It lists most companies currently active in the pleasure-boating field, covering boats, motors, and all kinds of equipment and accessories. A new addition to the field of marine directories is *The Directory for Motorboats, Accessories and Fishing Tackle*, published by Salt Water Sportsman, 10 High St., Boston, Mass. 02110.

Or, you can visit local marine dealers and ask to see the annual directory issues put out by marine trade publications. *The Boating Industry* magazine publishes an annual called *Marine Buyers Guide Issue* and *Boat and Motor Dealer* publishes an annual *Market Manual*.

The above mentioned three directories list currently active firms. But sometimes a company fails to get itself listed for some reason such as failing to fill out and mail back an annual confirmation card. Smaller companies are sometimes not listed because they never took the initiative to tell the publishers about their existence.

If none of these directories lists the firm you seek, it is possible they have either gone out of business, changed their name, merged with another firm, or switched to manufacturing non-marine items. At most medium-sized and large public libraries you can consult a multi-volume directory called *Thomas' Register of American Manufacturers*. It lists all known manufacturing companies in all fields. There are other business directories, too. The libraries in technical

Many catalogs and directories are available to help the boat owner locate needed maintenance items. Your local marine dealers probably have some of them in their offices.

colleges and the design offices of manufacturing companies in your area are likely to have *Thomas' Register*.

Many libraries have telephone directories from prominent cities in other states, so ask for and look into these. If you are fairly sure of the name of the company you seek and of the state and community in which it is located, try dialing Information.

If the above methods fail, write to the Department of Corporations at the pertinent state capital and ask if they have any information on the status of the firm.

If you suspect the company you seek is out of business but you urgently want information about the boats they made, ask your librarian to look in reference books and get the name and address of a newspaper that covers the area where the factory was located. Write a letter to the paper, asking any former employees of the company who might have information to contact you, and ask the paper to print it in their reader-letters column.

Parts for Imported Boats

Q. I own a European-built boat and need to replace several items of marine hardware on it. I do not have the manufacturer's address. How can I contact them?

A. Send $1.00 to the United States Chamber of Commerce, 1615 H St., N.W., Washington, D.C. 20006 and ask for a copy of their booklet, *Guide to Foreign Information Sources*. It lists embassies, consulates, information offices, and trade commissions maintained in the U.S. by foreign countries. Write to the most appropriate-sounding office for the country of origin of your boat, and ask them to help you. They might find the company listed in their reference library. Failing that, they can contact their home office. Or they may be able to supply you with leads, such as the name and address of the pleasure boating trade association in their country, or perhaps the names and addresses of boating magazines to which you can write.

A word of advice. It is sometimes frustrating to deal with overseas firms. In some countries, formal customs and traditions govern business transactions to an extent that easygoing Americans can find baffling. If you have not been properly introduced by a mutual acquaintance, some foreign businessmen will remain cold and aloof. Some governments force manufacturers to export to the U.S. to earn dollars, and while companies obey by shipping completed boats, motors, and equipment to the U.S., they have little incentive or interest when it comes to supporting these goods with parts and service. An unbelievable amount of red tape can be involved in exporting small orders of spare parts, so some firms find they simply cannot afford to reply to individuals who write asking for a few small spare parts. Others will refer one's inquiry to their export agents, where it may be pigeonholed by some clerk with an anti-American grudge. If

you run into problems in getting cooperation, try writing to the office of the U.S. Chamber of Commerce in the capital city of the country concerned.

Sometimes American businessmen attend foreign trade fairs looking for products to import. When they see something they think they can sell, they sign up as importers. Then, if their hopes fail to materialize, they drop the product and go in search of something else to import. So a fair number of imported boats, motors, and accessories become what the trade calls "orphans." It can take some diligence and initiative to get parts!

Locating an Owner's Manual

Q. Where can I get an owner's manual for my old cabin cruiser?

A. There is no company we know of that specializes in reprinting and selling old marine service manuals. In many cases, especially in the case of older wooden boats and low-volume metal and fiberglass ones, the manufacturers never had any manuals at all. They assumed the long-established boatyards that acted as their dealers would have people on their staffs who could answer all maintenance questions likely to arise. When only a few dozen or a hundred or so of a particular model of a boat were manufactured, the cost per copy of writing and printing a good manual would have been prohibitive. Many "manuals" were simply ten or a dozen mimeographed pages bound in a theme binder; these soon fell apart or got lost.

If you urgently need a manual, the best thing to do is make use of reader-letter columns in various boating publications and hope to make contact with someone who has the one you need. Answers to most maintenance questions can be had by digging into the several good books now in print on boat and engine maintenance. The principles that apply to one craft apply fairly well to another of the same material.

Where to Find Boat Maintenance Books

Q. Is there a bookstore anywhere that carries all the boating books currently in print?

A. None that stocks absolutely everything—one reason being that a lot of book publishers don't know where and how to sell books to the boating trade. But there's one place that has most of the available books. Write to International Marine Publishers, 21 Elm St., Camden, Maine 04843 and ask for their current catalog. The Seaport Store at Mystic Seaport Museum, Mystic, Conn. 06355 has a large bookstore. They have no complete catalog, but write and describe what you need—they may have something appropriate.

Finding Hardware for Old Boats

Q. I need several hinges, some deck hardware, and portlights for my older sloop. The builder has been out of business for many years. Do you know if anyone bought out the factory's stock of hardware when it closed?

A. Most older boats and low-volume production craft used stock marine hardware manufactured by old-line firms such as Wilcox-Crittenden, Perko, and a few others. These firms and others who have entered the boat business still offer more or less standardized hardware of traditional pattern, especially in the field of chocks, cleats, eyebolts, turnbuckles, hinges, brackets, locks and door bolts, etc. Your chances of finding matching replacements are good if you study current marine hardware catalogs.

The previously mentioned directory, *Boat Owners Buyers Guide*, lists firms in the mail order marine hardware business. You should get current catalogs (they cost $1.00 to $2.00 each) of firms such as Wilcox, Perko, Manhattan Marine & Electric, E&B, Defender Industries, James Bliss & Co., Crook & Crook, Mail Order Marine, Goldberg's, etc. With these catalogs you can find practically any hardware item.

Manufacturer Won't Answer Letters

Q. I have written three times to the maker of my boat asking for maintenance information and have not received a reply. The fact that my letters have not come back stamped "Undeliverable" shows they received my messages. What kind of way to run a business is this?

A. Welcome to the club! Each year we write to many companies for information and material needed in our own work. Out of every 100 letters sent out, we receive replies to only about fifty. And out of the replies we do get, only a few are really adequate and helpful—most are brusque or inept. We know many others who have had the same experience.

There are various explanations for this sad state of affairs. Very large companies sell to millions of customers and they cannot possibly cope by mail with all the service problems that arise. This is the responsibility of the dealer—to represent the manufacturer at the local level and deal directly with customers' needs. Unfortunately, a considerable number of dealerships are not very well managed and fail to follow up when a letter from a customer in their area is forwarded to them for action. In fairness to the dealer, it has to be acknowledged that boating is a very seasonal business. There are times when they are overworked, and it can be hard to find and hold capable employees in a seasonal business.

Another reason why manufacturers don't always reply expeditiously to letters is this. TV came onto the scene in the late 1940s and now the first generation of kids to grow up glued to the boob tube is showing up in management

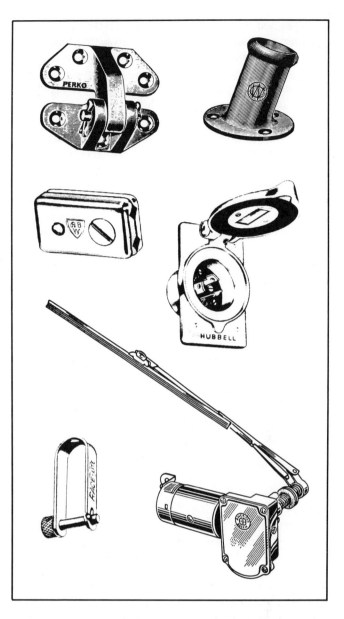

Inspect hardware for telltale trademarks when searching for parts. "PERKO" stamped on hinge, top left, identifies a product of Perko, Inc., well-known marine hardware firm. Superimposed initials "W" and "C" on flagpole socket, upper right, is trademark of another well-known firm, Wilcox-Crittenden. Initials "ABW" on tiller rope clamp, center left, stand for Attwood Brass Works, now called Attwood Corp. "Hubbell" on power line socket at center right shows this part was made by Harvey Hubbell, Inc., a specialist in marine wiring items. "RACE LITE" on sailboat shackle, lower left, shows it was made by Racelight South Coast, a sailboat hardware specialist. Initials "AB" on cover plate of windshield wiper stand for American Bosch, a prominent marine and automotive electrical equipment company. With a little detective work you can locate sources of supply. Always remember companies can change or modify their names with passage of time.

positions. These younger executives are the ones about whom "Why Can't Johnny Read?" articles are written. Their functional illiteracy shows up in their inept handling of company correspondence.

5

Also, the consumerism movement has manufacturers worried sick over the possibility of lawsuits and bureaucratic intervention. They are often extremely cautious about answering complaining letters, suspecting that some of them may be from people seeking damaging admissions through the mail.

When one actually visits them, some well-known firms in the marine business turn out to be surprisingly small organizations. They are understaffed and poorly set up to handle correspondence, while letters to large firms sometimes get passed from desk to desk and end up pigeonholed.

The best thing to do when a company does not reply to your letters is to address your next communication to a specific person or department. Then the recipient cannot so easily evade responsibility by passing your letter along to someone else. Don't hesitate to write directly to the President or General Manager. If possible enclose copies of your earlier letters and the unsatisfactory replies they brought. That usually gets fast results.

You can also try telephoning the firm. The person taking your call cannot as readily brush you off as he or she can pass your letter along to someone else. Speak calmly and reasonably, and identify yourself as the owner of one of their products by mentioning the model and serial number at the outset. Regardless of your feelings about a malfunctioning product, if you sound belligerent or abusive on the phone, you will put the person taking your call on the defensive and a satisfactory solution to your problem will be harder to achieve. Playing it polite and reasonable often produces surprisingly effective results.

Can't Find a Certain Product

Q. I am building a boat and the plans call for the use of Kuhls cements and compounds. Several marine stores in my area say they don't have it, some never even heard of it. How can I contact Kuhls?

A. The firm has been out of business for several years. Some publishers reprint old plans from time to time, as certain types of boats don't go out of style. And some boating books now in circulation have been around for a long time. Try to ascertain the original date of publication before accepting as valid and current everything you find in print!

To locate modern equivalents of various Kuhls products, obtain product lists and descriptions put out by prominent marine paint and sealant manufacturers. You can get their names and addresses in the *Boat Owners Buyers Guide* previously mentioned.

Can't Find Dynel Cloth

Q. I have plans for a boat that recommend the use of

"Dynel" cloth in place of glass fabric for sheathing the craft. Local marine stores never heard of it. Help!

A. When it was originally introduced by the Union Carbide company, the firm promoted it vigorously and received a lot of publicity. Boating literature that carries mention of Dynel is still in circulation, so people keep going in search of it. But some years ago the company decided to turn its energies and facilities to other pursuits and dropped "Dynel." Today, other firms make similar polypropylene cloths. One marine supply house that keeps abreast of new products in the fabrics and coatings fields is Defender Industries, Inc., 255 Main St., New Rochelle, N.Y. 10801. They list this and other fabrics in their annual catalog, which costs $1.00 as of this writing.

Military Surplus Parts

Q. I have a compass that I bought from a military surplus store. It is in good condition but I need a few small parts and a service manual for it. Where can I get them?

A. You're going to have problems! When the armed forces buy new equipment, they order spare parts along with it. Combat equipment tends to be distributed to a great many field stations, but spare parts tend to be held at supply and repair depots. When it is declared surplus and sold at auction, it is rare for a bidder to get both the basic equipment and the main stock of repair parts. One reason military surplus equipment sells for low prices is because vendors know that parts and service will be hard to get. If markings and labels indicate your compass was made by a prominent firm still in business, you might write to them. But don't count on getting parts easily, because the company probably sold all the spares to the military and kept nothing for civilian sales. Look for compass repair shops in the *Boat Owners Buyers Guide*—they just might have parts, or can make them if yours is a good, popular compass that is used by many boat owners. Visit military surplus stores, ask to see the trade publications they receive that carry announcements of surplus sales, advertisements by specialists in surplus gear, etc., in hopes of finding some source of parts.

Finding a Boat's Designer

Q. I have a fine yacht built in the 1950s and would like to get in touch with the man that designed it. Can you help?

A. The *Boat Owners Buyers Guide* contains a list of currently active naval architects. A "naval architect" is a person who designs boats—it's an old and tradition-honored term. If you don't find your boat's designer listed there, he may either be deceased or may have sold his business to another party who changed the company name. If you have information that leads you to believe he lived in a certain part of the country, you can write to designers in that area who are listed in *B.O.B.G.* and ask them if they know where your party can be reached. Naval architecture is a small field in which "everybody knows everybody," and you should have good luck.

If the designer used the initials "S.N.A.M.E." after his name on the plans, he was (and may still be) a member of the Society of Naval Architects and Marine Engineers. Write to them at One World Trade Center, Suite 1369, New York, N.Y. 10048. If he used the initials "S.S.C.D." he was a member of the defunct Society of Small Craft Designers. That group was associated with the Westlawn School of Yacht Design which is still active and can be reached at 733 Summer Street, Stamford, Conn. 06904. The people there are well informed on "who is who" in pleasure craft design and might have a line on your designer.

Getting Your Boat Appraised

Q. We have a boat that has been exceptionally well cared for. Now we wish to sell it. How can we determine its fair and proper market value?

A. If it is a name-brand boat, it may be listed in a marine trade publication called *Used Boat Price Guide*. Updated editions are published at intervals by BUC International Corporation, 1881 Northeast 26th St., Suite 95, Fort Lauderdale, Fla. 33305. Marine dealers in your area probably have copies. Individuals can purchase copies directly from BUC, but be prepared for a fairly high price since it is a 750 page volume. Small-boat dealers make use of "Blue Books" containing outboard motor and trailer prices, published by Abos Marine Division, Technical Publications, 1014 Wyandotte, Kansas City, Mo. 64105.

If you want a more formal, personalized appraisal, contact a marine surveyor. Such a person "surveys" boats and appraises both their condition and value. Like naval architect, marine surveyor is an old and tradition-honored term. If you live near a major yachting port, you may find surveyors listed under "Surveyors, Marine" in the Yellow Pages. Many naval architects do surveying as well as designing, so look also under "Architects, Naval." Marinas and boatyards can tell you about surveyors active in their areas. If you still can't find one, write to the National Association of Marine Surveyors, 86 Windsor Gate Drive, North Hills, N.Y. 11040 and ask for a list of surveyors in your area. Before telling a surveyor to go ahead, make sure you both understand what is to be done and what the fee will be. When either buying or selling a boat worth a substantial sum of money, having a survey done is well worth the cost.

There is an English book by Ian Nicholson called *Surveying Small Craft*, available from International Marine Publishers, 21 Elm St., Camden, Maine 04843. A new American book is *Fiberglass Boat Survey Manual* by Arthur Edmunds, published by John de Graff, Inc. and distributed by David McKay Company, Inc., 2 Park Ave., New York, N.Y. 10016. You can order it from McKay or International Marine, or you can have your local book shop order a copy. Its identification number is ISBN 0-8286-0083-X.

Wants to Donate Boat

Q. I have a powerboat that I wish to donate to the Sea Explorers and claim an income tax deduction for the gift. How can I establish its value to the satisfaction of the IRS?

A. Have a marine surveyor appraise it and give you a letter stating his expert opinion of its market value.

Identifying Marine Hardware

Q. I have a navigation light with no identification on it other than the name "Dietz" molded into the lenses. People at the boatyard never heard of this company and cannot find it listed in any of their trade guides. Can you help?

A. It is likely that the metalworking company that made the navigation light had the lenses made for them by a glass

When parts for older marine equipment can't be bought locally, some detective work may be in order. (Permatex Company, Inc.)

company named Dietz. Most manufactured products are assembled using many components purchased from outside suppliers. If you wanted to spend the time, you could look up the Dietz company by methods suggested in other parts of this chapter, and ask them what marine hardware companies they supply lenses to. Sometimes it helps to use a little of Sherlock Holmes' brand of observant and imaginative detective work to track down manufacturers. We have seen "Dietz" kerosene lanterns in hardware stores—this might be the company you want! Ask your hardware store to look them up in the directory issue of *Hardware Age* magazine.

Needs Discontinued Hardware

Q. My speedboat has a vee-shaped windshield held in place by three metal brackets. One is bent and another is missing. I can't find duplicates in any marine supply catalog. Any suggestions?

A. Inspect the parts carefully for some identifying mark. The initials "WC" superimposed one over the other identify items made by Wilcox-Crittenden. The word "Perko" identifies Perkins Marine Lamp and Hardware Company, recently renamed Perko, Inc. A trident mark on pulleys and other sailboat hardware identifies it as a product of the Merriman company. If you can find some such identification mark, look into *Boat Owners Buyers Guide* and write to the company. While they may not list the item in current catalogs due to lack of demand, they may have a few of the parts left in stock, or they might have the patterns and can cast a new set for you.

Many custom-built yachts employ made-to-order bronze castings for such parts as the stem plate, shroud tangs, rudder and tiller fittings, centerboard fittings, etc. If you can determine the shape of the original part and make a wooden pattern of it, a bronze foundry in your area could cast new parts.

Looking for Prefab Hardtop

Q. The folding top on my runabout is flimsy. Where can I get a kit from which to assemble a rigid, more leak-resistant hardtop?

A. We've never seen such an item listed in any marine literature. One would think there would be a good market for such an accessory. But some things just don't get into production for an assortment of practical reasons. There are so many makes and models of boats on the market that getting accurate measurements and designing tops to fit a useful number of them would be a costly undertaking. It would be expensive to do the amount of advertising necessary to reach enough runabout owners to generate a feasible

volume of business. Because they would be bulky to package, ship, and warehouse, distributors and dealers might be reluctant to stock them. You get the idea. One can think of several other desirable accessories that are not marketed for reasons like these.

Consumers Union for Boats

Q. Is there an organization that tests and rates boating products in a manner similar to the way the Consumers Union does it for general merchandise?

A. Yes and no. There's no big organization that tests everything that comes along. The Marine Testing Institute tests various products for their supporting manufacturers and those products they find acceptable are entitled to bear their seal of approval. It is rather a sales promotion device, similar to *Good Housekeeping* magazine's "Seal of Approval." There are some laboratories that test boats for compliance with Coast Guard flotation regulations, and gasoline tanks for Coast Guard reliability regulations.

A private organization puts out a newsletter called *The Telltale Compass*; their address is 18418 Old River Drive, Lake Oswego, Oregon 97034. It is a mixture of owner reports on experiences with various boats and items of equipment and staff reports on investigations into various boat owners' problems with boats and manufacturers. Most of the material deals with larger pleasure boats in the sail and power yacht categories. The Boat Owners Association of the United States, 880 S. Pickett St., Alexandria, Va. 22304 offers a variety of services to its members, including help with defective products.

As far as maintenance materials like paints and adhesives are concerned, the problem in publishing test reports on them is that whereas fair and objective test reports must be based on controlled laboratory conditions, such products tend to be used under a wide variety of conditions, on boats in all manner of conditions, and by people whose skill and willingness to read and follow instructions varies infinitely. A product rated highly in a controlled test can of course fail miserably if applied incorrectly or under bad working conditions. So it can be hard to rate such products in a way that will satisfy everyone. At the time of this writing, the Coast Guard was holding hearings to look into the possibility of establishing a boating consumers office.

Needs Glassware

Q. I own a Perko marine lantern so old that not even the Perko firm can supply a replacement glass chimney for it. What can I do?

A. This is a good example of how it is often necessary to

go outside the marine trade to find odd items. Try looking up a company that specializes in making up special glassware items for chemical laboratories. Chemistry teachers in high schools and colleges in your area would probably know of such a place.

Stainless Steel Fire Extinguishers

Q. I go boating on salt water and fire extinguishers soon turn to rust. Does anyone make them of stainless steel?

A. Not that we know of. Fire extinguishers are a typical **mass**-production item. Stainless steel poses special manufacturing problems of its own. We suspect extinguisher manufacturers would consider it too expensive to make them of this metal for the benefit of the comparatively small saltwater boating market. If you want to look into the matter, ask your local fire station for names of extinguisher supply houses and see what such firms have to say. Remember that to be used legally aboard a boat, an extinguisher must be labelled as having been approved by the Coast Guard. A commonsense solution to your problem would be to remove the original, general-purpose paint from new extinguishers and repaint them with rust-resistant primer and a good enamel, possibly some kind of epoxy finish.

Fire extinguishers used aboard pleasure boats must carry Coast Guard approval to be legal. Always keep existing safety regulations in mind when working on your boat. (U.S. Coast Guard)

Patent Numbers

Q. We bought a used boat and while cleaning it out found a strange item of hardware in one of the lockers. Nobody can figure out what it's for. There is no name or trade mark on it, only a patent number. If we sent it to you, could you tell us what it is for?

A. No need to mail it to us. Write a note to the U.S. Patent Office, Washington, D.C. 20231 and ask them to send you a copy of the patent. Give them the number that's on the object and enclose 50¢ check or money order.

Needs Bushings

Q. I'm reconditioning some blocks from my sailboat. To do the job I am going to need some new bushings. None of the marine supply stores in my area have them and they cannot find them in their wholesalers' catalogs. Do you know where I could get them?

A. Here's another example of where it pays to search outside the marine industry itself. In almost every city of any size you will find one or more companies that specialize in bearings and bushings. They stock bushings in a wide variety of sizes. If they can't come up with something that will fit, a local machine shop can probably make bushings for you.

Flying Bridge Plans

Q. Where can I get plans for a flying bridge for my cabin cruiser?

A. We know of none. Several firms make up flying bridge kits around basic fiberglass forms. The best-known is Rickborn Industries, Inc., 175 Atlantic City Blvd., Bayville, N.J. 08721. You can find advertisements for others in the boating magazines—it's an uncertain business and companies come and go in it.

Obsolete Steerer

Q. My old houseboat has a strange steering system. It consists of a hand-held unit at the end of a long wire. You can sit anywhere in the boat and steer it by thumbing the switch. Now I need parts. Where can I get them?

A. We remember the device. But we have seen no mention of the company in the boating press for over a score of years. Most electrical and electronic devices are put together from stock coils, condensers, switches, connectors, etc., so what we'd do is take the device to radio and electrical supply houses and see if they can find replacements for the defective parts. If they can't, you'll have to install a modern mechanical or hydraulic steering system such as made by Teleflex and Morse. These systems can be put together so as to afford two separate control stations at different places in a boat.

Books Disagree

Q. I have several books on boat maintenance and they often disagree on how a certain task should be done. Why can't the experts agree on things?

A. You overlook some things. Some of these books were written years ago. Some were written in England and Australia. Some were written by men who were writers first and boatmen second. Others were not written by any one man but were put together from items written by different people. You just have to allow for this wide range of writers' backgrounds, changing times, etc. and take some of the statements in these books with a grain of salt. Boat maintenance covers such a wide range of materials, methods, products and problems that even a computer would find it hard to be 100% accurate on every possible aspect of the subject. Furthermore, new ideas come along all the time. Doing boat maintenance work effectively is not a matter of rote, it is a matter of using horse sense and imagination. The best any book can do is give you a general idea of what it's all about.

Manufacturers' Slow Replies

Q. Why are many advertisers so slow in replying to my requests for information on their products?

A. Many reasons. Some firms wait until the minimum of 200 pieces of literature are ready to mail to qualify for bulk mailing rates—and bulk mail travels very slowly. Some have a computerized mailing company handle their inquiries, and have to wait their turn to be serviced by the computer. Sometimes a firm is waiting for new literature to come from the printing shop. Sometimes when you answer an ad and never get a reply, it's because you wrote your name and address illegibly. If you write to a company in the summertime, the only person there who can answer your question may be on vacation.

Getting Action on a Guarantee

Q. I bought a boat that has had a lot of problems. I can't get a bit of satisfaction out of the dealer or the manufacturer. Why do companies give guarantees and then welch on them?

A. We can understand your exasperation, but we all have to be realistic. If a part fails in a car or motor, new parts can be shipped to dealers and dealers can unbolt old ones to fit in new ones. A boat is a different problem. Often the defect is not something that can simply be unbolted and replaced— bad gel coat on a hull for example. Few dealers are gel coat experts. To repair that kind of problem, a boat may have to go back to the factory. If it's a big boat or the factory is far away, you can see the difficulty. A lot of boat guarantee problems are the outcome of people rushing to buy glamorous-looking boats they have fallen in love with without their having taken time to find out something about the company that made it, its financial condition, reputation, service facilities in the area, and so on. About all you can do is have your lawyer read over the guarantee and render an opinion. But even he cannot wave a magic wand and have a 36-foot boat waft itself back to a factory 1500 miles inland. Sometimes the best course is to realize that you are not in an ideal situation and see what kind of a settlement can be arrived at by talking things over with the dealer as calmly and reasonably as possible.

Books on Surveying

Q. Is any literature available on "surveying"; that is, inspecting used boats for condition?

A. There is a new book in print. Called Surveying Small Craft, it is authored by Ian Nicholson and published in England. Copies sold in the U.S. contain a supplement in pamphlet form that contains addenda on how U.S. surveying practices vary from English ones. It is available for $9.95 from International Marine Publishing Company, 21 Elm St., Camden, Maine 04843. Available from the same source is a book dealing exclusively with fiberglass; Marine Survey Manual for Fiberglass Reinforced Plastics by Gibbs & Cox, Inc., $8.00 from the same source.

Chapter 2

Boat Owners' Common Problems

Seagulls Love His Boat

Q. Seagulls constantly alight on and mess up my boat but leave nearby ones alone. What makes me so special? I really don't enjoy this kind of popularity!

A. Without even seeing it, we can guess the answer—your boat has comparatively flat, clear topsides, and the ones moored near it are probably sailboats with their topsides well covered with masts and stays. Airplanes do not voluntarily land on short, rough, obstruction-bordered fields; they choose airfields with clear, smooth runways and uncluttered approaches. Same with gulls. People get so mad at gulls they don't have enough presence of mind left to realize that a gull is just a flying machine designed by God rather than Grumman! All large birds prefer to land and take off facing into the wind, just as do airplanes. It helps them to come in as slowly as possible and to take off and climb out as easily as possible. The stern of a powerboat is generally uncluttered; the stern of a sailboat will have a tiller, boom, and backstay "guarding" it against landing gulls. The pilot of an airplane trying to land on a road would be very concerned about his wing tips clipping trees beside the road, and similarly a gull will shy away from landing close to obstructions that might clip his wing tips. Watch gulls landing on your boat for an hour and you will see where to erect simple obstructions that will send them elsewhere. People spend a lot of time trying to figure out how to scare gulls away with dummy owls, dummy dead gulls, noisemakers, fluttering objects, etc., when all the time the right answer is in front of their noses in the form of the nearby sailboats whose rigging obviously discourages gulls' attempts to land.

The "Gullsweep" device has red plastic tabs on the end of a rotating arm. A light breeze will set the device to rotating. It keeps gulls off not so much by frightening them as by discouraging them from trying a landing.

Proliferation of Gulls

Q. For years we had little or no gull problem. Then last year our mooring area swarmed with them. Do they breed in cycles, or what?

A. The key point is to understand that gulls are scavengers. They will eat the most repulsive things. A sudden increase in gull population may often be due to a new source of pollution in a given area. If gulls appear to be finding food in the area where you moor your boat, move to another place—even a few hundred yards could be enough. Gulls are creatures of habit; they often have well-defined flight paths from areas where they nest or sleep to places where they feed. If your town has changed the location of its dump, gulls may have developed a new flight path to it which brings them over your mooring area. If a commercial fishing boat has taken up docking at a nearby wharf, it will bring gulls in with it and they will hang around hoping for offal. If a parking lot nearby has recently been paved, it will attract them as they will use it as a fine place to drop and break open shellfish. A yacht that habitually dumps garbage overboard will draw gulls to a mooring area. Watch your gulls for several days to get an idea of their flyways and feeding spots—then either alter the conditions that attract them or move your boat elsewhere.

Seagulls are creatures of habit. They have favorite places for feeding and for roosting. Watch the ones in your area to learn their flight paths and destinations. Then moor your boat where they don't go. (Mercury Marine)

Boat Hauling Firms

Q. I've been transferred across the country and am in a quandary as to how to get our 35-foot yawl to our new home. Can you offer any suggestions?

A. There are companies that specialize in yacht hauling. Ask yacht yards in your area if they know of any active in your region. There is a list of hauling firms in the Boat Owners Buyers Guide. If you live near a large city where there is a lot of boating, look under "Yacht Hauling" or "Boat Transport" in the Yellow Pages. If you live near a boat factory, ask them if they patronize a hauling firm. It's common for such companies to be on the lookout for loads to carry on return trips or enroute to pick up boats at distant places. A few experienced boatmen advertise in the yachting press; they will sail a client's boat from one coast to the other via the Panama Canal.

There are companies that specialize in boat hauling. Some cater only to boat manufacturers, some specialize in large yachts, others will haul anything that happens to be going where they're headed. With some asking around, you may find one who can move your boat to a distant location. When several boats go at a time, cost is shared. (Chrysler Corp.)

We hope your employer is paying your relocation expenses because yacht hauling is an expensive proposition! You might visit local yacht brokers and work out a deal under which you'd sell your old boat before moving, and he or an associate broker would help you find a similar boat in your new location. That could be a lot cheaper.

Boat Insurance

Q. Where can I get a list of firms specializing in yacht insurance?

A. There's a list in the "Services" section of Boat Owners Buyers Guide.

Insurance Run-Around

Q. Local insurance agents shy off from giving me coverage on my homemade boat. It is well built and complies with Coast Guard safety requirements. So why the run-around?

A. Insurance people don't go by what their eyes see, they go by what their company's rulebooks say to do. These books in turn are written by people who are not very well in touch with the grass roots scene. Coast Guard requirements deal with safety matters such as fuel systems, electrical wiring, emergency equipment, navigation lights, etc. but say nothing about the quality of workmanship in amateur-built boats. Your insurance man may hear you when you say your boat complies with safety regulations, but he can still worry about such things as a loose knot in a bottom plank or too-short screws in the planking. Some homemade boats are works of art, admittedly, but many atrocities have also been built, launched—and sunk! Try to find out just what it is that bugs your insurance man and try to calm his fears. Better still, consult him and get his feelings *before* building your dreamboat!

Operating Costs

Q. Is there a rule-of-thumb for comparing the cost of maintaining a wooden boat versus a fiberglass one? Is there a formula for calculating the probable operating cost for any given boat?

A. We have not chanced to encounter anything like this in our years around boats. There are so many different kinds of boats, made so many ways, by so many companies, that any formula would be subject to so many variables as to produce wrong answers as often as right ones. Talk to people who already own boats closely resembling the one you are thinking of buying and average out the answers they give. One thing to bear in mind in times of inflation—a well-made boat of a popular type and make is apt to suffer little, if any, from depreciation, and some custom-built boats actually increase in value provided they are well maintained. And, many owners keep annual costs within reason by chartering their boats to responsible and qualified persons.

"Y" Valve for Bilge Pump

Q. When my boat is under way, it goes down by the stern enough to make bilge water flow aft. When it is at rest, it goes down by the bow enough to make water flow forward. Where shall I locate my electric bilge pump?

A. Bilge pump makers can supply "Y" valves. Mount the pump in any convenient location. Then one pickup hose from the "Y" valve is run to the aft part of the boat, and another is run forward. Switch from one pickup to the other, depending on whether the boat is under way or docked.

"Y" Valve For Sea Closet

Q. My cruiser is fitted with a holding tank as required by federal regulations, but there are no pump-out stations in the waters where I cruise. What should I do?

A. The regulations dealing with sea closet discharges by pleasure craft have been on a merry-go-round for some time now. Bureaucrats who don't know a barnacle from a

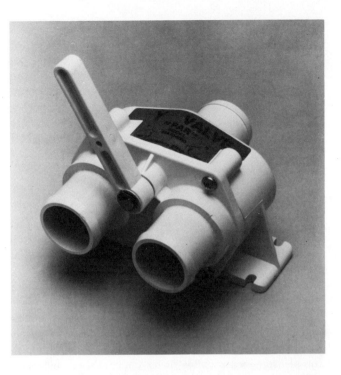

This is one type of so-called "Y" valve. Some are actually Y-shaped; others, such as this one by ITT Jabsco, is T-shaped. But all serve the same purpose.

A companion for the Y valve is a combination deck fitting like this one by ITT Jabsco. Called a "Dual Deck Waste Fitting," it provides for emptying holding tanks by either shoreside suction equipment or onboard discharge pump.

binnacle write idealistic regulations that have a way of colliding head-on with practical realities. These collisions require the regulations to be altered. The uncertainty of what the regulations will require a few years from now discourages equipment manufacturers, boatbuilders, and marinas from sticking their necks out too far in the marine sanitation facilities field. The currently popular solution to the holding tank problem is to install a "Y" valve in the tank's discharge line. It enables the tank to be pumped out when and where facilities exist—yet you can go out beyond the three-mile limit and discharge the contents overboard. On inland waters, portable toilets such as those used by campers and recreational vehicles are the interim answer. We would not be surprised to see somebody start marketing imitation cedar buckets molded from fiberglass!

Sea Closet Odor

Q. *I have constant problems with bad odors from my sea closet installation and wonder what to do. Deodorizing chemicals often make a worse smell themselves or emit vapors that are dangerous to breathe.*

A. The only thing to do is to visit marine supply stores often and keep posted on new ideas and products in this field. You're a classic example of the little guy caught in the midst of a herd of elephants—Big Government on one side of you and Big Business on the other. BG insisted on holding tanks for pleasure boats (while doing nothing about billions of gallons of raw sewage being discharged by many cities), so BB put them on the market. Then the currently available deodorants were offered in a hurry to cope with the obvious problem. Work goes on to develop deodorants that don't make you gag from their own emissions. In the meantime, make sure all parts of your system are working properly and make sure people who use it know how to operate it.

Wrong Lamp Fuel

Q. *I love to sail on the open ocean, far away from the madding crowd. But even out there I run into problems. Such as the one with my kerosene navigation lights—they just won't keep burning through the night and often go out in bad weather. Help!*

A. The composition of petroleum products varies. Your trouble may be that the kerosene you buy today differs from that which was available long ago when your kerosene lanterns were made. It may be all right for the few stoves, etc. that still use it ashore. It may contain impurities. An experienced cruising man tells us that he contacted some petroleum firms and found out where to get oil specially prepared for railroad lanterns—says it keeps his navigation lights burning very steadily.

Work on Wiring

Q. *I'm a radio freak and want to install a lot of electrical equipment in my sportfisherman. Where can I get information on boat wiring so as to do the job safely?*

A. Specifications for wire sizes, fusing, grounding, connectors, etc. appear in the pleasure craft safety standards manual issued by the American Boat and Yacht Council, the industry's official standards-setting organization. Their address is 190 Ketcham Ave., Amityville, N.Y. 11701. Get a copy of *Your Boat's Electrical System* by Conrad Miller, published by Motor Boating & Sailing Books, 224 West 57th St., New York, N.Y. 10019.

Boat Wiring vs. Car Wiring

Q. *I've been told that good automobile mechanics have a bad time of it when they try to work on a boat's wiring system. Is this so? Why?*

A. In a car, the battery is grounded to the frame. Electrical accessories, lights, etc. mounted in the metal of the car's bodywork are thus attached to one terminal of the battery via the frame, and have only one wire that goes to the junction box where it connects with power coming from the battery's other terminal. But boats lack steel frames. Each electrical item thus has two wires going to it, one connected to the battery's positive terminal and the other to its negative terminal. Until one comes to realize this simple but vital fact, working on boat wiring can be confusing, as everything will seem to be "wrong" and "different."

Fire Extinguisher Malfunctioned

Q. *The pressure gage on my boat's fire extinguisher indicated it was fully charged. Then one day we had a fire and after a tiny initial burst of white dust, nothing but gas came out of the extinguisher. We were able to put the fire out with seawater. Why didn't the extinguisher work? A fine "safety device" it turned out to be!*

A. Under the vibration experienced in a fast powerboat, the powder in a "dry" type extinguisher can in time pack down a little too solid for gas pressure to be able to pick it up. Several times each season, take your dry extinguishers off their brackets and thump them hard with the palm of your hand or on a solid surface to loosen up the powder and thus keep it free-flowing. You might have made your hard-packed extinguisher start working by banging it against a solid surface to break up the packed powder.

Spray Rails

Q. *My fiberglass cruiser throws too much spray. Is there any way I could install spray rails? Why do many fiberglass boats have such small, ineffective spray rails?*

One has to know safety requirements to do work on boat electrical systems. For example, one requirement is that battery terminals be protected so that tools or other metal objects cannot touch them and cause a shower of sparks. These oil-resistant neoprene rubber terminal caps by Moeller solve the problem. (Moeller Mfg. Co., Inc.)

Occasionally remove a dry-powder fire extinguisher from its bracket and thump it on a hard surface to loosen up packed-down powder. (Outboard Marine Corp.)

A. Many boat owners have installed wooden spray rails. They can be attached with generous-sized wood screws run through the hull from inside, through holes drilled in the fiberglass, and into the wood. Rails can also be bolted by using carriage bolts running from outside in and with washers and nuts inboard. Bending a usefully large strip onto a hull can be a rough job—consider laminated spray rails. Wax the hull, spread glue on the strips, lay them in place and hold on the hull until the glue has cured hard. Then remove to clean off glue and use a plane and sander to smooth up the wood. Soak it well with wood preservative and allow to dry. Paint it and set it in a tough, durable, adhesive-type bedding compound. The reason why some fiberglass boats have superficial spray rails is usually because bigger ones might pose awkward laminating problems, or pose problems in lifting the finished hull out of the mold.

Spray rails on fiberglass boats are a compromise. If too large or deep they can cause problems during the fiberglass molding process. If the wrong shape, they can prevent hull from lifting out of the mold. It is a challenge to shape them so they will work well at both low and high speeds. (Seamaster Boats, Inc.)

Speedboat Runs with a List

Q. My 17-foot outboard boat, with a 125 h.p. motor, tends to list to starboard all the time when going at cruising speed or faster. I have checked the bottom and am sure it is not warped. I am sure there is no trapped water inside the hull. Do you suppose the hull could have a soft spot in its bottom that flexes at speed and throws a warp into one side of the hull?

A. That is of course possible, but not really probable. We think you have overlooked propeller torque. A big propeller turning fast in one direction will apply an opposite force to the boat—through the motor and transom—which tends to make the boat run heeled to one side. That's normal. Shift the gas tank, battery, etc. to the high side. That failing, use contact cement to stick temporary, experimental wooden trim tabs to the bottom on the low side. When you determine what size and angle of trim tab will lift the low side so the boat is level at normal operating speed, make a better tab (more properly called a "wedge" or "shingle") of wood, finish it durably, and affix permanently.

Outboard Yaws to Right

Q. I have to hold the steering wheel of my outboard boat constantly; if I let go, the wheel and the boat will turn off to the right. What's wrong?

A. Nothing. The force of the pistons turning the crankshaft in one direction makes the power head—and thus the lower unit—want to keep turning in the opposite direction. Most large outboards cope with this in one of two ways.

Some have a built-in, adjustable trim tab. On others, the exhaust outlet snout is made unsymmetrical—it bulges out more on one side than on the other. You can see this by viewing the lower unit from astern. The adjustable ones can be set to compensate for torque at one particular speed; the non-adjustable ones can be built up with Devcon plastic metal (it comes in tubes and cans) and sanded smooth. Your boat may be going at a speed greater than the trim tab is set for. Talk to a smart outboard mechanic.

Cruiser Yaws Badly

Q. We bought a big cruiser without having a chance to try it out. It was in a storage shed when we got it. It's now in the water and I am upset to find that it yaws this way and that over the waves. The steering system has no apparent looseness. The boat was re-engined a while back and I wonder if the propeller-to-rudder relationship might have been altered? What is your opinion?

A. We can guess that this may well be your first boat with a conventional inboard engine. A rudder-controlled boat lacks the quick, positive steering associated with outboards and stern drives, which are steered by deflecting propeller thrust. A lighter, more understanding touch on the wheel might cure the problem. Is the bottom "hogged"—that is, sagging down at the ends and bent up in the amidships area so as to upset the hull's tendency to go straight? Did someone add a new cabin in the past so as to upset the relationship between the boat's side areas above and below the waterline? Do the rudders have too much balance area? If they do, the balance area will act too powerfully and make the rudders want to turn too easily to one side and then the

Trim tabs permit faster planing and smoother running on rough water, eliminate "porpoising" or "hobby horsing," and compensate for motor torque and temporary load changes to keep the boat on an even keel at all times. Installation is easy. They will fit on the transom of any boat whether the bottom is flat or deep-V, and are fastened directly to the hull with six stainless steel screws in each tab. (Tempo Products Company, 6200 Cochran Road, Cleveland, Ohio 44139)

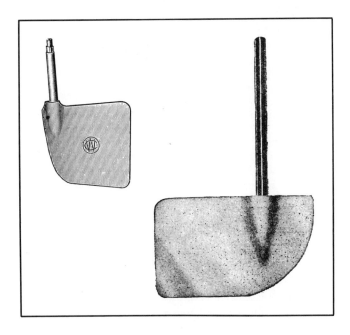

Balance area on rudders varies, as these two examples illustrate. Proper area is chosen by the original designer and modified as necessary by trial runs to arrive at final area for any given boat. When changes are made in engine, propeller or steering system later on, balance area may have to be altered to maintain good steering characteristics.

other. Reduce the balance area. If we were you we'd have a good naval architect look her over and try to evaluate these and probable other factors to pinpoint the fault.

Yaws When Reversing

Q. My small cruiser just won't back down straight and true. The bow goes up in the air, the stern goes down, and the bow yaws this way or that, willy-nilly. Why?

A. This behavior is typical of modern planing hulls, especially those with the weight of large outboard motors or stern drive engines on their sterns. When you reverse, the broad transom pushes against a lot of water. It eddies down the transom and under the bottom, apparently creating downward suction on the hull. Motor weight plus this suction lowers the stern, so the bow has to go up. The forebody of the boat then loses its grip in the water and any slight wind or steerer force will make it start to yaw. Once it starts, it gains momentum and is hard to stop. A deep keel that would remain down in the water when reversing would help—but that would give too much bow-rudder effect and make control altogether too sensitive when going ahead at cruising speed. Try having passengers move forward in the boat when you are about to back away from a dock. Their weight might keep the bow down in the water so it won't swing off so easily. If yours is a stern-drive boat, install a steering wheel that has a rudder position indicator built into its hub. This will show you where the lower unit (and hence propeller thrust) is pointing before you shift into reverse. That will stop a lot of yaws caused by the prop pulling in the wrong direction.

Stern Drive Steers Poorly

Q. *My stern drive boat steers sluggishly at low speeds. The lower unit does not seem to pivot as far to each side as I think it should. I wonder if there is something wrong with the steering system?*

A. Popular mechanical steerers have enough motion for any installation, provided the linkage between the ram on the aft end of the cable and the motor is not incorrect so as to lose some of the available motion. We think your trouble is the make of stern drive you have. Various makes turn from side-to-side anywhere from 30° to 45° off dead ahead, all depending on the design of the universal joints that transmit motor power to the top ends of their lower units. They will all pivot enough to afford good control at cruising speed, but some are sluggish when slowed down. Try having passengers move forward when you are moving ahead slowly. Their weight will put the bow down, raise the stern a little, and perhaps make it swing better in response to propeller thrust.

Cable "Sings"

Q. *The stainless steel cable that raises and lowers the centerboard in my sailboat "sings" annoyingly. I have tried putting tension on it but that just changes the pitch of the singing. What should I do?*

A. We suspect that it sings because of the way water flows around the cable's rough surface. Try wrapping it with

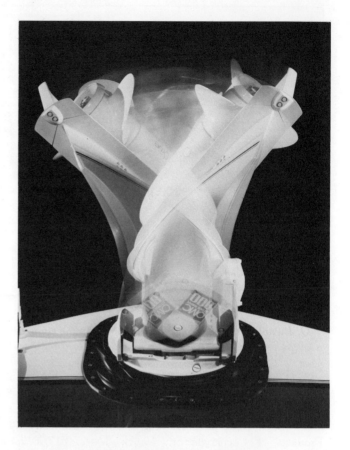

Depending on the mechanism used to transmit power, various makes of stern drive lower units pivot through varying angles. This OMC has a 90 degree arc. Its maker claims this to be at least 50% more than in other makes. A wide steering arc improves maneuverability at lower speeds. (Outboard Marine Corp.)

electrician's tape as an experiment. If that alters flow so as to stop the music, replace the cable with a plastic-coated one of the type used for steering small outboard motors. Or at a hardware store, get some brush-on plastic meant for putting a non-skid covering on tool handles and apply it to the cable. "Whip-End-Dip," a similar material sold in boat stores to keep ends of rope from unlaying, would also be worth trying. All that failing, try cable of a different diameter.

Loosening the Drain Plug

Q. *I am concerned that on a long cruise the garboard drain plug in my big cruiser might vibrate loose. What is the recommended tightening torque for such plugs?*

A. We know of no recommended figure. We think that one of these plugs installed in wooden planking with small bolts would not stand very much tightening. Try gasket shellac or a gasket cement that will set fairly hard. Or try "Lock Tite," a compound auto mechanics use to secure nuts.

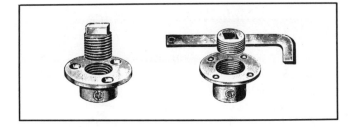

Some garboard drain plugs (left) have square heads for turning with any common wrench. Others (right) have a square socket and come with a special wrench. Note shortness of wrench. This is to minimize force one can apply to the plug. Too much force could pull mounting screws or bolts out of wood. (Wilcox Crittenden)

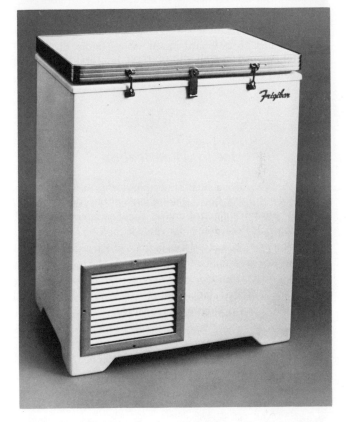

Marine iceboxes, refrigerators and freezers come in a variety of types. Front-opening type, top, offers ready accessibility to contents and is satisfactory for some situations. Top-opening type, bottom, is less convenient but high-water boaters often favor it. Top-opening minimizes loss of cold air when cover is opened, and contents will not fly out should the boat roll suddenly while cover is open. (Side-opening: Dayton-Walther Corp. Top-opening: Frigibar Industries, Inc.)

Unsuitable Soundproofing

Q. I want to insulate my inboard boat's engine compartment against noise. The men at the boatyard said not to use fiberglass house insulation, aluminum foil insulation, or acoustic panels available at lumberyards. Why?

A. They will not stand engine vibration. They soon crack and crumble, making a mess. Some will absorb engine oil and become a fire hazard. Write to American Acoustical Products, 9 Cochituate St., Natick, Mass. 01760 for literature on "Hushcloth." Specialty Composites Corp., Newark, Delaware 19713, makes "Tufcote Noise Barrier." They have a pamphlet on how to use it. Look under "Soundproofing" and "Sound Deadening" in the Yellow Pages of large cities. There are small companies that specialize in boat insulation located in or near major yachting centers; inquire of people at marinas, boatyards, and boat shops.

Insulating Outboard Motors

Q. Would it help to build and install a soundproofing cover over my large outboard motor?

A. It could, but sound control is a science that's full of quirks. You can experiment cheaply. Cut a large cardboard carton to shape and line it with opened-up egg cartons made of molded foam to get an idea of what a good hood could do. Keep some things in mind. The hood or cover must not cover the motor so thoroughly as to cut off its air supply. It must not tend to fill with exhaust smoke when the motor is idling or reversing, for too much smoke mixed with the air fed to the carburetor can upset the fuel-to-air ratio and literally gag the motor. The cover must not interfere with turning and tilting of the motor.

Marine Refrigeration

Q. We hope to cruise in the tropics. Where can we get information on refrigerators for boats?

A. The *Boat Owners Buyers Guide* has a section on refrigerators and freezers. Several companies make units in this field. You can also buy the *Marine Refrigeration Guide Book* by Howard M. Crosby, available from Crosby Marine Refrigeration Systems, Inc., 204 Second Ave. So., St. Petersburg, Fla. 33701.

RV Refrigerators in Boats

Q. *Could I use an RV-type refrigerator aboard my houseboat?*

A. You'd be in a grey area. Such an appliance would probably not be certified for marine use. If your houseboat has an inboard or stern-drive engine, it is possible that gasoline vapors might reach open flame in the refrigerator. If the boat has an outboard motor whose tanks, etc. are all outside and well removed from the refrigerator, it might be safe. We'd see our boat insurance man and get his reaction.

Ice for Boat Icebox

Q. *We are going broke buying bags of ice cubes at every stop to keep our outboard cruiser's icebox adequately iced. How can we slow down the rate of melting?*

A. Don't use ice cubes. Ten pounds of ice cubes has a lot more surface area than a ten pound block of ice, so of course the cubes melt faster. Ice cubes are intended for rapid cooling of drinks. Switch to block ice. It will last longer and still adequately keep a supply of food cold.

Marine Iceboxes

Q. *We were guests aboard a sailing yacht. The icebox had a top-opening door. The owner's wife complained about how awkward it was to reach down into it and sort things out to get at what she needed. We wondered why a high quality boat had such a dumb feature. Do you have any thoughts?*

A. Sure, dumb like a fox. It was made that way by a builder who knew what it's really like to go cruising. There's not many of that kind in the business today! The top opening keeps cold air from spilling out every time the door is opened, making a block of ice last considerably longer. And it's safer. If you open the door on a side-opening icebox or refrigerator while the boat is lurching over ocean waves, the entire contents of the box can come flying out into your lap!

Melt Water in the Bilge

Q. *We installed a portable icebox in our boat and led a drain tube to the bilge to conduct melted ice water down and clear of the galley. A friend said that is a poor idea. What do you think?*

A. We agree. If it's a wooden boat, past experience has shown that ice water tends to be full of rot spores and can cause wood-decay troubles quickly. Even if it's a fiberglass boat, it can lead to odor problems. Recommended practice is to drain melt water overboard by means of a through-hull fitting.

Dory Crabs Sideways

Q. *I built a 20-foot dory from plans and installed a motor-well inside it to take an outboard motor. It won't steer at all. When I turn the motor, the boat just sort of crabs sidewise and keeps pointing in the same general direction. What could be wrong?*

A. We've seen this happen before. You've located the well too far forward. When you turn the motor, the propeller thrust just pushes the whole boat to one side. If the motor was at the stern, it would push the stern to one side, the bow would swing the other way, and you'd be turning. Two possible fixes come to mind. Lock the motor pointing dead ahead and install a rudder at the stern to force the stern to move one way or the other when you use the tiller. Or install a long, shallow skeg on the keel ahead of the motor-well. Then when the motor pushes the hull sideways, water pressure will build up on the skeg so as to force the bow into a turn.

Installation of a motor well in a dory requires knowledge of boat design quirks. If it is located too far forward, propeller thrusts will tend more to make the hull crab sideways in the water than to push the stern to one side. This installation worked. (National Fisherman)

Motor Pulls Hold-Down Bolts

Q. I bought a sailboat that is regularly fitted with a four-cylinder gasoline auxiliary motor of 40 h.p. Intending to cruise extensively in remote waters, I ordered it to be fitted instead with a 20 h.p. two-cylinder diesel. To my chagrin, this engine has repeatedly pulled loose its mounting bolts. One would think that mounts able to take a 40 h.p. engine would be doubly dependable with half that power! I intend to sue and would like to know if your services are available as an expert witness.

A. Sorry, count us out! The 40 h.p. gasoline engine has four small pistons that feed a steady but modest amount of torque into the prop shaft. The two-cylinder diesel has two pistons and each thumps a lot more torque into the shaft on each power stroke. So, of course, the bolts that would hold the gas engine loosen under the jolting of the diesel. If this

Boatbuilding is an art. This single-cylinder 6 h.p. Acadia engine, manufactured in Nova Scotia for workboat use, requires a surprisingly strong engine mount. Single piston sends heavy, pulsating torque forces into a comparatively short bolt-down flange, so hold-down bolts get more of a workout than would the bolts holding down a more powerful multi-cylinder engine with smoother power flow and more spread-out mountings. (Acadia Gas Engines, Bridgewater, N.S.)

was the first time the boat's manufacturer installed that particular model of diesel in one of his boats, it'd be hard to blame him, even though common sense says he should have realized the difference. As soon as one begins to order changes made in a well-designed boat, one opens a Pandora's Box of unexpected problems. Good workmen are very hard to find; boat shops are caught between demanding customers on one hand and lackadaisical workmen on the other. It would make you feel better to go to Newport, R.I. some summer and see the amount of work that goes into getting everything aboard a carefully designed, fussily built America's Cup racer working well!

Mildew Trouble

Q. For several seasons we had no mildew trouble to speak of in our boat. Then last summer it hit like lightning and kept us scrubbing constantly. Can you offer an explanation?

A. Sure. Farmers have good years and lean ones. Sportsmen find there's plenty of game one year, little the next. Being a form of plant life, mildew fungus is affected by variations in weather patterns and environment. Your cabin might have become host to a strain of mildew that found its environment particularly attractive. You may have begun to use a different cleansing product that left the cabin interior covered with a residue of phosphate or other mildew nutrient. If an anti-mildew chemical was mixed into your cabin paint some seasons ago, last summer might have seen it reach the end of its effectiveness. Basically, some subtle change in the conditions inside your cabin triggered a mildew population explosion. It might take scientific study to pinpoint the exact cause. Make a stab at it by asking yourself, "What was different in the cabin last year compared to previous years?"

Mildew Likes Paint

Q. We redecorated the cabin of our ketch last winter. During the summer, mildew appeared profusely on the cabin ceiling but not on surfaces lower down. Why?

A. We think we can guess. You used flat paint on the ceiling for a soft look and gloss paint on the walls and lockers for brightness and ease of cleaning, right? The rough surface of the flat paint was easier for mildew fungus to attach to. Also, people moving around in a cabin are constantly brushing against vertical surfaces but seldom against overhead ones. This wiping action slows down mildew propagation on vertical surfaces. Hardware and some marine stores sell small bottles of chemicals to add to paint that will discourage mildew. Try some next year. Better still, go back to gloss paint.

Literature on Mildew

Q. *Mildew has gotten into the lockers, bedding, and upholstery in my boat's cabin. Where can I get some reading matter on mildew?*

A. Send $1.00 to the Superintendent of Documents, U.S. Government Printing Office, Washington, D.C. 20402 and ask for a copy of the Department of Agriculture's Home and Garden Bulletin No. 68, *How to Prevent and Remove Mildew*. It's written for homemakers but the information is generally applicable to boats.

Preventing Mildew

Q. *Can anything worthwhile be done to keep mildew from getting started in a boat?*

A. Certainly. Keep dampness down as much as possible. A well-ventilated cabin is important. Install additional ventilators if you suspect your cabin has poor air circulation. Marine stores sell electric heating rods under the trade name of "Dampp Chaser" (that *is* the correct spelling). A few of these set to work in lockers will warm the air, keep it circulating, and substantially reduce mildew problems.

Removing Mildew

Q. *We have scrubbed until we are blue in the face and still can't get all the mildew off surfaces in our boat. Is there an easier way to get it off?*

A. Yes. Hardware and marine stores sell containers of chemicals to spray on infected surfaces. It dissolves mildew like the morning sun melts frost on an auto's windshield. Then it is easy to wipe or rinse off. Whatever brand you get, try it on a small, obscure surface before going ahead just to make sure it will not discolor or otherwise affect some kinds of paint or fabrics.

Mildew in Synthetic Rope

Q. *On cleaning my boat out at lay-up time, I was dismayed to find a mess of mildew growing on the nylon anchor line in the forepeak. I thought synthetic ropes were mildew-proof.*

A. These ropes are mildew-proof in the sense that mildew will not eat away their substance and rot them as can happen with ropes made of natural fiber. But it certainly can breed on the surface of synthetic ropes, just as it can grow almost anywhere when the right conditions of warmth and dampness exist. It's all right to stow wet rope in the forepeak for a few hours or a day while cruising, but it's wise to let the rope dry out before stowing it when the boat is to be idle for several days or longer. As far as we know there is no cleaning method that will remove mildew discolorations from synthetic rope.

Chapter 3

Corrosion Problems

Electrolysis and Galvanic Corrosion

Q. *Since I bought a boat a few years ago, I've had a lot of advice from waterfront people about seawater corrosion. Some talk about "electrolysis" and some about "galvanic corrosion." It often sounds as if they're talking about one and the same thing. Can you set me straight?*

A. People do use these terms interchangeably. But there is a technical difference. Understanding it clearly is important in coping with corrosion problems.

Galvanic corrosion results when two dissimiliar metals are immersed in a solution capable of conducting electrical current and these two metals are in contact with one another either directly or by means of the conductive solution. If you put a galvanized iron nut onto a bronze bolt, galvanic corrosion results quickly when the assembly is immersed in salt water or water polluted by chemicals which makes it electrically conductive.

Electrolytic corrosion results when electrical current from some outside source starts flowing between two pieces of metal. They can be the same or dissimilar kinds of metal. The current can come from the boat's storage battery, from the dock current outlet, or from another boat moored alongside yours.

People use language very carelessly. "Electrolysis" has been used so often that newcomers have picked it up and applied it to all kinds of boat corrosion. All metals are made up of molecules. These are electrically-charged particles. You can put a strip of pure copper and one of pure zinc into a jar full of salt water (or plain water with acid added to it) and either let them touch or connect them with a wire. One metal, the "less noble" of the two, will disintegrate while residues from it will collect on the other. Or, you can mix two metals together in a melting pot to make an alloy. If you mix copper and zinc you will get brass. When the brass is put into the water, you will also get an internal galvanic reaction that will dissolve the zinc (the less noble of the two) out of the alloy and leave only a spongy form of copper. A brass wood screw immersed in seawater for a long time will become "dezincified," to use the boatyard man's language. This is internal galvanic corrosion.

You can also moor an aluminum boat to an iron pipe driven into the cove's bottom, using a steel chain and padlock to connect the two. Kids won't make off with the boat, but external galvanic corrosion will eat the boat's bottom into a metallic pulp!

On the other hand, you can put anti-fouling bottom paint containing copper onto a fiberglass boat powered with a stern-drive engine. The lower unit of the stern drive is immersed in seawater and attached to the engine, which is connected to the starting battery, which is in turn connected to the boat's wiring system. To this you connect something like a radio which has a ground plate on the boat's bottom. Current will go from that to the copper paint and then through the seawater to the stern drive lower unit. Because that's made of aluminum, which is a less noble metal than copper, after some months at the mooring it will also look like some kind of metallic pulp, thanks to *electrolysis*.

Have you got it straight? *Galvanic action*—metals in contact. *Electrolysis*—some stray current you didn't know was there until the damage has been done.

Corrosion in Fresh Water

Q. *Can electrolysis take place in fresh water?*

Many stratagems are used to protect metal parts of boats and their engines from saltwater corrosion. For a while some years back, a Florida firm offered demountable plastic bags to fit over stern drive lower units. Filled with fresh water from a dock hose, they kept seawater away from costly aluminum stern drive lower units. The "Hydro-Hoist" has tanks and a cradle to fit boat. When air is pumped into tanks, their buoyancy lifts boat out of water where it remains when idle.

A. Yes, but generally not as rapidly. Suppose you moor your boat in a river early in the spring. The water is slightly saline from salt spread on icy roads during the winter and which is still being washed into the river by rains. Or a factory half a mile upstream is still dumping used industrial acid into the river when the EPA isn't looking.

Electrolysis Appeared Suddenly

Q. For three seasons my cruiser showed no signs of corrosion problems. Then during the fourth season underwater metal parts began to corrode badly. Poor-quality hardware finally showing its cheesiness?

A. No. Something happened to upset the original electrical setup. You brought in dock current with reversed polarity. A boat with a bad electrical leak came in to the marina and was berthed next to yours. A wire broke or chafed through somewhere in your boat. You installed a new item of electrical equipment and in doing so introduced a stray current into the scheme of things. The zinc blocks on your underwater metal parts became eroded to the point where they suddenly lost potency. During the winter somebody dumped an old engine block into the water right over where your boat is moored. You started using a different kind of anti-fouling bottom paint. A new boatyard man applied anti-fouling paint over your zinc blocks, negating their ability to function. Sometimes one has to become a combination electrical and mechanical detective!

Books on Corrosion

Q. Is there a book on galvanic and electrolytic corrosion?

A. Yacht Corrosion Consultants, Inc., 1210 Beachmont St., Ventura, Cal. 93001 has a book called Boat & Yacht Corrosion Control. At the time we were writing, its price was $24.95. This firm also has instruments for use in testing boats for electrolysis problems. Your Boat's Electrical System by Conrad Miller, from Motor Boating & Sailing Books, 224 West 57th St., New York, N.Y. 10019 also has a good chapter on it. International Nickel Company, Inc., One New York Plaza, New York, N.Y. 10004, makers of Monel metal, have booklets on various aspects of the subject.

Stainless Steel Corroded

Q. My galvanized mooring cable has a stainless steel thimble in the eye splice at its lower end where it connects to the swivel and mooring block. On hauling it out at season's end I was amazed to find the thimble badly corroded. Did somebody sell me some phony stainless steel?

A. We don't think so. Stainless steel can suffer as much from galvanic corrosion as any other metal. An important fact in the science of corrosion is that the areas of two metals in proximity to one another are as important as the kinds of metal in determining what will happen. The area of the cable was greater than the area of the thimble, so despite the material from which it was made, the thimble was overpowered by the cable. Also, stainless steel gets its corrosion resistance through an ability of its surface to form a protective oxide as soon as it receives a scratch. To form this

Zinc sacrificial anodes are attached to the hulls of steel boats at various strategic locations. Here, several are located near the large bronze propeller on this commercial fishing boat to protect the steel hull from the bronze propeller.

oxide it must be exposed to oxygen, which is to say, to the air. Under water there is very little oxygen. So this put the stainless steel at a further disadvantage.

Corrosion is basically a chemical action. Just as a chemist can write an equation that tells exactly what happens when he mixes different chemicals together and gets a reaction, so can a corrosion engineer write an equation that scientifically describes exactly what takes place when any given metal or metals corrode under some particular set of circumstances. It is in fact a very complicated subject. People make lifetime careers out of specializing in the study of corrosion.

Underside of Hardware Corroded

Q. *We removed some stainless steel deck hardware from our boat and were surprised to find corrosion on all the* *surfaces of these items where they contacted the deck. We think some dummy bedded them in some kind of compound that was corrosive. What do you think?*

A. You do not understand how stainless steel works. It does not corrode in the sense that it rusts. Rather, its chemical characteristics are such that the moment it is exposed to the atmosphere, its surface develops an invisible but very present and very tough oxide coating that at once shuts off further access of the air (and the oxygen in it) to the metal. In a rather unscientific way, it is like what happens when you cut your finger—blood flows, then the blood quickly hardens to form a scab that seals and protects the wound while nature goes about healing it in a more permanent way. We suspect your hardware was not bedded in any kind of compound. Seawater from spray collected under it after being drawn into the small spaces between the hardware and the deck by capillary action, and stayed there long enough to shut out the air and allow salt water to start corroding the metal. The corrosion progressed through lack

25

of oxygen. If the hardware was set in a good compound that shut out water, no corrosion would get started under the pieces.

"Active" and "Passive"

Q. In various pieces of boat literature I have encountered the words "active" and "passive" in regard to stainless steel. What's this all about?

A. They are words metallurgists use to describe the chemical state of the surface of something made of stainless steel. This metal comes in various alloys and treatments, just as do other metals, in order to fit it to various jobs to best advantage. "Active" stainless steel is in such a condition that it can readily corrode. "Passive" stainless is in a corrosion-resistant condition suitable for use on boats. Note that "passive" stainless occupies a more noble position in the Galvanic Scale than does "active."

Galvanic Scale

Q. What is the "Galvanic Scale" I see mentioned so often in corrosion literature?

A. It is a table listing metals in the order of their susceptibility to galvanic corrosion. There are various Galvanic Scales, each dealing with the characteristics of metals used in various types of construction or engineering work. Below is the one used in boat work.

Corroded End—Least Noble

Magnesium
Magnesium Alloys
CB75 Aluminum anode alloy
Zinc
B605 aluminum anode alloy
Galvanized steel and wrought iron
Aluminum 7072 (cladding alloy)
Aluminum 5456
Aluminum 5086
Aluminum 5052
Aluminum 3003, 1100, 6061, 356
Cadmium
2117 aluminum rivet alloy
Mild steel
Wrought iron
Cast iron
Ni-Resist alloy
13% chromium stainless steel, type 410, active
50-50 lead tin solder
18-8 stainless steel, type 304, active

18-8 3% NO stainless steel, type 316, active
Lead
Tin
Muntz metal
Manganese bronze
Naval brass, 60% copper, 39% zinc
Nickel, active
Inconel alloy, active
Yellow brass, 65% copper, 35% zinc
Admiralty brass
Aluminum bronze
Red brass, 85% copper, 15% zinc
Copper
Silicon bronze (various alloys)
Nickel, passive
18-8 stainless steel, passive
18-8 3% stainless steel, type 304, passive
Titanium
Platinum

Protected End—Most Noble

The general rule is that the closer together two metals are on this list, the less powerful will be the electrolytic action between them. Thus, aluminums and type 410 active stainless steel are often used together since they are close, and the stainless is usually in the form of screws, etc., having less area than the aluminum parts they hold together. Silicon bronze is much used

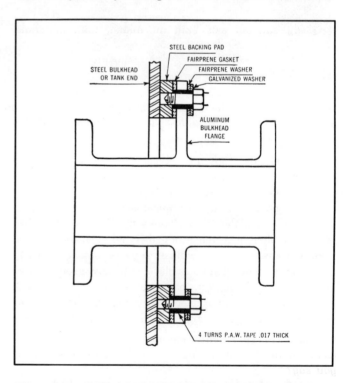

When ferrous and nonferrous metals are used together in a boat, good practice is to separate the two with appropriate gaskets, bushings, washers and compounds. Here is how a shipyard handles the problem of routing an aluminum flange through a steel bulkhead. (Kaiser Aluminum)

for screws in wooden boats, and as zinc is a long way from it in this list, the zinc disintegrates rapidly and thus, by sacrificing itself, protects the bronze.

Centerboard Pin Corrodes

Q. My sailboat has a lead keel and the iron centerboard pivots on a bronze pin. Many boats in this class have had their pins fail from galvanic corrosion. Can I do anything to make my boat's pin last longer?

A. International Nickel Company, manufacturer of Monel metal, has a pocket calculator they give out to designers who use their metal. It lists many metals in common use and has little windows in which green, yellow, and red dots appear when the calculator is set to any two dissimilar metals. If a green dot shows, it's probably safe to use the two together. If a red dot, the combination is prone to trouble. A yellow dot means even the experts can't be sure and they would want to run lab tests before settling on that combination. This calculator says a Monel pin used in proximity to a lead keel is probably quite likely to be durable.

Freshwater–Saltwater Corrosion

Q. My sailboat was built far inland, with materials generally used in freshwater territory. I want to make a cruise on the sea. Will there be a corrosion problem between the bronze propeller and the galvanized steel rudder hinges?

A. Very probably. The galvanizing is done with zinc. The bronze is likely to make the zinc dissolve, just as it will make a zinc sacrificial block dissolve. As rudder hinge failure at sea is a very serious matter, it would be well to switch to bronze hinges before setting sail.

Zinc Blocks Get Eaten

Q. The boatyard installed zinc blocks on the underwater parts of my boat and assured me they would prevent electrolysis. When the boat was hauled out in the fall I was greatly upset to find they had been badly eaten away. Obviously they were defective in some way and are not working. The yard refutes me and says they are working well. I think they are giving me a baloney story. What do you say?

A. We say the blocks are working as intended and the yard is telling you the truth. We often get letters from newcomers who are upset, like you are, upon finding zinc blocks badly corroded. People often don't understand that the zinc is *supposed* to be eaten away. Technical men refer to

them as "sacrificial anodes." They are comparatively cheap and easy to replace compared to bronze rudders, propellers, struts, etc. While engineers might boggle at the scientific inexactitude of this statement, an easy way to understand their principle is to consider them as sort of underwater lightning rods. Electrical currents eat them away because zinc is a less noble metal than the others used in a boat. Relax, all's well!

When to Replace Zincs

Q. Can you give me advice on when to replace corroded zinc blocks?

A. There is no firm rule. Often it is a matter of what common sense and convenience dictate. If they are somewhat corroded, say 25% of the original metal is gone, and you are relaunching the boat early in the spring, it makes sense to put new ones on to give best protection and peace of mind as the months afloat pass. In general, when about half of the metal seems to have dissolved, it is best to replace the blocks since the smaller they get, the faster they will dissolve and the less protection they'll give. As you gain experience with your boat you will come to know their average rate of loss and can decide when to leave the old ones on and when to play it safe with new ones.

Zinc Blocks Cause Vibration

Q. I have had bad vibration in my boat's propeller shaft ever since I put a new zinc collar on it. Do these collars have to be balanced?

A. No, they are accurately made and are well balanced as they come from the marine supply house. You probably made a mistake by installing a collar of square cross-section on the shaft at some point forward of the propeller. It is upsetting water flow into the prop and thus causing the prop to bite into disturbed water and set up vibration. Split, egg-shaped zinc blocks are available for installation in this location—they are more streamlined and upset water flow much less. The ring-shaped collar of square cross-section is meant to fit in places where it won't cause turbulence, such as the slight gap between the aft side of a prop shaft support strut and the front face of the prop hub.

No Space for Zinc Collar

Q. My boat has a skeg. The prop shaft emerges from the skeg and there is not enough space between the stern bearing and the prop for any kind of zinc collar. Is there anything I can do?

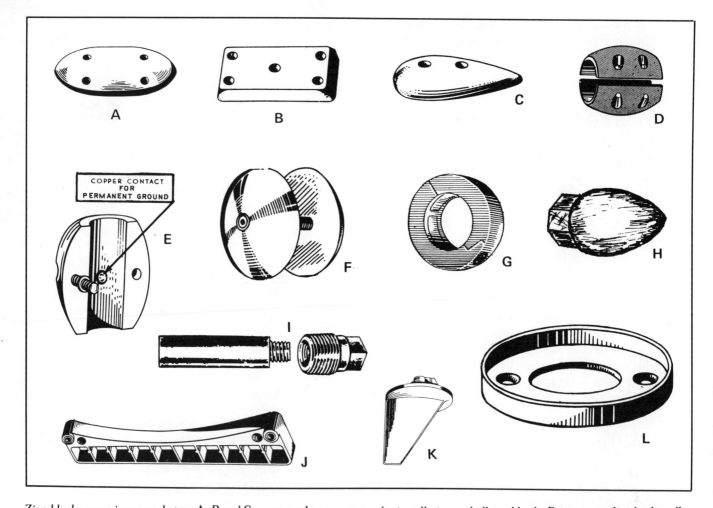

Zinc blocks come in many shapes. A, B and C are general-purpose types for installation on hulls and keels. D is a streamlined split-collar type to be installed on long, exposed propeller shafts; it does not disturb flow of water back into propeller. E shows copper contact inside such a collar to maintain firm, dependable electrical contact with shaft. F is a streamlined split type of block for installation on metal rudders; shape minimizes water resistance. G is a split collar that will fit in the narrow space between stern bearing and propeller hub of an inboard boat having a skeg. H is a streamlined zinc block cast onto a bronze nut threaded to fit on tail end of propeller shaft; useful where there is insufficient space on shaft of propeller. I is a "zinc pencil" that fits into an appropriate hole in a cast iron engine block to protect the block from saltwater corrosion. J is a zinc block designed to fit Outboard Marine Corp. stern drives. K is a combination trim tab and sacrificial anode for larger Mercury Marine outboard motors. L is a zinc block shaped to fit in aft end of lower unit's gear housing.

A. The companies that make zinc blocks offer bronze nuts with egg-shaped blocks of zinc cast onto them. Screw one on the aft end of the propeller shaft, after the main propeller nut has been installed. The bronze core provides strong threads and the zinc will protect the propeller and stuffing box.

Too Many Zinc Blocks?

Q. Is it possible to use too many zinc blocks on a boat?
A. Yes. But it's not such a problem with today's fiberglass boats as it was with wooden boats. After a wooden boat has been in seawater for a long time, the wood in the area of the skeg and shaft alley can become waterlogged with salt water, which of course makes the wood conduct electricity. Then, believe it or not, it can either sacrifice itself to metal or become a sort of spongy or porous metal itself. The wood can become soft. The condition is often diagnosed as rot. A little less zinc in the setup will let metal corrosion occur, a little too much will cause wood to suffer from galvanic corrosion. The telltale sign to look for is a fluffy growth coming out of the wood around shaft and rudder bearings. It looks rather like the corrosion growths on the terminals of an auto battery. If the metal parts show no signs of corrosion but the aforementioned condition exists on the wood, there are probably too many zincs. The problem is that a neutral condition calls for a fine balance between too few and too many zincs; it's hard to guess how many to install in the first place, and the normal dissolving of the zincs makes it

The round bulges on these rudders are the zinc anti-electrolysis blocks. (Coastal Yachts)

impossible to maintain an ideal balance. Another indication of too many zincs is blistering or peeling of bottom paint around stern bearings and propeller strut attachments, various through-hull fittings, etc.

Paint Zinc Blocks?

Q. My boat will sit at its mooring for several weeks between the time it is launched and the time I will start using it on my vacation. Shall I have the yard put antifouling bottom paint on the zincs to keep barnacles off of them while the boat floats idle?

A. No. The paint will keep the blocks from protecting the boat's metal parts, or will just come right off of them, depending on its type. Not enough marine growth will form on the zincs to worry about; they may even repel some kinds of growths by their own chemical nature. If there are some growths, someone can dive under the boat and brush or scrape them off.

No Zincs on Some Boats

Q. My fiberglass sloop did not have any zinc anodes on its underwater parts when it was delivered to me. But I see them on many boats at the local yards. How can I tell if they are needed or not?

A. In today's mass-production boating scene, manufacturers ship boats out in considerable volume to many parts of the country. They do not always know to whom their dealers will sell each individual boat. So they cannot know if a boat will need zincs or not. They leave it up to the dealers to

decide, depending on what the dealers know about where each customer will keep his boat and what protection is needed.

Do Fiberglassed Boats Need Zincs?

Q. My wooden boat has had its bottom sheathed in fiberglass. Does this keep seawater away from the planking fastenings enough to obviate the need for zinc anode protection?

A. Provided the wood was allowed to dry out thoroughly before fiberglassing (which is necessary to assure good fiberglass adhesion), the screws are probably safe enough. One can't say they are 100% safe, though. If the boat has only one layer of fiberglass cloth on it, cracks can develop and seawater will get in. If bilge water gets the bottom planking wet again, and if there is salt in the wood, the fastenings could in time suffer. You begin to see—there are so many "ifs" and "buts" in a situation like this! But to get back to your question, you may as well put zincs on because exposed bronze parts such as the propeller, shaft, and rudder fittings will still need protection.

His Zincs Eroded Fast

Q. At haul-out time I have noticed that the zincs on my boat have been eaten away more than those on boats moored near mine. Is something wrong?

A. Probably not wrong in the drastic sense of that word. But have a good marine mechanic look the boat over for problems that could be present. Ask him to look for possible sources of stray current, breaks or poor connections in the bonding system, or any other deficiency that could be causing stray currents to flow and accelerate the erosion of your zincs. When the boat is out of water he can check the electrical system with a meter for such defects that don't show up during visual inspection.

Do you use your boat a lot more than the ones moored nearby? That could explain the increased rate of zinc block erosion. Rushing water makes any metal erode faster than still water does.

His Zincs Eroded Very Little

Q. At haul-out time we found the zinc anodes on our boat had scarcely been eaten away at all, even though the boat had been in the water for some time. Does this mean we have no electrolysis problem and don't need the zincs?

A. We'd take them off and see if the mechanic who installed them neglected to clean the bronze struts and shafting thoroughly before installing the blocks. If a lot of old corrosion film or old paint has been separating the zincs from the metal they are attached to, that's your answer. Or, you might have moored the boat in a cove in which a small stream or storm drains are discharging fresh water. The resulting brackish water of course isn't such a strong electrolyte as is undiluted salt water, so your electrolysis rate is probably being lowered and the zinc blocks indicate it. There are all kinds of things that can affect the rate of dissolution of zinc anodes, and one really has to have Sherlock Holmes' powers of observation and deduction to do a consistently good job of explaining what has been going on in any particular case.

What is a Bonding System?

Q. I'm new to boating. I've heard more experienced people talking about the bonding systems on their boats. What's that?

A. A heavy copper wire or strap runs the length of the boat. Short connecting wires lead from it to all the metal parts below the waterline in the hull. By bonding them all together it gives each item the same electrical potential. It helps control stray currents, decreases radio static, protects

the system better during lightning strikes, etc. Chapter Five in the book *Your Boat's Electrical System* by Conrad Miller explains it in detail.

Where to Get Zincs

Q. We live on a remote island. Where can we get zinc anode blocks for our boat by mail order?

A. Several firms make them and most marine hardware stores carry them. Some well-known makers are Essex Machine Works, Lehman Mfg. Co., Perko and Wilcox-Crittenden. All are well known to people in the marine trade and are listed in marine trade directories.

Zinc Pencils

Q. What is a "zinc pencil?"

A. A short zinc rod and a threaded plug. The assembly screws into a threaded hole in a marine engine's block that is provided for this purpose. The zinc projecting into the engine's water jacket does for the engine what the zinc blocks on the outboard hardware do for the other metal parts on the boat.

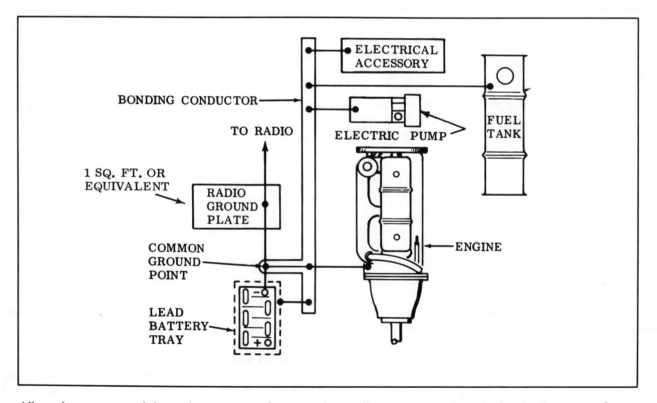

All metal components and electrical units in a motorboat or auxiliary sailboat are connected together by a bonding system. It gives every item the same electrical potential, with benefits as cited in the text.

Zincs on Aluminum Boats?

Q. Is it necessary and is it safe to install zinc anode blocks on an aluminum boat?

A. It is done, but there are also aluminum alloy anodes tailored to the job. Pat answers are risky because there are so many variables present—complexity of the electrical system, degree of insulation of bronze and iron parts in the boat from the aluminum structure, presence or absence of corrosion-retarding primer and paint. There is a page on the subject in the softcover book *Aluminum Boats*, published by Kaiser Aluminum as mentioned in our Chapter 13, "Aluminum Boats." If your boat is of some value, it would be best to consult with its manufacturer before rushing to bolt on anodes. It is possible you could just louse things up through ignorance.

Compensating for Variables

Q. It's obvious to me that it is hard to determine the exact number of zinc anodes needed on a boat, and even harder to maintain their area once they are on so as to obtain just the right amount of protection. Is there any other way of approaching the problem?

A. Yes, through the use of what is called the "impressed current" system. A device called a "reference anode" is installed at a suitable place on the hull bottom. It is a kind of electrical sensing device. It senses how much stray current is present and sends a signal to an electrical controller inside the boat. The controller then feeds just the right amount of current to another anode which feeds exactly the right current into the seawater so that just the right amount of protection is provided, even when boat speed and water temperature and salinity vary. The CAPAC™ system made by Engelhard Industries is often used on larger boats, while the Mercury Marine firm makes a "Mercathode" system for stern drives and outboards that can't be tilted completely out of salt water when moored.

Fuzzballs on Fastenings

Q. My lapstrake wooden boat has the planks held together with numerous small brass machine screws with washers and nuts on the inner ends. Most of these fastenings have fuzzy white growths on them. What's going on?

A. It looks like a case of "internal galvanic corrosion," in which the copper and zinc molecules in the brass alloy are reacting electrically in the presence of salt water. The white fuzz could very well be zinc oxide. As this reaction progresses, the zinc will gradually go out of the alloy completely. The copper that remains will be spongy and very weak. Looks like you'd better plan on a tedious refastening job in the near future.

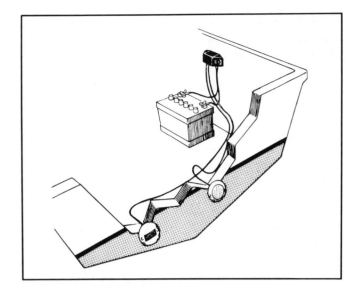

Here's Mercury Marine's "Mercathode" impressed-current anti-corrosion device. The little black box senses variations in corrosion-causing electric current acting on an outboard motor or stern drive lower unit and sends a neutralizing current into the water via the electrodes on the transom.

Electrolysis in Trailered Boat

Q. Do I need to worry about electrolysis problems in my big outboard boat, which is kept on a trailer when not in use?

A. Basically, no. It's the boats that sit at moorings or that are tied to docks for weeks and months on end that suffer. The constant immersion of the underwater parts in salt water (or electrically-conductive polluted fresh water) does the damage. But after use in salt water, rinse any boat off well with fresh water to avoid as much as possible the collecting of salt water from spray in the many places aboard where it can do damage—in hinges, on plated surfaces, inside light fixtures, and the many other spots where there are two or more different metals and a tendency for the water to remain for some time.

Outboard Motor Corrosion

Q. Wouldn't a good bronze propeller be better on my outboard motor for use in salt water than a much cheaper aluminum one?

A. No. With a bare bronze propeller in the water close to an aluminum lower unit with the inevitable scratches in its paint, you have a good setup for galvanic corrosion and it will be the aluminum that will suffer—often badly. The only advantage of a bronze prop is that the blades can be thinner due to the tougher metal, so it will help performance a little. And if they get bent, bronze blades can be hammered straight with less danger of cracking than aluminum ones.

Chapter 4

General Hardware Problems

Costly Sea Cocks

Q. Bronze sea cocks used in boats have come to cost altogether too much. Why don't the marine supply companies make them out of plastic? Surely modern plastics are good enough for the job. They'd cost less and would not be subject to corrosion.

A. At least one firm has put them on the market, but took them off again. The basic problem is that they have not yet found a plastic that will solve a seemingly simple, but nevertheless important, problem. After long immersion in water, such plastics as are otherwise suited to this application tend to slightly swell—just enough to make sea cocks jam and difficult to close, or make their handles subject to breaking off. Because of this weakness, safety standards specify that only bronze be used. This discourages those who would develop a good plastic one, for after they had perfected it they would have to struggle to get the standards changed. When and if a plastic sea cock is developed and approved, its availability will be widely publicized in the boating press.

As this book went to press, RC Marine East, 862 Mantoloking Rd., Brick Town, N.J. 08723 had introduced a plastic valve. They do not say if it is ABYC-approved in their ads, but claim several prominent boatbuilders are using their valves.

Brass Substitutes?

Q. Why can't I use brass shutoff valves from a plumbing supply store in place of bronze sea cocks in my powerboat's cooling system?

A. Because safety standards do not approve brass, use of valves made of it could void your boat's insurance. Real sea cocks are of the "ball valve" type; plumbing cocks are usually of the "gate valve" type. In many, the gate is rather thin and it could corrode through rather quickly. Brass, made of copper and zinc, will lose its zinc through internal galvanic action and the remaining copper will be weak.

Sea cocks like these are made of bronze to comply with existing safety standards.

Why Plastic Through-Hulls?

Q. *Since they don't allow sea cocks to be made of plastics, why do they allow through-hull fittings to be made of plastic?*

A. There are no moving parts in through-hull fittings, and therefore nothing to swell and jam from exposure to water.

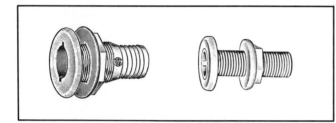

Plastic through-hull fittings are acceptable on pleasure boats because they have no moving parts that might swell and jam.

Swapping Used Hardware

Q. *I'm sickened by what it is going to cost to buy marine hardware to complete the large schooner I am building. Is there any company or club that specializes in buying, selling, and trading used and surplus marine items?*

A. There have been attempts to start such a service, but as far as we are aware there is no well-established, well-known operation like this. From time to time people try to start such services. You can find their small and usually intermittent advertisements in specialty periodicals such as *National Fisherman, The Woodenboat, The Small Boat Journal,* etc. The basic problem is that there are so many items that are being or have been used on boats that collecting, sorting, stocking, advertising, and selling endless odds and ends could require so much time and paperwork that the items might have to be priced so high as to offer boat owners no savings. Your best bet is to place a "wanted" ad in one or more publications such as those mentioned above.

Not Enough Hardware

Q. *I am rather unhappy with the meager amount of hardware on the decks of my new boat—things such as chocks, cleats, etc. Why do boatbuilders skimp so much on such vital equipment?*

A. Admittedly, partly to keep the price tag down. But there is another and quite legitimate reason. In a mass-production factory, there is no way to tell how each boat will be used by whomever buys it. Some owners will keep their craft on trailers, some will keep theirs at docks, some at moorings, yet others will make use of dryland marinas where boats are forklifted onto racks. One man will use his boat for fishing, another will never fish. Some will tow water skiers, others never will. If hardware is installed to meet every conceivable use, many owners will complain about the cost and clutter. It is best to sell boats with a bare minimum of equipment and let owners choose what they want.

Boatbuilders have no way of knowing where and how each craft they build will be sold and used so they install only a minimum of standard equipment and leave it to individual purchasers to choose and install whatever supplementary items may be desired. (Evinrude Motors)

Polishing Stainless Steel

Q. *None of the hardware store metal cleaners and polishes I have tried do any good in brightening up dulled stainless steel fittings on my boat. Where can one get an effective polish?*

A. Marine Development & Research Corp. of Freeport, N.Y. makes a "Stainless Steel Cleaner-Polish" that is sold through marine supply stores. You may find other products in this category in marine stores.

Polishing Aluminum

Q. I have been using hardware store and marine store metal polishes on the aluminum hardware on my boat. It works fairly well but does not get rid of pitting. Is there anything I can do?

A. For good results on stubborn polishing jobs you really need to use a buffing wheel driven by a bench grinder. A variety of buffing compounds in stick form are sold for use with cloth wheels; they are made to get best results on various kinds of metals so it's important to use the proper compound. Try a factory or industrial supply house or hardware stores catering to shops and factories.

Polishing Cheap Hardware

Q. My mass-produced boat has deck hardware made of die-cast zinc, chrome plated. It is covered with pits and blisters. Can anything be done?

A. Marine supply stores sell cleaners for chrome. "ABC Cleaner" by Marine Development & Research Corp. is one. There comes a time when low-priced hardware is beyond saving. You will find that some "chrome plated" light fixtures are nothing but molded plastic with a type of plating called "zinc chromate" that is found on the bright trim of toys, novelties, etc. Volume manufacturers have to put fancy trimming on their boats to sell to people who judge by glitter, and they have to keep all this trimming cheap to appeal to those who buy by price.

Protecting Stored Chrome

Q. Is there anything wrong with the idea of spreading a thin film of Vaseline on a boat's bright-plated deck hardware to protect it from corrosion during long periods of storage?

A. There's no real objection to it. Some boatyards in coastal areas do it all the time, on the assumption that it will get into pits and blisters and tend to keep salt specks remaining there after wash-down from doing too much damage. The main objection is that it will collect dust and dirt as time passes and become a messy job to clean off. If hardware is mounted on teak decks, Vaseline could stain the wood around the bases of the coated hardware. So will a light oil. We have seen good results from spraying parts with WD-40 and then wrapping them in Saran Wrap. Our own preference is to wash salt and dirt off, let dry well, go over the hardware with a suitable cleaner/polish, and then apply a few coats of auto or boat wax. There is no draining into wood and no spring cleaning-off fuss.

Removing Old Chrome

Q. What is the best way to remove old, peeling chrome plating from marine hardware?

A. We know of no practical method. It's put on by the electroplating process, and professional plating shops would remove it by using their equipment in such a way as to reverse the process. Chrome plating isn't a simple matter—a great many materials and processes are used by professionals to deal with various kinds of metals, object shapes, cost requirements, etc. There is a manual that they use which contains some 700 pages of plating information! You will get nowhere with abrasive paper because chromium is one of the hardest metals known. If you try sandblasting, by the time the chrome is off you will have eaten into the softer metal underneath where it was exposed by the peeled chrome.

Homemade Chrome Plating

Q. Where can I get instructions on how to chrome plate boat hardware?

A. The home workshop magazines printed material on this subject quite a long time ago. But it was mostly doing-it-for-fun material. We doubt if any of the crude methods described would produce as attractive and durable a plating job as you'd want on good marine hardware. There are many tricks in this work, just as there are in boatbuilding, photography, etc. Electric current tends to flow from the electrode to the higher points on the object being plated. This puts too much chrome on the high spots and can leave the depressions between them with scanty plating. An experienced operator can coax the best possible results out of his equipment. Chrome does not adhere to some metals as well as it will to others; it is common in high-quality chrome plating work to first apply a plating of copper. This can improve adhesion and brilliance, and sometimes minimize galvanic corrosion problems. You have seen chrome plated auto bumpers in which the steel was almost rusted away and only a fragile shell of chrome was holding things in shape. This is an example of such corrosion. You won't do much chrome work on a typical boat overhaul job; the time and money you spend on equipment and supplies would better be spent by having a good professional do a top quality job for you.

Transom Drain Tubes

Q. The brass tube at the bottom of my outboard boat's transom, into which the rubber drain plug fits, has corroded and cracked apart. I bought a new one and made a mess of trying to fix it in place by tapping a flange onto it with a machinist's hammer. How do boat shops do such a smooth job of installing these items?

A. They use a special flanging tool available from marine hardware distributors. A number of firms in the "OEM" marine hardware field make them. OEM means "Original Equipment Manufacturers," a fancy trade term for factories. Many smaller boat shops do not have one of these tools. If you don't want to buy one, just ask around among local shops; somebody is bound to have one. Moeller and Attwood are two firms that make them.

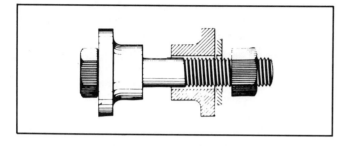

Transom drain-plug tubes are installed with a special flanging tool available from marine supply firms. (Olson Industries)

Drain Tube Holes

Q. I want to install a few more transom drain tubes in my big outboard boat so some low spots will drain faster and better, but I'm afraid to just rush in and bore holes in the transom. Please tell me how to do the job right.

A. On one hand, you want the tubes to be as close to the floor level on the inside as possible, so all water will drain. But on the other hand, you have to locate the tubes far enough above inside floor level to allow space for the flange—as a rough rule, at least one-eighth of an inch, with a quarter of an inch being more than ample. It is best to hold one of the tubes against the inside of the transom and mark the circle with a felt-tip pen. If you start from the outside, you can easily get the hole too high or too low on the inside. It's a mistake to bore right through with a high-speed wood bit driven by an electric drill; due to the hard layers of fiberglass mat between the layers of plywood in the transom core, the bit can start to dull on its way through the two inches or so of transom thickness. Soon after that happens the point will begin to "wander" and you can end up with a hole that does not go straight through. Then it's difficult to install the tube well.

A better way is to make a pilot hole all the way through with about a one-eighth inch twist drill. Take care to hold the drill as vertical as possible to the transom surface. This pilot hole will make a larger tool tend to go straighter. The neatest work can be done by using a round hole saw to go through the thicker layers of fiberglass on the outside of the wood. Saw in about a quarter of an inch or until wood dust begins to show. Stop, withdraw the hole saw, and use a screwdriver to

pry out the fiberglass disc on the inside of the saw's cut. This will expose the plywood core. Go through that with a high speed wood bit. Go all the way through; if you go halfway through from inside and then halfway from the outside, your holes may not line up where they meet.

Once you have the hole, brush several applications of preservative onto the exposed wood transom core. Let dry. Smear bedding compound around in the hole, pressing it vigorously into the wood grain. Tap the brass tube in with a rubber hammer or lay a small square of wood on the tube and tap against that to avoid denting the tube. The tube should extend about an eighth of an inch from the inside of the transom. Less than that won't give an adequate flange, more than that can lead to a split flange or crumpling of the thin brass tubing. If the tube needs to be shortened, do the job with a sharp plumber's tube cutter to get a clean, square cutoff.

Bigger Transom Tubes

Q. My boat has a one-inch transom drain tube. It takes forever for a cockpit full of rainwater to drain out. Does anyone make larger ones?

A. A few firms make slightly larger ones, about one and a quarter inches. That's enough to let appreciably more water out. Look in the Moeller and Feik catalogs at a marine supply store. The usual drain tube has an inside diameter of seven-eighths of an inch and fits into a one-inch hole. We have asked boatbuilders why they use such small drains. They say, "We have to use whatever we can get from the hardware firms." We asked the hardware firms why they don't offer larger sizes as standard. They say, "We make one-inch tubes because that's the size the boatbuilders specify when they place orders." It's just another example of the inertia that characterizes the hardware field.

Remote Control Drains

Q. Due to arthritis, it is hard for me to reach under the slop well in the stern of my boat to get at the transom drain plug. Does anyone make a remote controlled plug?

A. Such plugs have been on and off the market for years. At the time we write this, we know of none that are on the market. The big hardware firms don't often add new things to their lines, and the small firms find it hard to penetrate the market well enough to stay in it. Various remote control drains we have seen all had one disadvantage or another—too small an opening to pass much water, a tendency to stick part way open due to bits of debris on their seats, awkward or complicated installation or controls, you name it. Your best bet is to install one of the fine small electric bilge pumps.

Water flows out a typical seven-eighths-inch diameter tube at around 200 gallons per hour, where the smallest electric pumps will handle 400 gallons a minute and slightly larger ones will get rid of 1200 to 1800 gallons in the same period. If your problem is the plug in a trailered boat, try putting the plug in from the outside. That's much easier to do. The likelihood of a snugly-fitting plug falling out at sea is very small, and you can affix an extra one on the inside with a small length of chain to have a spare plug which can be installed from inside the boat in the remote event that your outside one drops out.

Hatch Track

Q. The hatch on my old cabin cruiser slides back and forth on a track that is made of some kind of brass or bronze, I'm not sure which. It is cracked and bent. The company that made the boat has been out of business for 30 years. What are my chances of finding a replacement?

A. Pretty good. Our hunch is that what is on your old boat's hatch is nothing other than common sail track as used on the wooden masts of sailboats. Some of it was made of brass, some of nickel silver. Now that wooden masts have been replaced almost completely by aluminum ones, not so many dealers stock it but you can find some at a yard which caters to sailboats. Using sail track for hatch slides is typical of the ingenuity displayed by custom boatbuilding shops.

This is a section of sail track, together with a slide made to fit on it. The original purpose was to connect sails to wooden masts but boatbuilders found other uses, such as for sliding hatches.

Transom Braces

Q. I am going to install a larger motor on my outboard boat and am worried about transom strength. Does anyone make metal transom bracing brackets?

A. Not today. We remember seeing them in catalogs a score of years ago when wooden outboard boats were still common. But the market for them dried up when fiberglass and aluminum took over. You can stiffen your transom with oak strips or a thick plywood plate. Set the wood in bedding compound and fasten with bronze carriage bolts run through the transom with their heads outboard.

No Transom Knee

Q. My son is in the Coast Guard and is a nut on boat safety. He frets because our large outboard boat has no transom knee. He says any well-made boat should have one to transmit motor forces from transom to keel. The boat is made of fiberglass. Is there any way we could install one?

A. What is true of traditional wooden boats is not always true of those made from other materials. A bolted-on wooden knee would concentrate forces under the bolt heads and nuts; the fiberglass would flex and perhaps eventually crumble. Designers of fiberglass boats use other methods of coping with motor weight and thrust. The curved transom on Boston Whaler boats, for example, is naturally stiffer than a flat one. The typical fiberglass outboard transom has a plywood core at least an inch and a half thick, and may have fiberglass sheathing on both surfaces from one-eighth to one-quarter of an inch thick. This is very strong. Then, it is common practice to bond the slop well to the transom with several layers of glass fabric. That makes the well stiffen the transom and motor loads are transmitted to the hull with no localized stress points. So, no knee!

Because the slop well, which is built into the after end of the deck molding, is usually built strongly and well-fastened to the transom, it does an excellent job of stiffening the transom against motor forces. Thus, transom knees are not required on modern fiberglass outboard boats.

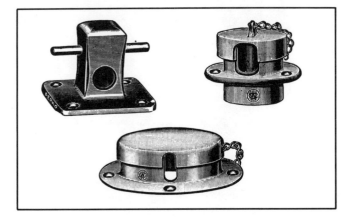

There are different ways of doing things. The mooring bitt, left, has a hole so anchor line can be fed into a locker below the deck. Small size of hole makes this a tedious proposition. The rope deck plate, center, has a cap that comes off and lets rope be fed in much faster. Chain deck plate, right, has a slotted hole to accept one of the last links in the chain, enabling rope and chain to both be fed into locker quickly and neatly.

Different Deck Plates

Q. *Following recommended practice to improve holding power, I have a length of chain between the end of my anchor line and the anchor. Now I find that the chain will not pass through the hole in the bitt on the foredeck. I hate to file the hole oversize as that will fracture the chrome plating. What would you do?*

A. It pays to make a habit of browsing in marine supply catalogs. There are one-piece bitts that have just a round hole in them. It takes a lot of time to feed rope through such a hole and such a bitt is good only for a short mooring line. Also available are "rope deck pipes" and "chain deck pipes." A cap comes off to allow rope to be fed rapidly into the locker. One type has a round hole for the rope to fit into when the cap is on. The other type has a hole with a slotted shape, to fit the links in a chain. If you install the latter type you can stow things quickly and neatly.

Chapter 5

Screws, Nails, and Fastenings

Cost of Wood Screws

Q. I am building a plywood dinghy and am appalled at the cost of bronze wood screws—about nine dollars for a box of 100 small ones! The boat will be out of water when not in use, so can't I use galvanized steel screws?

A. You are right, the cost of bronze and brass screws is discouraging to the boat owner. There are two kinds of galvanizing—"bright plated" and "hot dipped." The bright plated ones have a thin coating of zinc that is applied by the electroplating process. Such screws are all right in household and general use. But the coating is too thin to offer much rust protection in a severe marine environment. However, they can be used in small boats like yours where exposure is not severe and the wood is not likely to become and remain waterlogged. We have used them successfully on many plywood boats which were fiberglassed; in such construction the screws are so well buried in the wood and insulated from water that they will last a long time.

Most small plywood boats use glue or adhesive compound between the plywood and the frames. When this has set or cured, it is what really holds the boat together. As a stunt you could remove all the screws and the boat would stay together! The screws serve mainly to hold things while the adhesive sets. So it follows that your small boat would remain serviceable even if a number of the screws eventually rusted away.

Theoretically, hot-dipped galvanizing is better than bright plated. The metal parts are immersed in molten zinc and

come out with an appreciably heavier coating. The problem is that in the sizes commonly used in small boats, such as #6, #7, and #8, the zinc tends to fill in and round off the screw threads and to fill in the screwdriver slots. The threads are often so shallow and blunt that they will not cut into wood cleanly and will not hold well. You will also throw away several out of a boxful because the slots are too heavily filled to accept a screwdriver blade. What is needed is a line of wood screws made of a hard, corrosion-resistant aluminum alloy. But, we have found in 35 years of working around boats that there is a vast amount of inertia in the hardware industry. "If it was good enough for grandpa, it's good enough for me" they will say, when asked to give us something better suited to present needs.

This is a typical size of wood screw used in small boat work. Hot-dipped galvanized ones tend to have the threads and slots filled with zinc so they drive in poorly about two times out of ten.

Serrated Nails

Q. The plans for the small boat I am making call for annular ringed nails, also called serrated nails. A friend has advised me against them. Is his advice good?

A. Could be. These nails work well some places, poorly in others. The bronze ones came into wide use during World War II when numerous boat shops were banging out wooden utility boats for the armed forces as fast as they could. Makers of these nails were hurt by the turn to fiberglass, so now they try to maintain a toehold in the pleasure boating trade by selling the nails to marine dealers in blister packages mounted on display boards.

We have used them and can make some comments. Although the shanks hold very tenaciously in wood, the rather small heads will let the piece of wood being retained pull past them somewhat easily. The serrations seem to weaken the thinner sizes of these nails so they often bend when being driven. To prevent this, you have to drill pilot holes. The thicker ones have a lot of resistance when going into wood, so to enable them to be driven without undue hammer force, you also have to make pilot holes. If you drive them without making pilot holes, the force of the hammer blows will flex the wooden parts on a typical lightly built small boat, and the hammer will bounce and be hard to manage. Since you usually have to drill pilot holes, you save no time here over using wood screws.

Screws can be turned down tight with a slow, firm twist of a screwdriving blade mounted in a bit stock. This squeezes glue out of the joint so you get a snug joint. You cannot do this very well with serrated nails, especially on "bouncy" wood. When using screws, you can hold wood parts in place temporarily to check fit, remove, apply adhesive, reinstall, and snug down. You can try these nails. If they work well on your job, fine! If not, you will know you're not alone in finding that screws often work out better.

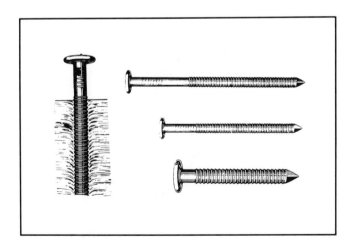

Serrated or "ringed" nails hold very well but have their peculiarities. Pieces of wood they hold in place can pull off their small heads. The long, thin ones tend to bend when being hammered. They have so much resistance when being driven that it is usually necessary to drill pilot holes so the saving in time is not as great as anticipated.

Copper Rivets

Q. *I am reconditioning an old lapstrake boat and am unable to get copper rivets at any of the local marine stores. Where can I get them?*

A. Wholesalers and retailers in today's pleasure boating scene stock items that will sell to the people who own modern mass-produced boats. They stock less and less of the traditional, old-time wooden boat items. A prominent firm specializing in all kinds of marine fastenings is Clendenin Bros., Inc., 4309 Erdman Ave., Baltimore, Md. 21213. Look for specialty supply companies in the classified advertising section of *The Woodenboat* magazine, such as Skookum and Duck Trap. A sample copy of this magazine can be purchased from the publisher, whose address is Brooklin, Maine 04616.

Boat Nails

Q. *We are going to build a reproduction of an old dory and wonder where to get galvanized boat nails. Local marine stores don't carry them and don't know where to get them.*

A. Sure! More and more of the people behind counters at today's marine stores were born after 1950. You can't expect them to know where to get obsolete hardware that the ship chandlers of 1920 stocked. See the previous paragraph on "Copper Rivets." Also, send a self-addressed stamped envelope to Tremont Nail Co., P.O. Box 111, Wareham, Mass. 02571 for current price list of roves and cut steel boat nails. A "rove" is a kind of rivet and washer combination sometimes used on heavier lapstrake boats, such as those of Scandinavian origin.

Blunt Points on Boat Nails

Q. *A friend is restoring a fine old schooner. He showed me some of the boat nails he's using in the work. I was amazed at their blunt points. One would think they would have the sharpest possible points to go into hard woods well. Why the bluntness?*

A. We moderns are forgetting a lot of the lessons the old-timers learned from experience. The blunt ends shear wood fibers as they penetrate, punching a hole that has a minimum tendency to split the wood. A long, slim point would have a wedging action and would encourage splitting. It's about the same idea as the "wad cutter" bullets used for pistol practice on paper targets, as compared to the round-nosed bullets used for outdoor shooting.

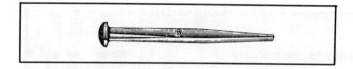

Boat nails have rather blunt points that punch holes through the wood, minimizing tendency to split.

Boat is "Nail Sick"

Q. *A friend owns an old boat and says it probably isn't worth reconditioning because it is "nail sick." What does this mean?*

A. The iron nails are badly rusted. Although they were treated by the hot-dip galvanizing process, the zinc coating does not last indefinitely. Further hammering on the heads and bending over the points (clenching) fractures the galvanized coating at the places where nails are most exposed to water. As nails rust away, they loosen in the wood. Nail sickness shows up in the form of rust streaks in the paint, weeping downwards from every point in the hull planking where there is a nail. Galvanized boat nails typically were used in wooden workboats. A workboat is given rough use and often wear and tear bring its useful life to an end long before the nails begin to rust seriously. When a pleasure craft is built with them and is used carefully and usually only in the summertime, its wood lasts a long time and gives nail sickness more chance to show up and become a serious problem.

Removing Old Nails and Screws

Q. *How does one remove the remains of corroded nails and screws from a wooden boat?*

A. There is no simple, pat way. If the boat is old and will probably not last many more years, old fastenings are often left in place and new ones put in near them. One can try grinding the jaws of a pair of pliers or Vise Grips to parrot-beak shape and use the tool to twist and pull old screws out. Or, one can use a small electric grinding tool to remove as much of the old fastening head as possible and "paint" the bare metal with epoxy cement to seal it and hopefully stop rust from bleeding through the putty or deck plug used to fill the hole.

Lapstrake Fastenings

Q. *What is the best kind of fastening to use at the plank overlaps of a lapstrake boat?*

A. There's no pat answer to this question. One must remember that lapstrake hulls have been made of various kinds of wood, in various thicknesses, and with various kinds of seam compounds or even none at all. So, various builders have chosen different fastenings to suit particular circumstances. Whatever you find in a particular boat, think over the conditions the fastenings had to fulfill and you will usually realize that whatever fastenings were used, they filled the particular need well.

Iron vs. Steel

Q. *A variety of books about traditional wooden boat construction have given me the strong feeling that galvanized iron fastenings are the ideal answer to the conflicting requirements of low cost and durability. But the galvanized screws available in my area are made of steel. Is this just as good? If not, where can I get iron ones?*

A. The evidence is that virgin wrought iron made long ago had excellent resistance to rust. Much of that old stuff was hand-made. Today, what is labelled "wrought iron" is not virgin. That is to say, it has been made by melting down old iron or at least some scrap metal has been blended in with the newly-mined or "virgin" metal. While this new metal may be made by the same process, it can contain alloying metals not found in the old-time iron. So corrosion resistance may not be as good, and can prove to be quite unpredictable. The galvanized steel screws stocked by today's marine hardware stores would probably be the same as you'd get in hardware stores. There simply is not enough demand today for this kind of thing to justify stocking something special. These stores cater to the yacht trade and assume most customers would want bronze screws for their high-grade boats.

Silicon or Silicone?

Q. *Where can I get silicone bronze screws? And by the way, can you tell me how they manage to alloy a chemical like silicone with the copper and tin in bronze?*

A. People get confused between "silicon" and "silicone." The two are entirely different. In regard to bronze, the proper form is "silicon bronze." It is an alloy that has good strength and corrosion resistance. Silicon is a nonmetallic element, very common in nature. Silicone is a product of modern chemistry.

Everdur Screws

Q. *In marine catalogs I see references to "Everdur" screws. What are these?*

Lapstrake boats have been made of many kinds of wood, fastened together by a variety of fasteners. There is no pat answer to "what kinds of fasteners are best?"

A. Everdur is the trade name for silicon bronze alloy screws made by The Anaconda Company. It is an alloy well suited for marine use.

Testing Screws

Q. My cruiser is now 25 years old. I am beginning to wonder how well the plank fastenings have stood up. I took a few screws out of the cabin structure while making some modifications and they broke off easily, so of course my thoughts turned to the hull fastenings.

A. We can tell from the name you mentioned that yours is a mass-produced boat. Small shops making custom boats tend to use one kind of screw metal throughout their craft, because it is easier to order one kind in the modest quantities needed. But in mass production—especially of boat equipment aimed at the mass market which often means 10% sales in saltwater areas and 90% sales in freshwater areas— there is a tendency to use a variety of materials. Screws are bought in such huge quantities that substantial savings can be realized by using lower-cost metals where such metals can be expected to serve adequately. Thus, your boat probably has brass screws in her superstructure and internal finish work, and bronze screws in the hull. Brass and bronze both come in many alloys, with varying durability under different conditions. It is anyone's guess what was used in your boat. It is common for large firms to buy in quantity at the lowest prices they can find from suppliers of a wide range of materials. Often they buy from firms that are not specialists in the marine trade. Your boat could have very good fastenings or rather poor ones.

Uncover screw heads by digging out putty or wooden plugs over their heads. With a bit stock fitted with a screwdriver blade, take out several screws from scattered locations. When screws are driven in, they "wipe" wood fibers in the direction of rotation. These fibers then serve as tiny "ratchets" that resist backing-out of the screws. It can be hard to "start" old screws to come out. First try increasing pressure on the bitstock handle. If that fails, "bump" the handle with the palm of your hand. Or fit an adjustable wrench to a square-shank screwdriver and use the wrench as a handle to twist the driver. While twisting, have a helper rap the screwdriver handle smartly with a medium-weight hammer.

If attempts to remove several scattered screws fail, it's obvious the screws are in sound condition and holding securely. If you manage to get several out, a quick inspection will show whether or not they are sound. If there is some corrosion and you are in doubt, put one screw at a time into the jaws of a vise and try bending with a hammer; if they snap off they are brittle, probably from corrosion. Then you have to use judgment to decide if the ones remaining in the boat are good enough to be trusted for a while longer.

If screws come out easily, yet appear to be in good condition, the ease with which they were removed could mean the wood around their threads is soft. In such a case it would be wise to replace them with screws of the next larger diameter. It is basically a matter of thinking about what you see and then doing what common sense indicates is right.

Trunnels

Q. What are "trunnels"? I've heard the word around boat shops.

A. They are wooden fasteners. Trunnels is a contraction of "tree nails." They are simply dowels made of a hard, durable wood pounded into holes bored in ships' framing where two pieces of wood are joined. Ends are then sawn off and hardwood wedges driven into both ends to expand the wood and lock the trunnels in place. Rarely found in pleasure craft, they are usually found only in ships and heavier old-time yachts where timbers are large enough to take holes for trunnels of acceptable strength. Locust is a typically used wood, being tough and highly rot-resistant.

Brass Screws

Q. I bought many boxes of brass screws at a flea market. Can I use them in a 15-foot plywood outboard boat I would like to make? A friend says I'm foolish to do it.

A. If you were building a conventionally planked 30-foot boat for use in salt water, we'd advise against using them. Your friend probably heard someone speak against them in this context and jumped to the conclusion that what might be

true of some boats is true of all boats. This is common; we encounter it all the time.

We have been working on boats for 35 years and have written over 2000 articles on boating. Yet every so often, some local character who does not know anything about our background comes along, watches what we are doing on a particular job, and says, "You're doing it all wrong! You should do it my way! My grandfather was a sea captain and told me all about how boats should be built!" When we try to explain that what we are doing is logical and acceptable for the very different circumstances applicable to the small boat we happen to be building from modern materials, he refuses to listen and stalks off calling us "nuts."

We suspect that the "instant-gratification" culture in which we live has produced a breed of person who expects pat answers to any and all questions and problems. When this type finds that there are in fact many "ifs," "buts," and "maybes" involved in a situation, he is shaken and hides his discomfiture behind a smokescreen of bluster.

Years ago when using brass screws in plywood boats, we dipped an artist's paint brush in Plastic Wood Thinner and put a drop of this fluid on the head of each screw before covering it with a dab of Plastic Wood. That made the Plastic Wood adhere tenaciously. Subsequent coats of primer and paint completed an excellent sealing-in job. We recently had a letter from a man who had bought one of those boats 25 years previously; he commented on how pleased he was with its durability! Today, we use common polyester auto body putty over screw heads in plywood boats; it is compounded to cling well to metal, hardens much faster, sands well, and does not swell upon exposure to water. So you see—it all depends on the particular circumstances.

Driving Wood Screws

Q. My old plywood boat has oak frames. While replacing corroded screws I had a bad time driving new ones in—at least half of them broke off when they were about three-quarters of the way in. I got big blisters on my palm from the screwdriver handle. How do professionals do it to make it look so easy?

A. You've given us a perfect example of what we have been saying. You've made the mistake of assuming there's a simple, pat way of doing everything. We don't know why the builder of your boat used oak for framing. Oak is fine for ribs in round-bottom boats because it is easy to steam and bend onto a building form with no wasted scraps. But it is stronger than necessary for the sawn frames used in vee-bottom boats. That is why a wood like Philippine mahogany is often used for sawn frames—it's easier to bandsaw, takes glue better at joints, and is much easier to drive screws into while still having good screw-holding power.

However, you are stuck with those oak frames. In oak, pilot holes are even more important than in softer woods. The pilot-hole tools sold in hardware stores under such names as "Screw-Mate" are designed for general carpentry use in the soft woods common to home workshops and everyday carpentry, but they can make a pilot hole a bit too tight for easy driving of screws into oak. Experiment on scraps to find a size of drill that will enlarge these holes just enough to make driving screws into oak acceptably easy while still leaving enough wood for good thread "bite." Wipe screw threads across a block of beeswax so enough clings to the threads to afford lubrication—soap will work too but could encourage corrosion. Use a ratchet screwdriver to put screws in speedily; when resistance builds up so it's hard to keep turning them with this tool, switch to a bit stock fitted with a screwdriver blade for the final turns.

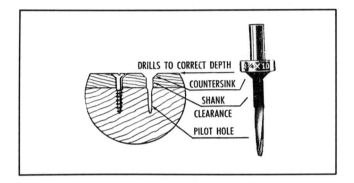

DRILLS TO CORRECT DEPTH 1/4 X 10

COUNTERSINK

SHANK

CLEARANCE

PILOT HOLE

The "Screw Mate" tool does quick work of drilling pilot holes for wood screws. Sold at most hardware stores.

Stanchion Screws

Q. The life line stanchions on my large sailboat are held down with No. 12 stainless steel wood screws. But they tend to work loose. Any suggestions?

A. Due to its height, a modest force on the top of such a part will develop a lot of leverage. How long are the No. 12 screws? Fairly long, slim ones are awkward and slow to drive, and screwdriver blades will often slip from their slots and scratch or chip nearby areas. The exigencies of mass-production might have obliged the boat's manufacturer to use shorter ones. Few factory people do any serious boating and sometimes it falls to boat owners to learn that things that seemed logical in the shop don't stand up on the sea. If your No. 12 screws are, say, two inches long, try three- or four-inch ones. Actually, stanchions should be installed with bolts and nuts, with washers under the nuts. This calls for one man on deck and another below decks—in volume production there's the cost-control man's ever present temptation to get the job done by putting one man on the deck with a power-driven screwdriver. If you feel this is gypping the boat buyer, take a look at prices asked for custom-built boats put

together by perfectionists! Whether we own, build, or repair boats, we all have to change with changing conditions.

Getting Nuts on Bolts

Q. The way my fiberglass boat is built, in some areas there's just no way to get at the lower ends of stanchion bolts to put washers and nuts on. Any ideas?

A. Some simple surgery might work. With a hole-cutting saw, make holes of from one to one and one-half inches in diameter in the interior fiberglass. Use a "mechanical finger" to put washers and nuts on. If washers keep dropping off, use a long-handled artist's brush to dab contact cement onto the area and on the washers. Then they'll stay put while nuts are threaded on. Plug the holes with the small, round, molded plastic ventilating louvers sold at hardware stores. They will look so natural and appropriate that people will not realize they were installed to plug the holes you had to make.

Pop Rivets

Q. I bought a used outboard boat. Soon after starting to use it, rust streaks started to appear on the sides below the gunwales. On removing the vinyl gunwale material to investigate, I found the pop rivets were all rusty. Have I bought a "gyp" boat?

A. We don't think so. It looks as if the previous owner replaced the gunwale material and got confused between aluminum and steel pop rivets. The latter are plated and, unless you are aware of the difference or put them side-by-side so you notice the difference, it's easy not to realize there are both steel and aluminum rivets on the market. The steel ones are good where strength is needed, but on a boat you need the aluminum ones. Looks like you will be doing some drilling out and replacing!

Pop rivets are widely used in fiberglass boats because they make a lot of sense. There are no nuts or washers to be installed—sometimes painstakingly—on inner ends. There are no threads to be cut in holes. In production work, power-driven guns "pop" them rapidly. If the holes are the right size and the rivets the proper length for the work (not too long; long ones bend over, don't swell tight in the hole area), they hold very well. They are amply strong for many hinges, light hardware, trim strips, etc. They make a fast job of holding deck and hull moldings together snugly and accurately while fiberglass seam compound or strips of resin-soaked mat cure for more permanent assembly.

Like anything else, pop rivets can be misused. But then blame the boatbuilder, not the rivets! They should not be used for attaching hardware that will be subject to heavy loads or which is vital to safety. It's wrong to the point of unethical to assemble fiberglass decks to hulls solely with pop rivets; the vibration and flexing puts excess loading on the rivets and on the fiberglass around them and loosens things up. Aluminum pop rivets used with plain brass or bronze hinges can quickly suffer from galvanic corrosion, but aluminum rivets with chrome plated brass and with stainless steel work satisfactorily in this regard.

Two sizes are in common use, one-eighth inch and three-sixteenths inch. Use drills of the same size so the rivets are a light press fit in holes made in fiberglass. Choose length so the inner ends project from the backside of the work far enough to readily expand but not bend over. Old pop rivets are very easy to remove; just use a high-speed twist drill of either one-eighth or three-sixteenths inch diameter. It will take the head off and either push or drill out the shanks of the old rivets. Just feed the drill in slowly so it follows the "pilot hole" formed by the mandrel hole. A variable-speed electric drill is best as it allows a slow start and gentle feed.

Stripped Threads in Fiberglass

Q. Some of the smaller items of equipment aboard my fiberglass boat are held on with self-tapping stainless steel screws. Vibration has caused the screws to chew the laminate around them and loosen so they are all dropping out. What should I do?

A. Various things. If you can get at the back sides of the panels where the screws are, thread the screws in as snugly as possible, then cover the exposed threads on the back side with small dabs of polyester auto body putty. If you can't get at the back sides, whittle a popsicle stick into a small putty-knife and use it to press this material into the holes, thread the screws in, hold them until the putty begins to set, and later turn the screws a quarter-turn or so to snug tight. Or fill the holes in similar fashion with quick-set epoxy glue. Many

SCALE IN INCHES 5/8 1/4 1/2 1/8		RIVET DIA. (In Inches)	RIVET LENGTH Work Thickness In Inches	DESCRIPTION
Short Rivets		1/8	1/8	Short Aluminum
				Short Aluminum White Painted
				Short Aluminum Closed-End
				Short Steel
				Short Steel Countersunk
				Short Steel Large Flange
				Short Copper
Medium Rivets		1/8	1/4	Medium Alum.
				Medium Steel
Long Rivets		1/8	1/2	Long Alum.
Long Rivets				Long Steel
EXTRA SHORT RIVETS		3/16	1/8	Extra Short Aluminum
Short Rivets		3/16	1/4	Short Aluminum
				Short Aluminum Closed-End
Medium Rivets		3/16	1/2	Medium Alum.
Long Rivets		3/16	5/8	Long Aluminum

Pop rivets come in a variety of sizes. Their use is very common on fiberglass boats.

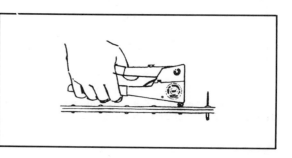

Hardware stores sell pop rivet guns. They save much time when it is difficult or impossible to reach the back side of the work to put nuts on screws.

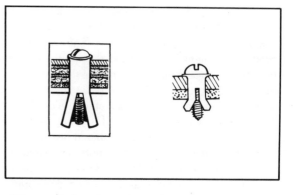

"Fibergrip" plugs from Marine Development & Research are made of tough plastic and make quick and dependable work of putting screws into fiberglass.

marine stores carry plastic inserts made by Marine Development and Research Corp. of Freeport, N.Y. Pick a suitable size, press or tap into the hole, and drive the screws. They work almost identically to "expansion shields" sold in hardware stores for making screws hold in holes drilled in masonry. With these ideas as starters, you can think up other ways of doing it. In a pinch, a good boat mechanic might even make up small pieces of plywood, drill pilot holes in them, hold them in place on the back side of the fiberglass, and drive the screws into these "nuts." There's always more than one way to do something—use your imagination!

Hard-to-Find Clips

Q. Some of the equipment in my fiberglass boat is held in place with some odd-looking clips. Local marine stores never saw anything like them. I need some replacements. What do I do?

A. Here's another case where mass-produced boats use items not available at the retail level. You will find the same situation in your car, refrigerator, etc. Production men are always looking for clever products that will facilitate quick assembly. Many of these items are designed to be used with automatic or power-driven installation tools. Inspect the clips closely for some name or trade mark. If you find some identification, go to the library and look up the name and address of the maker in *Thomas' Register of American Manufacturers*. If there are no identifying marks, you'll have to use your ingenuity. It often pays to visit non-marine shops and stores and look around for some item that will solve your problem.

Deck Plugs

Q. I have always admired the way screw heads in fine wooden boats are hidden under wooden plugs that perfectly match the surrounding wood. How is it done? Is it hard to do?

A. It's very easy to do. The plugs can be bought in various sizes and kinds of wood, by the bagful, from marine supply houses. Or you can make your own a few at a time with a plug cutter, also available at marine stores. Another tool with an adjustable depth of cut makes a counterbored hole. After the screw has been driven, a plug is dipped in glue and gently tapped into the hole. When the glue has dried, the projecting end of the plug is carefully trimmed off with a chisel and sanded smooth.

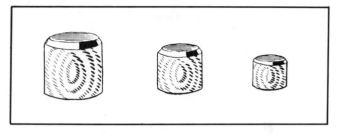

Deck plugs come in several sizes. Chamfer on one end facilitates guiding them accurately into hole in boat planking.

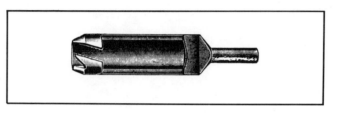

A plug cutter can be used to make up small quantities of deck plugs, using either a drill press or an electric drill.

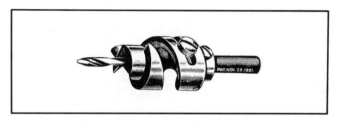

This tool, adjustable for depth of cut, makes a counterbored hole to receive the screw and the deck plug that covers it.

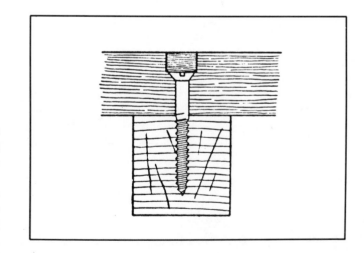

How a wooden deck plug looks when installed over a screw head. If surface is to be painted, a very durable alternate way to do it is to fill the counterbore over the screw head with epoxy glue or thickened epoxy putty. It will stay in place tenaciously.

Loose Deck Plugs

Q. Many of the deck plugs in my wooden boat have come loose. This does not happen on other boats here. What could be the trouble?

A. If the screw holes were not counterbored deep enough, the plugs may be so shallow that there is insufficient glue area, or they will warp and loosen under the effects of weather. In general, if a deck plug is three-eighths of an inch in diameter, it should go into the counterbore at least one-quarter of an inch to hold well and be stable. If too much glue is slopped into the counterbore before a plug is tapped in, it will keep the plug from going in far enough. If the glue is of a type that becomes brittle when hard, the glue under the plug will break up and have little holding power. A good way to apply glue is with a small artist's brush, wiping just enough on the sides of the counterbore to give good adhesion but not enough to form a pool of glue under the deck plug. A chronic plug-popping problem could be solved by installing the new ones with epoxy glue.

Chapter 6

Understanding Wood Rot

Why Wood Rots

Q. I have been assigned to overseas duty for two years. A relative is going to let me store my classic wooden speed-boat in one of his outbuildings. It's a clean place, the roof is tight, and there are no kids or animals around, so on those scores I am happy. But tell me, what are the chances the boat will suffer from dry rot during those two years?

A. Zero. Under the conditions you describe, it will be entirely safe from rot. There is no such thing as "dry rot." That's a figure of speech, in the same class as "deader than a doornail"—you never saw a doornail, did you, and you can't tell what one looks like, can you? We will have to look into the matter of wood rot here, because people know so little about it.

First, let's explain dry rot. It is a term that originated a long time ago, before modern science gave us an explanation of what causes wood to rot. Badly-rotted wood is always noticeably crumbled and shrunken. Because of this condition, a piece of rotten wood is of course well ventilated. If you wet it, it will promptly dry out again. So, workmen on old-time wooden ships often encountered timbers in ships that were crumbled, cracked, and *dry*. Not knowing the real cause of rot, they called it dry rot and the phrase has become part of the language. But you never saw furniture inside your house just begin to rot away, did you? If there was really such a thing as dry rot, rotting furniture would be a common sight!

Wood rots because it is attacked by certain kinds of fungus. This is a primitive form of plant life. Trees, flowers, and vegetables send their roots into the earth to find nutrients, but fungus sends its roots into wood to get food. The microscopic filaments that form fungus roots tap into wood cells and draw off the cellulose for food. This is what causes the wood to first turn soft and punky, and finally to shrivel and crack.

Fungus-caused rot is nature's way of ridding the forest floor of dead trees. If there were no rot, the ground would be so covered with dead wood that tree seeds could no longer reach the soil to germinate and grow. When a fungus plant is mature, it is visible in such forms as toadstools sprouting from dead wood in the ground and leathery conks growing out of the sides of dead trees. These "fruiting bodies" release millions of microscopic seeds called spores. Air currents carry them far and wide and they settle onto wood everywhere.

Spores behave exactly as do other seeds. The prevailing temperature must be mild—wood *does not* begin to rot in wintertime, and existing rot spots become dormant when the weather turns chilly and then cold. There must be moisture to soften them and stir the life within. And there must also be oxygen. Because wood that is in the water long enough to become waterlogged is very deficient in oxygen, rot cannot occur in it. You can prove this by sealing a piece of wood inside a bottle—the wood will become soft and may discolor, but when removed many years later and dried out will prove to be sound.

It is *dampness* that starts and promotes rot. It isn't the outer surface of the bottom planking that starts to rot first—it's really the last place rot shows up, after the inside has suffered extensively. Where rot really starts in a wooden boat is in cabin and deck joints where rainwater can seep and remain long enough to keep the wood damp, not soaked. It also starts in confined spaces below decks where there is poor ventilation. Water that leaks in from above remains, and some water gathers there from condensation.

Only fresh water will start and promote rot. Salt water will kill fungus just as it will kill grass and shrubbery when a storm carries salt spray to vegetation back from the beach line. When rot appears in boats used on salt water, its cause can be traced to rain and condensation on the topsides and deep inside.

Salting the Bilge

Q. Some local old-timers tell me I should scatter rock salt around in the bilge area of my wooden boat to prevent rot while it is in winter storage. What do you think?

A. They are exhibiting their ignorance. In the long-ago days of wooden sailing ships it was common to use salt in a certain way. In such ships the timbers are much heavier than in any pleasure boat. Big timbers are easy prey for rot because they do not dry out very quickly after being soaked with fresh water and because of the generally poor ventilation in the depths of a ship. Also, as they dry out under favorable conditions, they often develop deep cracks and checks which later admit and hold water. To combat the rot problem thus created, old-time shipbuilders fitted small wooden shelves against the inside of the planking and between the ribs. Rock salt was piled on these shelves and replenished as necessary. Fresh water leaking down from deck seams would encounter these shelves, dissolve some of the salt, and act thereafter as a fungus-killing agent as it worked its way farther down the timbers. Since such ships were held together with wooden pins, called trunnels, there was no danger of corroding metal fastenings. Such metal as there was tended to be virgin wrought iron, which had high corrosion resistance.

In a modern pleasure boat, the conditions are entirely different. Rot takes place in the cabin joints, in the upper ends of ribs where deck water leaks in, and in other places generally well above the bilge area. Putting salt in the bilge will not do a bit of good in preventing rot in such places. Since boats of this kind are held together with metal fastenings and tend to have many metal parts in their bilge areas, salting the bilge not only won't stop rot, it will usually aggravate metal corrosion problems. And, of course, since fungus becomes dormant in cold weather, salting the bilge to prevent rot during storage is like spraying insecticide on shrubbery in mid-winter—an act of futility.

Forget salting the bilge. Instead, make a cover for the boat that will shed rain and snow so as to keep fresh water out of topside joints. Leave hatches, floorboards, drawers, and lockers open to encourage constant and generous ventilation. Position the boat in a level attitude so that any fresh water that does get inside will flow down through the boat's limber holes and into the bilge. Finally, remove the drain plugs in the bilge so this water will flow out. These procedures make sense in the light of a working knowledge of wood rot.

Limber Holes

Q. I encountered the term "limber holes" on some old blueprints of a wooden boat. Was that a misprint for "lumber holes?" If so, what are those?

A. Limber hole is an old boatman's term, derived from the French word "lumiere," meaning light. You could see light through one of these holes; hence the Anglicized form of the French word made its way into our language. It's just a hole, notch, groove, or gutter cut or bored into some part of a wooden boat to allow water to drain out of a spot where it might otherwise tend to be trapped. Assuming a boat will float level on her waterline when at rest, the holes are made so water will drain out of the lowest parts of recesses when the boat is in that position. Storing it on a cradle or trailer ashore so that one end of the boat is lower than the other usually stops such drainage, hence the importance of blocking up a boat's cradle so her waterline will be horizontal while in storage. In some old boats, you can find brass chains running fore and aft through the limber holes along the keel. At one end of these chains you will find coil springs. One could pull on the chains against the springs' tension and the movement of the chain links back and forth in the limber holes would clear out accumulated silt and scum that might block the free flow of water.

Detecting Early Stages of Rot

Q. I bought a wooden boat that had been covered over with black sheet plastic. The plastic had been snugly sealed all around the gunwales with wooden strips nailed on over it. The inside of the boat has a strong musty smell that has not gone away and the boat has been airing out for a month. I am worried there may be rot. How can I tell for sure?

A. A musty smell with a peculiar sharpness to it is characteristic of actively rotting wood. Before wood is painted or varnished, it is bound to have some airborne rot spores settle on its surface. They are too small to be seen by the naked eye, and are sealed in against the wood by the finish. Paint and varnish have no fungicidal power so they do

Arrows point to "limbers," notches to each side of the stringers on the bottom of this frame for a plywood boat. Limbers allow water to drain freely from all spaces within a wooden boat that could possibly trap and retain water. A vital rot-preventing detail!

Mature fungus plants take the form of leathery growths on the surface of the wood. These give off spores in vast numbers, which are spread far and wide by air currents. (Forest Products Laboratory)

A typical specimen of rotted wood. Lacy pattern is the "hyphae," or roots, of the fungus plant which causes rot. As roots draw cellulose out of wood cells to nourish fungus plants, wood gradually softens and crumbles as its substance is drawn out of it. (Forest Products Laboratory)

not affect the ability of spores to germinate—and they can germinate after years of dormancy.

The first traces of rot are small moldy spots, which are actually the beginnings of fungus growths. These spots tend to be blackish and scattered. They can be seen under varnish, but, of course, not under paint. They are also visible on bare wood. It takes an expert to tell if a particular collection of spots are rot-causing fungus, or harmless fungus, or harmless stains. If the spots you find are in wood that has probably been warm and damp for some time— several weeks perhaps—you can suspect rot.

The first evidence of spreading rot is that the wood becomes "brash," that is, it is still hard and sound but has become somewhat brittle. Stick the point of a very sharp knife (an X-Acto modeller's knife, for example) or a large needle diagonally into the wood for a fraction of an inch. Then lift up on the wood. If the splinter is long and sharp, the wood is sound, but if the pieces of lifted wood are short and blunt-ended, it is brash. The "hyphae," or tiny, filament-like roots of the fungus plant, have spread appreciably and have been actively drawing cellulose out of the wood cells—enough to weaken the wood but not yet enough to make it crack and collapse. Brash wood is not reliable for load-carrying members. It is a warning that rot is starting.

What to do then depends on circumstances. Find out where the fresh water is getting in and stop it. Consider scraping the paint or varnish from the wood to allow it to thoroughly dry. Brushing on wood preservative might or might not help—it depends on how deeply into infected wood this solution chances to penetrate. When wood begins to suffer appreciably from loss of cellulose it begins to feel soft and punky. Marine stores sell small bottles of epoxy resin with a variety of trade names that have the word "rot" in them. This resin will soak into punky wood (provided it is thoroughly dry) and will rigidize it when it cures hard. It is expensive and thus not always the thing for big rot problems, but is often a good rot-stopping procedure to catch localized rot before it spreads.

Due to sap ducts, rot spreads with the grain much more readily than across it. The hyphae follow the sap ducts. When you find a spot that is obviously rotted, it is safe to assume the hyphae have spread along the wood to each side of that spot for a distance of about ten times greater than the extent of the rotted place. Thus, if you have a one-inch spot of rot, you should if possible remove wood for ten inches to each side of that spot, going with the grain. If you remove the rotted spot only, hyphae left in the seemingly sound wood nearby have the power to commence growing again should the wood become suitably warm and damp. It is much like cancer in humans—the critical question is how far it has spread from the spot where it was first discovered.

Creosote the Bilges?

Q. Would it be a good idea to brush creosote all over the framing and inside of the planking of a 30-foot cruiser under construction in order to discourage rot?

A. No. That material is an excellent preservative and is widely used for fence posts, utility poles, etc. But those things are used outdoors. Inside a boat hull, the strong smell will linger for a very long time. And as long as traces of creosote remain in the wood, it will tend to repel paint, making attractive interior finishing impossible. These shortcomings have led to the development of more suitable preservatives.

How Preservatives Work

Q. How do wood preservatives work?

A. They are "fungicides"; that is, toxic to fungus plants. There are many chemicals that will kill fungus. But a practical commercial wood preservative must not be toxic to humans when used according to directions, must not repel paint or varnish, must not corrode metal fastenings, etc. Chemicals often found in the preservatives on sale in marine and hardware stores are copper naphthenate, zinc naphthenate, and pentachlorophenol. The liquids sold to the public contain suitable amounts of fungicidal chemical dissolved in some liquid, usually a common petroleum solvent, that will readily penetrate wood. The solvent carries the chemical into the wood with it, where it remains. After a number of days the solvent will have evaporated from the wood, allowing it to be painted.

Preservative Color

Q. Marine stores sell proprietary brands of wood preservative in both clear and green color. What's the reason? Is the colored kind more powerful?

A. There's no difference in potency. The green color helps workmen make sure all areas in a boat that require treatment have been taken care of. There is probably also a psychological value from the sales department's point of view—it is reassuring to prospective boat buyers to look into the bilge area and see for themselves that the green color they associate with wood preservative is there. The clear type is useful where a green color would be undesirable underneath varnish. A beautiful spruce mast would look utterly repulsive with bright green glowing under its clear varnish!

Using Preservative

Q. A friend built a porch onto his summer cottage and liberally brushed preservative onto the framing. Only four or five years later, though, the framing showed much sign of rot. Did he buy some "gyp" preservative? Can you recommend a better kind for me to use in the boat I am building?

A. Merely brushing preservative on one time does not guarantee protection. Much depends on how well saturated the wood is. If the lumber your friend used was wet inside from being stacked out in the rain for some time at the lumberyard, the preservative would not have been able to

The last place rot shows up is in the bottom planking. It is caused by fresh water from rain, spray, condensation, etc. remaining in places that tend to trap it. Rot begins in upper parts of a wooden boat and progresses downward as deteriorating woodwork allows more water to enter. Top Left: Mounting block for radio whip antenna was located so that it prevents free drainage of deck water. A wet spell will let water stay there long enough to seep into joints. Rot will eventually breed in this moist area. Top Right: Rubber step pad has gaps that will let rainwater soak under it. Slow drying-out will keep wood damp enough to breed rot. Bottom Left: Wooden flagstaff rotted because it was left for a long time in a socket that had no drain holes. Rainwater trickling down staff was trapped in base of socket and kept wood damp. Bottom Right: Gap where heavy deck trim moldings come together will open and close with changes in weather. A dry spell will make it open up, so water will seep in at next rainy spell. Water going into end grain will seep in and remain long enough to start rot.

Wood preservative products are sold in most marine and hardware stores and at lumberyards. They consist of a suitable liquid vehicle into which has been dissolved a fungicidal chemical.

Flowing wood preservative into dried-out cracks and open seams on the deck and cabin woodwork is a good way to help a wooden boat last. Fresh water from rain is what starts and nourishes rot in a boat.

penetrate the wood very well. A single brushing-on amounts to a superficial treatment. If preservative was applied after the framing was finished, it probably did not reach hidden areas of wood at joints and ends. If the wood was green, (inadequately seasoned) the large amount of sap in it would prevent the preservative from soaking in well.

In boat work, the ideal way to do it is to brush preservative onto finished parts several times *before* they are permanently fastened in place. This assures complete coverage. If one's shop is large enough and can stand the cost, a dip tank full of preservative is a fine thing. Finished pieces can be soaked in it for a few hours or even overnight. Some factories making 10- to 20-foot lapstrake boats a score or more years ago had tanks large enough to dip completed hulls into preservative. Others set hulls up onto strong supporting cradles and filled them with preservative. This not only let the fluid soak well into the wood, it also tested the hulls for leaks.

Period of Protection

Q. How often should a hull be given a fresh wood preservative treatment?

A. There is no pat answer. A lot depends on how thoroughly the wood was impregnated in the beginning. Actually, a great many fine boats have been built with no treatment at all and have lasted for years with no rot problems. Much also depends on how skillfully the boat was made and how well it is ventilated and cared for. Rot is not a great problem in open wooden boats like canoes and rowboats simply because such craft are very well ventilated; if it gets damp, the wood can dry out before rot takes root. It is known that preservative chemicals will gradually leach out of wood, but again, no specific timetable can be established

because there are so many variables. If the wood was well impregnated while the boat was being built, certainly she should go for several years before one need be concerned about the preservative. If she is poorly drained and ventilated, preservative alone will not guarantee freedom from rot; if she is well drained and ventilated, she may last for scores of years and have no rot problems. A sensible view is that since preservative is low in price compared to a boat's overall value, using it in the beginning makes sense—but it is not essential and is not a guarantee of long life.

Misuse of Preservative

Q. I bought a used wooden runabout in good condition. No information was available about its history, though. In order to take no chances, I brushed a good grade of wood preservative all over her interior, which was varnished but had many thin and peeling spots in the varnish. It dried to a sticky mess which took days to wipe off with rags and kerosene. What went wrong?

A. You misunderstood the use of preservative. It is meant to go onto bare wood. When you put it over a varnish finish that is in poor condition, it can't soak in in many places. As the solvent slowly evaporated on the varnish, it thickened and left a gummy deposit. If you used a preservative that was made for use on shingles, outdoor furniture, etc., it may have contained some kind of oil, in addition to the preservative chemical, put in it to help keep unpainted wood from checking and splitting with alternate wet and dry weather. So when you put this kind on your boat, the oil over the varnish had no place to go and thickened to a sticky coating. It would have made more sense to put preservative into an oil can and squirted it into all the small gaps and crevices on the cabin and decking where rain water could leak in. This of course should be done when the wood is very

Wooden boats of canoe-type construction often last 50 years without rotting. Their all-open construction allows them to dry out after use, and when not in use they are normally stored upside down so that inside water drains out and rainwater is shed. Under these conditions, rot fungus cannot get started. (Old Town Canoe Co.)

dry, such as at the end of winter storage in a shed. And any excess left on the surfaces should be wiped off.

Use an oil can to run preservative into deck seams. Do this only when wood is very dry.

Bilgewater Chemical

Q. Is there any chemical I can add to the bilgewater in my wooden boat to prevent rot?

A. We have never seen anything like that in marine stores or in boating literature in the many years we have been active in boating. What with the bilge pump working during the boating season and the garboard drain plug opened during the storage period, a batch of treated bilgewater would not remain in the boat long enough to do any good.

Fungicidal Chemicals

Q. Where could I buy the chemicals used in commercial wood preservatives so I can mix my own preservative and save money?

A. As far as we know it is sold only in bulk to chemical-products firms. It is mixed in a petroleum-base vehicle which is also available only in bulk. If you tried commonly available solvents such as kerosene, range and heating oils, diesel fuel, etc., you might encounter serious problems—slow evaporation, odor, fire hazards, etc. If you need a lot of preservative, hunt around and find a way to buy it wholesale.

53

He Built a Rot Hatchery

Q. I built a sailing surfboard using plywood for planking. Since it is decked over and completely enclosed, I often wonder—is it prone to rot?

A. You've got a rot hatchery on your hands! Make vent holes in the decking fore and aft. Marine hardware catalogs show a variety of drain plugs, hand hole covers, deck plates, etc. Choose a suitable style and install them in these holes. Leave them open when the boat is not in use. Next spring, after the boat's interior has been drying out for some months, pour a gallon of wood preservative into the hull, close the vents, and turn the hull over and over to spread the preservative. Drain the excess and thenceforth open the vents when the boat is not in use.

Formaldehyde for Rot?

Q. Would dosing a boat with formaldehyde prevent or stop rot?

A. We doubt it. We've never encountered mention of this idea in rot literature. It might knock out existing fungus plants but it will soon evaporate, leaving the wood unprotected since it is not a durable fungicide.

Cruising in Fresh Water

Q. Our high-quality wooden cruiser has always been used in salt water. We are planning a cruise on inland rivers. A friend warns us the fresh water will make the boat rot out quickly. What do you think?

A. Notions like this are common due to the average person's vast ignorance of rot. Wooden boats *constantly* used in fresh water do have more rot problems. In your case, the hull's bottom is safe because it is well-soaked with water. For the duration of a normal vacation cruise, your boat will be in motion and its doors and windows will be constantly opened. If rain comes, it will dry off promptly enough—besides which the boat gets soaked with rain just as much when it is back home on the sea. Go have your fun!

Bilgewater and Rot

Q. I have two bilge pumps in my big sportfisherman, but there is still some seepage water here and there. I worry about rot. What should I do?

A. Go fishing! Assuming your big boat is used for offshore fishing, it's being used in salt water. The seepage in your bilge is therefore salt water—which will kill rot fungus. No reason at all to worry about a little water in the bilge!

Is Rot Contagious?

Q. My old wooden boat expired from a terminal case of wood rot. Is it possible for a new one to pick up the infection from articles brought aboard from the old one?

A. It's theoretically possible, but highly unlikely. Rot will spread from one piece of wood to another, but they have to be in close contact. That's how rot spreads in wooden boats. If a wooden gaff handle were actually rotting and you laid it alongside some damp wood in the bilge area of your boat, the infection could take place. But you would notice rot in any such wooden object and discard it as useless or inappropriate aboard the new boat. If rot ever starts in the new boat, it will probably do so from spores that are ever present in the air currents. Just don't bring aboard a lot of rotting stuff like old rope, mops, cushions, boxes, etc. There's no chance of the new boat picking up rot mysteriously as though rot were an invisible virus.

Rot in Wooden Core Material

Q. Rainwater seeped under deck fittings and got into the balsa-wood core material in the deck laminate of my fiberglass sloop. The deck has become flexible in the areas around the fittings—we can see it give when pressed. What can be done?

A. Doing it from below decks, if possible, to avoid marring the outer surface, drill exploratory holes in the fiberglass with, say, a three-sixteenths or quarter-inch high-speed drill. Start close to the fittings and work gradually outward. Feel and smell the wood chips. In this manner, determine the extent of the wet and rotted areas. It would be best to have a good fiberglass man decide what to do. First thing is to let the wood completely dry out. This might be accomplished by drilling scores of small holes and letting the sun's heat drive the dampness out. If the boat could be inverted, or a pump-and-nozzle device cobbled up, you could work epoxy-type wood rot fixer into the balsa to firm it up. Or it might be necessary to grind the inner fiberglass layers off the laminate to expose all the rotted balsa, replace the balsa or substitute a suitable foam material for it, and cover over with fresh fiberglass. Send the bill to the fool who installed the deck hardware without using bedding compound to keep rain and spray from seeping under it and into the wooden core!

Wood Durability

Q. How can one tell which woods are rot-resistant and which are not?

A. Wood technicians have studied the matter at length and published tables. One is given herewith containing North American, European, and various tropical woods that have been or could be used in boats. The usual test method is to drive wooden stakes into the ground and observe how long the underground portions last before rotting. Durability testing can also be carried out in climate-controlled test chambers at wood laboratories.

Some Ribs Rotted, Others Didn't

Q. We bought a wooden boat built by commercial fishermen in the Maritimes. The price was low and we liked its uncluttered, functional design for our purpose of sport fishing. Within a few years some of her steamed oak ribs rotted completely away, others remained sound, and on others there were some rotted and some sound areas. What do you make of this?

A. It was a cheap boat, built to be used as a fishing tool, then replaced and written off as a business expense. The wood used for ribs was a mixture of sapwood and heartwood. Sapwood is rather more susceptible to rot than is heartwood. In a cheap boat built for a comparatively short life, there was no point in carefully sorting out piles of lumber to get only heartwood in the ribs. And you will also find that some backyard boatbuilders don't know the difference between the two. Various kinds of wood are very different in their rot resistance; red oak is much less durable than white oak and your boat may well have been full of red oak. There is a lot to building a good wooden boat that does not meet the eye! Read a lot of literature on wooden boatbuilding and on wood technology if you are seriously interested in wooden boats.

Rot Holes Around Bolts

Q. Wood has rotted away around several iron bolts in my old boat, but the wood beyond these areas is perfectly sound. What happened?

A. The iron affects chemicals that are naturally in the wood and give it its inherent good rot resistance. This breaks down the rot resistance in the area around the bolt. This phenomenon is to be seen often where iron fastenings go into old, weathered wood such as fence posts, railroad ties, and barn boards. Deck hardware should always be set in bedding compound. This keeps water from seeping under the hardware and down between the fastenings and surrounding wood. Every time you bore a hole in wood to install a new item of equipment, it is a good precaution to use a small paint brush to soak the exposed wood with preservative before installing bolts.

Common Name	Botanical Name
VERY DURABLE	
Afrormosia, kokrodua	Afrormosia elata
Afzelia	Afzelia spp.
Ekki	Lophira alata var. procera
Greenheart	Ocotea rodiaei
Iroko	Chlorophora excelsa
Makoré	Mimusops heckelii
Opepe	Sarcocephalus diderrichii
Tallowwood	Eucalyptus microcorys
Teak	Tectona grandis
DURABLE	
Agba	Gossweilerodendron balsamiferum
Chestnut (sweet)	Castanea sativa
Freijo	Cordia goeldiana
Guarea	Guarea spp.
Mahogany (Central American)	Swietenia macrophylla
Oak (American white)	Quercus spp., chiefly Q. alba
Oak (English)	Quercus robur, Q. petraea
Pitch pine (Honduras)	Pinus caribaea
Utile	Entandrophragma utile
Western red cedar	Thuja plicata
MODERATELY DURABLE	
African walnut	Lovoa klaineana
Baltic redwood	Pinus sylvestris
Danta	Cistanthera papaverifera
Douglas fir	Pseudotsuga taxifolia
Gedu nohor	Entandrophragma angolense
Gurjun	Dipterocarpus spp.
Krabak	Anisoptera spp.
Larch (European)	Larix decidua
Mahogany (African)	Khaya spp.
Oak (American red)	Quercus spp.
Sapele	Entandrophragma cylindricum
NON-DURABLE	
Elm (English)	Ulmus procera
(Rock)	Ulmus thomasi
(White)	Ulmus americana
(Wych)	Ulmus glabra
Gaboon	Aucoumea klaineana
Spruce	
Baltic whitewood	Picea abies
Canadian spruce	Picea glauca
Sitka spruce	Picea sitchensis
PERISHABLE	
Ash	Fraxinus excelsior
Balsa	Ochroma lagopus
Beech	Fagus sylvatica
Yellow birch	Betula lutea

Dry Rot in England

Q. I have an English book that has a whole section in it on dry rot. What do you mean, there's no such thing as dry rot?

A. There is a species of fungus in England that will thrive under conditions of somewhat less moisture, so they call it dry rot.

Adequate Ventilation

Q. People say a wooden boat must have adequate ventilation to keep her free of rot. How much is "adequate?"

A. There's no firm rule. Generally, enough to eliminate any feel of dampness. Much depends on the interior layout of the boat. A powerboat with a small cabin and large cockpit will tend to ventilate better than a big sailboat with deep keel and cabin appointments fitted low down in the hull. All enclosed boats have at least some fixed ventilators, often as part of the provisions to keep gasoline vapors from accumulating. If a boat is kept at a mooring so she can swing into the wind all the time, these ventilators will work all the time too. But the same boat kept at a dock will experience a mixture of head, cross, and tail winds and will ventilate less steadily. Some regions are more humid than others and will pose more ventilation problems. A boat stored outdoors gets the winter winds, where one stored indoors seldom feels a breeze. You just have to take a close look at the individual boat, the local conditions, and how she is moored and/or stored, and act accordingly. Marine-supply catalogs are full of ventilators; you have plenty of types from which to choose to solve whatever your boat's problems might be. When a boat is in storage, all hatches, floorboards, lockers, etc., should be opened or lifted so air can freely circulate.

Don't Insulate Boat

Q. We bought a big old cruiser and plan to use her as a live-aboard craft on a year-round basis. While rebuilding her cabins we will have the paneling out. This would be a good chance to install lumberyard-type fiberglass insulation, to make her more comfortable in both summer heat and winter cold. What is your opinion?

A. We would be very cautious about doing it. It will stop air circulation in a lot of enclosed spaces and in a marine environment could lead to widespread rot. If the boat is to be afloat when you are living in her, remember that the water she floats in keeps summer heat and winter winds from getting at her undersides. The hull topsides are probably more tightly built than the siding of a house. The hull volume will almost surely be less than in a normal house. We think we'd settle for installing one-inch foam-board insulation under the decks, putting it on with a suitable cement, and using strips of wood to provide from a quarter- to a half-inch clearance between the undersides of decking and roofing and the top of the foam. This will help with summer sun and winter winds without posing too much of a rot problem. We think you will find that a moderate fire in a modest stove will keep you amply warm. We'd consider making "storm windows" for the cabin out of rigid sheet plastic; a boat's windows are not designed to keep out winter's cold and doing this is probably the best thing you could do.

Salt's Effect on Wood

Q. Will salt water hurt wood more than fresh water will?

A. What do you mean by "hurt?" Because salt water will corrode metal, people often have a feeling that it will somehow also be hard on wood. But as we have pointed out elsewhere, salt was often used in old wooden ships to preserve the wood. If salt water corrodes metal fastenings, it can indirectly affect the nearby wood. Marine creatures living in seawater can bore into and eat away wood. But salt water by itself is quite harmless to wood.

Seaweed on Skiff Bottoms

Q. Some years ago I visited Cape Cod in the wintertime. Driving past some coves, it was common to see wooden rowboats left for the winter turned upside down with seaweed piled several inches thick on their upturned bottoms. What was it for?

A. The layer of weed keeps the bottom planks from drying out under the influence of winter winds. The boats are then usefully watertight when launched in the spring. It's too cold for fungus to rot the wood and also the salt in the wood and seaweed would kill any fungus that might become active during a late-winter mild spell. If you put hay on top of a wooden boat left upside down by a Florida pond, we think the heat and the constant dampness from rain showers would make its bottom start rotting out rather quickly. So again you see there are no pat answers; everything about boats depends on prevailing conditions.

Oak in Tropics

Q. We bought a fine sloop that was built by craftsmen in Maine. It is now on Long Island Sound. We have been talking about taking it to Florida with us when we retire. An *old fellow at the marina told us not to do it because the oak ribs would rot out quickly down there. Everyone knows oak is one of the most durable woods; was he feeding us baloney?*

A. We don't think so. We have talked to boatbuilders in Florida and they prefer other woods for framing, claiming their experience has been that white oak in northern-built boats often rots quickly in Florida. Apparently, the climate and/or some species of rot fungus found in warmer regions readily gets into oak and rots it sooner than is usual up north where the oak is a native wood. A lot would depend on how your boat is put together, how well it is ventilated, etc. Find a marine surveyor or naval architect with Florida experience and have him look at it.

Chapter 7

Wooden Boats in General

Trailered Boat Leaks

Q. We inherited a big dory-like skiff and a trailer to go with it. Every time we try to use it, it leaks badly. What can be done?

A. Boats with conventional planked wooden hulls were never intended to be kept on trailers. The earliest trailerable boats were lapstrake craft with one kind of compound or another in their riveted seams so they would be watertight when launched. Then plywood came along and trailerable boats became enormously popular. Fiberglass and aluminum, being better suited to mass production, supplanted plywood. But there are now many newcomers to boating who don't realize that conventional wooden boats need several days of soaking to swell their planks and close the seams. You can pull out the old cotton caulking and replace it with one of today's rubber-like seam compounds sold in standard 11 ounce gun tubes; whether or not it will work will depend on how wide the planks are, how wide the seams are, and how much the flexible compound will compress when the planks get wet. If you leave the boat in the water for several days, the planks might swell so much as to "spit out" the compound or start buckling under the swelling pressure. But the wood should not swell that much if the boat is in the water for only a day at a time.

Time Out of Water

Q. How long can I leave my carvel-planked cruiser out of water before the planking begins to dry out and open the seams?

A. There's no pat answer to this. It all depends on circumstances—the width and thickness of the planks, the kind of wood, how much the boat is exposed to direct sunlight and steady wind, how much internal air circulation there is, whether the climate is humid or dry, and so on. Haul it out and from there on keep an eye on it.

Controlling Leakage

Q. Our old boat was extremely dry after several years in a barn. We kept it wet for several days with a hose to try to swell the bottom planks. But it still leaked so badly when we launched it that we had to haul it out. Now what?

A. Borrow an electric basement pump with an automatic switch. Install it in the lowest part of the bilge and route its discharge hose overboard. Tie the boat to a dock with shore power outlets. Stay around for most of the day to make sure

Conventionally planked wooden boats were never meant for trailering. Those who tried it in the early years of the postwar boating boom had endless problems with leakage. When plywood boats came along, trailering suddenly became feasible and the boating boom took off.

the pump is able to keep ahead of leakage. Have someone around to keep an eye on things. As the days pass, the pump should come on less often, and for shorter periods, if the seams are closing and tightening satisfactorily. When leakage is slowed to a moderate rate, remove the cellar pump and permanently install an electric bilge pump. Remember that if this pump comes on fairly often and you don't use the boat much, the battery can run down and the pump then will not take care of leakage.

Sawdust Box

Q. I was at a boatyard and saw some workmen doing a strange thing. They had a small wooden box with a long handle on it and a sliding cover. It looked just like a corn popper but was bigger. They kept sticking it under three or four boats tied to their dock. I was too far away to ask what they were doing. Do you know?

Planked wooden boats had to soak for several days after launching to allow planks to soak up water, swell and close seams.

A. We can tell that those boats were made of wood, right? The box contained sawdust. When pushed under a floating boat, the cover is opened by pulling a string and the box releases sawdust. The sawdust floats up along the bottom and some of it lodges in leaks where water is flowing into the boat. It slows down the rate of leakage while the planks are swelling, sometimes keeping a boat from sinking if the pump cannot keep up with the rate of flow.

Building a Boat in the Desert

Q. *We live in the desert country of the southwest but we are determined to build a wooden boat to get the features we want. What problems can we expect with the wood in this dry climate?*

A. There is no pat answer. The wood will obviously become so dry that when the boat is finally launched, it may swell excessively. How serious the problem will be would depend on the boat. If the planks are narrow, there will be many seams and the caulking in them will allow for swelling. But if the planks are wide and few in number, there quite possibly will not be enough "give" in the seams to keep the planks from buckling or pulling loose from their fastenings. We have visited wooden boat factories in the past, that were heated in wintertime by ceiling-mounted gas heaters. They had rigged copper lines and nozzles so that a gentle spray of water would play into the warm air coming from the heaters. This kept the air from getting too dry.

If the size of the boat and the workshop construction are adaptable, one or two household humidifiers would help. We would look into making the hull of epoxy-saturated veneer layers. This construction is less affected by the tendency of wood to swell and shrink with changes in moisture content. More on this method later in this chapter.

Should Insides Be Painted?

Q. *We bought a used wooden cabin cruiser. There is no paint at all on the framing and inside surfaces of the planking. We are afraid the wood will rot, and think it should be painted to protect the wood. But it would be hard to get at some of the areas. So what can we do?*

A. There is a difference of opinion among wooden boat experts about painting the bilge area. In open boats it is done as a matter of course, to give a good appearance and to protect the wood from both chafing underfoot and from weather-checking. But paint will not protect wood from rot because rot is caused by fungus and paint is not a fungicide. In fact, a lot of rot is caused by paint—particularly too many coats of paint—because the paint holds water in the wood for a long enough time to enable fungus to start growing. Old paint with many cracks in it is often a rot-breeder; the cracks let water in when the bilge is flooded, then the overall coating of paint slows down the drying-out. Paint will help to prevent rot only when it is in good condition. To keep all cracks out of paint calls for almost continual attention, which is obviously impractical.

One reason some boat builders paint the bilge area is to give the wood a coating that—they claim—will keep the wood from soaking up dripped engine oil floating on the bilgewater. They say this makes for a cleaner, better-smelling, less fire-susceptible bilge. Some settle for a compromise. They brush onto the wood as many coats as it will absorb of a mixture of equal parts raw linseed oil and turpentine, kept warm and thin by setting the container in a bucket of hot water. Boat books printed prior to World War II often recommended this, and some modern wooden boat experts advocate it too. They claim this mixture soaks deeply into the wood and therefore minimizes soaking up water. They feel it also reduces the tendency of wood to check and reason that the less checking, the less water will enter. Some old books claim turpentine will kill rot spores but literature put out by rot prevention experts during and after World War II doesn't mention linseed oil, concentrating on chemicals known to be fungicidal. Turpentine will evaporate soon enough and linseed oil, being a vegetable material, has no fungicidal properties. Indeed, it attracts the kinds of fungus that create mildew! Raw linseed oil dries slowly—a matter of several days—and leaves rather little in the way of a skin. Boiled linseed oil will dry in a day and form a rubbery skin. It is reasoned that the penetration of the raw oil and turpentine mixture will fill the grain so as to repel water, but not create a skin which, like paint, can in time dry hard and develop water-admitting cracks. Once it has evaporated, the turpentine could have no effect on spores that subsequently get onto the wood through air currents.

One will find no agreement between believers in old-time boat techniques and modern wood preservation scientists. We cannot try to settle the matter here. If you wanted the best of both worlds you could apply preservative to the insides of your boat's hull, and when its solvent has throughly evaporated in a week or so, seal the wood against water and bilge oil with the linseed oil/turpentine mixture.

By keeping water that has soaked into wood from drying out rapidly, paint can actually encourage rot to begin.

Preservatives and Glue

Q. Will applying wood preservative before gluing a part onto a boat affect the glue's holding power?

A. It will if the product's mineral oil vehicle is not allowed to dry out thoroughly before gluing. It's hard to say exactly how long to let it dry; it depends on the kind of wood, amount of moving air and sunshine reaching the wood during the drying period, etc. In general, allow at least a few days of drying time under favorable conditions and several days under unfavorable conditions.

Epoxy and Wood

Q. I have encountered the term "cold molded construction" in a few boating magazines. What is it?

A. It is a modern version of the old "double planking" method. Plywood bulkheads are sawn to the shape of the cross-sections of the hull at various stations. They are set up on a floor or building jig and numerous longitudinal stringers are affixed to them. This creates a light framework in the shape of the hull that is to be built. Strips of veneer, usually about an eighth of an inch thick and from a few to several inches wide, as befits the hull shape, are laid diagonally onto this mold and stapled in place. When the first layer is finished, a second layer is put on over it at a 90-degree angle. Epoxy adhesive, suitably blended for the job, is spread on before each strip of the second layer is laid in place and stapled. Depending on the size and speed of the boat, from

two or three to five or six layers of veneer are used in the laminate. When removed from the building mold, the complete hull is given a number of coats of epoxy resin, the first of which is thinned out to assure deep penetration. The hull is then so well saturated with epoxy that swelling, shrinking, and rot problems are rendered insignificant. The method has been used on everything from kayaks to large sailing yachts.

A number of firms have been active in developing and promoting the process. They include Gougeon Brothers, Inc., P.O. Box 908, Bay City, Mich. 48707, Chem-Tech, Inc., 4669 Lander Rd., Chagrin Falls, Ohio 44022, and Clark Craft, Inc., 16 Aqua Lane, Tonawanda, N.Y. 14150. They all have how-to literature ranging from pamphlets to thick books; write to them for literature prices. Their epoxy materials have all kinds of uses in boat repair work. Most hardware-store glues require snug wood-to-wood contact in joints and substantial pressure while drying to develop strength but epoxy adhesives do not. You should understand that there are many formulations of epoxy adhesives tailored to a wide variety of applications and problems.

Epoxy Allergy

Q. I have heard stories about people being more allergic to epoxy resin than to polyester resin. Is there anything to this?

A. Yes. It's different from most allergies. Very few people are allergic to it in the beginning. But after working with it for a while—a few days, weeks, or months depending on the individual—one will suddenly become "sensitized" to epoxy. The skin breaks out in a rash, which can be quite severe and exceedingly uncomfortable, and which often will not respond to common allergy remedies. From that time on, the individual cannot tolerate epoxy at all—he will break out when merely in the same room with epoxy materials. One can become sensitized to epoxy in a short time by being careless when using it. The prime safeguard is to always wear rubber or plastic gloves when working with it. If some does get on the hands, it should be washed off with hand soap and water. Wiping it off with a cloth wet with solvent is bad, for the thinned-out epoxy can penetrate the skin and enter one's system.

Epoxy products now being sold for boat use have been carefully tested and chosen to minimize the problem, and there are many people around who have been working with epoxy for a long time without trouble. Before working with it for the first time, read the directions that come with it carefully and be sure to follow them. The Andrew Jergens Company, whose skin care products are often seen in drugstores, makes a line of industrial skin-protection creams under the "SBS" label. Some are helpful as added insurance when working with epoxies. The Chem-Tech company previously mentioned sells them by mail order to boatbuilders using their epoxy products.

Try Laminating

Q. We lost the tiller from our old sailboat. It was of steamed oak and had a nice curve to it. We drew its curves from memory on a sheet of plywood, bolted wooden blocks along the curve, steamed a length of oak, and let it dry on this form. It promptly straightened out when removed from this jig. What did we do wrong?

A. Perhaps you did not allow the wood to dry adequately before removing it from the jig. Perhaps you did not exaggerate the curve when making the bending jig, to allow for the wood's spring-back when removed. Remember, when you bend a rib onto a building frame, nearby parts keep it from springing back. We'd try making the new tiller by using the laminating process instead of steam-bending. Several thin strips of wood can be glued together to build up the necessary thickness. This is a job that a modern epoxy glue could do very well. Not only will it tenaciously adhere to the wood, it is also a neutral color and will not emphasize the glue lines.

Cracked Ribs

Q. Some of the steam-bent oak ribs in my old sailboat have cracked through. How can I repair them without a steam box?

A. You can soften oak strips well enough for the purpose by boiling them in hot water. Plug one end of a length of pipe that is long enough to hold the oak strips. Prop one end against a wall and fill the pipe with water. Get a blow torch going with the flame against the lower end of the pipe. Put the oak in, close the top of the pipe with a piece of cloth, and let things cook. The pipe can be fully filled or you can put water just in the lower end. A full pipe will boil the wood, a partly-filled one will steam it, but you have to check the water often to make sure it does not boil away. An iron pipe will tend to blacken the oak; try an aluminum one. A length of oak with a cross section about one inch by one inch will soften enough to bend with about an hour's boiling, but you will have to experiment to find the right time with your particular setup.

If the ribs that are broken are scattered about in the hull, you can bend new ones in alongside the old ones, clamp as well as possible, and pull the hot oak snug against the inside of the planking with screws driven from outside. If a number of ribs adjacent to one another are cracked, you may have to

resort to timbers, blocks, and jacks to push the planking in and take out any bulges caused by the broken ribs. It is common to snug new ribs against the sides of old ones but the inevitable slight gaps between old and new ribs will collect dirt and hold moisture long enough to breed rot.

In recent years some good rib repairs have been made by cutting out the old wood for several inches to each side of the break and fitting in laminated repair pieces using epoxy glue to secure things. Sometimes repair inlays bandsawn from pieces of wood with suitable grain have been used instead of laminating in several thin strips. One man's cleverness is as good as another's when it comes to rib repair work.

Steam-bent ribs are fast and easy to make. A volume-production wooden boat shop kept its steaming tank busy heating oak strips. When sufficiently pliable, strips were pulled out and quickly bent and clamped onto building forms. Then planking went on. When these ribs crack in an older boat, there are different ways to repair them.

Buying New Ribs

Q. There are some broken ribs in my lapstrake outboard boat hull. Where can I buy new steam-bent oak ribs to replace them? The manufacturer is out of business.

A. Nobody makes wooden replacement parts like these, except for a few wooden canoe manufacturers who still have the same forms they used two and three generations ago. You do not need to buy wooden replacement parts because you can make up new ones. If you desired to replace a complete old rib, you could boil or steam the wood as previously described. Or, by trial and error, cut a stiff cardboard template to the shape of the hull's cross section on the inside. Mark the resulting curve off on a sheet of rough plywood. Glue and screw wood blocks along the line. Rip up several strips of oak, each about one-sixteenth or one-eighth of an inch thick and as wide as the ribs. They'll bend onto the form easily and by spreading epoxy glue on them as you lay them on you'll laminate up a rib as good as the original—probably better, as it will resist localized cracking.

Books on Lapstrake Repairs

Q. Does anyone publish a book on lapstrake boat repair and maintenance?

A. Not that we are aware of. Various books on boat maintenance treat this type briefly. In the old days, pleasure boating centered around well-established boat yards whose workmen had learned about these boats from experience. So, no books. After World War II, a lot of small lapstrake boats were made by wooden boatbuilding firms trying to produce craft adaptable to the new trailer boating craze. Fiberglass soon took over so there was hardly time for anyone to gain necessary experience, write a book, and get it published before the need for it began to dwindle. Chapelle's book, *Boatbuilding*, has a chapter on lapstrake planking in general, and the English book, *Dinghy Building* by Richard Creagh-Osborne, has a chapter on "Clinker planking," another name for the same thing. Data on how to build these boats can be applied to repair problems. Various books on boat maintenance devote a page or two to lapstrake maintenance, hardly enough to bother with.

Varnish on Lapstrake Interiors

Q. I bought a shabby lapstrake boat and spent ages patiently scraping old peeled varnish off the countless surfaces on the inside of its planking. Why did boat factories use this unhappy method of finishing off interiors?

A. It was a matter of keeping cost within reason. You can't spray paint on such an irregular surface with uniform results. Thick and thin spots on the inside of a lapstrake hull show up much less because varnish is transparent. So it was the fastest way to get an acceptable-looking production finish.

Undercoating a Lapstrake

Q. My lapstrake boat leaks at many points. How about spraying the bilge area with automotive undercoating compound to seal things up all over?

A. It's a fascinating idea but we'd hesitate to try it. It might be difficult if not impossible to get a thorough coating, especially under ribs. It might trap dampness and encourage wood rot. Spilled gasoline might soften and loosen it.

Interiors of once-popular lapstrake boats were finished with varnish as the fastest, most economical way to get a uniform-looking finish in volume production.

Besides, you do not need an over-all coating because all the leaks have to occur at the seams.

Caulking a Lapstrake

Q. Please explain how to caulk a lapstrake boat.

A. If you mean caulking by driving cotton strands between the planks with a caulking iron, don't do it! Uninformed boat owners have ruined a lot of good lapstrake boats by jumping to the conclusion that all wooden boats are caulked the same way. Some lapstrakes, such as the dories made of pine boards, had no caulking. When the wood got wet and swelled, it had a self-sealing action. Other old ones were "caulked" with strips of muslin soaked in marine glue while being built. Mass-produced powerboats built in the 1950s and into the 1960s used a variety of synthetic sealing compounds. These were supposed to last longer than the boats but in some cases it has not worked out that way!

Hull Too "Rubbery"

Q. My old lapstrake outboard boat leaks all over and the planking is obviously coming loose along the seams. What should I do?

A. Most lapstrake outboard boats were lightly built for reasons of speed and cost. Any outboard boat takes quite a rattling as it speeds over choppy water. Many have been left outdoors all winter without covers. There comes a time when such a boat will loosen up so much, on an all-over basis, that

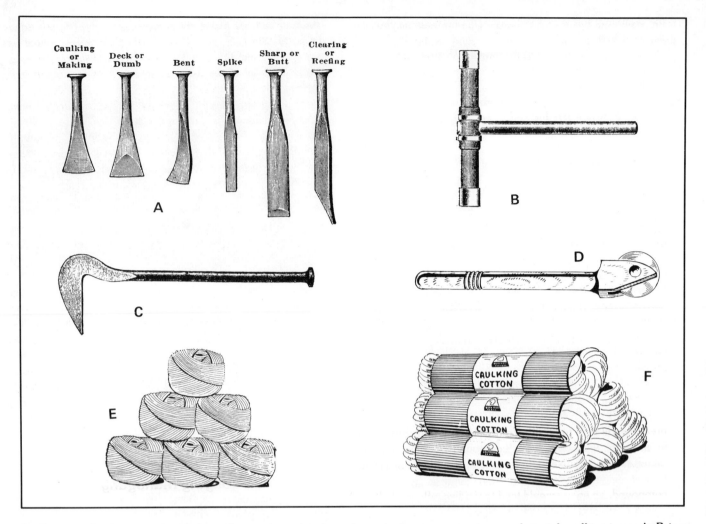

Caulking wooden boats requires tools rarely seen in modern boat shops. At A are some common and special caulking irons. At B is a caulker's mallet. It is not swung through an arc as is a hammer but is used to tap the irons more or less gently. Its force is generated more by the momentum of its mass rather than by a long swing. At C is a "reefing iron" used to remove old caulking. The device at D is a "caulking wheel" used to press the first course of wicking into the bottom of a seam. Twine or wicking, twisted for the purpose as shown at E, is used for thin planking in small boats and for first courses in thicker planking. Caulking cotton, F, comes in hank form and is lightly twisted. The caulker pulls off what he needs and twists it to suit.

there's just no magic cure. Fiberglassing might stiffen it up. It's a question of whether the boat is worth what fiberglass costs today.

Rubber Bottom-Paint

Q. My lapstrake cruiser is in generally good condition but leaks all over—tiny, weeping leaks that are hard to find. Is there some kind of rubber paint I could spread all over the bottom?

A. Such paints have been on the market but we have not chanced to see them in marine stores lately. Demand may be declining as the flood of lapstrake boats built in the 1950s and '60s become worn out and are discarded. Look up the makers of sealers and compounds in the marine trade directories and write to them, asking if they have anything. You might find one willing to mix up a batch for you. How well it would work is anyone's guess. Such a paint won't fix loosened fastenings, it might not adhere well to oil-soaked motorboat wood, and might stretch and get peeled off by trailer roller-pressure.

Tightening a Leaky Lapstrake

Q. What is the best way to tighten up a leaky lapstrake boat?

A. There is no one "best" way. It depends on how your particular boat is made. If you have one of the lapstrake outboards popular several years ago that used plywood for the planking and is of generally light construction, you can do as follows.

First, let the boat dry out thoroughly. With a high-pressure compressed air jet, go along each of the plank laps from the inside, blowing as much silt and sand out of the seams as possible. An awl or hacksaw blade might help dislodge imbedded stuff. It's this sand that works in between the planks as the boat flexes in use that tends to push the seams apart from the inside.

Then study the fastenings. It may be possible to tighten them up as common sense suggests. Then invert the boat. With a beercan opener or similar tool, rake along the lines where each strake contacts the one below it, pulling out old paint and dirt and at the same time scraping a V-groove into the wood. You will find a variety of sealing compounds in marine stores. Some are white liquids in squeeze cans, some are paste-like materials sold in caulking-gun cartridges. Choose whichever one you prefer, considering cost, ability to adhere well to wood, and the characteristic of curing into a tough, tenacious, rubberlike material. Work this into the V-grooves, wiping it into a smooth, uniform fillet with your fingertip or some tool such as a popsicle stick, wood pencil eraser, etc.

When cured, this fillet will be paintable. Water pressure from the outside will always press it more tightly against the wood. Anything you might apply from the inside, water pressure will tend to lift off. You could look into epoxy resins in place of a flexible seam compound. Various powdery materials can be mixed into them to modify their consistency to suit various tasks. Even more than a good flexible compound, an epoxy would tend to rigidize a floppy hull, and it might go on easier than fiberglass.

Softening Seam Compound

Q. I started to repair the transom of my lapstrake inboard and soon found the rubbery seam compound used between the planking and transom is extremely tough and tenacious. Is there any kind of solvent that would soften it?

A. Not that we know of. The stuff is sold with the idea that it's supposed to be rather permanent! Separate the wooden parts by inserting a hacksaw blade into the joints and cutting them loose, taking out as much of the compound and as little of the wood as possible. It will be slow going.

Undercutting Seam Putty

Q. I bought a good used wooden boat that has carvel planking. During winter storage the planks had shrunk slightly and opened the seams. I fixed them by applying seam putty, then painting the bottom. In the fall, on hauling the boat out, we found the bottom was covered with ridges of putty that had been pressed out by pressure when the seams had closed up after launching. These ridges must cause a lot of water drag. How can I prevent them from forming next season?

A. After applying the seam putty, drag a nailhead along each seam to scrape out excess putty and leave it slightly concave. When planks swell, there will be less of the putty to be squeezed out. With luck, your undercutting will leave just enough so that when swelling is complete the putty will lie level with the planking surface.

"Putty Bugs"

Q. What is "putty bug?" I have heard boatyard men mention such a creature.

A. It is a small sea creature that does resemble a bug. For some strange reason, it is attracted to the older types of seam putties made from natural materials. A sound coat of anti-fouling bottom paint should keep them out of your seam putty. When putty bulges out from seams when the planks swell, the paint skin is ruptured and these creatures can get at edges of exposed putty.

Buying Mahogany

Q. I am rebuilding a 40-year-old cabin cruiser. She has some fine cabinet work in her—one rarely sees its equivalent in later boats. I will need some mahogany to replace some cracked pieces. Where can I get it?

A. What kind of mahogany? Honduras, African and Philippine mahoganies are used in boat work, each having different appearance and properties. "Philippine mahogany" is not a real mahogany but has been imported and widely used under that name. It comes in a variety of grains, colors, hardnesses and qualities—some quite nice aboard a boat, some of poor appearance and thus used mostly for framing, etc. As good woods go, it is not particularly costly, nor is it fabulously hard. It works quite easily, holds glue and screw-threads well, is fairly light in weight, and has good rot resistance. It has a grain that usually is easy to recognize, with many little check marks breaking up the solidity of the color.

African and Honduras mahoganies are real mahoganies and are generally found in high-quality, custom-built wooden boats. One needs to be familiar with boatbuilding woods to recognize them and tell one from another.

Many local lumberyards and millwork shops carry Philippine mahogany, as it is used for furniture, interior decoration, novelties, etc., in addition to boats. Or they can get it for you. It usually comes in the form of rough-sawn boards, often of varying width. You will have to seek out specialty lumber companies in or near large cities to find African and Honduras mahogany. These woods are available by mail order from a company that specializes in boat lumber—the Maurice L. Condon Co., 250 Ferris Ave., White Plains, N.Y. 10603.

Sitka Spruce

Q. The mast of our sailboat was smashed in a storm. We wish to try to make a new one ourselves. Where can we get long pieces of high quality Sitka spruce?

A. It's not easy. Look in the Yellow Pages of big city phone books for listings of specialty lumber dealers. Ask local boatyards. Go to the local airport and ask to be referred to local members of the Experimental Aircraft Association, a nationwide organization of people who make their own airplanes as a hobby. They will know of some sources of spruce. Sitka spruce is used in wooden ladders; try contacting ladder manufacturers. The Maurice L. Condon Co., mentioned previously, could probably supply it. Write to the Forest Products Laboratory, U.S. Department of Agriculture, P.O. Box 5130, Madison, Wis. 53705 and ask for a copy of their mimeographed *Partial List of Wood-Using and Allied Associations.* Look up likely-sounding associations to query in it about spruce sources.

Luaun

Q. I have seen a few mentions of a wood called "luaun." What is it?

A. It's the proper name for what is usually called Philippine mahogany, pronounced lu-an. If you need a smaller piece of mahogany for a repair job and it's obvious your boat is made of Philippine mahogany, go to a lumberyard or even a discount house and ask to see luaun shelving. Be warned that the hardness and strength can vary, so pick a piece with this in mind.

Teak Plywood

Q. Is there such a thing as teak plywood? Seems to me this wood would be too oily to hold glue.

A. As a matter of fact, there is teak plywood. It's even available with score lines in it filled with a black or white compound to make it look like the seams of a real teak-planked deck. Some mass produced boats have "teak planking" decks made of this stuff. M.L. Condon and, also, The Harbor Sales Company, 1401 Russell St., Baltimore,

Md. 21230 are sources for mail-order teak plywood. Harbor, by the way, stocks a variety of plywoods suitable for boat use, ranging from domestic Douglas fir to several imported kinds made of assorted African and other woods. They will package and ship to you.

Seasoning Wood

Q. I want to cut some trees in my woodlot to use in rebuilding an old sailboat. How long will it take to season?

A. The general rule is that timber should be allowed to season for one year for each inch of thickness. In theory, a ten-inch tree trunk would have to season for ten years— much too long to wait! Usual practice is to fell trees in the winter, when it is presumed there will be a minimum of sap in the wood. Then have a sawmill rip it into boards of the desired thickness, stack them with strips of wood between to allow air to circulate, and either put them under a roof or build a tarpaper or tarpaulin rain shield over the pile. Some woods will tend to develop checks at the ends of boards when they begin to dry. Some lumbermen will put a thick type of paint on board ends to prevent too-fast drying; some will brush linseed oil on ends. As there are many kinds of wood and they season at varying rates, it is hard to give pat instructions—one has to have some knowledge of woods to do seasoning without encountering unpleasant surprises.

Literature on Boat Woods

Q. Where can I read up on the various kinds of wood used in boats?

A. For a starter, read the chapter on this subject in *Boatbuilding in Your Own Backyard* by S.S. Rabl. Get boat-book catalogs from International Marine Publishers, 21 Elm St, Camden, Maine 04843 and The Woodenboat, P.O. Box 78, Brooklin, Maine 04616. For specialized literature on a vast range of wood subjects you can always write to the Forest Products Laboratory previously mentioned. They will also answer specific questions about wood and wood technology.

Why No Wooden Boats Today?

Q. Why are they manufacturing so few boats of wood today?

A. Very simply, labor and finishing costs. You can use up every drop of resin in a drum and every foot of cloth in a roll when working with fiberglass, but boat lumber comes in random pieces with various defects, it has to be sorted out, and there is always waste. Glass cloth is easy to cut and needs only to be of approximate shape, but all wood parts have to be cut to exact shape. Several inexperienced workers can spread resin on cloth and roll it out quickly, but skilled hands are needed to fit wood parts together in workmanlike manner. When a fiberglass part comes out of a mold, the gel coat on its outside is smooth and needs only a little buffing to finish it off, but a wooden boat requires sanding, priming, and several coats of paint and varnish. We can love the looks and feel of a wooden boat, but we have to admit that the amount of labor required makes its use uneconomical in volume production.

Double Planked Hulls

Q. We have an older yacht with a double-diagonal planked hull. Externally it appears to be in fine condition, but once in the water the bottom leaks in countless places. What should I do? Is there a book on maintaining double-planked hulls?

A. There are various forms of double planking and they have all been used on a variety of boats, for the most part before and during World War II. It was popular for naval PT boats, for example, because it produced light, strong hulls. When speed is a designer's main objective, long-term durability is not apt to be a consideration. After one layer of planking has been put on, the next one is laid in some kind of bedding material. In different boats, this could be something like Kuhls or Ferdico marine glue (no longer manufactured) or a mixture of white lead and linseed oil. Some kind of cloth, such as muslin, was often used in connection with the glue or bedding compound. After many years the glue and cloth becomes dry and brittle. Short of removing the outer planking to replace the dried-out materials (a dreadful job), there is little one can do. One might consider fiberglassing, but on a boat of any size, such as your cruiser, a single layer won't work. Two or more will be needed to achieve rigidity and strength. It will cost a lot. The various boatbuilding books have a few paragraphs in them about making double-planked boats but there's nothing helpful in them about maintaining them in their old age. There's no book on double-planked boats; such boats were built in small numbers in widely scattered places and no author could manage to gain sufficient experience with all forms of this construction to handle a book adequately. And the market for such a book would have been too small to make its publication a feasible business venture. There comes a time when any boat must be retired from service. Some museum might be happy to get yours, and you could claim an income tax deduction for the gift.

Oil in Wood

Q. Just before my wooden sloop was hauled out for the winter, it passed through a patch of oil floating on the water. When hauled, the bottom was oil-covered. Do you think oil could have seeped through thin and bare spots in the paint so as to impair adhesion of bottom paint next spring?

A. We would not worry much. The wood under chipped spots in the paint would have been so water-soaked that we doubt it would have absorbed any oil. If it was our boat and we had reason to think oil was in the wood, we would sand paint off around the suspected spots and use pieces of stiff cardboard, Masonite, etc. and small nails to press wads of soft cloth or cotton against the oily spots in order to draw as much of the oil out of the wood as possible during the months of storage. This is a good example of an improvised but common-sense solution to an odd maintenance problem.

Wooden Thwarts Warp

Q. The wooden thwarts in my utility outboard boat are made of single wide boards that have cupped with exposure to the weather. Now they hold rainwater. What should I do?

A. Take them out. Adjust a table saw to make cuts about half as deep as the wood is thick, or a little more. Run the boards over the saw to make kerfs running from end to end and an inch or so apart. These kerfs will usefully reduce the tendency to cup. You can pull the boards flat if necessary with a few cross-cleats screwed and glued onto the bottom surfaces.

"Gunk" and Wood

Q. I have regularly used Gunk cleaner on the engine in my inboard boat. Now I wonder—is there any possibility that products of this type could injure the wood below the engine?

A. We would not worry about injury to the wood. After all, cleaners of this type have been used for years to clean not only the engines on small airplanes, but also to clean engine oil off of the fuselages. There's a lot of wood fairing and cotton fabric covering on these planes and we never knew mechanics to worry about Gunk harming these materials. There are several brands of engine cleaner on the market; if we were worried about side effects from the one we were using in a boat, we would write to the manufacturer for advice. If you want to play safe, spread old newspapers under the engine before spraying cleaner to catch and absorb the drippings.

Chapter 8

Plywood

Books on Plywood

Q. Where can I get a book on plywood boat care?

A. We know of no book that treats this subject in detail. Plywood boats enjoyed a rather brief period of popularity in the years following World War II. By the time any potential author could have gathered the necessary knowledge of them, fiberglass had begun to take over and the market potential for such a book began to shrink. The various boat maintenance books now in print each have a page or two on plywood, none being particularly informative. About the best is *The Master Handbook of Boat and Marine Repair* by Daman C. Fenwick, available by mail from Tab Books, Blue Ridge Summit, Pa. 17214. Plywood information is scattered through various sections of it. If you can build a plywood boat you can fix one, so get *Boatbuilding With Plywood* by Glen L. Witt, from Glen-L Marine Designs, 9152 Rosecrans, Bellflower, Cal. 90706. Clark Craft Boat Co., 16 Aqua Lane, Tonawanda, N.Y. 14150 has a book called *Boat Building With Plywood*.

"Exterior" and "Marine" Plywood

Q. I understand that "exterior" plywood is made with the same waterproof adhesive used in making "marine" (sometimes called "boat hull") plywood. Can I use it in boat work? How do the two differ?

A. You are correct; they are both made with the same adhesive. Core veneer for marine grade is carefully selected to be free of knotholes, splits, etc. that would create hollow places inside a sheet of plywood, and the pieces of veneer are fitted together snugly so there will not be gaps between them. When you inspect exterior plywood in a lumberyard, you will see gaps along the edges where core pieces do not fit together snugly. Knotholes are a problem because sometimes one will be in the way of a metal fastening, and so the fastening will not hold well. Voids between the core veneer are a problem when plywood has to be bent onto a hull. They will either encourage the plywood to crack along the line of a void, or a ridge will appear on the surface and will show through the paint. Knots and voids are starting points for rot. Exterior plywood can be used for decking, cabin roofs, etc. where the plywood will not be in constant contact with the water and where it will not be bent much. It can be used on small, cheap utility boats where there is not much bend or twist in the hull panels. One can pour activated fiberglass resin down into voids to fill them and firm up the laminate usefully. The quality of exterior varies widely; one batch will have many voids, another rather few. Although the plywood industry has a set of standards, individual factories occasionally deviate from them for such reasons as supply and demand, cost, quality of logs coming in from the forests, etc.

Testing Plywood

Q. Someone gave me a few sheets of plywood, insisting it is exterior grade. I can find no identifying marks on it to substantiate that claim. I don't want to use it in a boat only to have it come apart once it gets wet. How can I make sure it is satisfactory for boat use?

A. Cut small pieces out of each sheet—a few inches square will do. Put them in a porcelain pan (a metal one might cause discoloration and lead to some confusion) and soak them in water for a few days. Bring the water to a boil for a short time every so often, say four or five times a day. If the plywood is still sound after a few days of this treatment, it should be all right to use in a boat.

Buying Marine Plywood

Q. I've been to several lumberyards looking for marine plywood. None have it. Some say they can order it for me but it will take time and it will cost a lot. Why is it so hard to get a commonplace material?

A. Wake up, bud! Marine plywood in the 1980s is not really commonplace! After all, you don't see plywood boats being offered at boat shows and marine sales yards, do you? Too much hand labor is involved in shaping, assembling, and finishing any kind of wooden boat for today's mass-production scene. The demand for marine plywood has fallen off markedly. Only a few plywood mills still make it. It sells for approximately three times the price of exterior plywood at lumberyards. Imported marine plywoods of mahogany-like tropical woods cost even more. Marine plywood can be bought by mail order, but then trucking costs must be included in the final price. Two firms prominent in the business of selling marine plywood by mail order are Harbor Sales Co., Inc., 1401 Russell St., Baltimore, Md. 21230 and Maurice L. Condon Co., 250 Ferris Ave., White Plains, N.Y. 10603. If you live near a large city, look in the plywood section of the Yellow Pages for ads of firms that carry marine plywood. Write to American Plywood Association, 1119 A Street, Tacoma, Washington 98401 for a copy of the current APA Directory: Members, Products, Services. It will tell you which few firms still make marine plywood. Also ask for a copy of Guide to Plywood Grades.

Utile, Occume, Gaboon, Khaya

Q. While reading wooden boat literature I encounter strange words such as utile, occume (or okoume), gaboon (or gabon), khaya, tanguile, etc. What do they mean?

A. They are names of tropical woods used in imported marine plywoods.

Overlaid Plywood

Q. Instructions that come with some small-boat plans mention "overlaid plywood" as a good material. What is this?

A. It is regular fir plywood with a special treatment. A resin-treated fiber sheeting is bonded to the plywood's surface and virtually becomes a part of it. The surface appearance is reminiscent of Masonite but is lighter in color. This overlay bonds the grain and virtually eliminates weather checking and grain raising. It comes in "medium density" and "high density" forms; use the former for boat work because it holds paint best.

Don't Sand Fir Plywood

Q. We replaced the foredeck on our big old runabout with new fir plywood. Wanting a good painted finish, we sanded it well with an orbital finishing sander before priming and painting. To our dismay, the wavy grain showed through the paint with clearly visible high and low spots. Could the primer possibly have raised the grain like this?

A. You made a very common mistake. Sanding bare fir plywood is wrong. The abrasive grains tend to slide over the darker, harder portions of the grain and to eat into the lighter, softer areas. There's no need to sand plywood—the entire surface is uniformly sanded by huge drum sanders as part of the finishing process in the factory. Because of its length, the working surface of such a big drum straddles all the hard and soft areas and puts uniform cutting action on them to leave a flat surface. If it is necessary to sand putty or plastic wood over screw heads, do it after the first coat of primer has dried. The primer will "lock" the fibers of the soft grain and minimize the tendency of abrasive grains to scour away the wood grain.

Wood Preservative and Plywood Glue

Q. Will wood preservative soften or weaken the glue in plywood?

A. The liquid is just a petroleum product. Since glue used to make marine plywood obviously must resist the gasoline and oil likely to be found in motorboats, a little preservative is harmless. Just let the solvent dry out completely before trying to glue treated plywood onto the boat. Better brush on the preservative after the gluing has been completed and the glue or other adhesive has set firmly.

Plywood Delamination

Q. I bought a used plywood boat and was assured it was made of marine plywood. Now, on pressing various areas on the bottom, I find that the outer ply has come loose from the inner plies, especially at the bow. Was I gypped?

A. Your boat would have fallen apart long ago if it were made of "interior" grade plywood. Delamination often happens as plywood boats age. It is the material's Achilles heel. You can test a sample of marine plywood by sealing it in a bottle of water. It will still be sound 100 years later, but that does not prove its durability in boat use! Plywood consists of veneers glued together with each layer at right angles to the other. Moisture can and will penetrate almost all finishes except a deeply penetrating epoxy, such as the resins offered by Gougeon Bros., Clark Craft, and Chem-Tech. Moisture also seeps in at the edges, especially when a builder has not been really careful about sealing them. When the plywood gets wet, the veneers expand at right angles to one another, putting a shearing load on the glue lines. When a sheet of plywood is bent onto a boat hull, the outer glue lines are put under further tension. The pounding and flexing a boat experiences when under way puts even more stress on the glue lines. With repeated swelling and shrinking and application of tension, the wood fibers at the glue lines gradually break free and the plywood delaminates. The glue has not failed, rather the wood itself has broken loose from the glue. Delamination up forward is common—the wood is bent more there, hence more tension on the glue lines.

Molded Plywood Boat is Delaminating

Q. I have a boat made of molded plywood. Here and there I find some of the strips of veneer are coming loose from the laminate. Why is this happening and how do I fix it?

A. The cause is basically the same as in the preceding question. Molded plywood boats were an offshoot of development work on molded plywood aircraft components done during World War II. When peace came, a few firms that had autoclaves (large tanks for heat-and-pressure treatment) turned out a vast number of molded hulls. They sold the bare hulls by the truckload to numerous boatbuilding firms who finished them off and sold them under their own brand names. The trim was different but the basic shapes were all the same. Then fiberglass came along, making it possible for each boatbuilder to create his own shapes and styling, and molded hulls vanished from the market. There is no standard way to fix a delaminated molded hull. You could try running some kind of adhesive into the open places, use small bolts and nuts to pull things tight, and hope it works.

Patching Plywood

Q. My kid hit the dock while coming in for a landing and knocked an eight-inch hole in the side of our plywood outboard. How do I fix it neatly?

For several years following World War Two, molded plywood boats like this "Dunphy" were popular. But the material was not as strong or durable as fiberglass and gradually lost favor with both boatbuilders and the public. An amateur could build a boat like this himself today using the "cold molded" process made possible by modern epoxy adhesives.

A. Use a sabre saw to cut out the damaged wood. The resulting hole can be either rectangular or circular. Bevel its edges from the outside with a wood rasp and sandpaper block. Cut and bevel a piece of plywood to fit in this hole. Make another piece of plywood, about two inches larger than the hole, to go on the inside. Marine stores sell general-purpose epoxy glue in 8-ounce cans and tubes. Set the pieces in this glue and fix them in place with small wood screws. When cured, sand smooth, level off with surfacing putty, prime, and paint.

Three-Sixteenths Inch Plywood

Q. My small plywood sailboat got adrift and ground its bottom up badly on a rocky beach. The bottom plywood is some kind of mahogany measuring three-sixteenths of an inch thick. Local lumberyards never heard of such stuff. Where can I get some to fix the boat?

A. We think the plywood on your small boat is in all likelihood some imported marine plywood that was manufactured to the metric system. Three-sixteenths of an inch corresponds to 5 millimeters. Try Harbor Sales, mentioned previously, to get some.

Plywood Longevity

Q. We're making a catamaran from magazine plans.

They call for fir plywood for the deck. How long would this last out in the open?

A. Things don't last a certain number of years and then just suddenly fall apart. Deterioration is gradual. A poor finishing job will let deterioration set in sooner, a good one will appreciably prolong something's serviceability. A well-finished, cared for plywood deck should certainly last many happy years.

Fir Plywood Checking

Q. Why does fir plywood develop so many weather checks so soon? Is there any way to prevent it?

A. The matter has been researched at length. It appears to be characteristic of the wood's grain structure. We personally suspect it has something to do with the way the thin veneer is sliced off the logs by a huge knife blade—a sort of combination lathe and oversize apple peeler. The check lines always show up parallel to the edge of the knife blade. There are various primers that are claimed to do well, such as "Firzite." Our observation is that fir plywood surfaces that are horizontal check more than those that are vertical, probably having something to do with getting the brunt of mid-day sun and night-time dew. A plywood deck can be covered with canvas or with fiberglass to stop checking.

In recent years a number of epoxy resins have been marketed. Their prime purpose is to serve as adhesives in a method of boatbuilding in which many long, thin strips of veneer are laid onto a building form to create a modern version of the old "double diagonal" type of planking. The firms that market it claim that an adequate coating of such resin on fir plywood will bind the wood against checking. Such resin must be covered with paint to shut out destructive sunlight. Get literature on these boatbuilding and boat maintenance resins from: Clark Craft, 16 Aqua Lane,

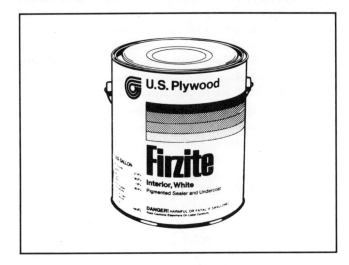

"Firzite" is one of the primers made especially for use on Douglas fir plywood to minimize weather checking.

Tonawanda, N.Y. 14150, Gougeon Bros., P.O. Box 384, Bay City, Mich. 48706, and Chem Tech, 4669 Lander Rd., Chagrin Falls, Ohio 44022. Professional boatbuilders prefer to use non-checking, mahogany-type plywoods on surfaces exposed to the elements—this can cost less than a cheaper fir plywood covered with a rather expensive epoxy coating.

Removing Paint from Plywood

Q. I wish to refinish my plywood sailboat. Can I burn the old paint off with a propane torch?

A. No, don't do it! The heat will penetrate the wood enough to affect the glue under the outside layer of veneer. The glue will probably blister or foam, losing its holding power. Remember, any time you're in doubt about how something will work on or around a boat, make up some test samples and see for yourself what will happen.

Painting Prams

Q. This winter I plan to make up several fir plywood prams to sell next spring. Can you suggest a good but moderately priced painting scheme for them?

A. The first coat should be a checking-deterrent plywood primer, such as "Firzite," with white pigment. Firzite is made by United States Plywood Corp., Kalamazoo, Mich. and is available at many hardware stores and lumberyards. Some marine paint firms also make plywood primer. Then apply one, or better two, coats of marine undercoater. If the final coat is to be other than white, you can add a little of the chosen paint to the undercoater to tint it and make scratches show up less. Let the first coat of undercoater dry hard so it can be sanded without gumming the abrasive paper. The second coat can be thinned out slightly to make it spread smoothly. Sand less vigorously. Finish with two coats of the marine paint of your choice, making sure it is a type suitable for use on wooden boats.

Kit Boats

Q. I got an urge to build a small boat. On asking around, I was surprised to find that marine dealers don't carry kits and don't know where to get them. Kits used to be so popular. What happened?

A. After World War II many highly improved outboard motors came onto the market. There were far fewer boat manufacturers and dealers than there are today. Kits enjoyed a short spell of popularity, then faded away as mass-produced fiberglass and aluminum boats began to appear in quantity and were sold on time-payment plans. Only a few firms remained in the kit business, advertising mostly in the mechanical magazines to get business from do-it-yourselfers. As we write this, there are signs that inflation is generating new interest in kits. The kit manufacturers now find that plywood is not as readily available in satisfactory quality as it once was and costs a lot more than it did. Some are thus looking into other materials, such as fiberglass panels and cedar veneer laid in epoxy resin. When you pay retail prices for boatbuilding materials and spend a lot of time assembling and finishing a boat, you can find you have not saved as much money as you hoped. We recently built a 16-foot plywood johnboat for a client and the raw materials cost just over $400.00. One can buy a plain but serviceable factory-built aluminum johnboat for less than that! Figure material costs carefully before starting to build and don't forget to include lumber for the jig as well as the cost of tools, sandpaper, paint thinner, masking tape and other incidentals not shown on bills of material. Many people today build their own boats more for the satisfaction of creating something, or to get a type of boat they can't buy, than to save money.

Plywood kit boats enjoyed a spell of popularity in the period around 1945 to 1955. But the coming of fiberglass and mass-production caused the public to gradually lose interest. A key point to remember is that when all the materials are purchased at retail prices, a homemade boat can cost about the same as one that has been factory-built using mass-production techniques.

Plywood Boat Plans

Q. Where can I get plans for homemade plywood boats?
A. Write to American Plywood Association, 1119 A Street, Tacoma, Washington 98401 and ask for a copy of their free *Plywood Boat Plan Directory.*

Magazine Plans

Q. I started to build a plywood boat from plans in a newsstand publication put out by a magazine. I soon found it was hard to get some of the materials called for. Why don't they design these boats to use readily available materials?
A. Some publishers print the same old plans over and over. We have recently seen plans in print that are for designs 25, 30, and even 40 years old! Publishers keep getting letters from readers asking for boat plans, so they feel compelled to get something into print. There are very few people who can design, build, test, draw, and write up good how-to-build-it projects. And fewer still who can or will do it at the rates of payment the magazines can afford. So the magazines are starved for good up-to-date material. Some of these books of plans are put together by office employees who have had little or no boatbuilding experience. Sometimes they choose clunkers to reprint, or don't spot things

that have become out of date. Don't let magazine hype stampede you into building some boat on the spur of the moment. Take time to look around. Get plan catalogs from Clark Craft, 16 Aqua Lane, Tonawanda, New York 14150; Glen-L Marine Designs, 9152 Rosecrans, Bellflower, Cal. 90706; and Texas Dory Boat Plans, P.O. Box 720, Galveston, Texas 77550. Write to them on postcards and ask the price of current catalogs. Get a few copies of *The Woodenboat* magazine, P.O. Box 78, Brooklin, Maine 04616 and *The Small Boat Journal*, Highland Mill, Camden, Maine 04843. Read articles and ads in them to get an idea of what's being done today in the homemade boat field. There are also two modest but interesting newsletters about small craft built by amateurs; *The Ash Breeze*, c/o Samuel M. King, Francestown Turnpike, Mont Vernon, N.H. 03057, and *Ripples*, published by Small, Antique and Unusual Boats, 3725 Talbot St., Suite B, San Diego, Cal. 92106.

Another word of advice about plans—they are drawn up by people with widely varying knowledge and skill. Some are gems, some are turkeys. Once you get a pile of literature on small boat construction, you will quickly develop an ability to sort them out. For example, be wary of plans for a boat where the finished craft is illustrated only by an artist's rendition. The fact that it is not illustrated with a photograph could mean that a prototype was never built; therefore, flaws in the plans or the design were never discovered!

Plywood has strong appeal to those who would like to build a boat of a type they cannot buy from mass-production companies. These are big, able fishing and utility dories designed by Texas Dory Boat Plans.

Chapter 9

About Very Old Boats

Antique Boat Restoration Books

Q. We have a fine old launch in the barn that was built around 1920. Right now it's a mess, but basically it's sound. If we could get it fixed up it would be a living museum piece. Is there a book on restoring old boats?

A. Yes. It was written by an Englishman and deals as much with restoring ships as with small boats. At first you might think its cost ($20.00 as of this writing) is high, but it could be worth it considering the value of your boat when fully restored. It's available from International Marine Publishing, 21 Elm St., Camden, Maine 04843. Better send them a postcard and get the current price plus postage.

A beautifully-restored old-time boat and engine is a source of great satisfaction to its owner. The woman here is showing a scrapbook containing photos of restoration work to admirers at an antique boat rally. One of these old boats in good condition will increase in value with passage of time.

Antique Boat Clubs

Q. Is there a club for people who love to restore antique boats?

A. Yes. Write to the Antique Classic Boat Society, Box 199, Cloverdale, N.Y. 12820. The Chris Craft Corporation, 555 S. W. 12th Ave., Pompano Beach, Fla. 33060, has a club for owners of older Chris Craft boats. There is an Antique Outboard Motor Club whose address is 3724 N. Briarcliff Rd., Kansas City, Mo. 64116. There are clubs for various makes of old boats besides the Chris Crafts; they come and go and change addresses. Contact them by writing to the various boating and yachting magazines.

Antique Hardware

Q. Is there any source for replacement hardware for an antique boat?

A. Many basic items such as chocks and cleats, hinges, etc., have changed little down through the years and they can be obtained from today's marine hardware firms. Brass and bronze parts can be reproduced by foundries from your wooden patterns.

Plans for an Old Boat

Q. We think our old sailboat is a classic; that is, designed

publication you seek. Some marine museums have bound volumes of old magazines in their libraries.

Activities such as the "Op Sail" programs, which bring fleets of sailing ships to various ports, have generated interest in old boats of all kinds. Here a reproduction of the fishing schooner "Blue-nose" sails into Halifax, Nova Scotia. (Nova Scotia Communications & Information Center)

by some famous old designer and thus possibly worth a lot of money. We've written to various boating magazines asking if they ever published plans for this design and if so could we buy photocopies from them. But they all reply they have no information. What do you make of this?

A. Magazine offices are not archives; they are places of business. They regularly clear out their files to make room for the fresh material that is constantly coming in. Although a magazine may have been around a long time, there is a constant turnover of people in its office. The present editors are probably younger people who not only don't know what went on in the magazine's office in 1925 but had not even been born then! Magazines change ownership and they move from one address to another with the passage of years. Although a magazine might have its present office in New York, its files of very old issues may be in a warehouse 50 or 100 miles away from the city. Some famous old yacht clubs maintain files of bound volumes of most of the yachting magazines and persons with a legitimate reason for wanting to look into these files are usually allowed to do so. If you live near a large city, ask the public library if they have bound volumes or microfilmed copies. If you live far from a large city, ask your local librarian for suggestions on how to contact big-city libraries to learn which might have the

Treating a Dried-Out Boat

Q. We found an old sailboat in a barn. It had been there for many years and the wood is as dry as a dog biscuit. The seams have opened up very wide and it's easy to see daylight through them from inside the hull. If we launch it, it will leak like a shotgunned colander. What should we do?

A. Get an assortment of garden hoses, lawn sprinklers, and the kind of garden hose that has hundreds of tiny holes that send jets spraying every which way. Arrange things to keep water flowing steadily but gently over the hull. Let it soak this way for as long as is needed to get the planking wet again and close the seams. The old caulking compound is probably dry and hard and will have to be replaced. Few modern boatyards have men who really know the fine art of caulking. Ask around. If you can find no one, various books on wooden boatbuilding have information on caulking. (See Chapter 1, Locating Parts and Information.) Write to *The Woodenboat* magazine, Box 78, Brooklin, Maine 04616 and ask if they can provide copies of material they have printed on caulking.

Treating a Waterlogged Boat

Q. While scuba diving in a local lake, we discovered a boat on the bottom that is obviously very, very old. It might even be of historical importance. Can you give advice on raising it?

A. Leave it where it is and seek expert advice. If a very old and completely waterlogged boat is brought up and left exposed to the air, the wood can dry out so fast as to be in danger of cracking and crumbling. The usual procedure is to build a plastic tent over it as soon as it is brought ashore. Then hoses and sprinklers are started to keep it wet and it is allowed to drain and dry out very, very gradually. It's a job for experts. Sometimes they chemically treat the wood to strengthen it and keep it from disintegrating. Don't get excited; act deliberately and logically. Ask your local historical or archaeological society to notify the state authorities of your discovery. It is better to let experts handle the old boat. If you try to do it all yourself, you may lose the boat and everyone will be angry at you for ruining an historical treasure.

Old-Style Fastenings

Q. Where can we get old copper rivets, etc. to use in reconditioning an antique boat?

A. Things like this are getting hard to find. Marine museums such as Mystic Seaport, Mystic, Conn. 06355, employ experts at restoring old craft. They will be glad to tell you what they know of sources for such items. The few firms that remain which deal in marine fastenings can be located through *Boat Owners Buyers Guide*. (*See* Chapter 1, Locating Parts and Information, and *The Woodenboat* magazine previously mentioned in this chapter.)

Marine museums like the Mystic Seaport in Connecticut can often help owners of interesting old boats restore them to prime condition. An interesting old boat that has been carefully restored can be worth a lot of money and its value will almost surely increase. (Evinrude Motors)

Working on older wooden boats often calls for special skills and tools. This man is using a special tool to rake old oakum out of seams in the deck of a schooner. (John Gardner)

Refinishing an Old Boat

Q. We have begun to recondition a wooden boat that is at least 40 years old. It has countless layers of old paint on it, the varnish is discolored, blistered, and cracked and we've got a job on our hands to clean and brighten it up. Any advice?

A. The major marine paint firms put out literature on painting problems and techniques. Most will gladly offer advice by mail or phone on specific and unusual problems. (*See* Chapter 7, Wooden Boats, and Chapter 16, Painting.)

Pleasure Boat Museums

Q. I am restoring my 1938 cabin cruiser to as near original condition as possible. Where can I get photos or advertising brochures that will show its original equipment and color schemes? Is there a museum devoted to pleasure boats?

A. As far as we know, all marine museums now in existence seem to concentrate on traditional boats. Apparently, pleasure craft are not old enough or romantic enough to appeal to museum types. Best thing to do is locate bound volumes of boating magazines for your boat's period—see the question under "Plans for an Old Boat" earlier in this chapter. It would help to attend meetings held in various parts of the country by antique powerboat lovers and hope to meet people who can help. One such museum is the Thousand Islands Museum, Clayton, New York 13624.

Pennants for Old Boats

Q. We are restoring a fine cabin cruiser built before World War II. The original pennant with the maker's trademark on it still exists but it's too faded and tattered to use. Where can we find a replacement?

A. All kinds of flags and pennants can be made to individual order by such yacht flag companies as Dettra Flag Co., Oaks, Pa. 19456. Sailmakers and canvas shops near boating centers can also make flags—look for them in the Yellow Pages.

Curved Cockpit Coamings

Q. The old launch we are rebuilding has a curved oak cockpit coaming. The sharp bend at the forward end of the cockpit worries us. We don't like the thought of making a steam box with which to bend this one piece of wood. Any ideas?

A. Consider laminating. Modern adhesives, such as the epoxies, will hold wood in a way early glues wouldn't. It's easy to bend thin strips used in laminating work.

Price of Older Boats

Q. We have an old Matthews cabin cruiser and would like to determine its present value. Have you any thoughts?

A. Get a copy of *Older Boat Price Guide* from BUC International Corp., 1881 Northeast 26th St., Suite 95, Ft. Lauderdale, Fla. 33305. It gives prices for hundreds of small, medium, and large pleasure boats built between 1905 and 1968. Send them a postcard requesting the current price. A new edition comes out each year.

Chapter 10

General Maintenance
of
Fiberglass Boats

Fiberglass Life Expectancy

Q. I have been told so many conflicting things about the life expectancy of my new fiberglass boat that I don't know what to believe. What's your opinion?

A. The life expectancy is impossible to predict. An automobile driven only on weekends in the dry climate of the Southwest will last longer than one used for daily commuting in heavy traffic on salt-treated winter roads in the Northeast. This is to say, so much depends on circumstances! A cheaply built fiberglass boat will begin to break up long before a solidly built one will. In this case, the blame should not be placed on the fiberglass, as such, but on the way in which it was used.

A cheap or unethically built fiberglass boat may contain a variety of shortcomings. There will be a minimal number of layers of glass cloth in the laminate. There will be inadequate internal stiffeners. Unethical boatbuilders have been known to make a given amount of resin go farther by adding assorted powders to it to increase its bulk, at the same time decreasing its strength. A cheap boat will have its deck molding fastened to the hull molding with nothing but pop rivets. A better boat will have some kind of fiberglass putty in the joint to supplement the rivets. A top grade boat will have

strips of mat along the joint to provide an almost indestructible fiberglass-to-fiberglass connection between deck and hull.

One way to judge a boat is by its reputation. Ask around at the waterfront and talk to owners of the make you are considering. Since glass cloth and resin are priced by the pound in the wholesale market, the weight of a finished boat can be taken as an indication of how much material is in it and therefore of how sturdy it is. If one outboard runabout weighs 700 lbs. and another one very similar to it weighs 1000 lbs., the latter is *probably* built better. You have to take into account the probable weight added to each boat by upholstery, windshield, deck hardware, seats, etc. Some hulls are made of solid fiberglass, others have their bottoms and sides made thicker and therefore stiffer by incorporating lightweight core materials into the laminate. These core materials can be some kind of tough foam plastic like "Airex" and "Klege-Cell," or end-grain squares of balsa wood called "Balcor" or "Contourcore." A new lightweight laminating cloth called "Kevlar" is coming into wider use as this is being written. The various glass fabrics and core materials come in different weights and thicknesses, and they can be combined in a laminate in an infinite variety of ways.

As the old saying goes, "It doesn't matter so much what a boat is made of as it does who made it!" A rather general rule is you get what you pay for when buying a boat. A 26-footer costing $30,000 almost certainly will have to be a better built boat than one of similar size and type selling for $15,000.

A lot depends on the care given to a boat. One man rinses salt spray off his boat after each outing, another lets salt specks accumulate. One waxes his fiberglass twice a year, the other never. One stores his boat on a good cradle and covers it over, the other stores his on a makeshift cradle and leaves it exposed to winter weather. One touches up his varnish regularly, the other neglects his until it's badly peeling. A boat used three months of the year in Maine will suffer less sun damage than one used nine months of the year under Florida's sun. A boat used in fresh water will suffer negligible damage from corrosion, one used in salt water by an owner who knows nothing about corrosion problems and protection will be a mess at the end of its first year. Boats owned by people who read this book will of course last longer than boats owned by those who don't!

Laminate Thickness

Q. How thick should the hull laminate be on a 27-foot boat?

A. There is no pat rule. A good hull can be made with a wide variation in the weights and number of fabric

Life expectancy of a fiberglass boat depends on various factors: how well it was designed, how well it was made, the choice of materials used in its construction, how it is used, how it is cared for, the climatic conditions under which it is used, and so on. There is no pat answer to the common question, "how long will a fiberglass boat last?" (Bob Hewes Boats)

laminations. Core materials come in various thicknesses, and thicker does not always mean stronger. A hull having many internal reinforcing strips can get by with a thinner skin than one with much less reinforcing. Large flat surfaces will "flutter" where large curved surfaces have built-in resistance to fluttering. A fast offshore cruiser will have to be tougher than a slow sailboat. A sailboat having heavy lead ballast will have to have more fiberglass laminates in its bottom around the keel, to support the lead's weight, than a centerboard sailboat will have to have around its centerboard trunk. A fiberglass canoe intended for portaging trips in the wilderness might logically have a thinner laminate than one that is going to be used by a boys' camp or canoe livery.

You can give the drawings of a new hull to ten good fiberglass men and each will come up with his own idea of an appropriate lamination schedule. And all will produce sound boats. You can give the plans to ten unknowledgeable men and each will come up with a lamination schedule lacking in one way or another. Unfortunately, there have been a lot of fools in the fiberglass boat business—you can spot them by their big mouths and the $$ signs glowing within their eyeballs!

Wood vs. Fiberglass

Q. I sold my wooden cabin cruiser and bought a new fiberglass boat. Now several friends have told me I made a bad mistake because shipworms will riddle its bottom. What is your opinion?

A. The world is full of people who love to talk but don't know what they are talking about! Saltwater creatures, such as barnacles, and a variety of sea plants, generally called "grass" by boatmen, will attach themselves to the *surface* of fiberglass. In addition to making an unsightly mess, the roughness they create hurts performance. So it is normal to put anti-fouling paint on fiberglass boats that will be moored or docked in salt water. Since these paints will also repel shipworms, some lubbers have jumped to the conclusion that fiberglass is somehow susceptible to shipworm attack.

Common sense says shipworms eat wood to survive. Obviously, they would get bellyaches from eating fiberglass. Shows how little common sense there is! Some years ago a boating magazine printed a tongue-in-cheek story about a new breed of marine borer called the "polyestermite" that supposedly would devour fiberglass. Fiberglass boats have been around since the mid-1940s. Common sense says it takes nature much longer than that to evolve a new species. But some people believed that story about "polyestermites," talked about these critters at cocktail parties, and threw a scare into many a new boat owner. We know this is true because we have received dead-serious letters from boat owners anxiously wanting to know how to protect their craft from these little monsters!

Resin and Gel Coat

Q. *I'm confused by the oft-used terms "resin" and "gel coat" in fiberglass talk. Can you please explain them?*

A. Resin is the liquid that is brushed and rolled into glass fabric to fill and stiffen it. Gel coat is a type of pigmented resin formulated to be used as the outermost finish coat, to impart color and glossy appearance. Gel coat belongs to the same class of chemicals as resin. It is really just a modified resin, blended to give the best possible resistance to cracking, scratching, and exposure to the elements. Resin is of syrupy consistency and transparent save for a slight yellow, purple, green, or milky cast to it. Gel coat is of a semi-paste consistency and is colored with pigments. A vast range of colors are made by gel coat manufacturers.

How Deep Is Fiberglass Color?

Q. *I had heard that the color goes all the way through a fiberglass hull. But my boat has a few scratches and I can see the color coat is very thin and there is nothing but greyish fiberglass under it. Is my boat of poor quality?*

A. No. In the early days of fiberglass, they had to make do with a much smaller range of materials. Gel coat was in its infancy. It was common to impart color to early fiberglass boats by mixing pigment into the clear laminating resin. So of course the color went all the way through. As the pigment did not make the resin 100% opaque, one could see the glass filaments close to the surface. You can still see this sort of appearance in molded fiberglass chairs, food trays, etc. As soon as good gel coats became available, manufacturers switched to them to give a less translucent look and a richer, more brilliant coloring to their boats.

Gel Coat Thickness

Q. *How thick is gel coat?*

A. The ideal thickness is about .015 inch. If it is thinner than that, it is possible for the underlying laminate to show through in a sort of mottled appearance. If thicker, it tends to be brittle and just like a too-thick coat of paint will have a tendency to develop a multitude of hairline cracks on its surface as time passes. This is called "crazing" in the fiberglass trade. It is often impossible for a gel coat spray gun operator to attain real uniformity of thickness due to the peculiarities of the molds being used. A deck mold, for example, will amount to a mixture of flat areas broken up by ridges and grooves that form toe rails, coamings, windshield mounting pads, etc. In trying to spray an adequate thickness of gel coat on the surfaces in the depressions, it is almost impossible to avoid some overspray that will make the gel coat thicker on the flat surfaces close to the depressions. Keeping as close as possible to the ideal thickness requires a spray gun operator who has a fine combination of experience, dexterity, and sense of responsibility. Sometimes the fault lies with the designer, not the spray operator, for having created a mold that is hard to spray uniformly.

Sees Sunlight Through Deck

Q. *While installing accessories in my new fiberglass boat, I crawled into the bow locker and was horrified to see sunlight filtering through the foredeck and hull sides. Have I bought a poorly-made boat?*

A. We doubt it. It's entirely normal for sunlight to show through laminates of the thickness commonly used in pleasure craft. After all, the sun shines through fiberglass canopies over patios! Boat manufacturers have found that seeing sun through decks and hulls has an adverse psychological effect on prospective purchasers—though harmless, it somehow just does not seem "right." Rather than risk getting into arguments by trying to explain things to upset people, they resort to doing the insides of their boats with thick spatter paint, vinyl upholstery, outdoor carpeting, and cockpit liners (double-wall construction). This saves awkward situations in salesrooms—but it sets people up for quite a shock later on when they go underneath an unpainted or unupholstered area and see sunlight shining through! Relax. Remember the patio fiberglass.

He Sees Ghosts!

Q. *My sailboat is ten years old and I have always polished and waxed it each season. Now I am beginning to see scattered greyish discolorations all over the white gel coat on the hull. I have tried a variety of cleaners and polishes but none will improve the appearance. In fact, the discoloration seems to be getting worse. Could this be a chemical problem caused by polluted harbor waters?*

A. Your gel coat is getting thin and allowing the

underlying fiberglass laminate to show through. The person who sprayed the gel coat might have gotten it a little thin, perhaps on a hot day when the viscosity of the gel coat made the thickness of the spray coat hard to judge. He might not have stirred up the gel coat in its five-gallon shipping container before using it. The shop might have been using a brand of gel coat that was a little on the shy side in pigment content. Talk to a boatyard that has had experience painting fiberglass boats. A good paint job is in order.

Electric Polisher on Fiberglass

Q. *The gel coat on my boat's deck is starting to dull. I tried a well-known brand of cleaner-polish on a small section and it restored the shine nicely. But it's a big boat and I dread hand-rubbing the whole deck. Is it safe to use a sheepskin polishing head driven by an electric polisher?*

A. Yes. It's done all the time by professionals. Keep it moving so as not to build up heat and possibly cause a scorched spot. Bear down lightly on corners and edges so as not to buff through the gel coat there. Blunt an old screwdriver blade on a grinding wheel; when the sheepskin fills with compound, touch this tool lightly to the spinning pad to break off the caked material. If the boat is afloat alongside a dock, be very cautious about using electric tools. Ask competent yardmen about safe extension-cord hookups and other precautions against dangerous shocks.

Faded Red Gel Coat

Q. *My runabout has a red deck. Alas, the red has faded so much that no amount of polishing will bring back the color. Now what?*

A. Try fiberglass rubbing compound, using an electric polisher. It has a more vigorous cleaning action than liquid or paste cleaners. If that fails to brighten things up, it is time to think of painting. Sunlight passes through fiberglass laminates. That means it passes through the gel coat, too. When a boat is relatively new, cleaning the gel coat's surface will restore a brighter color. But after long exposure to sunlight, the pigment in the gel coat *below the surface* also becomes faded. When you use polish or compound on the surface, you simply expose gel coat that is filled with pigment that has faded from its original brilliance. So, no amount of polishing will then restore original coloring.

Grinder vs. Polisher

Q. *Is there any difference between what hardware stores call a "grinder" and a "polisher?"*

A. Yes. They look alike, but a grinder is geared to drive its rotating pad at a higher speed. The faster the abrasive grains on a sanding disc strike the work surface, the more vigorous the cutting action and the less the tendency to load up with material. But a sheepskin or cloth polishing pad driven by a grinder can turn so fast that there is a tendency to flick compound off the work surface rather than to work it under the pad where it can do its thing. Also, a pad that is turning too fast can "burn" a surface that is being polished. Some of these tools are combination grinder-polishers. A switch controls speed. Typically, the speeds might be 3000 or 3500 r.p.m. for polishing and 4000 or 4500 r.p.m. for grinding.

Gel Coat Color Durability

Q. *Do some fiberglass gel coat colors fade more than others?*

A. Yes. Reds, medium and dark blues, and greens seem to fade to a greater degree and sooner; white, light greys, and tans show most fade resistance. Other colors are in between. The pastel colors you see predominating at boat shows are in general the ones that boat manufacturers have found offer good fade resistance. You may have noticed that you see fewer bold colors used on new fiberglass boats. But please remember, pigment manufacturers are always developing improved products, so it is unwise to flatly state that such-and-such a color will definitely fade more than some other color.

Brushing on Gel Coat

Q. *Could I buy some original color gel coat from the manufacturer of my boat and brush it on to spruce up a faded deck?*

A. It won't work. Gel coat is about the consistency of slightly chilled molasses, and cannot be brushed out smooth like paint. Mix a bowlful of plaster of paris and try brushing it out to get an idea of how gel coat would behave and look if you tried brushing it.

Painting Fiberglass

Q. *I bought some high grade boat paint and used it on my*

fiberglass boat. In a few weeks it started to peel off. Did I buy some "gyp" paint?

A. No. Was it paint intended for wooden boats? If so, that's the trouble. The surface of fiberglass is simply too hard and nonporous for ordinary paints to have a chance of adhering well. Paints made for use on fiberglass are usually of the epoxy or urethane types. They are specially compounded to spread and adhere well when applied to fiberglass. Some go right onto well-sanded fiberglass, some require the use of a primer. To do a good paint job on fiberglass you will have to obtain and read the literature provided by paint makers. Do not use one brand of paint with some other manufacturer's instruction sheet. Each paint must be used exactly as its maker intended.

Sandpaper Scratches Show Through

Q. Following instructions, I sandpapered the surface of my fiberglass boat before painting. After the paint dried, the entire surface showed countless scratches through the paint. Does it need more than one coat to cover well?

A. What grade of sandpaper did you use? Sounds to us as if you used much too coarse a grade of abrasive. The special paints made for fiberglass tend to form a rather thin film when they dry, so scratches show through easily. This is an example of why it is so important to follow paint manufacturers' instructions when using modern, sophisticated finishes.

Spraying Gel Coat

Q. I have a booklet on fiberglass repairs. It says that when the patching of a hole is completed, spray the area with gel coat of a matching color. But it says nothing about what type of gun to use and gives no tips on spraying gel coat. Can you help?

A. A lot of boating literature floating around these days was written by office people who have never worked on a boat themselves! For repair work, gel coat can be sprayed from an ordinary paint spray gun. The problem is not to let it "kick" while it is still in the gun. (*See* Chapter 12, section on "Fiberglass and Weather," for explanation of "kicking.") If this happens, you will certainly have a horrid clean-out job ahead of you. It's wise to reduce the amount of hardener as a safeguard against too-early kicking. Have everything ready and spray immediately after mixing the hardener into the gel coat. Use more air pressure than for paint.

One has to experiment with how much to thin the gel coat to make it spray satisfactorily, and one has to know the gun's adjustments perfectly to get it to spray the gel coat perfectly. Acetone will do for a little thinning, but it will affect the gel

coat's composition less if styrene monomer is used when much thinning is necessary. Gel coat will not level out into a glossy surface as will the types of paint designed for spray gun application. You will have to do a lot of wet-sanding and buffing to smooth it satisfactorily.

When using some colors, especially darker ones, the sprayed area will never match the surrounding surfaces. It will tend to be a bit lighter, slightly cloudy perhaps. Fiberglass experts have differing opinions on why this is so. Some feel that air entrained in the gel coat spray is incorporated in the material deposited on the surface, and that this changes the material's light reflection characteristics and hence its tint. Others feel that since it is the high polish on the surface of the manufacturing mold that makes the surface of gel coat so glossy and rich, a sprayed surface that is given its polish by wet-sanding and buffing simply does not reflect light the same way.

Matching Gel Coat Color

Q. I got a good buy on a fiberglass boat that had been on display in the dealer's yard for over a year and had been scratched by a passing vehicle. The dealer gave me a can of gel coat from the factory with which to repair the scratches. On finishing the job I find the gel coat in the scratches is darker in color than the surrounding surfaces. The dealer says he gave me an exact duplicate of the original color. I don't believe him! Do you?

A. Yes. The original color of the boat faded in the months it was out in the sunlight. Gel coat colors fade, just as automobile, house, and toy paints fade. The fading is so gradual that boat owners don't notice it for a few years. Then, depending on the particular color, they are shocked when they put their boat beside a new one of the same model and color, or when a scratch is touched up with "original color" gel coat. Tinting fresh gel coat to make it match some faded color on a boat is a job for a fiberglass artist. There are very few such men around. Ask boatyards in your area if they happen to know of one. Otherwise, you'll just have to wait for the new gel coat in the scratches to fade and blend into the rest of the surface less conspicuously. When a large area of a fiberglass boat is repaired, the usual way to restore uniform appearance is to paint the whole boat so as to cover the patchwork.

Paint Brushes Vary

Q. A friend and I painted our fiberglass boats the same color, on the same day. His paint job turned out to be beautiful, mine was a mess of brush marks. Why?

A. Did you use one kind of brush and he another? Brush

prices vary widely and so does the quality. Cheap brushes have bristles that are clipped off square at their ends. Fine ones made of natural bristle use animal bristles that taper toward the ends, sometimes to the extent of being forked. Such a brush spreads paint more thoroughly and leaves fewer brush marks. Some synthetic paints affect synthetic bristle materials so as to further impair their already poor paint-spreading ability.

Found His Boat Was Painted!

Q. I bought a large used fiberglass boat and while readying it for launching was appalled to discover its hull had been painted and there was no gel coat under the paint. Did the seller stick me with a dog?

A. We don't think so. It is fairly common for larger fiberglass boats to be finished this way. Some have a dull, matte-like gel coat that takes paint well, some have a lot of good primer over the underlying laminate to give a tough, fair base for hull paint. The reasoning is that large boats inevitably collect scrapes in the course of a season afloat when they rub against docks and when tenders rub against them. Since pride of ownership is very much present in the big boat field, a logical thing to do is to paint such boats. In the long run it can cost less to lightly sand the hull and apply fresh paint than to find a fiberglass expert and have him spend hours doctoring scores of scratches. In the case of custom-built fiberglass boats, it makes sense to mold up a batch of hulls in a neutral color, then finish them off by painting each one whatever color the customer favors.

Burning Paint off Fiberglass

Q. Someone tells me it is all right to remove old paint from a fiberglass boat by softening it with a blowtorch so it can be scraped off. What do you think?

A. We think you have encountered a good example of the wild hearsay that floats around waterfronts. Enough heat to effectively loosen paint will almost surely cause the gel coat to overheat and blister or crack off in small flakes. If you have doubts about any kind of maintenance procedure someone tells you about, you can always try it out on a piece sawn out of an old boat or on a test specimen made up of whatever materials might be involved. That way you can see for yourself what will actually happen.

Removing Paint from Fiberglass

Q. How can I remove old paint from a fiberglass boat?

Sanding it off would be very tedious work indeed. And I'm afraid paint remover will take the gel coat off too.

A. For some reason, probably complete lack of familiarity with fiberglass, a great many boat owners jump to the conclusion that paint remover will injure fiberglass. But well-cured fiberglass is one of the most chemically inert substances around—only a few very special, sophisticated chemicals will dissolve it. The solvents in paint remover won't hurt fiberglass.

The job should be done with a little caution, though. Try the remover of your choice on a small, inconspicuous part of the boat first. Once satisfied that it will do no harm, do small sections (two or three square feet at a time) and scrape the paint off *as soon as* it is adequately loosened. This will minimize the time the remover can be in direct contact with the gel coat surface.

The worst that paint remover can do is to slightly dull the surface of glossy gel coat. But on removing old paint, you are quite likely to discover the gloss had already been sanded off to improve paint adhesion.

Can't Buy Gel Coat

Q. The manufacturer of my boat is out of business. Where can I get some gel coat with which to repair some scratches? Boat stores in my area don't know.

A. Gel coat is hard to get in small quantities. You'd think it would be a stock item in boat stores but it isn't. There are reasons. When one buys a can of paint, it is taken for granted that you will use it to paint an entire deck, or the entire hull, etc., thus achieving a uniform color all over. But one buys a small container of gel coat to fill scratches, not cover the whole surface. One problem is the great variety of colors and shades that have been used by boatbuilders. Another is the fading problem mentioned previously. Yet another problem is that there is apt to be a rather small and infrequent demand for gel coat. The stuff has a rather short shelf life and will begin to harden after a number of months. This hardening is due to molecular rearrangement and just trying to thin it out with solvent won't reverse the molecular action. The stiffening gel coat has to be thrown out.

A well-stocked marine supply house will have colored pigments in the primary colors that can be used to tint clear resin to make a gel coat good enough for touch-ups. But it's hard to duplicate the many pastel tints commonly used in boats unless you have some background as an artist or auto-painter. It's fairly easy, however, to find touch-up putties and sticks for white hulls, which are the most common.

Old Name Haunts Him!

Q. I bought a used sailboat and used paint remover to get

the old name off the transom. Now I find the images of the letters still show in a lighter shade of white against the rest of the white transom. Any way to banish these "ghosts?"

A. The old lettering enabled the gel coat under them to fade less than the surrounding gel coat, which was exposed to sunlight. Try buffing with rubbing compound. If that fails, try sanding the transom all over with fine wet sandpaper—start with, say, 400 grit and go over again with 600 grit, then with buffing compound and wax. If this fails too, you have two choices—let time do the fading for you, or paint the transom with a white fiberglass paint tinted as closely as possible to match the white of the hull.

Using Lacquer on Fiberglass

Q. I'd like to give my fiberglass speedboat a flame-style paint job such as those seen on racing cars. How should I do it?

A. There's nothing in marine literature on the subject—not enough interest in it among boat owners to justify the cost of printing. The best thing to do is visit shops catering to hot rods, race cars, customized vans and "chopper" motorcycles. They have had experience with doing fancy paint jobs on fiberglass and can help or give good advice.

Gel Coat Is Flaking Off

Q. After only two seasons of use, the gel coat on my boat's deck is in such bad shape that it is actually coming off in chips about the size of fish scales. What would cause this—exposure to polluted air?

A. This is an unusual condition. Sounds like defective gel coat. Many boat manufacturers run incoming raw materials through various quality tests before using it in their boats, but they can't run endless tests to show up all possible shortcomings. You should take photos of your boat and send them to the boatbuilder. He might find his suppliers sold him some defective gel coat and get a settlement for you from them.

Cloudy Spots on Gel Coat

Q. My runabout is only a year old but already there are scattered spots of a cloudy or milky sort of discoloration on the gel coat of its deck. What might cause this?

A. Go over the deck with fiberglass cleaner-polish. Our bet is that the spots will then be gone. A likely cause is that you used a wax not intended for fiberglass or for outdoor use and dampness in the air made it turn milky. Automobile, household, floor, and fiberglass waxes look and smell very much alike, but there are subtle differences in their composition. A car wax might prove to be too slippery when used on a boat deck. A household wax might develop water spots. They could be small, distinct ones from drops of spray, or widely spread clouded areas from evening dew. Fiberglass waxes cost little if anything more than other quality waxes, so use them on your boat and save yourself any unpleasant surprises.

Stains on Gel Coat

Q. I spilled some teak oil on the deck of my boat and it made some spots on the gel coat. I wiped them with rags dampened with gasoline, lacquer thinner, and cleaning fluid but they remain there. What should I do now?

A. Try acetone—it's the closest thing there is to an all-purpose solvent for cleaning resin, paint, tar, glue, and many other things from fiberglass. If that fails try fiberglass rubbing compound. If that too fails, about all you can do is let time and sunlight fade the stains. This advice also applies to stains caused by other unusual substances, ranging from brown-tinted stanchion bedding compound to spilled gasoline stabilizing liquid, which is put into gas tanks at layup time.

Stain at Waterline

Q. I moored my sloop in a harbor having rather dirty water. Now there is an ugly brown stain all around the hull just above the waterline. I tried various fiberglass cleaners and polishes without luck. How can I get it off?

A. To look at it you'd think gel coat was as dense and impervious as a piece of plate glass. But under a powerful microscope you would find a specimen slice of it to be somewhat porous—after all, a very sharp razorblade edge becomes surprisingly jagged under a powerful lens! Polishes and compounds touch only the surface, but these brown stains (from all the kinds of foreign matter in dirty water) are to some extent lodged in the porosity of the gel coat, so polishes don't get at them. There are some special cleaning products on the market which, when brushed on such stains, penetrate into the gel coat and go after the imbedded stains. A widely sold one is called "Y-10" made by Propco, P.O. Box 217, Old Greenwich, Conn. 06870. It is stocked by many marine supply houses. Rule Industries of Gloucester, Mass., has a product called "Miracle Coat." They claim that when it is applied over waxed hull surfaces, grass, scum, etc., will adhere only loosely to the waterline areas.

Preventing Hull Stains

Q. When I took my new boat to the mooring basin to put her out for the summer, I noticed all the other boats in the basin had brown stains above their waterlines. It's a local problem. Anything I can do to minimize it on my fiberglass boat?

A. Two coats of fiberglass wax on the hull as a whole, and an extra one in the area just above the waterline, would be well worth trying.

Why Wax Fiberglass?

Q. Fiberglass boat surfaces are so hard and shiny I can't see the point of waxing them—they are already quite shiny enough.

A. The objective is not to make boats shine even more—it is to maintain that shine as time passes. Gel coat is really just another type of plastic. No plastic stands up to weather forever. The surface of gel coat oxidizes, however slowly. It does not turn to rust as does iron when it oxidizes but it does "die" and turn into a dull film. Waxing at regular intervals— say twice a year—seals the surface, slows down the rate of oxidation, and lets you clean and polish the boat without taking off an appreciable percentage of the thin layer of gel coat. It also keeps dirty water, dead leaves, etc. from staining the surfaces. A boat that is kept waxed and out of direct sunlight when not in use will retain its good looks for years. Anyone who thinks fiberglass is so durable that a boat made of it can be abused and neglected is deceiving himself.

A variety of cleaners, polishes and waxes are on the market especially formulated for use on fiberglass. Their use can materially help to maintain the appearance of a fiberglass boat. (Rule Industries, Inc.)

Gel Coat Got Scorched

Q. One evening we used a hibachi on the deck of our cruiser, and in the darkness did not notice until too late (we finally smelled it!) that the heat was scorching the gel coat on the deck. Now there's a dreadful-looking brown place there. Can anything be done?

A. It depends on how far into the gel coat the scorching goes. First try fiberglass rubbing compound. If this fails, go over the area with 400 grade wet sandpaper. If that removes the discoloration, go over it again with 600 paper to reduce the surface scratches made by the 400 and then use rubbing compound and wax. If that too fails, a professional fiberglass repairman can spray new gel coat and polish it. The color match may not be perfect but will become less noticeable as fading takes place. Or, you can hide the burned area under some non-skid material, under a teak fish-cleaning board, or under a rubber step pad.

Repairing Fire Damage

Q. A galley fire in my boat burned some of the non-structural fiberglass areas around the stove. It left some of the glass fibers exposed. Could this be repaired?

A. Since the fibers are still there and have not melted into globules, they should be capable of once again serving their purpose of reinforcing the resin. You can probably brush new resin onto and into the affected areas. Care will be needed not to fracture the filaments. When the first careful coat has hardened, more can be applied to build up the surface. Sanding and filling of depressions with fiberglass putty will prepare the surface for fiberglass paint. The job should leave the area looking like new if it is done well.

Does Fiberglass Burn?

Q. While cooking in our boat, I got to wondering about the inflammability of fiberglass. Will it burn? Explode? Create poisonous fumes? Or what?

A. It will start to scorch and blister well before bursting into flame, so you would have some warning of impending trouble. Once ignited, a small burning area will behave something like damp plywood—it will produce a slow, sputtering flame and emit a lot of sooty smoke, so you would have time to grab and use an extinguisher. As the flame grows and generates a greater volume of heat, nearby unburned fiberglass will be heated up ever more rapidly, and so a fiberglass boat enveloped in flame can burn madly. Some quality yachts are made with fire-resistant resin and can qualify for reduced insurance rates.

Chipped Gel Coat on Corners

Q. The edges of the transom of my outboard boat are chipped from bumping docks and rubbing on launching ramp pavement. What's the best way to touch them up?

A. If the boat is white, you can get fiberglass patching putty at well-stocked marine stores. If you can find some white gel coat, that too can be used just like putty. If it tends to sag away from the touched-up spots, hold it in place with a small dam made of masking tape. Apply the putty or gel coat so it is higher than the surrounding surface; when cured it can be sanded down to blend in very neatly.

Cracks from Flexing

Q. I had a very heavy person as a guest aboard my boat. Now I find hairline cracks in the gel coat on the cockpit floor. They seem to be at the places where he walked. Does it sound reasonable to you to blame his weight?

A. Yes. We suspect the floor in your boat was built a little on the thin side. Under the weight of an unusually heavy person it flexed enough to make the gel coat crack. Since gel coat does not have any glass fibers to reinforce it, it will crack more readily than will glass laminate. The cracks do not extend down into the laminate and thus do not weaken the boat or shorten its life expectancy. They are an appearance problem only. A typical fix is to use a modelmaker's electric grinding tool to rout out the cracked lines in the gel coat and make vee-grooves in it. Then putty new gel coat (if obtainable) or fiberglass patching putty into the cracks, let cure hard, and then sand and polish.

Cracks from flexing tend to be localized at the point of stress; for example, at the corners of the motor cut-out in an outboard boat's transom, around the edges of the daggerboard slot in the bottom of a small sailboat, along the angles where decks blend into cabin sides, along gunwales where boats bump against docks, etc.

Cracks from sharp, localized blows such as caused by striking dock corners also tend to be localized. But they radiate out in jagged lines from the point of contact. Typically, they are caused by bumping dock corners and other objects that concentrate the impact at one place.

Random hairline cracks all over the surface are usually caused by too-thick gel coat, which tends to develop such cracks as it ages.

Sees Image of a Crack

Q. In a couple of places on my fiberglass sailboat I see blemishes that puzzle me. They amount to faint images of cracks caused by localized blows; that is, they amount to

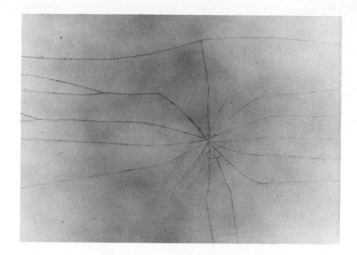

This gel coat cracking is typical of that caused by a localized sharp blow. Lines radiate out from the point of contact. (Pittsburgh Plate Glass Industries)

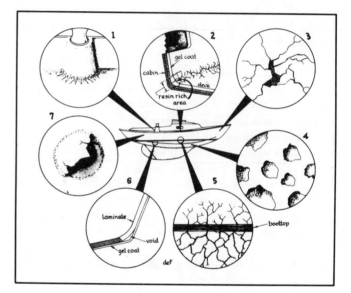

Cracking in gel coat has various causes, such as: 1. Stress concentrations at places where one surface blends into another, such as at this winch mounting. 2. Flexing of area where cabin joins deck, due either to weakness of a too-thin or unreinforced laminate, or to a localized "resin-rich," and therefore brittle, area. 3. Typical irregular, radiating cracks where surface received a hard blow. 4. Small pimples in gel coat below waterline due to long immersion and some abnormality or irregularity in the formulation or application of the gel coat. 5. General overall crazing with passage of time, usually due to gel coat being too thick. 6. Air bubble or void at corner, due to glass cloth pulling away from gel coat after being rolled into place and before resin hardened. 7. Large air bubble between gel coat and laminate. First coat of glass fabric was not rolled down thoroughly, or vapors expanded a tiny bubble between time resin was brushed on and time when it hardened. An inspector could have seen such a bubble in the first layer of fabric, cut or sanded it out, and repaired it by applying a small glass fabric patch with resin.

irregular lines radiating out from a central point. I looked at the gel coat surface under a magnifying glass and while I can see these lines as faint ridges, they show no evidence of cracking. What could have happened?

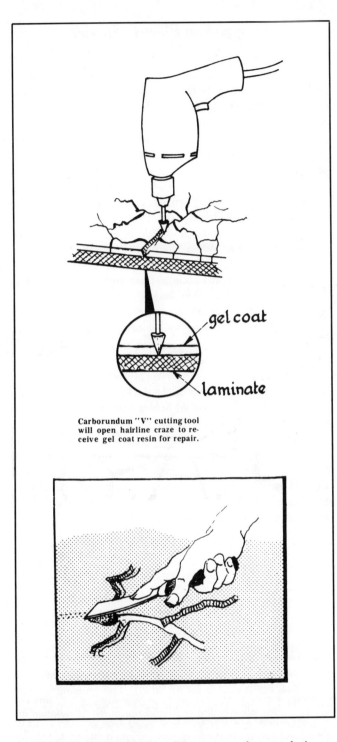

Carborundum "V" cutting tool will open hairline craze to receive gel coat resin for repair.

Crazing can be repaired fairly well but is very tedious work. A vee-shaped burr or sanding stone is used to cut out crack lines. A high-speed modelmaker's grinding tool would be more effective than the electric drill shown here. Gel coat patching putty is then troweled into grooves, sanded and polished. A perfect color match may be difficult to attain. (Owens-Corning Fiberglass Corp.)

A. You see images in the gel coat picked up from cracks in the mold. Sometimes workmen strike molds with rubber hammers to help loosen parts that don't want to lift out of a mold easily. Once in a while one of these hammer blows will be a bit too hard, the fiberglass in the mold will flex, and the gel coat on the working surface of the mold will crack. From then on, no matter how much the area is sanded and polished, an image will be made on every part made in that mold. The more one wet-sands the area, the more one simply exposes the gel coat cracks. Small shops can't afford to replace molds just because of one or two such cracks, so they make do with them until they have been amortized. The images imprinted in the gel coat of boats made in a cracked mold can be removed most of the time by wet-sanding and polishing.

Boat Leaks Resin!

Q. Soon after I bought a new sailboat a strong-smelling, sticky, amber-colored material began oozing out of an irregular crack in the gel coat on the aft bulkhead of the cabin. The dealer cannot explain it. Can you?

A. We have a hunch. Our guess is that you have encountered a fairly rare but quite possible bungle in the fiberglass shop. If the material smells like fiberglass resin, that has to be what it is. A very probable cause is that a workman forgot to add hardener to a pot of resin, or failed to mix it into the resin thoroughly, resulting in an uncatalyzed spot. If a number of layers of glass fabric were put on one right after the other (a common practice), this uncatalyzed wet spot would have been covered over by succeeding layers of cloth that hardened properly. Then, when your boat was exposed to hot sunlight, the soft spot began to expand and then to leak out through a fragile area between it and the gel coat.

Prod the area with a sharp awl to feel out the extent of the soft area around the weeping crack. Talk to the dealer about it calmly. Fiberglass work is messy, smelly, and boring; forgetting to add hardener to a pot of resin is a mistake every worker is bound to make sooner or later. Usually the soft spot is noticed in the factory, but once in a while it is encapsulated in the laminate without anyone realizing it. And it would be left to hot sunlight to show it up, as happened on your boat. Be calm and reasonable, but firm, about it. If the manufacturer has any sense of responsibility, he will arrange for repairs.

Hollow Spots Under Gel Coat

Q. I leaned a portable ice box on the cockpit gunwale of my fiberglass boat and was dismayed to hear a sharp crack. On inspecting the place where the box had touched the surface, I found the gel coat was shattered and there was a void under it, with the fiberglass laminate visible a quarter of an inch below the surface. What is this and what shall I do?

A. You chanced to discover an air bubble that the factory missed. When the first layer of glass mat is laid in place over the gel coat, resin is brushed on and rolled out. A worker will push the mat into the angles along corners and ridges with his resin brush, using a dabbing motion as the brush moves along. This will expel air bubbles between the gel coat and the mat. But the stiffness of the glass filaments will make it attempt to straighten out, and here and there the mat will pull away from the gel coat. Workers form the habit of looking back over areas they have done to catch these air bubbles as they form and press them down again with the brush. But if they put the first layer of mat on just before quitting for the day, air bubbles may form when no one is around to pat them down again. So the resin "kicks" and the bubbles are locked in. (See Chapter 12, section on "Fiberglass and Weather," for explanation of "kicking.") Sizeable bubbles are easy to see. The hardened mat forming them can be carefully cut away and new mat worked into the bubble area to fill the void. When parts come out of molds, inspectors usually go over edges and corners with a small hammer or metal rod, tapping gently and listening for the dull sound that air bubbles will make. An expert fiberglass worker can repair them soundly and inconspicuously, but a few manage to get past inspection.

Break out all the gel coat over the air bubble. Obtain some gel coat from the manufacturer, add hardener to it as directed, and work it into the depression with a spatula. Fill in slightly above the surrounding surface. When cured hard, wrap abrasive paper around a wooden sanding block and carefully take the patched area down to level. Use progressively finer grades of wet sandpaper to smooth the area and finish by using rubbing compound and an electric polisher.

Will Fiberglass Rot?

Q. There is an area a few inches wide and several inches long on the bottom of my fiberglass outboard boat that looks a bit rough and yields slightly when pressed. A local boat shop says it is a rotten spot in the fiberglass under the gel coat. Will fiberglass really rot like this? What should I do?

A. There are people who will dream up fanciful explanations for things like this to cover up the fact that they don't know the real answer. We think you have found a resin-starved area. For some reason—a damp or oily spot in the mat or carelessness while brushing and rolling resin into the mat—that spot did not get enough resin to firm up the mat. It's a bit soft and it's been subjected to the normal water pressure under a fast hull long enough to make it begin to show. Grind out the bad area with a disc sander, fill the depression with fiberglass patching putty and then sand and polish.

Dropped an Electric Sander

Q. I dropped an electric sander on the deck of my boat and before it stopped it chewed quite a scar into the non-skid pattern molded into the gel coat. Is it possible to repair such damage inconspicuously?

A. A good fiberglass man might be able to make a passable repair. The job would take a "feel" for fiberglass and some patience. First step would be to wax a section of undamaged non-skid surface—four to six coats of mold-release wax being best. Then, gel coat would be brushed on (it could be any available color). When hard, about three or four layers of mat and resin would be laid on top of it and allowed to harden. When lifted off, it would amount to a mold with the non-skid pattern imprinted in it. Then the damaged area would be cleaned up with a model-making hand grinder and suitable burrs. Now the tricky part—spreading some gel coat the same color as the deck into the damaged area and trying to get neither too little nor too much of it into the depression. The mold previously made would next be waxed and lowered carefully over the damaged area. A little careful movement would get its pattern to fit into the existing pattern on the deck. A moderate amount of weight placed on it would hold it down while the gel coat hardens. If you're lucky with the amount of gel coat put into the depression, the pattern in the mold would be completely filled, yet with no overflow. Later the mold could be lifted off and any slight roughness around the edge of the patch cleaned up. This isn't a repair for a newcomer at fiberglass to try; we describe it here because it illustrates the type of clever things a good fiberglass man can do.

Replace Bad Gel Coat?

Q. The gel coat on my sailing dinghy is a mess of cracks and scratches. Could it be ground off and replaced?

A. Yes, but it's a job for an expert! The grinding job will leave the laminate exposed and there will inevitably be high and low spots. The problem is to apply new gel coat so as to get a level surface that can be sanded and polished so it looks presentable. The amount of tedious labor involved could make the job cost more than a small boat is worth. It would probably be better to look around for someone who can do a good job of puttying the scratches and then give the boat a really good paint job. Some remarkable jobs have been done with a fairly new process called "Awlgrip." Ask boatyards in your area if they know of a yard that does this kind of refinishing. Or write to the manufacturer for literature and the name of their nearest representative. It's made by U.S. Paint Division, Grow Chemical Corp., 831 South 21st St., St. Louis, Mo. 63103.

Chapter 11

Fiberglass Repair Work

Schools for Fiberglass Repair

Q. Can you recommend a good school that teaches fiberglass repair work?

A. To the best of our knowledge there is no such school. If there is one, those in charge have done a great job of keeping its existence a secret from the boating press! A few fiberglass raw materials manufacturers and a few boat manufacturers have from time to time run small classes for dealers' mechanics. Most of today's really good fiberglass repairmen learned the trade by working in boat factories. In areas where there are many boat factories—such as around Miami, Fla.—it's easy enough to find expert repairmen who will fix a boat for you in their spare time. But in localities where there are no factories, all you can do is hope to locate a self-taught repairman. Why are there no fiberglass schools? Probably a combination of things—lack of good instructors in some areas; inertia on the part of trade school administrators, who'd rather stick to familiar subjects like cabinetmaking and auto body repair; costs of setting up specialized facilities; the problems of smell, fire risk, and insurance involved in doing some fiberglass work in buildings used for other purposes; you name it.

Bought Bare Fiberglass Hull

Q. I bought a bare fiberglass hull for a cabin cruiser. Now I'm apprehensive about doing a good job of finishing it off. Can you suggest some books for me?

A. *Modifying Fiberglass Boats* by Jack Wiley will be a big help on general methods and cabin details. It's put out by International Marine Publishing Company, 21 Elm St., Camden, Maine 04843. *Boat Repairs and Conversions* by Michael Verney is an English book that has been around for some time. It's mainly about converting lifeboats for pleasure use but has useful information for you. *Inboard Motor Installations in Small Boats* published by Glen-L Marine Designs, 9152 Rosecrans, Bellflower, Cal. 90706 will help in the engine room. *Fibreglass Boats* by Hugo Du Plessis is an English book full of details showing how various parts are made and put together. Some of the methods vary from the American way of doing things, but the book as a whole will give you ideas. The Du Plessis and Verney books can be mail ordered from International Marine, as can *Boatbuilding on a Glassfibre Hull*. This is another English book and it deals with turning bare hulls into completed boats.

Holes Won't Cause Cracks

Q. I drilled holes in the dashboard of my fiberglass boat so I could install some instruments. My neighbor threw a fit when he saw what I had done—says the holes will be starting places for cracks in the fiberglass. Will they?

A. Pshaw! People who know nothing about fiberglass come up with weird notions. The criss-cross disposition of the glass filaments in the several layers of fabric in the laminate make cracking impossible. Localized cracking, however, can be caused by putting self-tapping screws or pop rivets too near an edge. Laminates that are too thin for the loads

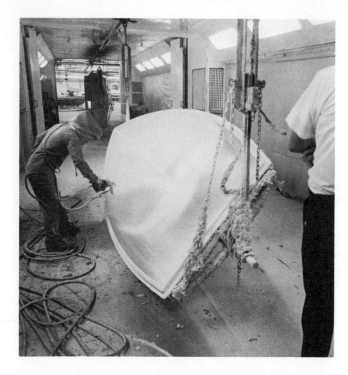

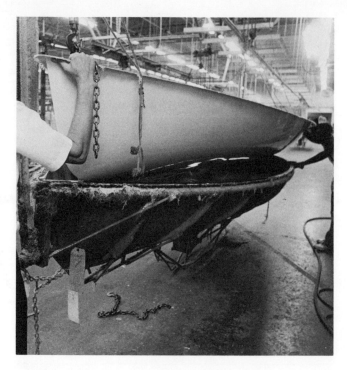

An operator is spraying gel coat onto the polished surface of a hull mold as first step in making a hull. When colored gel coat has hardened, a work crew will apply glass fabric and resin to build up the laminate. A wide variety of cloths and core materials are available from which manufacturers can choose a suitable laminating schedule for any particular hull.

Finished, cured hull is being lifted from mold. The high polish of the mold's surface is reproduced in the surface of the gel coat; no painting is required to finish off a molded hull.

Special jigs make fast, accurate work of positioning and holding down the floor support grid. Grid both supports floor and stiffens hull bottom.

Grids and stiffeners can take many forms. In low-volume production they may be of wood over which is draped several layers of glass fabric and resin; in high volume operations a mold may be used to make a molded grid like the one here.

Here a cockpit liner is being made on a mold that was designed and built for the job. When laminate has cured hard, liner will be lifted off this mold.

Molds in this shop are for making fiberglass runabout decks. Casters facilitate moving them from gel coat spray-booth to laminating shop, then to curing area.

imposed on them will crack, but that cracking isn't due to holes. Relax!

How to Make Holes in Fiberglass

Q. I bought some fish rod holders and have tried and tried to drive screws into the fiberglass, but the stuff is too tough. What should I do?

A. You have to drill holes for screws. It's common practice to attach small, light accessories with stainless steel, self-tapping screws. The metal is strong enough so these screws won't break when twisted hard. A back-and-forth motion of the screwdriver handle will make the screw cut threads in the fiberglass. The pilot hole size has to be found by experiment—it will be larger than you'd make for wood. Start with the smallest hole you think might work, and if the screws go in too hard, try the next larger drill bit. If the gel coat "lifts" around the edges of the hole when you start the screws, the hole may be too small. Lifting of gel coat around holes can be minimized by using a countersink to slightly chamfer the gel coat before starting the screws.

Pop rivets make fast work of installing many things and will hold a surprising load. Two sizes are common, one-eighth and three-sixteenths of an inch. Use aluminum rivets; steel ones will rust much too quickly. Make holes of a size that will produce a snug fit but not so small you have to force the rivets in. If you chance to make a hole too big, don't fret—the rivet will expand to snugly fill the hole.

Common high speed twist drills will easily make holes up to around three-eighths of an inch. As the hole size goes up, or when drilling in thin fiberglass, the drill lips may tend to "grab" as the drill breaks through. If this becomes a problem, try high-speed wood bits. The abrasiveness of the fiberglass will dull them sooner than will wood, but you can use old ones and sharpen their cutting edges with a patternmaker's file.

For holes from three-quarters of an inch up to four or five inches, round "hole saws" driven by an electric drill are ideal. Professional shops use them all the time. An adjustable "hole cutter," sometimes called a "fly cutter," will work if driven slowly and carefully by a variable-speed electric drill.

Larger round holes, rectangular holes, and those of irregular shape are easily made with a sabre saw. Drill a starting hole for the blade, and use a fine-tooth metal cutting blade. To prevent the "foot" of the sabre saw from marring the surface of gel coat surrounding the hole, put a few layers of masking tape onto the boat's surface before starting to saw. If wood chips come out when you make the starting hole, do not be alarmed. Use of rough plywood, thin balsa wood, and various types of foam plastic as core materials is common. It makes a thicker, more rigid laminate. Tools used constantly in fiberglass dull sooner than tools used in working with wood, but in typical equipment-installation work you needn't worry.

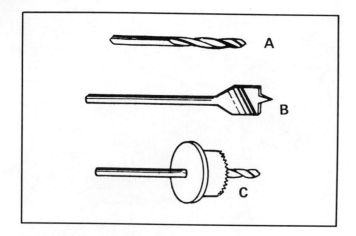

A. High speed twist drills can be used for making holes up to about ⅜″ diameter in fiberglass. B. High speed wood bits can be used for holes up to about one inch in diameter, a little more if care is used to avoid "grabbing." C. Hole saws are best for making holes much over an inch in diameter. Adjustable "hole cutters" can also be used if driven slowly and carefully by a variable-speed electric drill.

Heavy Fiberglass Cutting

Q. Engine support timbers have been heavily fiberglassed into the hull of my boat. We are installing a different engine and have to remove the old ones. How do we cut through the fiberglass, which is half an inch thick or more in places?

A. Get a husky rotary grinder of the type often used by auto repairmen for rough smoothing work. Fit it with a metal-cutting abrasive disc or a similar-looking masonry-cutting disc. As such a disc wears down it automatically presents fresh abrasive material to its cutting face. You will have to hold the tool steady with a strong grip and feed it into the glass carefully, lest it grab and jump. The work will produce a cloud of fiberglass dust, so wear a good respirator to protect your lungs. Wear old work clothing of dense fabric to keep dust off your skin and save yourself a spell of fiberglass itch, and if possible do this work outdoors. One of these discs can also be used in an electric circular saw. The saw's blade-guards will make the job safer, but cutting depth may be limited.

Hardware Backing Plates

Q. I am installing some deck hardware on my fiberglass boat. Some of it will have to withstand heavy strain. How can I keep fastenings from pulling out?

A. Use backing blocks of appropriately thick plywood for the job at hand—typically three-eighths-, one-half-, or five-eighths-inch material. Make the blocks at least a few inches

larger than the hardware's bolt patterns. As the inner surfaces of fiberglass laminates are usually rough and irregular, set the blocks in a thick bedding compound to spread the load and let them rest securely. Attach the hardware with bolts or machine screws of appropriate size and use large washers under the nuts to keep the nuts from pressing into the wood and ultimately loosening.

Plugging Holes

Q. What can one do about the holes left in fiberglass surfaces after an item of equipment has been removed?

A. A fairly normal-looking and therefore acceptably inconspicuous fix is to fill the holes with oval-head machine screws under which are placed finishing washers. Most people on seeing these will take them for granted. Or you can fill the holes with fiberglass patching putty; color matching will then be the problem and one way out is to apply self-adhesive wood-grain vinyl trim panels to the affected spot. On a deck, you can cover such a spot with one or another of the teak or rubber non-skid step plates sold in boat stores.

To fix a large hole such as one left in a dashboard when an instrument is removed, try this. Saw out a wooden plug the size of the hole, trim it to a press fit, and fasten it in place with wood glue, fiberglass resin, or polyester auto body putty—whichever seems most suitable for the situation. Affix this plug approximately one-eighth of an inch below the surface of the dashboard. When the adhesive has set, fill in the depression with auto body putty and sand flush to the surface. Then cover the dashboard with adhesive wood-grain vinyl in an attractive pattern. No one will ever realize you have hidden an ugly hole.

Plugging Underwater Hole

Q. I have to remove a sea closet's thru-hull fitting as part of the job of converting to a holding tank system. What's a dependable way to seal the hole in the hull?

A. Remove the fitting. Clean and roughen the area around the hole for three or four inches, on the inside. Put a patch made of three or four layers of glass cloth and mat on this area. When the resin has cured this inner patch will surely never leak or loosen. The bulk of the hole can be filled in various ways. A cheap, convenient, and completely reliable way would be to fill it with round pieces of cloth or mat, each laid in resin. Stop just below the outer surface. Finish off with fiberglass patching putty, sand and paint over. The patch will be invisible and you will never have to worry about it coming loose and letting water aboard.

Patching Torn Deck

Q. My fiberglass sailboat has a hole in its foredeck that receives the mast. A cable broke, the mast toppled and fractured the fiberglass around this hole rather badly. What would be a suitable repair procedure?

A. If the boat is small enough, roll it over and block it up so you can get under it and reach the mast hole easily. Sand the surface around the hole to clean and roughen the original fiberglass. Whittle some wood a foot or so long to the same cross-section as the mast. Wind three or four layers of masking tape around it to make the new hole in the deck large enough to let the mast slip easily in and out.

Carefully prop this dummy into position in the hole so it reproduces the mast. You may wish to install and rig the mast and tape thin strips of wood to the deck, just touching the mast, and then carefully lift out the mast and use these indicator strips to locate the dummy just right. Give the dummy several coats of wax to prevent resin adhesion. Bring together and clamp broken edges of surrounding fiberglass as well as possible. Cut several pieces of cloth, mat, and roving in whatever combination seems sensible for the job at hand. Make them large enough to extend some inches beyond the cracks around the hole. Fit them in place around the dummy mast, one at a time, applying activated resin to each layer as it goes on. Work out bubbles. Work up against the dummy but do not build up a thick flange that could lock the dummy into place. When the resin has cured, pull out the dummy and trim the hole edges with a wood rasp and sandpaper. Then turn the boat upright and smooth up the top-side of the deck with fiberglass putty, etc.

This will "key" the patch in place with absolute security.

Write to Owens-Corning Fiberglas Corp., Industrial Materials Division, Fiberglas Tower, Toledo, Ohio 43659 and ask for a copy of their free booklet, *Repair of Fiberglas-Reinforced Plastic Boats*. It describes patching methods with step-by-step photos.

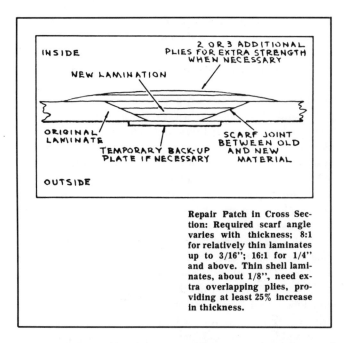

Repair Patch in Cross Section: Required scarf angle varies with thickness; 8:1 for relatively thin laminates up to 3/16"; 16:1 for 1/4" and above. Thin shell laminates, about 1/8", need extra overlapping plies, providing at least 25% increase in thickness.

Patching holes in fiberglass is easy. Fracture is cleaned out and edges beveled, then a simple patch of mat and resin laid in. Back-up plate on outside keeps patch flush with outer surface.

Repairing Small Hole

Q. My fiberglass boat struck a piece of pipe projecting from a dock and punched a hole about four inches in diameter in the side. How should I fix it?

A. Use a sabre saw to trim out broken and loose material around the edges of the hole. For a hole of this size, it would be best to make the trimmed-out hole a neat round one. At an automotive store, get a three-inch sanding pad of the type that takes self-adhering sanding discs. Use this to feather the edges of the hole from the inside. Tape a piece of waxed Formica as firmly as possible to the outside of the boat where the hole is. Stiff cardboard covered with cellophane would also work. Apply progressively larger round pieces of mat to the hole, working from the inside. An accompanying sketch shows the way this patch would look in cross-section. When cured, sand the outer surface and finish with fiberglass putty.

If the hole is on the bottom of a boat where accidental loosening would be dangerous, the outside of the hole can also be feathered, although not as much as on the inside.

Repairing a Fracture

Q. Another boat collided with mine. The impact did not puncture my hull but did crack the fiberglass laminate. There is a torn, jagged place on the inside and a firm push on the outside makes the area bow in slightly, confirming the existence of cracked laminate. How do I fix it?

A. Easy. Grind off paint or old, dirty fiberglass on the area around the crack on the inside. Use resin to stick two or three layers of mat or glass cloth to the weakened area, going several inches beyond it all around. This will restore structural integrity. Tend to external appearance with fiberglass putty.

Repairing a Large Hole

Q. My sloop went adrift and spent a night bobbing up and down against a large rock. This chafed a hole in the side about four feet long and two feet high. You can stand outside and look right into the cabin! The insurance company wrote it off and paid me. Seeking to salvage parts and gear, I bought it back cheap. Now some boatyard men tell me not to junk the boat, claiming the hole can be patched. Are they kidding me?

A. No. Boats damaged like yours have been repaired as follows. Find another boat just like yours and get the owner's permission to apply five or six coats of wax to its hull in an area corresponding to the damaged part of your hull. Carry the waxing a foot or so beyond the actual area. Mold release wax from a fiberglass supply house would be best, but you can make do with boat hull wax or bowling alley wax, if necessary. Let each coat dry a few hours and let the final one dry overnight so solvents will evaporate off.

Then, brush activated resin onto the surface and apply a piece of glass cloth cut a foot or more larger than the hole in your boat. Roll bubbles out with a fiberglass working roller. When this cloth is hard, apply three to six more layers of glass mat, depending on the size of the hole and the rigidity needed. Let cure overnight. This mold can then be popped off the side of the boat.

Next, sabre saw out the ragged edges of the hole in your boat and with a disc sander feather the edges as for the smaller patch previously described. Wax the surface of the mold you have made from the other boat and as an added precaution coat it with "parting agent," a green liquid that dries to form a resin-resistant skin. Accurately position the mold on the side of your boat and prop it very securely into place. Now you can work from the inside of your boat (use a fan or blower for positive ventilation of resin vapors), brushing resin onto the mold and laying glass cloth and mat in enough layers to equal the thickness of the surrounding hull. When all has cured hard, the mold can be removed and you will find an accurately curved patch filling the big hole neatly! You will probably want to paint the whole hull to cover this big repair and give the hull a uniform color.

Skeg Worn Through

Q. The heel of the skeg on my fiberglass dinghy wore through from being dragged over the concrete launching ramp. A flotation chamber is built into its aft end and makes it impossible to get at the skeg from the inside. How do I patch the hole neatly?

A. Clean off the edges of the hole and bevel them with a disc sander. Cut a piece of stiff cardboard about an inch larger all around than the hole. Punch four holes in the cardboard and put two strings in, one string in each two holes like your shoelace at the first set of eyelets. Slip the cardboard into the hole and use the strings to pull it up against the inside of the hole. Tie the strings to sticks, wires, or whatever you can rig up for the purpose. This will hold the cardboard against the inside of the hole and form a "dam" onto which you can lay the fiberglass fabric for the patch.

When the first layer of fabric and resin are hard, remove the supports, snip off the strings where they emerge from the surface, sand off the nibs, and proceed to lay on more fabric to build up the thickness of the patch. Sand smooth and paint or use gel coat if you can get it in a matching color.

Forefoot Wore Through

Q. The forefoot of my outboard boat wore through from running up on paved launching ramps. The boatyard fixed it by sticking a few layers of fiberglass tape over the hole. This looks awful. How can I do a more presentable patching job?

A. Pull off the patch. If you can't get at the hole from inside, use the cardboard dam method previously described. If you can get at the inside, sand all oil, dirt, and paint off the inside of the hull for a distance of four or five inches around the hole. Cut a piece of glass cloth to fit the area. This will probably work out to be a long oval piece. Brush resin on the inside surfaces of the hull around the forefoot hole and lay the cloth down. Press the cloth to the hull surfaces around the hole with your resin brush to stick it on. Then gently press on the central portion of the cloth to push it down and wet it with resin. Keep it about one-quarter to one-half inch inside the edges of the hole. When cured, lay on several more layers of cloth or mat to strengthen the area. Then, working from the outside, push shredded mat mixed with resin into the cavity, filling it to just below surface level. When this is hard, finish off with one layer of cloth and smooth with fiberglass putty. If your boat is white, white fiberglass patching putty will blend in fairly inconspicuously.

Loose Bottom Stringers

Q. The bottom of my fiberglass boat is stiffened by hat-shaped stringers running fore and aft. They are coming loose from the bottom at some places. Is there any way to refasten them neatly and securely?

A. If the affected areas are accessible, you can clean dirt and oil film off the affected areas, roughen the surfaces with sandpaper to provide "tooth," and lay strips cut from fiberglass cloth or mat along the loose flanges. Work the resin under the loose flanges as much as possible with the applying brush before laying the strips. If the boat is a large or fast one, two or three layers of fabric might be wanted to hold things rigid.

If the loose places cannot be reached by hand, a fiberglass man who knows his materials might contrive to clean the bilge area, dry it, and run a suitable epoxy resin back and forth by rocking the boat on its trailer to spread the resin fore and aft along the stringers. Epoxy resins tend to be tough, will not crack as will the rather brittle polyester resin, and will fasten the stringers to the hull without the need of glass cloth strips for reinforcing polyester resin. Also, epoxies adhere to surfaces made of other substances very tenaciously and should hold on this job. The trick will be to choose among the many epoxy formulations and thin it out so it will flow into place, yet not be so thin as to run out again before it has cured.

Rot in Wooden Stringers

Q. *The stringers in the bottom of my boat are made of strips of wood covered over and bound to the inside surface of the hull with fiberglass mat. Water has gotten into the wood through cracks in the fiberglass, and has caused the wood to rot. I found this to be so by drilling holes in various places and having wet, punky wood chips come out in addition to the familiar musty smell of rotting wood. What do I do now?*

A. The wood, in nine cases out of ten, is used simply as a convenient form over which to drape the fiberglass. The strength is not in the wood but in the fiberglass. Some boats use stringers of fiberglass made in trough-shaped molds to prove the point. Your stringers may well stand up for years despite the rotten wood inside them. If they seem to flex, you can clean and sand their surfaces and put a couple more layers of glass mat on their outsides to make them more rigid. You could make holes in the stringers with a one-inch high speed wood bit and try to break up and then wash out the rotted wood with a hose. As we've said before, much boat work is mostly a matter of a little ingenuity.

Outboard Transom Flexes

Q. *The motor on my outboard boat bobs in a fore-and-aft manner when going over choppy water. The transom clamps are tight. What would make the motor act like this?*

A. It is standard practice to use cores of heavy plywood in fiberglass boat transoms. It's fairly light yet it gives the needed thickness and rigidity. Since plywood is made of thin veneer, tree sap tends to evaporate from the wood rather quickly after veneer is peeled from logs. The heat used in the laminating process drives out more natural moisture. By the time plywood is shipped to a destination and sawn into transom blanks, the wood is very dry. Then if care is taken to seal it into the fiberglass work carefully, it is most unlikely to rot.

Occasionally such a transom core does rot, as a result of water getting in through poor fits or lack of bedding compound at the holes where transom drain plugs, slop-well drain tubes, and motor safety bolts are drilled through transoms. With your boat on its trailer, push forward on the propeller shaft rather firmly with your foot and watch the surface of the transom around the clamp bracket. If it flexes inward, you've probably got a rotten core. That can be a real problem!

Drill small holes through the fiberglass and into the wood. If the chips coming out are wet and punky and you detect a musty smell, a real job lies ahead! A professional glass man would probably use a masonry cutting wheel in a disc grinder to saw out a piece of the outer fiberglass several inches square, making an opening through which to inspect the plywood core more fully. From there on he'd make more holes to determine the extent of the rotten area. He might find it to be fairly small and fill the void with a mixture of resin, microballoons, and maybe even sawdust. A mixture of resin and sawdust will cure to be surprisingly hard and strong!

Or he might go around the edge of the transom, carefully cutting through the fiberglass so as to remove all of it from the transom, exposing all of the plywood. Then he might grind out all the old plywood, put a couple of layers of mat and resin on the inside fiberglass, brush resin on a new plywood core, and press this core against the wet glass with plenty of clamps and props. When cured, he might then fiberglass the outer surface with three or four layers of cloth to make it strong and able to absorb motor stresses. Then he'd fill in around the edges with putty, smooth up with a heavy-duty pad sander, and finish with a good paint job. The job might be done in different ways by different men, but this gives you an idea of how a good glass man might do it.

Wood Isn't Unethical

Q. *While installing some equipment in my fiberglass cruiser I made a bolt hole in one of the engine girders and was shocked to find wood inside the fiberglass girders. I feel this is a blatant example of unethical boatbuilding. When I am told I am buying a fiberglass boat, I feel entitled to get a boat that is all fiberglass. I am planning to sue and am collecting the opinions of expert boatmen. What do you think?*

A. We think you should calm down. The cost of product liability insurance is driving up boat prices just as much as is the rising cost of labor, materials, etc., and it is time the public realized it. Use of wooden reinforcements inside fiberglass is a common, accepted, and ethical practice. Laboratory work indicates that the resin spread on wood encapsulates rot fungus spores on the surface of wood so effectively as to inhibit their ability to germinate. Plywood is a favorite type of wood because among other things it is dimensionally very stable and resists cracking. The only unethical aspects of using wood is when a careless builder incorporates unseasoned or wet wood into a fiberglass laminate, or fails to cover it thoroughly and adequately with resin and fabric to seal out water.

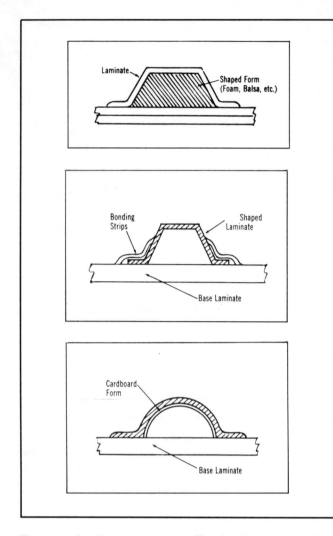

The internal stiffening stringers in fiberglass boats are made in various ways. Top, a strip of balsa wood, pine, plywood, foam, etc. can be stuck to the inside surface of the hull and covered with fiberglass laminate. Center, "hat" section fiberglass stringers can be made in separate, trough-shaped molds and affixed to inside of hull with bonding strips of glass laminate. Bottom, cardboard tubes can be sawn in half, laid in place and used as formers over which to apply glass laminate. The strength is more in the glass laminate than in the core material used to create the shape. (Owens-Corning Fiberglass Corp.)

Bottom Is Warped

Q. I bought a used outboard boat that had been sitting on a poorly adjusted trailer for a long time. When I was repainting its bottom I realized that it had a "hook" in it. This hollow amounts to about an inch off the straight and true and is located in the area a few feet ahead of the stern. If I leave the boat on a flat floor for some time with a weight in it to press down on the inside of the bottom, will this hook go away?

A. It probably won't. Once it has become appreciably distorted, fiberglass tends to stay that way. What to do will depend a lot on how the boat is built. If stringers are fiberglassed permanently to the inside of the hull, they are probably warped too. If the flooring can be taken up so you can get at the warped area of the bottom, you might position the boat on a solid floor and use weights or jacks and timbers running to the shop's ceiling to press the bottom down and back into shape, then fiberglass more stringers to the bottom to hold it true. These stringers could be strips of wood of whatever length and cross section seems feasible, and preferably three or more layers of mat should be draped over them and stuck to the bottom to give them high rigidity.

If no repair is possible from the inside, you may be able to bring the bottom back to straight and true by filling the hooked area from the outside. Overturn the boat, roughen the hollow area thoroughly with coarse sandpaper, and put a straightedge on the depressed area. This will let you judge its extent and depth. If it is of appreciable size, filling it with polyester putty is a chancy thing. The putty might hold, but it might also decide to develop cracks and break up.

We have had good luck doing it this way: cut a number of pieces of glass mat of varying size and shape to make enough to fill the area almost completely, but leaving from about one-sixteenth to one-eighth of an inch to be finished with putty. Spread the putty with a stiff straightedge. When hard, buy a sanding belt at the hardware store, cut it at one place so it can be opened up, and glue it to a piece of smooth and flat wood of matching width and length. Run this "plane" back and forth over the putty in long, sweeping strokes to smooth it down dead level and true. Then seal the surface with a layer of fiberglass cloth. Sand the cloth smooth and paint the bottom.

Mysterious Leaks

Q. Every time I use my powerful outboard boat I find water in the bilge. I can tell by watching what happens that it can't possibly come aboard in the form of spray. The dealer tells me it comes in through tiny cracks that open only when the boat is under way. He says it's a common situation and can't be fixed. What do you think?

A. We think you have encountered one of those dealers who will tell customers fairy tales to cover up their own lack of knowledge of the boats they sell. We have worked with fiberglass extensively and read much about it and have never encountered anything that would suggest there's a shade of truth to that story. If there were tiny cracks that could open enough to admit water, they would have to be ones that went all the way through the fiberglass laminate. And if they did that, they would surely weaken the hull so much that more serious effects than a few cups of water in the bilge would be experienced. We think that water gets in from other causes. Read on.

More Mysterious Leaks

Q. I keep finding a few cupfuls of water in the bilge of my outboard boat. I know it can't be getting in in the form of spray. The boat has been in use only a few months, so defective hull material can't be the cause. Any ideas?

A. Inspect the boat around the full length of the joint where the deck and hull moldings are joined together. Sometimes there are gaps here due to poor fit, poor assembly, or lack of adequate sealing compound or putty. Water flies up the sides of the boat when you meet waves, and some of it can shoot into these gaps and trickle down inside the hull. If the inside of the boat is finished off with upholstery or a fiberglass liner, often you do not see this water trickling down the insides of the hull sides and collecting in the bilge. Crawl under the foredeck, loosen upholstery, remove cover plates, do anything necessary so you can see what is going on in those areas on a test run. If you find water is coming in, fill the gaps between deck and hull moldings with a suitable rubber-like caulking compound from a marine or hardware store.

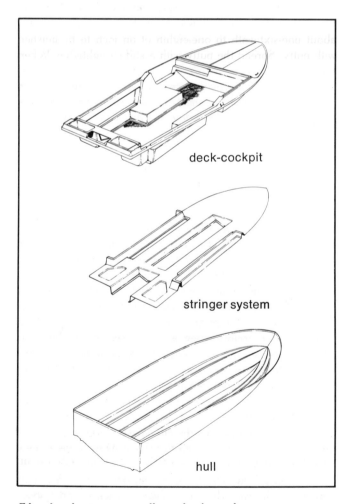

deck-cockpit

stringer system

hull

Fiberglass boats are normally made of two, three or more separate moldings. All molds are made to enable finished pieces to be lifted out easily.

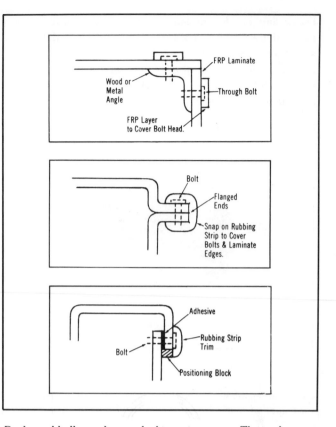

Decks and hulls can be attached in various ways. The angle gusset at top could be made from several thicknesses of glass mat cut in strips and affixed with brush and resin. The joints at center and bottom are designed to fit different types of gunwale molding. On small boats, the bolts would be replaced by pop rivets. Either joint could be taped with one or two strips of mat to make a very strong joint. (Owens-Corning Fiberglass Corp.)

Very Mysterious Leaks

Q. I keep finding fresh water accumulations in the bilge of my sloop, which is used in salt water. This happens even after prolonged rainless spells, so it can't be blamed on rain. Might I have an obscure leak in the galley's fresh water system?

A. Possibly. But do you moor the boat in water that tends to be colder than the air above it? You have seen water condense on the outside of a glass containing a cold drink. The same can happen in a boat, especially a fiberglass or metal one. These dense materials readily transmit heat or cold. The water chills the material and moisture in the warm, damp bilge air condenses on the material's surface. It trickles down into the lower part of the bilge and waits for you to discover it. Some boats do it a lot, some little or not at all. It all depends on how a boat is made. Some hulls are laminated with glass and resin alone; these sweat the most. Others use foam or balsa wood core material in the hull laminate.

Depending on the insulation value of the particular core material, the thickness used, and the temperature differential, sweating can be anything from slight to nonexistent. Location and effectiveness of the cabin's ventilators, and how much air circulation takes place in air spaces under and around the cabin walls and floor, also affect the matter.

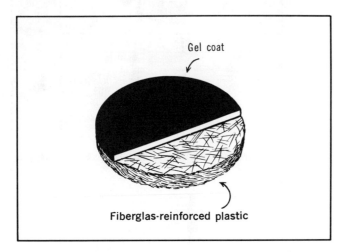

Gel coat

Fiberglas-reinforced plastic

Thin pigmented "gel coat" on outer side is a resin chosen for good weather- and abrasion-resisting properties. Laminate is any of many combinations of glass mat, glass cloth and glass roving. Each type of fabric has its own special properties.

Stopping Condensation

Q. The condensation on the insides of my cruiser's hull is a real problem. Down in Florida it was moderate, due to minimal difference between water and air temperature, but up here in cold Maine waters it can get pretty bad. Is there some insulation I can install that will stop or reduce condensation?

A. Not that we know of. One problem that seems to discourage entrepreneurs from marketing something is the matter of accessibility to interior hull areas in many boats—owners could not reach some important below-decks spots. We know a marine cushion company that for a while marketed a foam-texture vinyl upholstering material that could be cemented to the insides of cabin walls. It seemed to work, but inflation put its price so high the market all but vanished, so they discontinued it. Hardware stores sell a thick kind of paint intended to stop water pipes in basements from sweating, so we wrote to the maker inquiring about marine use. They had never looked into it and would not comment.

There is another thick paint used to apply non-skid surfacing to cockpit floors. We thought it might have insulating qualities so we wrote to the maker and never got a

reply. Your best bet is to look into better ventilation and electric heaters and dehumidifiers to keep the interior dampness at a lower level. It is getting harder and harder to get manufacturers to comment on new, novel uses for their products because they are more and more afraid that condoning such non-authorized use in any way could get them into product liability lawsuits. They will say "Don't rock the boat!" when you ask them if their products might work in unusual or special circumstances.

Finding Leaks

Q. One hull of my fiberglass catamaran leaks somewhere, but as it is an enclosed structure made by sealing two moldings together I can't get inside to see the areas I suspect of leaking. How could one find the leaks?

A. Prop the boat up so that any water put inside the hull will flow to the area of suspected leakage. As water weighs 62 pounds per cubic foot, prop the hull up well so it will not be strained. Using a garden hose, run water in at a gradual rate while maintaining watch on the suspected areas. Remember, though, that water can leak out at one place and run along some structural member for a distance before coming to a spot where it can come out and be visible. Another thing you could try would be to put the boat into shallow water and have enough people sit on it to submerge the hull completely. Then watch for telltale air bubbles.

Waterlogged Foam

Q. My boat's bilge area is filled with flotation foam. It has become soaked with water. I can feel the water squish around when I invert the boat and press on the hull surface. How do I get it out?

A. Good question! There are a lot of boats around with this problem and there are no standard fixes. Makers of foams used for this purpose insist these materials will not absorb water because they are of closed-cell composition. What happens is that after pounding and rattling over waves and chop for some time, the flexing of the bottom compresses the foam repeatedly and sometimes forcibly. Eventually the foam in contact with the bottom breaks down into a powderlike substance. Water from condensation or scattered small leaks in the fiberglass works around and under the floor and gets into this space. How to get it out is then an awkward and embarrassing matter to the boatbuilders. You can't blame them, because putting foam under the floorboards was standard practice and nobody quite anticipated the waterlogging problem. About all one can do is make drain holes at points suggested by common sense and hope the water will drain out. It would be easy to patch the holes but it would take a good fiberglass man to figure out how to fill the voids to prevent a reappearance of the water. Fiberglass supply houses catering to professionals sell aerosol containers of foam, used for filling small voids during repair work. One could try this to see if it would work in this particular problem.

Suspects Soaked Foam

Q. When at its mooring, my fiberglass boat sits lower in the water than it used to. I can tell because the water level is now above the painted waterline stripe; it used to be below this stripe. I suspect the foam under the flooring is waterlogged. How can I verify this suspicion?

A. If you get the boat's original weight data from its maker, you can then weigh your boat and see if it is noticeably heavier, making due allowance for the extra equipment you may have installed. Or weigh another boat of the same make and model to get comparative figures. If your boat is noticeably heavier, it's reasonable to suspect water inside. You can drill exploratory holes of about three-sixteenths-inch diameter at the bottom edge of the transom and see if water trickles out. If it doesn't, the holes can easily be sealed with fiberglass putty, flat-head self-tapping screws, etc.

Boat Floats with List

Q. My fiberglass stern-drive boat floats with a noticeable list to one side when at its mooring. There's no rainwater in the bilge or cockpit. What should I do?

A. Find out if the bulkheading and stringers in the reinforcement in the space under the floor and above the bottom have a pattern such that water could be trapped there. Haul the boat out on a trailer. Lift and lower the trailer drawbar to make any trapped water slosh back and forth while someone listens carefully to various areas of the bottom for telltale sounds. Place the boat on a flat surface. She will probably list to the same side she did when moored. Lift the low side and "heft" it to judge the magnitude of the force needed to lift it. If it is appreciable and the listing cannot be accounted for by such an off-center item of equipment as the storage battery, the probability of trapped water is high. Go over the bottom with a wooden mallet, tapping to detect by sound the area that is full of trapped water. Try to find out from the boat's dealer or builder what the under-floor structure looks like to decide on how to prevent a recurrence of the water leakage.

It used to be common practice to put all the flotation foam below the flooring. Today more of it is put higher in the boat to provide upright flotation. Foam is put in in various ways. In Boston Whaler, top, it is foamed in place between inner and outer fiberglass shells. In Kenner Ski Barge, bottom, blocks of foam are cut up and fitted in place, with some air gaps. With various methods and foams, as time passes there can be varying problems with the foam. Sometimes the foam never gives trouble, other times it manages to become waterlogged.

Rotted Core Material

Q. When we hauled my cruiser and put steadying props against the bottom of the hull, the fiberglass bowed in enough to make a noticeable depression. I do not understand this because the dealer said the hull laminate is three-quarters of an inch thick and thus very strong and rigid.

A. It sounds like you have rotted or waterlogged core material in the laminate. Various core materials are used. A common one is made of many small squares of end-grain balsa wood. All the squares are stuck to a flexible, screen-like material to hold them in proper relationship to one another and form sheets of core material that are easy to pick up and lay in place when a hull is being made up. Makers of this material insist it will not rot, and it is approved for hull use by Lloyd's of London. We know enough about wood rot to accept the argument that end-grain balsa thoroughly impregnated with and encapsulated in a fiberglass laminate should not rot. But we also know some very experienced and conscientious boatyard men who have found rotted balsa core material in boats that have come to them for work. Sometimes the trouble is traceable to skimpy application of resin to the balsa, sometimes to leakage into the core material at holes made for fittings. There have been troubles with foam-type core materials becoming soft or collapsing when subjected to the sun's heat on decks, cabin roofs, etc. Each case of this type must be individually evaluated by fiberglass experts who really know this material.

A small area of rotted balsa might be dried out by means of many small holes drilled in the fiberglass and then firmed up by using an epoxy rot-repair fluid. An extensive case of rot or widespread waterlogging might be beyond the limits of practical or economical repair methods. Fiberglass has not been around long enough for boatbuilders to have had time to learn all there is to know about it. Salesmen are constantly visiting boatbuilding factories trying to sell new materials. Some things in time work out well, others prove to have shortcomings that laboratory testing did not and could not have foreseen. You have to remember that wooden boats have developed rot troubles, too, and we have had well over 5000 years of experience with that material!

Goose Bumps on Bottom

Q. When we hauled my new boat from the water after its first season afloat, we found its bottom to be covered with thousands of small pimples in the gel coat. A local expert claims it was caused by the fiberglass surfaces below the waterline being unable to breathe. What do you say? And what do we do?

A. He was more or less right, although his terminology would strike a fiberglass man as being a bit on the elementary side. A glass man might prefer to say the water kept the fiberglass from "gassing off." It's not a simple matter that has a pat answer. Pimpling and blistering of gel coat is a fairly common occurrence and there are various causes. Gel coat specialists have done much research into the matter. Gel coats are constantly being improved; blistering problems are now less frequently encountered.

There are various causes for these problems, which are rooted in the intricacies of fiberglass chemistry. The cause of a specific case of blistering can be determined only by a gel coat expert. Some blisters are tiny, like gooseflesh. Others are as large as nickels and dimes. Some are in the gel coat alone; others originate in the laminate and work out to show as blistered gel coat.

A common cause is too much solvent in the laminating resin. Another is use of too little or too much hardener. Blisters may be more likely to form when a coarse type of glass cloth is used as the first layer in the laminate over the gel coat than when a smoother or denser grade is used. Sometimes over-pigmentation of a gel coat renders it slightly porous so as to encourage the soaking-in of enough water to produce pimpling. Too-thin gel coat can have an inherently low resistance to water absorption and hence is prone to blistering.

It is difficult to assign blame when blistering occurs. When several men are working at once on a large laminating job, one of them might find a barrelful of resin to be too thick to wet out the glass fabric readily enough, so a little more thinner is added. Or the shop heater may be malfunctioning, so some glass work is done in a cool room and curing is a little slow, allowing tiny droplets of solvent in the resin to form instead of evaporating off. Large fiberglass boat factories have facilities to run quality checks on incoming shipments of material; small ones don't and have to rely on the integrity of their suppliers. To learn exactly what went wrong and who goofed among the many individuals involved in the chain of events is like tracing the family tree of an alley cat!

The thing to do when blistering is found is to contact the boat's manufacturer in a calm and reasonable manner. Nine times out of ten real concern will be shown. Yours may be the first tip-off they've had that something has gone awry, and they will want to check into their shop procedures, quality control, etc., to isolate the reason. A mass-production company may offer to give you a new boat; a custom shop may offer to refinish the bottom of your boat.

The usual big-shop repair is to grind off all the gel coat, respray and go through the tedious process of smoothing and polishing the new gel coat. The usual small-shop or private-party repair is to break off the flaking gel coat around pimples, clean out each depression, fill with fiberglass putty, sand smooth, and cover the repair work with an attractive cosmetic of some appropriate bottom paint.

Blistering typically occurs early in a boat's life. If it does not show up after the second season at a mooring, it probably never will. Prolonged immersion of a new hull in water seems to be the common denominator. It isn't that the water necessarily keeps the fiberglass from "breathing," but that the wetness triggers or aggravates whatever the chemical problem may be.

A hull that is finished off and promptly put out to mooring for the season is a prime candidate for pimpling or blistering, assuming it has some quirk in its fiberglass that renders it subject to the trouble. One that stands around ashore for some months before being launched is allowed ample time for the curing process to taper off. If the potential for pimpling that dwells in it involves something like excess solvent or hardener, the tendency to form pimples will be less. If you plan to keep a boat at a mooring, choosing a hull that was molded in October rather than in May would be a wise move, if this is at all possible. Boats kept on trailers or davits, of course, are immune to pimpling.

Blistering of bottom gel coat in boats left at moorings for long periods has many causes. Here are three examples. Several other possible causes have been identified. To determine the cause of a specific case of blistering is often difficult; the following were identified by means of controlled tests on prepared specimens. (Ferro Corp.) (A) Side A was made with gel coat applied .020 inch thick. Side B was made with gel coat only .010 inch thick. (B) Side A was made using a flexible resin as the base for its gel coat. Side B was made using a rigid resin as the base for its gel coat. (C) Side A had a small amount of acetone mixed into the gel coat. Side B had an excessive amount of acetone mixed in the gel coat.

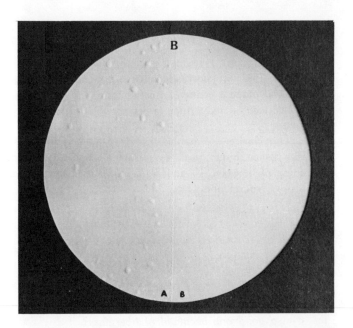

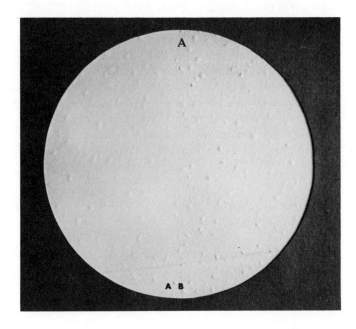

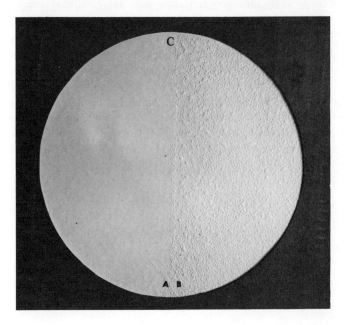

Bubbles on Topside

Q. There are a number of coin-sized blisters on the fiberglass deck of my boat. What might have gone wrong?

A. Blisters on above-the-waterline areas of fiberglass boats are not common. The most likely cause is air bubbles entrapped between the gel coat and the glass laminate. They do not show up when the factory inspector looks over the deck's surface, but later the hot sun outdoors expands the air in them and pushes up on the gel coat enough to form a blister. A less common, seldom found cause would be a spot of soft resin between the laminate proper and the gel coat. A glob of uncatalyzed resin or, perhaps, gel coat might drop onto the hardened gel coat, not be noticed or else considered to be catalyzed, and be covered over by laminate. It will form a soft spot that later will expand or leak under the sun's heat.

Barcol Hardness

Q. A marine surveyor went over a large sailboat I was buying and made a written report on its condition. At one place I noticed he had written in "Barcol—40." What does that mean?

A. The Barber-Colman company makes a hardness testing device much used by technical men. A Barcol hardness of between 40 and 50 is considered normal for well-cured, sound fiberglass.

Fiberglass Rudders

Q. A new cast-bronze rudder for my cruiser would cost a lot. Can a good one be made of fiberglass?

A. Probably. It has been done. Many sailboats have rudders and even centerboards made of fiberglass. Smooth, streamlined ones are made in molds. Right and left halves are waxed, a gel coat is applied, laminate glass and material and usually some kind of core or filler material are all put in place, and the two halves are clamped tightly together until the resin has cured. Simple flat ones can be made by waxing a sheet of heavy plate or auto glass, brushing on resin and as many layers of cloth, mat, and roving as is desired for the thickness and strength needed, and then putting another piece of glass over all this to push it down smooth. Washers can be used between the two sheets of glass to control thickness. The rough-edged sheet of glass laminate that results can be bandsawn to the needed outline and the edges rounded off as desired.

The problem with a blade-type motorboat rudder is attaching the fiberglass blade securely to the shaft. Typically, small bronze rods would be pressed into holes drilled in the backside of the shaft to "key" the glass and shaft together, then the glass would be molded up around this metal core.

Sponge Rubber in Fin

Q. We were working on my sloop, which has a molded-in fin on the bottom onto which the rudder is hinged. We found a sizeable piece of sponge rubber stuffed down inside this hollow fin. We threw it away, assuming it was junk. Later we got to wondering why it was there and if we should have left it alone. What do you say?

A. The presence of that sponge rubber puzzled us at first, too. It was a new one to us, but you can be around boats forever and still encounter new things! Our guess is that the sponge rubber was put down inside the hollow fin to serve as a pressure-reliever should water freeze inside that hard-to-drain fin in the wintertime. If you think things over long enough, you can usually hit upon a logical explanation for some very odd things you will discover around boats!

Chapter 12

Fiberglassing a Boat

Variety of Glass Cloths

Q. I am confused. Fiberglass supply catalogs talk of cloth, mat, and roving, and of all three in a variety of weights. How does one decide what to use?

A. You see a variety of woods in assorted sizes at a lumberyard because carpenters need different properties and sizes when making a house. The same applies to fiberglass— no one fabric will serve all purposes. There are three types of fabric—cloth, mat, and roving.

Cloth has a fine weave, generally comparable in coarseness to burlap. It has a smooth, lustrous appearance and is available in various weights, from about 6 to 20 oz. per square yard. The weight most commonly used is around 10 oz. per square yard. Because the strands of glass filaments are very slippery and the weave is loose and open, this cloth readily drapes onto the compound curves found in boats. Because it is smooth, it is favored for covering small boats, cabin roofs, etc. Because it is made by the weaving process, it costs more than mat. For this reason, it is not used very often in the laminates of medium- and large-size boats. Where light weight combined with good puncture strength is needed, as in kayaks and canoes, the laminate may be partly or wholly of this cloth. The smoothness of its surface sometimes leads to poor adhesion between successive layers of cloth, and so delamination is occasionally a problem.

Mat is made by chopping glass filaments into short lengths, averaging two inches, and blowing it, along with a starch-type binding agent, onto a flat surface. It looks like a very coarse sort of felt, and is white in color. Because the method of manufacture is quicker than weaving, the cost is lower. It has less tensile and rupture strength than cloth. Its big advantage is that it offers a rapid, economical way of building up the thickness of a laminate—and it is thickness that gives a hull its rigidity. It is very easy and quick to work with. Lay it on a Masonite-covered table and cut it readily with a common replaceable-blade carpenter's utility knife. It tears easily and is ideal for making small pieces used to build up or finish off laminates in corners, around gussets, etc.

Mat comes in several weights. Three-quarter, 1½, and 2 ounces per square foot are the most common. The first is so thin that air bubbles work through it easily, so it is often used for the first layer of glass over the gel coat in molding work. The second is a general-purpose type and by far the most frequently used. Two-ounce mat is used mostly for larger hulls.

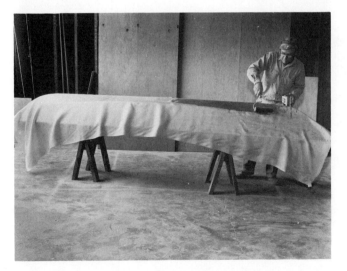

Glass cloth has a loose, slippery weave. As wetting-out with resin progresses, it readily drapes to fit the shape of a hull. Here a man is starting to fiberglass a "Can-Yak" kayak made from Glen-L Marine plans. (Glen-L Marine)

Glass cloths come in various types. At center, "mat" is a feltlike cloth made of short chopped strands held together with a binding material. Bottom, the familiar glass cloth you see in marine stores. Top, "roving" is a coarse cloth that imparts stiffness and puncture resistance to a laminate.

When you tear off a piece of mat for a patch or gusset, the torn edge is tapered and greatly facilitates blending a patch into a surrounding laminate very inconspicuously. It can be used for covering wooden boats in place of cloth. Be careful when using the roller on it because too much pressure can pull it apart and leave a thin spot.

Roving is a very coarse cloth, readily told from 10-oz. cloth by its much greater coarseness. The strands from which it is woven are flattened and average one-quarter of an inch in width. Its chief advantage is that it has high tensile strength. One layer of roving incorporated in a laminate made of several layers of mat will add substantially to a hull's resistance to cracking and puncturing. It's useful for repair work on heavier boats and boat parts, such as wooden masts, where its coarse, basketweave texture does not pose an objectionable appearance problem.

Adhesion of Old Fiberglass to New

Q. I have often wondered if the new resin used when patching a fiberglass boat will adhere dependably to the old laminate.

A. It will, if you roughen the old surface well with coarse sandpaper. But new resin applied to an old, very thoroughly cured and unsanded fiberglass surface is apt to have rather little adhesive capability. When an amateur spills or drips resin onto a part of his boat, he rushes to wipe it off, thereby smearing it. A professional may just let it stay there and cure hard—after which a little pressure with a putty knife will make it pop off easily and completely! When resin drips onto a concrete floor the pros do not fret—several days later when it is really hard (and brittle) they strike the droplets smartly with a hammer. The droplets pop right off the concrete!

Sources of Fiberglass Supplies

Q. I live on a ranch and the nearest waterfront city is far beyond my reach. How can I learn about working with fiberglass? How can I get supplies by mail order?

A. Most of the books on fiberglass now in print are stocked by International Marine Publishers, 21 Elm St., Camden, Maine 04843. The companies that make and sell fiberglass supplies have good literature in the form of assorted pamphlets. Write to Owens-Corning Fiberglas Corp., Fiberglas Tower, Toledo, Ohio 43659 and ask them to send you an assortment of their booklets on choosing and using fiberglass. The catalog put out by Defender Industries, Inc., 255 Main St., New Rochelle, N.Y. 10801 lists a page or two of useful books, as well as fiberglass supplies. Other firms well-known as suppliers of fiberglass to boatbuilders and boat owners are:

Fibre Glass-Evercoat Co, Inc., 6600 Cornell Rd., Cincinnati, Ohio 45242

Lan-O-Sheen, Inc., 1 W. Water St., St. Paul, Minn. 55107

Kristal Kraft, 900 Fourth St., Palmetto, Fla. 33561

Dunbar Marine Specialties, Box 531, East Longmeadow, Mass. 01028

TAP Plastics, Inc., 2041 East St., Concord, Cal. 94520

Kick-Shaw, Inc., 3511 Hixson Pike, Chattanooga, Tenn. 37415

Clark Craft, 16 Aqua Lane, Tonawanda, New York 14150

Allied Resin Products Corp., Weymouth Industrial Park, Pleasant St., E. Weymouth, Mass. 02189

There are others—look in the Yellow Pages for cities in your part of the country.

Information on "Kevlar"

Q. I see more and more mention in boating publications of a new fabric called "Kevlar." I've asked marine stores in my area for it but they don't stock it. Where can I get information about it?

A. It is just beginning to be used by the boat manufacturing industry. At this time it is not considered a maintenance material. It is usually used in combination with glass cloth in boat hulls. Technical knowledge and some experience are required to use it effectively. For example, where glass cloth is easy to cut with scissors, and mat is readily sliced with any sharp knife, Kevlar is surprisingly hard to cut. Some special tools have been developed for use with it. If you wish to learn more about it, get literature from the manufacturer, E. I. Du Pont De Nemours & Co., (Inc.), Plastics Department, Wilmington, Del. 19898.

Books on Fiberglassing Boats

Q. Does anyone publish a book on how to fiberglass boats?

A. Yes. Glen-L Marine Designs, 9152 Rosecrans, Bellflower, Cal. 90706 has a 120-page softbound book titled *How To Fiberglass Boats*. Clark Craft Boat Co., 16 Aqua Lane, Tonawanda, N.Y. 14150 has a 64-page softbound book, *How to Use Fiberglass for Repairing, Covering, Etc.*

Will Fiberglassing Cause Rot?

Q. If I fiberglass my wooden boat, will I increase the chances of the wood rotting?

A. The question has been hotly debated by boat experts and no conclusive answer has emerged. The fiberglass, all by itself, won't cause rot. The crux of the matter is how much fresh water will get into the hull from the topsides and stay there. It thus depends on the type of boat and the way in which it is used. If it happens that wood in the bottom of the boat is kept damp, rot is very possible. But if it is kept either quite dry or soaking wet, rot is rather unlikely.

Will Fiberglass Cause Itch?

Q. I am going to fiberglass a boat soon. Everyone I talk to tells me the fragments of glass that break loose while cutting and sanding fiberglass will cause my skin to itch terribly. Is this so? Can anything be done about it?

A. People exaggerate things they know nothing about. Most of the people you have talked to have never worked with fiberglass themselves and are just repeating hearsay. Early fiberglass cloths did cause a lot of itching, but the types now marketed are much improved in this respect. You will not itch all over, just on whatever areas of skin happen to be exposed when the work is being done—usually your arms. Wearing old coveralls with only your hands exposed all but eliminates the itching problem. Or, wear an old long-sleeved shirt and an old apron of some kind. The kind of glass-cloth cutting and trimming done when fiberglassing a boat does not raise such a great amount of dust. The use of a high-powered disc sander to trim surplus off of fiberglass parts in production work is what really fills the air with glass fragments and causes the most noticeable itching. Little or none of this work is done when glassing a wooden boat. In humid weather, the glass fragments will stick to sweaty skin and itching will be more noticeable than if the same job were done on a drier, cooler day.

Hardware and paint stores sell protective hand creams that prevent paint from sticking to the skin. These creams wash off easily. Du Pont's "Pro-Tek" is a widely available type. It dries into a protective film when rubbed into the skin, and will materially reduce the number of glass filament fragments that stick to the skin and lightly puncture it, which is the cause of the itching.

After finishing a fiberglass job, take your work clothes off and keep them outdoors so they won't dust up the house. Shake them well before laundering. Take a hot shower with plenty of soap to wash glass fragments out of your hair and off your skin. Don't worry about itching; it's not as bad as know-nothings imagine!

Hand creams such as "Pro-Tek" make fiberglass work pleasanter.

Fiberglass Hazards

Q. Are fiberglassing materials dangerous to work with? Are any of them poisonous?

A. They are as safe as other things likely to be found in a shop. Only an occasional individual proves to be allergic to the resin. A person with sensitive skin might have a mild itch or rash until his skin gets used to the materials, but a person who works regularly with solvents and finishes, such as an auto body man, will notice nothing. The *polyester* resin commonly used for fiberglassing is not toxic, but some of the *epoxy* resins can irritate the skin. Too much exposure to it can cause an allergic reaction, forcing some to stop using it altogether. A small drop of resin splashed or wiped into the eye will sting badly but will not do harm—wash copiously with water and use soothing eye drops.

There is one thing to be extremely careful about. The hardener used with resin to make it "kick" is terribly damaging to the eye tissue. Be extremely careful so that it does not splash when pouring and mixing it into resin. Don't put it in containers that can tip over easily. Don't get some on your fingers while pouring and then absent-mindedly rub your eyes. If you do have an accident, wash with copious amounts of water and rush to a doctor. Memorize the name of this chemical right now—METHYL ETHYL KETONE PEROXIDE, called "MEK Peroxide," "MEKP," or just "MEK" by fiberglass workers. Tell the doctor this is what you got in your eyes and have him go right to work. This chemical can cause the eye tissue to decompose and cause blindness. Be as prudent and deliberate when using it as you'd be when picking up a porcupine, and you'll be safe. Never lose your wholesome respect for it!

There is a solvent used for clean-up work and resin thinning in professional shops named Methyl Ethyl Ketone, also called "MEK" in some shops. It is totally different from Methyl Ethyl Ketone PEROXIDE. Don't get the two confused. MEK Peroxide is colorless but noticably heavier and a little more viscous than water. MEK, the solvent, is also colorless but is noticeably less viscous than water and has a very sharp, penetrating odor that MEK Peroxide, which has a sourish smell, something like a weak mixture of acetic acid and vinegar, lacks. The average amateur will not have any MEK around, so the danger to him is nil.

The acetone used to clean resin from hands, tools, and brushes is very flammable and must be treated with as much respect as gasoline. *No smoking* in or around the area where fiberglass work is being done! Be good and careful about using electric drills, sabre saws, etc., as a little stray acetone vapor meeting the sparks on the commutator of such a tool will flash, jump back to the acetone bucket, and let all hell loose! Acetone takes oil from the skin; use hand cream if your hands get chapped.

The familiar sharp, pungent odor of fiberglass resin is caused by another commonly used solvent called "styrene." Too much inhalation of acetone or styrene vapors will make you feel woozy and cause headaches. So work only in a well-ventilated place, such as a garage with its doors open. Styrene vapor is heavier than air and tends to collect in low places. If you do fiberglassing in a basement it will flow along the floor to the furnace. It will collect and remain inside anything shaped like a boat hull and slow down the hardening of resin, so if you do fiberglass work inside a boat, have a fan going or do the job outdoors on a breezy day.

When sawing, sanding, or grinding fiberglass laminate, wear a good dust mask. Prolonged exposure to fiberglass dust (such as one would get when working in a poorly ventilated fiberglass shop for months on end) is suspected of causing cases of lung cancer. There seems to be something about the shape of the fiberglass fragments that makes it hard for the respiratory system's self-cleaning apparatus to handle and get rid of them.

We warn you of the above not to scare you, but so that you will know all the potential common hazards. Fiberglass materials have been widely used for years and much has been learned. They are safe when used according to instructions and with some knowledge of the potential hazards.

Fiberglass and Weather

Q. Are there any weather conditions under which fiberglassing should not be done?

A. Yes. Ideal working temperature is around 70 degrees F. When it's noticeably hotter than that, the resin will start to "kick," or turn from liquid to solid state, sooner. You must either use it up faster or add less hardener to it to maintain useful pot life. When the temperature gets down to 60 degrees or below, kicking time begins to increase and the amount of hardener must be increased. If much work must be done when the temperature is below 60 degrees, ask your supply house for a few tubes of "cold weather promoter." It is a blue liquid added in small quantities to the resin *before* the hardener is put in. Stir well before adding the hardener. It will make the resin kick more normally and you can work in temperatures down to about 45 degrees. If polyester resin is used when it's colder than that, it may not kick for a long time, leaving spots of uncured resin here and there in the job, and the resulting laminate may be soft and weak.

Don't work in the rain or in very humid conditions. The cloth will absorb dampness and this will make the resin turn milky when it is worked into the fabric. The resulting whitish spots scattered about the laminate will be soft and weak. There is no way to get the dampness out of a glassing job. Wait for the weather to improve.

Direct sunlight speeds up the curing time; the resin will kick sooner. Experienced fiberglass workers sometimes push a finished job from the shade into the sunlight to make it kick faster. They do this when working in a chilly shop or doing a rush job. But if you lack experience, better stay in the shade.

Pot of Resin Started to Smoke

Q. I mixed hardener into a quart of resin and went to work. Some dirt got onto the work and I had to stop to clean it off. When I turned to pick up the pot of resin, I was startled and frightened to see that it was bubbling and emitting an evil-smelling, yellowish-white smoke. When I picked it up to carry outside it was so hot I screamed and dropped it. What did I do wrong?

A. You failed to read the instructions carefully before starting to work! Resin always generates heat when it "kicks," or, once again, turns from liquid to solid state. It's the chemical reaction that goes on. The amount of heat generated increases appreciably with the volume of activated resin. If you measure out the hardener carefully and add the same proportion to a gallon container of resin that you also add to a quart container, the gallon of resin will generate a lot more heat and start kicking faster, often fast enough to generate too much heat and start smoking. You added a little too much hardener and your quart of resin started generating heat behind your back. If you had not stopped to clean off the dirt and gone ahead to spread the resin, you would have spread it out before it began to kick and it would not have gotten that hot, due to the low volume at any one spot when brushed out.

One has to learn by experience how much hardener to add. Experienced glass workers know how to vary the amounts of hardener added to any particular volume so as to get a fast or slow kick suitable to the shop temperature, or the type and size of job they are doing. But when you're new to glass work, follow instructions as to how much to add. As you become more familiar with resin's curing rate, you can begin to vary the amount of hardener slightly to get a slower or faster kick.

On a hot day, keep a bucket of water handy, and if your can of resin starts to boil, dunk it in the pail to cool off the reaction. Fire or explosion is not very likely but the smoking can give you a bad scare. Watch your can of resin; as soon as a slight curdling becomes apparent, use up that batch of resin fast so it won't kick in the can and be wasted.

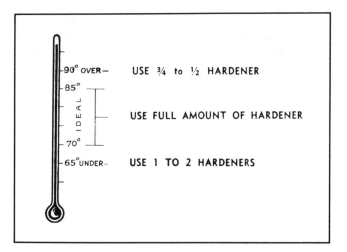

This thermometer serves as a guide for increasing or reducing the amount of hardener added to resin to compensate for changes in room temperature.

What Kind of Resin?

Q. How does one decide between using polyester and epoxy resin for a job?

A. Epoxy resin costs a lot more and has to be used carefully lest it cause skin irritation. Epoxy bonds by molecular attraction and is extremely tenacious. Polyester bonds well to itself, such as in the laminates in a fiberglass part. You'd use epoxy when fiberglassing over an oak or teak deck or over metal. Nine times out of ten you will use polyester for typical boat jobs.

What Brand of Resin to Use?

Q. I am going to fiberglass my wooden boat and I'm undecided between two competing brands. Which do you think is best?

A. Only a rather small number of firms make resin and they are all reputable. If one firm is appreciably nearer to you than the other, you might save something on freight by patronizing them. As far as basic quality and durability are concerned, don't worry about brands. But it's useful to know that every firm in the business makes a variety of resin blends. This is mostly for the benefit of factories that use fiberglass for many things—boats, car bodies, furniture, food processing equipment, bathroom fixtures, machine parts, and so on at length. Slight variations in blending can make useful changes in assorted characteristics. A boat resin should be tough and resilient. A resin for making molds should be hard and stable, but need not be weather resistant. Resins intended for use with boat-type cloths should be thin enough to soak in and saturate the cloth readily, yet not be so thin as to drain out of the cloth on vertical surfaces before beginning to kick. If you visit a fiberglass warehouse to buy at wholesale, you may be offered a choice of several different resins. But when you buy at retail, you will be sold a blend that is suitable for general patching and fiberglassing wooden boats.

Resins have a peculiarity worth noting. The side of a freshly laid laminate that is against a mold or the wood of a boat is shut off from air and has a tendency to cure with a dry and hard surface. But the other side, exposed to air, cures with a slightly soft, tacky feel to its surface. This assures good bonding when another layer of cloth is put on. This is called "laminating resin."

But as a tacky surface is hard to sandpaper and paint, a laminating resin is not suitable for repair work or covering wooden boats. So, a wax-like paraffin is dissolved in styrene solvent (technically called "styrene monomer" in the trade) and a little of this is mixed into a batch of laminating resin. That converts it into "surfacing resin." The wax will float to the surface, shut out the air, and cause the surface to cure hard and dry, ready for sanding and primer. The kind of resin you buy in cans at marine stores is "surfacing resin."

What Went Wrong?

Q. I fiberglassed my surfboard with some resin a friend gave me. Now, weeks later, the job is still soft and tacky. What went wrong?

A. You may have used a laminating resin, or some oddball resin made for some special purpose. You may have done the job during extremely damp weather—resin-impregnated laminate cures much more slowly under such conditions. The hardener you used may have been old and lacking in potency. If you did the job under all three of these circumstances, they'd work together to make for a very slow cure. Try putting the work out into the sunlight for a number of days. If that does not make the resin harden, you can try to salvage the job thusly; wipe the surface with a cloth wet with acetone to clean off any foreign matter that might be present in the tacky surface, then brush on a coat of surfacing resin. With luck, it will cure dry and hard and will adhere well to the soft resin below.

Fiberglassing a Big Boat

Q. We have an old boat that is in fine condition overall, and the quality woodwork in her cabin is a joy to behold. But the bottom has many small leaks that are a constant problem and menace. She's 40 feet long. Should we fiber-glass the bottom?

A. You should have a local fiberglassing expert evaluate the situation. The cost of fiberglassing materials has substantially gone up in recent years. Ten or twenty years ago

the cost of fiberglassing such a large boat might have been within reason. Today you should make sure of what it'll cost before going ahead. The job might save the boat, but can your budget stand the outlay?

Fiberglassing a Double-Planked Hull

Q. My boat is of the once popular double-planked type of hull construction. Would I encounter any problems if I fiberglassed it?

A. If the outside is sound and dry, there should be no adhesion problems as such. It's what you can't see below the surface that could turn the job into an eventual failure. If the canvas or muslin used between layers on double-planked boats is rotten and damp, or if there is separation here and there between inner and outer layers of planking, there could be damp spots that are ideal breeding grounds for rot. The fiberglass will keep such places from drying out when the boat is not in the water, aggravating the rot problem. It comes down to being not a fiberglassing question but a question of what the fiberglass might do to encourage rot in the wood. If the interior of the boat can be well and thoroughly ventilated, and if its topsides are such that little or no rainwater gets into the bilge area, there might be small hazard of rot. Another problem could be widespread loosening of fastenings to the extent that the outer layer of planking is not very well secured to the inner and thus to the boat. A thin fiberglassing job could crack up rather soon. A job consisting of two or three layers of glass cloth would resist cracking quite well but then it becomes a question of cost.

Scattered Wet Spots on Fiberglass Job

Q. After I fiberglassed my skiff, there were several scattered patches where the resin did not cure dry and hard. Several days out in the sun eventually made these spots kick. I'd like to know what I might have done wrong.

A. Did you stir the hardener into the resin? Did you let the acetone drip out of the roots of the resin brush before using it? Did you use wax-containing paint remover and fail to wash the stripped wooden surfaces with solvent to remove all traces of wax? Did the wet spots match oily spots in the wood?

Added Weight of Fiberglass

Q. If I fiberglass my fine old wooden speedboat, will it add enough weight to harm the performance?

A. Probably not. If the boat is kept in the water all summer, as is customary with boats of your type, the wood in the bottom will soak up water and become quite heavy. You might find that fiberglass will have the end result of keeping the boat lighter by slowing down or stopping waterlogging of the bottom planking.

In the case of a rowboat, sailboat, or other non-planing craft that does not lift onto the water's surface to go fast, the thickness of a fiberglass sheathing job adds a little more to the hull's volume, and hence to its buoyancy. In general, then, a typical fiberglassing job brings in counterbalancing factors such that one usually need not worry about added weight.

You might worry about weight if you were going to put two or three layers of fiberglass onto a canoe that has to be portaged, or do very extensive and heavy fiberglassing on the topsides, decks, and cabin of a larger boat. Fiberglass supply houses can give data on weights of various laminates from which one can calculate how much will be added to a boat's weight. Or you can wax a piece of glass, make up a test laminate on it, trim it down to exactly one square foot, and weigh it to get the data yourself. The actual job will come out a little heavier per square foot due to some resin going into the wood. Just how much heavier will depend on the kind of wood.

Fiberglassing a Workboat

Q. We have a 38-foot workboat. It makes a profit so we want to keep it going. The bottom leaks all over. We'd like to fiberglass it but the idea of trying to work overhead with something as messy as resin and resin-soaked cloth is discouraging us. The boat is too big to be inverted. Is there an answer?

A. The job will be appreciably easier if you can manage a way to heel the boat over on one side and then the other. A really dependable fiberglassing job on a big boat can be assured by putting on the first layer of fabric, then mechanically fastening it to the wood with a large number of stainless steel or Monel staples driven with a production-type staple gun. Running of the resin on sloping surfaces can be controlled by adding "Cabosil" or equivalent. This is a silica product made by the Cabot paint company. It is a very light, fluffy, powder-like material that is white in color. Added to resin and stirred in thoroughly, it will thicken the resin enough to control running—the right amount to add is found by trial and error. You will use so much resin and cloth on this boat that you should buy it at wholesale price from a fiberglass warehouse. Ask local boat shops about such companies in your area. Or find them in the Yellow Pages for the nearest cities. They may know of people in your area who have had experience with fiberglassing larger boats.

Suction Did It!

Q. I fiberglassed the bottom of my wooden cruiser. A few weeks later, a large section of glass on the hull above the propeller ripped loose. Various people have told me it was due to loosening by vibration pulses in the water from the propeller, to oil in the wood from supplies stored in the lazarette in the stern, and to softening of the wood in the rudder and propeller area by "wood electrolysis." I'd value your opinion.

A. This kind of thing has happened many times. People just do not realize how much suction is created on a boat's bottom just ahead of and above the propeller. The prop creates it in the process of drawing water into its area. Some tugboats, while straining to move heavy ships, have had the planking rip off their frames in this area! A good fiberglass job calls for generous use of big staples to mechanically fasten the glass to the wood. If you lack such a staple gun, when you replace the missing fiberglass you can drive many small Anchorfast serrated boat nails through the first layer of glass cloth to serve the same purpose.

Patch Comes Off

Q. On three occasions, a patch of fiberglass over a leaking seam in my boat has come off shortly after the boat was relaunched. Why won't it stay on?

A. Chemical firms originally developed resin and glass cloth with the idea of using it to laminate boat hulls, airplane parts, auto bodies, etc. They never intended it to be a tenacious glue. Merchandisers hit on the idea of fiberglassing wooden boats as a means to sell more of the product and gain wider public acceptance for it. So you start off with a resin that isn't an especially tenacious adhesive when used on wood.

If the wood is of an oily species, if it is soaked with oil from the engine compartment, deeply impregnated with old primer and paint, or not 100% dry when fiberglassed, the resin will adhere indifferently. When a piece of fiberglass cloth is used for a patch on a boat's bottom, its edges are exposed to the flow of water and the rush of water can get hold of the edge, lift it, push under, and billow the piece off easily.

If the planking is wet and will obviously take a long time to dry, you might be better off with a patch made from a strip of copper laid in bedding compound and liberally fastened with Anchorfast nails. No one ever said fiberglass is a cure-all!

Removing Oil from Wood

Q. How does one get old engine oil out of the wood on a boat's bottom before fiberglassing?

A. Fiberglass vendors used to recommend carbon tetra-chloride. But this chemical was found to be too hazardous to the health and its sale has been stopped. Now the vendors don't seem to know what to recommend. Acetone might work but it is costly and even more volatile than gasoline. One can't suggest unleaded gasoline without the safety monitors becoming terribly agitated. About all one can suggest is a strong detergent—but it's anyone's guess whether it will get to and pull out oil that is below the surface of the wood. A solution of lye in hot water will work, but it is dangerous to use. One might try using epoxy resin on the area of the bottom that is soaked with oil and hope it will cling better than polyester.

Glass Lifts over Seams

Q. We fiberglassed an old smooth-planked boat and after a time the glass began to loosen and form ridges along the seams. What might have gone wrong?

A. Are the seams "payed with"—an old-time seaman's term meaning "filled with"—a seam compound having an oil base? If so, that's the trouble. Fiberglassing literature stresses that only non-oily fillers and compounds should be used in seams in a surface that is going to be fiberglassed.

Durability of Fiberglassing Jobs

Q. A friend and I fiberglassed our homemade boats on the same day, helping each other. We did one boat in the morning and one in the afternoon. Now mine, done in the morning, is developing small cracks in the surface and his isn't. What might have gone wrong?

A. Assuming the weather did not significantly change, our guess is that you were a bit liberal with the resin on the first boat, yours. Then, finding you had used more than half of your resin supply, you went easier on the second boat. So your boat has what glass men call a "resin-rich" job. When there's too much resin in the laminate, the result is a rather brittle laminate that cracks more readily. It does take some experience and skill to learn how to brush in just the right amount of resin. The tendency, in one's eagerness to get the fabric wetted out quickly and thoroughly, is to apply too much of it. A resin-rich job tends to have a glossy look to its surface. A resin-starved job is likely to have some of the glass looking a little whitish and rough, obviously from lack of enough resin to encapsulate the filaments well. A good job has an obviously dense, sealed surface resulting from adequate resin, yet it has a slightly rough, dulled look indicating there isn't excessive resin which would cause a glossy appearance.

Fiberglassing Lapstrake Hulls

Q. Can a lapstrake boat be fiberglassed?

A. Yes—if you know how. Although each tiny glass filament will bend easily, it is made of a springy material that wants to remain straight. When you brush cloth down into and over the corners of the laps, the cloth tends to slowly lift up off the surface at the laps and form long bubbles. Not being a glue or a real adhesive, the resin has little effect in holding the cloth down prior to the "kicking" of the resin. Once it begins to kick, it will be a little sticky and attempts to push down the bubbles with a brush or tool will often end up in lifting the cloth some more.

There are various tricks. Use a lighter and therefore more flexible cloth than those sold for general-purpose work. Round off the corners of the planks with a small plane and make putty fillets in the valleys with a popsicle stick to reduce the abruptness of the curves the cloth must form to. Rip up some wooden battens, wax them and nail them with thin brads against the cloth at each lap to hold it down until the resin kicks. Instead of using woven cloth, make the first layer of fiberglass using three-quarter-ounce mat. This is a very thin type of mat, so thin one can easily see through it. The many small openings in it let air pass through easily. It is used by fiberglass boat and body shops as the first layer of fabric after the gel coat. It aids in avoiding air bubbles between the gel coat and laminate. Get it from a fiberglass supply house. It could lay over the corners and valleys of the laps much better. Then the second layer, of woven cloth, will almost surely stick down better and bubbles will be minimized.

Fiberglass Smell

Q. I fiberglassed a small boat in my garage and the neighbors raised an uproar about the smell. They claimed it gave them headaches and menaced the health of their children. Is the smell that hazardous?

A. No. People work with fiberglass for years without ill effects. The problem with neighbors plagues everyone who uses fiberglass. People react to it strongly simply because the smell is different from anything else they have encountered, just as they will react in agitated fashion to a house painted in weird colors or to a teenage girl wearing outlandish dress. Their reaction to fiberglass smell is also strong because so many are worried about air pollution. Unlike smoke, odors from a stable, etc., fiberglass smell tends to dissipate rapidly with distance from the work. It will hang around more on damp, still days than on dry, breezy ones. If you have crabby neighbors, do your fiberglassing when the wind is blowing away from their house. The resin will "kick" in an hour or less, after which the smell will taper off noticeably. Or, find out when neighbors plan to be away for a while and do the job then.

Fiberglassing a Plywood Boat

Q. I am finishing up a homemade plywood boat and am wondering whether or not to fiberglass it. I get conflicting stories from the people who drop in to watch me work.

A. People who think they know everything, but in fact know nothing, are a menace anywhere, anytime, when boats are concerned. More boat jobs have been spoiled through following bad advice than from all other reasons combined! What most people know about fiberglass can be written with a felt-tip pen on the head of a common pin!

If your boat is made of fir plywood, a fiberglass job can sheath it so as to practically eliminate weather checking. If your boat is planked with one of the mahogany-type woods, checking will not be a problem so a good priming and painting job would be cheaper and easier than fiberglassing.

If your boat has wooden protective strips over the keel seams, chine seams, etc., so that the edges of the plywood are sealed against chafing and entry of water, fiberglass really wouldn't be necessary. But it could be a good way to firm up those weak spots on a boat that does not have hardwood strips at such points.

If your boat is to be used off a sandy beach, bottom abrasion will be a minor worry. But if it is to be used off a rocky or gravelly shore or in rock-strewn waters, two or even three layers of fiberglass on the bottom will make it last much longer.

If your boat is to be moored in fresh water, marine borers will not be a concern. But if it is to be moored for long periods in coastal waters known to be infested with teredos—marine borers—fiberglass can save the bottom from a riddling. Plywood manufacturers point out that the water-proof glue they use is indigestible and will repel borers as soon as they eat through the first ply. They say borers can't attack plywood. But we have seen samples of borer-riddled plywood from a number of different boats! It is true that a coating of anti-fouling paint on the bottom will repel borers as well as creatures that merely attach to the surface. But such paint soon collects scratches, and juvenile borers are quite small enough to get at the exposed wood there. Then they burrow in and go to work. So a fiberglassed bottom is useful.

Fiberglass Tape Comes Off

Q. Rather than stand the expense of fiberglassing the entire hull of my plywood sailboat, I used fiberglass tape to cover the exposed edges of the plywood along the chines, etc. A few weeks after launching it, the tapes began lifting off. The plywood was new, clean, and dry. Any idea of what went wrong?

A. Did you drag coarse sandpaper over the areas that would receive the fiberglass, to roughen the surface of the wood? Sometimes new plywood has traces of wax on it from the metal platens used in the gluing press at the factory. So use sandpaper!

How Many Layers of Cloth?

Q. I have a wooden day cruiser, 19-feet long, that has smooth planking. The wood seems to be some species of cedar. Logic tells me the swelling and shrinking of the planks with changes in weather would tend to split the fiberglass along the plank seams. What do you think?

A. We agree. Time and again fiberglass jobs using a single layer of cloth have developed cracks along the plank seams. The only answer is to apply two or more layers of cloth. This is why a good job can be expensive.

Solvent for Old Fiberglass

Q. I made a mistake in securing an item of equipment into my boat using fiberglass. Now it's in so securely I'm afraid of damaging the equipment while getting it loose. Is there a solvent on the market that will soften cured fiberglass?

A. Some supply houses sell a solvent that has special uses in industry, such as dissolving fiberglass or resin housings of small electrical units for the purpose of salvaging defective units. But it's nothing that would work in general maintenance areas and also it might be hard for you to get. It requires complete immersion of the object being treated, for many hours or a number of days. No commonly available solvents will soften fiberglass resin. That is why it is much used for containers and vats in industrial plants.

Pulling apart old fiberglass work is a matter of using common power tools such as electric drills, sabre saws, disc grinders, and metal- or concrete-cutting abrasive blades in portable electric saws.

Rollers Came Apart

Q. While fiberglassing my boat I had much trouble with the paint rollers I used to spread and work the resin into the cloth. Glass filaments kept sticking to them and building up. Acetone got inside them and kept dribbling out on the work, and after a short time they came apart from the acetone's solvent action. I've seen other people use rollers for fiberglass and they never had such troubles. Why not?

A. Rollers sold in paint and hardware stores are entirely different from those meant for fiberglass work. Most fiberglassing rollers are made of aluminum or solvent-resisting plastic. They are solid, not hollow, so they won't fill

111

with acetone when put into the acetone bucket. The fabric rollers sometimes used have a rather dense, hard stippled surface that will not pick up glass filaments. Few marine stores sell fiberglassing rollers; get them from fiberglass supply houses.

Polished Fiberglass Deck

Q. I am building an outboard racer with a fine mahogany plywood deck. I have seen boats like this at shows that had the plywood covered with fiberglass to make it hard and durable. The fiberglass jobs were marvels of smoothness and brilliance—just as highly polished as plate glass! I have been making up squares of plywood with fiberglass covering and trying various methods of smoothing and polishing them. But I can't match the jobs I see at shows and boat races. How do they do it?

A. There's a trick to it. The surface is well sanded with a powerful industrial-type orbital sander and/or with a rotary sander driving a soft, foam-type sanding disc. Then if the weave is still visible, another coat of resin is brushed on, allowed to cure, and sanded. When the surface is uniformly smooth it is given a very careful varnishing. A urethane varnish will adhere quite well to a well-sanded fiberglass surface. What you see is not polished fiberglass resin but a very good varnish job over a fiberglass base.

Resin in Place of Varnish

Q. Every boatman has seen how durable fiberglass is. I'm tired of maintaining the varnish on my boat's woodwork. Could I strip the varnish off, sand the wood, and give the wood a coating of resin?

A. We very much doubt if it would work. Resin would be very, very hard to brush out smooth like varnish. You would have an irregular, lumpy surface and probably some runs that would call for a great amount of tedious sanding to bring down to level. Even if you got an acceptable looking surface after much work, the resin film would be brittle and every bump from a boat hook, etc. would fracture it. Stick to varnish.

Copying an Old Boat

Q. I own a finely shaped old rowboat that rows like a feather. I'd like to make a fiberglass copy of it. Can I use it as a form over which to mold a hull?

A. Yes, but we have reservations. If the sides have any more than a very slight amount of tumble-home, you will have a very bad time trying to lift the fiberglass hull off the old boat. You might have to saw the fiberglass hull down its middle along the keel to get it off, then tape it together again. To make the new hull acceptably rigid, you will need at least three or perhaps four layers of glass fabric in the laminate. Any appreciable humps and hollows in the surface of the first laminate will show up in the next layer, perhaps even to a greater degree. So you may have to do some sanding down, patching, and puttying on the first layer or two to get the surface as smooth as possible. A lot of sanding and puttying may be needed to get the final, outer surface acceptably smooth.

If the finish of the boat is in poor shape, it will have to be refinished some day if you want to continue using the original craft. So you may as well start by doing a good job of refinishing her as a first step in making a fiberglass copy. The smoother and more uniform you can get her, the better the fiberglass copy will be. Using masking tape and/or staples, cover the inverted hull as smoothly as you can with cellophane or Mylar plastic sheeting. This will keep fiberglass resin from sticking to the boat's surface. If in doubt about the ability of your chosen sheeting to resist penetration by resin, make small test samples. Waxing the old hull's paint before going on to the fiberglass work would be good insurance against the new boat sticking to the old one if resin leaks through cuts or gaps in the plastic. Read about the various types of fiberglass fabrics and choose a laminate that will produce a strong hull. Glass cloth, mat, and roving can be used in various combinations to get good strength, durability, resistance to delamination, good appearance inside and out, etc.

Repairing a Glitter Finish Boat

Q. Our fiberglass speedboat has "glitter" finish—clear fiberglass with multicolored metallic flakes in it to add sparkle. We got a bad hole in the side. How can we repair it and retain the appearance?

A. You've got a problem! Reproducing the glitter effect in a patch is a challenge. A common way of making a "glitter" laminate is first to spray a coat of clear, colorless gel coat on the mold. When this has cured hard, the glitter is applied. Some shops might mix it in clear resin and spray it on. Some might brush a thin coat of laminating resin onto the hardened gel coat and sprinkle glitter onto this. When that's hard, work would proceed with the cloth. The basic point is, the glitter is encapsulated in the fiberglass, it is not brushed on after the boat is made. Hence the problem in reproducing its looks. There is nothing in any boat maintenance book on working with glitter. Your best course would be to visit shops that specialize in dune buggy, race car, and motorcycle fiberglass work. They would have more experience with glitter work than any boat shop.

Making Parts from Fiberglass

Q. Where can one get plans for making gasoline tanks, marine engine mufflers, and sea closet holding tanks of fiberglass?

A. Publishers shy away from printing such plans because of the engineering involved on one hand and the liability problems on the other hand. Water and gas tanks can be made of fiberglass but this requires knowledge. A water tank must be made so glass filament particles can never form and be carried into people's bodies by drinking the water. Gas tanks must comply with Coast Guard strength and safety requirements. *Fiberglass Boats* by Hugo Du Plessis has a little in it about making tanks. Other books that contained such material are now out of print. Making mufflers requires knowledge of the heat resisting qualities of various resins. The design and construction of holding tanks gets one involved with Coast Guard requirements for the performance of Marine Sanitation Devices.

Fiberglassing a Canoe

Q. Where can I get information on how to fiberglass a wooden canoe?

A. Contact your local or district Red Cross office. Ask them to help you get a copy of the 400 page book published by the National Red Cross on "Canoeing." The book number is ISBN 0-385-08313. Do not confuse it with the smaller booklet on the same subject that sells for 50¢—the one you want sells for $3.95 as of the time of this writing. It has a section on fiberglassing canoes.

Why Glass Fabric?

Q. Why do they use glass cloth, mat, and roving in boats? One can think of other fabrics that could be impregnated in resin and would cost less, such as burlap.

A. Most people don't realize it but the resin does not completely exclude water. If one made a hull of fiberglass and kept it moored in the water instead of on a trailer, enough water could get to the burlap to provide the degree of dampness needed to cause it to rot. Glass is used because it will never rot and it also has high tensile strength. Some other cloths may contain oils from the manufacturing process or sizings from the finishing process that would impair wetting-out with resin.

We have heard of kayaks being made of polyester resin and burlap as an experiment in lowering cost and weight. Such boats are put in the water only for short periods and they don't go fast, so burlap was considered usable. We have also seen cabin interiors decorated in burlap stuck on with resin and given a few extra coats of resin to fill the weave. And we have seen cockpit floors decorated with printed beach towels laid flat and stuck down with resin. Navigation charts can be "laminated" to the tops of inboard engine boxes with a few layers of resin.

Once one has learned the basics of fiberglassing, all kinds of fun can be had with it. We know a builder of custom boats who makes his own Coast Guard capacity plates as follows. The information is typed on heavy paper or light cardboard and the paper is trimmed to size. Two pieces of heavy plate glass are waxed. Resin is brushed on one and a piece of glass cloth laid into it, then more resin is brushed into the cloth. The card is laid onto the cloth. Another piece of cloth is laid over the cardboard, resin is liberally brushed into it, and the second piece of glass laid over it. Spring clamps are put on this "sandwich." Glass cloth becomes transparent when soaked with resin. Pressure from the clamps drives out air bubbles. When the resin has kicked, the laminated card can be lifted off the glass and trimmed to a smooth edge. It looks like something out of a commercial laminating machine!

Cracks in Cabin Roof

Q. The cabin roof on my outboard cruiser is made of plywood covered with a layer of fiberglass cloth. Many cracks have appeared in the fiberglass, especially where it goes around corners. How shall I fill these cracks before repainting?

A. The strands of glass in the cloth are probably broken, due to flexing of the cabin on your light, fast boat. You have a situation comparable to a concrete bridge in which the steel reinforcing rods are broken. Nothing applied over the breaks will restore the original strength. If you putty the cracks, they will open up again. You may as well take time to fix things properly and be rid of a recurring headache. We'd remove all the paint with paint remover and then use a heavy-duty orbital sander to smooth off rough spots and put "tooth" into the surface to make fresh resin adhere well. Then we'd clean loose material out of the cracks and fill them with polyester auto body putty. When that had hardened, we'd sand it flush with the surface. Then we'd put strips of fiberglass tape over all the cabin edges where the cracking has occurred. When cured hard, we'd feather the edges into the surrounding surface with sandpaper and a little more resin if needed to fill low spots. Over this, we'd put glass cloth to cover the whole cabin. This would provide a double thickness over the corners where flexing occurs, yet keep cost and weight down by putting only one new layer of cloth over the flatter areas that don't develop cracks. This is a good example of what boat work amounts to—using common sense and a little imagination to figure out a good solution to a particular problem.

His Cabin Sweats!

Q. I bought an old police patrol boat at an auction. I removed deteriorated canvas from the cabin roof and put fiberglass in its place. Now the underside of the roof sweats badly. Policemen who worked aboard this boat say she never did that when there was canvas on her roof. Does fiberglass cause sweating?

A. Vapor transmission of the fiberglass covering is probably less than for canvas, but no technical data is available to prove it. Your old boat probably has a few small portholes in the cabin, compared to today's style which has many large windows. We suspect that you don't have enough ventilation. When the boat was doing police duty, and people were aboard all the time, doors and ports were opened and closed much more frequently. Install more ventilators. If you keep the boat at a dock having a 115-volt power supply, put a common household room dehumidifier in the cabin when you are not using the boat. Experiment with its controls to find a setting that will keep the cabin free of sweating while still running the dehumidifier as little as possible. Always shut off this device before refueling and before starting the engine—it probably does not have an explosion-proof motor.

Here are basic fiberglass working tools. Brushes have plain wooden handles and natural bristles that won't be affected by acetone. Rollers shown are but two of many styles and sizes available from supply houses. Common carpenter's knife is ideal for cutting glass fabrics; use plywood or Masonite on workbench surface. Always use a dust mask when sawing or grinding fiberglass.

discard the gooey stuff in the can and put the brush into a small can of fresh acetone. This will keep it clean and soft.

Brushes for Fiberglass Work

Q. What kind of brush would be best for spreading fiberglass resin?

A. Professional shops use "chip brushes." You can get them at any fiberglass supply house and at some marine stores that sell fiberglass, or your hardware store might order some from their suppliers. You may have seen these brushes occasionally at hardware stores. They have unpainted wooden handles and the bristles are of a straw-colored natural material. Acetone used to clean fiberglassing brushes will dissolve plastic handles and soften some synthetic bristles. But it won't touch these "chip brushes." One tip we can give you is that when you put a resin brush back into the acetone can, push it up and down against the can's bottom three or four times to work acetone into the roots of the bristles. Otherwise, resin in the root area will harden and soon you'll have a brush that's too filled with hard resin to be of any use. As work progresses, acetone in the can will become more and more filled with dissolved resin. If left overnight, it can harden and lock your brush into the can. Also, the acetone evaporates, leaving a thicker and thicker mixture of resin and acetone in the can. At day's end,

Work Gloves for Fiberglassing

Q. Does anyone make special gloves to wear while fiberglassing?

A. Disposable plastic gloves sold in hardware stores can be used. Also, cheap rubber gloves that can be discarded will work. Many professional fiberglass men prefer to work barehanded. Gloves soon become so covered with resin and matted glass filaments that the ability to handle tools and use the fingers to press down edges and corners is seriously impaired. It is hard to rinse gloves off, but easy to rinse hands off. If you work barehanded, each time you rinse your hands take a moment to get all resin off your fingernails. As work progresses, resin tends to build up on nails and cuticle—after which it can be very hard to scrape off. Supply houses that sell to professional fiberglass workers often have hand creams designed to work well with resin and special hand cleaners that don't dry out the skin as much as does acetone. Another tip—cured fiberglass has a lot of sharp edges and hard slivers. It's easy to get your hands full of many small cuts. Acetone used to clean the hands will then sting excruciatingly. Wear heavy cotton or leather gloves when handling untrimmed fiberglass parts in order to minimize the number of cuts and scratches your hands will collect.

Chapter 13

Aluminum Boats

Fixing Loose Rivets

Q. *Several rivets have loosened in my aluminum outboard boat. What should I do to stop the leaks?*

A. A workable temporary fix for loose rivets (and weeping seams) is to brighten the metal with abrasive paper around the area to be repaired and then brush on "Pliobond" cement, available in small bottles in most hardware stores. A quick-setting epoxy glue would work well, too.

Also available at hardware stores is a relatively new kind of glue. It comes in very small containers and is advertised as a miracle glue able to fix anything; just a few drops will do the trick. Whatever the brand, it's basically a cyanoacrylic chemical. It dries—or cures—*in the absence of air*. A drop of it on a surface will remain liquid for some time, but a drop of it between two surfaces will quickly set. With a compressed air jet, blow water out of the seam, or let the boat sit in the hot sun long enough to drive all the water out of the seam. Then a few drops of this miracle cement will flow into the seam by capillary action and set. The resulting fix is not only strong and durable, but doesn't show up, as will other adhesives or compounds.

If the rivets are so loose they rattle, find a heavy metal object such as a hammer. Tape the end of it. Place this "bucking bar" against the outside end of the rivet and hold it firmly against the rivet while rapping the inside end of the rivet lightly but smartly several times with another hammer. The tape on the first hammer keeps the heads of the rivets from marring. If this tightening does not work, the rivets may have to be drilled out and larger ones used in their place.

Locating Aluminum Rivets

Q. *Where can I get aluminum boat rivets? Local marine stores don't have them.*

A. That's right—few if any retail stores stock this item. The reason is there is too little call for them. Maybe it shows how little maintenance aluminum hulls need! As there are many alloys of aluminum, one can't use just any "aluminum" rivets one might find. If possible, ask the dealer who sold you the boat about getting some rivets. If he can't help, go to a dealer for some other well-known brand. Any rivets you might get from him will be of a suitable marine alloy. If you live in a remote area, get the names and addresses of one or more manufacturer of aluminum boats in a marine trade directory (*See* Chapter 1, Locating Parts and Equipment).

Paint Remover for Aluminum

Q. *What kind of paint remover is safe to use on an aluminum boat?*

A. Practically any kind sold in hardware and marine stores for general use. But stay away from heavy-duty or homemade removers containing lye. Any caustic-base remover will corrode aluminum. Some removers contain wax, which makes them thick enough so they will stay in place when spread on vertical surfaces. If you use one of them, wax residue must be thoroughly cleaned off with rags and solvent.

Boats, motors, airplanes—all are made with aluminum. But the vital thing for maintenance people to remember is that specially-made aluminum alloys are used in each. When repair work must be done it is important to use the correct alloy. (Alumacraft Boat Company)

For a while, it was common practice to apply several "barrier coats" to an aluminum bottom before applying regular anti-fouling paint. This was a special coating designed to effectively separate the aluminum from the copper paint. It worked on large boats, but on small ones that were often beached the paint soon became scratched, so that the copper could go right to work on the bare aluminum exposed by scratches.

Today we have special anti-fouling paints for aluminum boats. They contain one or another chemical compound based on tin. You will see abbreviations such as "TBTO" and "TBTA" on the labels. They stand for tributyltin oxide and tributyltin adipate. They're chemical compounds that will repel marine growths but which will not harm aluminum. Most major marine paint manufacturers offer a paint of this type and have literature explaining how to apply it.

Early paints of this type sometimes had indifferent anti-fouling capabilities, but much improvement has been made in their power in recent years.

Painting Aluminum Boats

Q. Where can I get instructions for painting my aluminum boat?

A. All major marine paint manufacturers have primers and paints suitable for use on such craft and detailed literature on how to properly use it. If your marine dealer does not have this literature for the brand of paint he sells, insist that he contact the manufacturer and get it for you. Or, get names and addresses of the marine paint firms from a marine guide (*See* Chapter 1) and write to them for it. Painting aluminum boats is not difficult but does have to be done properly to produce good results.

Bottom Paint for Aluminum

Q. I wish to moor my aluminum boat in salt water. Is it all right to put anti-fouling bottom paint on it to repel marine growths?

A. Yes and no. A great big NO for most bottom paints—they contain copper in pulverized form, or copper salts and sometimes other metals, such as mercury. (Mercury bottom paints have been banned in some areas, and are gradually going off the market since they leach mercury into the water, eventually finding its way into the ecological chain.) Any metal in the paint will react galvanically with the aluminum, to the great disadvantage of the aluminum! Some aluminum bottoms have been quickly eaten to next to nothing by bottom paints having a high copper content.

Copper-containing anti-fouling bottom paints can ruin aluminum boats quickly. Marine paint manufacturers thus offer special non-corroding coatings such as this, which contains "TBTA"—short for tributyltin adipate. (Pettit Paint Co., Inc.)

Mysterious Corrosion

Q. Although I used a "safe" bottom paint on my aluminum boat, I find some areas of the bottom are noticeably suffering from corrosion. Should I sue the paint maker?

A. No! It would be wrong to automatically blame him. There are various causes of "mysterious" aluminum corrosion. If an aluminum boat is regularly tied to a dock supported by steel piles, the result is literally to make a bimetallic electric battery there—and it's the aluminum hull which will suffer. Even an old engine laying on the harbor bottom underneath where your boat lies at an otherwise safe dock will cause the aluminum to corrode. If the harbor water is polluted with certain chemicals, that too can corrode an aluminum boat. If there is a badly designed or poorly maintained electrical system in the boat, current from the battery can leak into the hull or into the water under it and cause electrolytic corrosion.

Non-skid Paint for Floor

Q. I like my aluminum fishing boat except for one thing—when it is wet the floor is slippery. How can I put a good non-skid surface on it?

A. Minnesota Mining and Manufacturing Company makes a non-skid product called "Liquid Carpet." Two coats applied with a brush result in an excellent non-skid surface. It looks rather like ordinary paint with sawdust mixed into it, and it feels like a rough sort of crepe rubber underfoot. It also helps deaden noise. When put on in accordance with instructions it works very well.

Attaching Hardware to Aluminum

Q. Please give us some information on how to attach hardware to aluminum boats.

A. If the hardware is of bronze, brass, iron, or steel, it must be separated from the aluminum surface with some kind of insulating gasket. This can be anything that convenience and common sense suggest—a piece of fiber board, a piece of formica, or a gasket made of one or two layers of fiberglass cloth and resin formed into a sheet by laying the cloth out on a piece of glass, soaking it with activated resin, and letting it cure hard, or some kind of sealing compound brushed onto both surfaces and allowed to cure into a rubbery surface, etc. This separation will prevent galvanic corrosion between the dissimilar metals. It is usually safe to attach small stainless steel items to aluminum without such a gasket. (*See* drawing on page 26)

Use stainless steel bolts, machine screws, or self-tapping screws as suits the size, design, and working load of the particular piece of hardware. Although this puts two dissimilar metals in contact with one another, it works satisfactorily in practice and is standard procedure. One reason is that the area of stainless steel is usually relatively small in proportion to the area of aluminum. Another is the fact that the two metals are fairly close together on the Galvanic Scale, which keeps electrolytic action at a low level.

Literature on Aluminum Boats

Q. I want to learn as much as I can about aluminum boats. Is there any book on the subject?

A. Write to Kaiser Aluminum & Chemical Sales, Inc., Technical Publications, Room 1136KB, Kaiser Center, Oakland, Cal. 94643 and inquire about their book, *Aluminum Boats*. It is partly a textbook for designers and fabricators, partly a general guide to aluminum boats for the layman. The price in 1980 was $7.50 plus $2.50 for handling and mailing. *The Boat Owner's Maintenance Manual* by Jeff Toghill, published by John de Graff, Inc., 34 Oak Ave., Tuckahoe, N.Y. 10707 and *Modern Marine Maintenance* by John Duffett, published by Motor Boating and Sailing Books, 224 West 57th St., New York, N.Y. 10019 both have chapters on metal boats that have several pages each on aluminum. The various firms making aluminum boats often have promotional and maintenance literature on aluminum boats, reprints of magazine articles about aluminum boats, etc., so write to them. Reynolds Metals has a booklet called *Dealers Repair Manual for Aluminum Boats and Canoes*. Interested persons can get a copy by writing to Industry Director, Pleasure Boat Market, Reynolds Metals Company, 6601 West Broad St., Richmond, Va. 23261. The Aluminum Association, Inc., 818 Connecticut Ave. N. W., Washington, D.C. 20006 acts as an information center and promotional agency for aluminum products.

Fiberglassing an Aluminum Boat

Q. The bottom of my old aluminum utility has so many loose rivets and small seam leaks that rebuilding it would be about the only way to really fix things. Could I fiberglass the bottom instead?

A. Generally speaking, yes. But the work has to be done properly or the effort can be wasted. Proper preparation of the surface is vital. Sandblasting would be best. It has to be done with care as the blast from a large, powerful rig used to clean heavy machinery, buildings, ships, etc. could eat right through thin aluminum. As an alternative, careful and thorough sandpapering, to leave the metal bright and full of scratches to give "tooth" for the resin, will work. It's necessary to work close up to all the rivets, while at the same time not taking metal off the tops of them.

Epoxy resin would be best, as it will adhere to the metal very much more dependably than will the commoner polyester resin. Manufacturers and vendors of resins and fiberglass supplies have how-to literature. A problem will be that if you fiberglass the bottom only, the edges of the covering must terminate someplace part way up the sides. If there are spray rails on the boat, the fiberglass sheathing can terminate up under them. If there are none, the problem is that the edges of the fiberglass can tend to start separating from the aluminum. With epoxy resin, there's a fair chance things will hold together. Depending on the value of the boat, the amount of work you want to put into the job, etc., you could cover the top edges of the fiberglass with half-oval aluminum strips, or with added-on spray rails made of white oak, mahogany, or teak. Anything that will mechanically clamp the edges and prevent loosening will work. The fiberglassing could be carried all the way up to just under the gunwales in a smaller boat without undue expense on materials.

New Aluminum Boat Leaks Badly

Q. I bought an aluminum runabout because I wanted durability and freedom from maintenance. Now, after only one season of use, I find the bottom has several leaks. The dealer says it's my fault for not trailering it properly. Can I believe this?

A. Yes. If the trailer has too few hull-support rollers, if they are badly adjusted and press unequally against the bottom, and if the tiedown strap isn't tight enough to hold the boat down against the rollers very firmly, the bumps the boat gets when it is trailered can indeed loosen rivets and open seams. If it's a light boat and the trailer has rather stiff springs, you would be surprised what a hammering the hull's bottom can get! This is bound to flex the skin and strain the rivets.

Corrosion on New Boat

Q. My aluminum boat is only a few months old but already the bright surface of the metal has turned a dull grey. I thought these boats were corrosion resistant. What do I do now?

A. There's nothing wrong. The problem is that too few people understand how marine aluminum resists corrosion. It does so by forming an oxide coating on its surface. This has the effect of automatically shutting off further access of the oxygen in the air to the metal. You could compare it to the "self-extinguishing" action of fire-retardant fiberglass—as

soon as it begins to burn it reacts so as to put out the fire. If you prefer the bright, shiny look, you can restore it with aluminum polish.

Tightened Rivets Still Leak

Q. I tightened the rivets on my aluminum boat but the scattered small leaks remain. What do I do next?

A. Many things can go wrong with driven rivets, as can be seen from the following illustration:

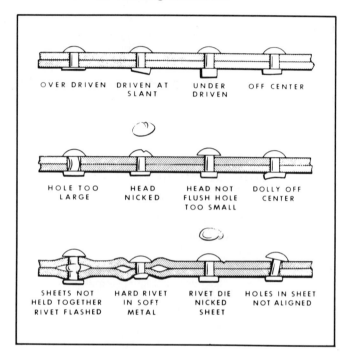

Many things can go wrong when driving rivets.

How to Remove Rivets

Q. Is there any special technique to use when removing old rivets from an aluminum boat?

A. Yes. As the drawing in the preceding question illustrates, if the original hole is enlarged or otherwise distorted, the new rivet cannot be put in accurately. Here's how to do it:

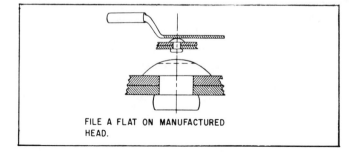

FILE A FLAT ON MANUFACTURED HEAD.

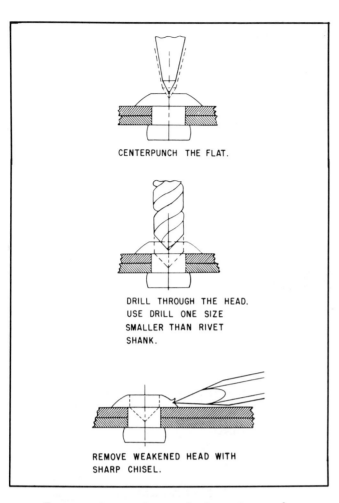

CENTERPUNCH THE FLAT.

DRILL THROUGH THE HEAD. USE DRILL ONE SIZE SMALLER THAN RIVET SHANK.

REMOVE WEAKENED HEAD WITH SHARP CHISEL.

Four steps in removing an aluminum rivet neatly.

Q. *The rivets I was able to get to repair my aluminum boat are obviously too long and must be trimmed down. To what length should I trim them?*

A. The projecting part of the shank should be one-and-a-half times as long as the shank is thick. That is, if the shank is one-eighth of an inch in diameter, trim the rivets off (with a pair of mechanic's diagonal cutters) to a length of three-sixteenths of an inch. See the drawing below, which also shows the ideal amount of setting to give the trimmed-off end:

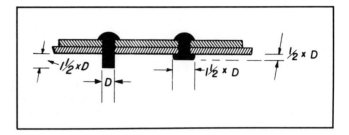

Chapter 14

Steel Boats

Repainting a Steel Hull

Q. I bought a steel cruiser that's in need of painting. Would you be able to advise me on how to do a good job? Do you recommend red lead or zinc chromate primer?

A. Most of the marine paint manufacturers offer lines of primers and paints designed for use on steel boats. Get their literature. We'd recommend choosing one brand of products and using them throughout the job to assure that the primer and paints used will be both suitable to the job and compatible with one another. The recommended way to clean off old paint and prepare the metal for refinishing is by sandblasting. Not only does this get old finish off quite rapidly, it also does it thoroughly and leaves the metal with a surface to which primer can bond most dependably. The work cannot be done by small portable compressors, for they do not have the combination of pressure and volume needed to supply a sandblasting gun. Visit tool rental services in your area and see what they have in the way of gasoline-powered contractors' type compressors mounted on two-wheel trailers. The results can be well worth the rental fee, in time and labor saved and quality of results.

Pitted Surfaces

Q. There are numerous rust pits, below the waterline, in the surface of my steel boat's hull. How should they be filled before priming?

A. An advantage of sandblasting is that the flying grains of abrasive will go into pits and clean them out as completely as the rest of the surface. The marine paint firms offer metal putties to cope with pitting and dents, along with special primers and paints.

Can't Sandblast

Q. There's just no way I can locate a capable sandblasting outfit here in the north woods. How do I best prepare the hull of my steel workboat for painting?

A. Use a heavy-duty disc grinder of the type often seen in auto body shops. Use heavy-duty automotive abrasive discs with it; they will stand the flexing and heat. If you unwittingly use lighter floor-sanding discs, you will find they will crack and break up quickly. Hardware stores sell various kinds of "paint-removing" tools that have assorted small star wheels or free-swinging, hard-wire bristles; we have found they do not have the clout needed to knock old paint off and get right down to bright metal. But some kind of small cup brush in an electric drill, or a pointed grinding stone, will be useful in cleaning out pits.

Paint Job Blistered

Q. I did a good job of refinishing my steel boat, but now a year later there are blisters in the paint. Why?

A. There's no everlasting finish for steel hulls in salt water. After all, when there's nothing else to do, the Navy keeps its sailors happily occupied with the task of chipping rusted spots! No finish is 100% impermeable to water. In time, some moisture gets through to the bare metal under the primer. When iron rusts, it becomes iron oxide, which occupies more space than did the iron itself. It's this expansion underneath the paint that makes blisters form. When the blisters get large enough for the finish to rupture, seawater gets at the metal directly and the rust spots spread rapidly. Then it is time to repaint. That's what shipyards are for!

Paint Job Disintegrating

Q. I had the hull of my steel workboat sandblasted. They did it on a weekday and on the weekend I applied primer. Meaning to do a really good job, I let the first coat dry hard and on subsequent weekends applied several more coats of primer. But only a year later the paint is practically falling off. Wrong primer, bad paint, or what?

A. You goofed twice. Primer must go on immediately after sandblasting, otherwise oxygen in the air will start to work on the very naked metal. It does not matter that it did not rain—oxide formed on the metal from water vapor in the atmosphere and provided a breeding spot for rapid rusting once dampness started coming through the paint skin. And, you put on too much primer. You built up a thick but mechanically weak coating that just would not hold together. The primer sticks to the metal and provides a bond coat for succeeding layers of paint. Paint is formulated to create a tough, durable skin. You begin to understand what we were getting at when we said to choose some brand of paint, then follow that particular manufacturer's instructions to the letter!

Oil Drums into Pontoons

Q. I would like to make a pontoon boat by welding several old oil drums together end-to-end to make the two pontoons. Is this practical?

A. No. The steel is too thin. It is not a matter of mechanical strength. Any well-designed steel boat will be made of metal thick enough to allow for some rusting and still retain adequate strength. Old steel ships are retired when the bottom plating has rusted away so it has become too thin. Your pontoons will last one or two seasons, depending on the paint job and the waters, and then let you down.

Lifeboat Longevity

Q. We bought a surplus steel lifeboat at an auction. It seemed to be sound, but only a few months after we launched it we started finding small leaks all over the bottom. We thought these boats were well made and would last and last. What went wrong?

A. A ship's lifeboat is designed and built to spend years suspended from davits fifty feet above the seawater, then to spend a few days in the water after the mother ship has sunk. If they were made a lot heavier they could be much harder to launch in an emergency. You could try fiberglassing the bottom using epoxy resin but it will cost a lot. Always remember that surplus military equipment is a pig in a poke. Sometimes it's sold off because the forces have too many of an item or just don't need it anymore. Other times it's sold because it has been inspected and found not to be worth the cost of reconditioning.

From Lake to Ocean

Q. We have a fine old steel yacht that has spent its life on a large lake. Now we have retired and live near the sea. Will the paint job that served well on fresh water stand up in salt water?

A. We can't say without knowing more about the boat and the paint now on it. Our gut feeling is that if the boat is worth anything, a new paint job would be very much worthwhile. It will have to be done eventually, so you may as well do it now and be sure that the new paint job is a good one that will protect the boat in its new environment. We would contact a marine paint firm and get their advice.

Zinc Blocks on Steel Hull

Q. On wooden yachts, zinc blocks are installed on the bronze rudder, propeller shaft, shaft strut, etc. Are they also used on steel boats, and if so, how many and where?

A. Yes, they are used. A fair number of them are attached at various places all over the bottom. Contact makers of zinc blocks for their advice as to how many and in what locations they should be installed on your particular boat.

Cannonballs on Compass

Q. In a marine surplus store we saw a compass that had come from a steel workboat. It had arms projecting to each side of the stand and big iron balls—they looked like cannonballs—mounted on these arms to each side of the compass. Why would they bother to put cannonball decorations on a workaday compass?

A. The mass of metal in those balls plays an important part in getting a compass to work properly when it is mounted inside a steel ship's pilot house. They are located so as to have a neutralizing effect on the steel structure's influence on the compass.

Chapter 15

Flotation

Adding Flotation

Q. I've seen a lot in print about new small boats being made with upright flotation. I would like to add this feature to my 14-foot aluminum utility which was made almost 20 years ago. Where can I get instructions on how to do it?

A. To our knowledge there are no instructions designed for do-it-yourselfers. It is not a simple, cut-and-dried procedure. Boat manufacturers employ a 100-page Coast Guard manual. If you want to try to use it, contact your nearest Coast Guard base and ask for the address of the headquarters of the Coast Guard district in which you live. Write and ask for a copy of *Level Flotation Compliance Guideline.*

You would probably not want to do your job with the formality required by a boat manufacturer producing boats for sale. After all, the figuring and testing involved in putting flotation into a boat so it will meet Coast Guard requirements are based on calm water conditions. This is because it would be impossible to reproduce a "standard wave" for testing purposes anywhere, anytime. A boat that will pass the tests in the calm waters of a swimming pool will not necessarily remain upright when it swamps in stormy waters.

Your best bet is to look around at boat shows, marine dealers, and launching ramps for boats similar in design and size to yours. Observe how much flotation they have under seats and gunwales and where it is located. It is not easy to find space in a boat for the needed amount without its obtruding into space needed for the boat's load. Manufacturers don't always get their flotation in just right on the first try; often a number of tests are necessary.

Foam for Flotation

Q. I'm a carpenter. At various lumberyards I see assorted foam materials in board form. Can I use one of these foams for flotation in my homemade boat?

A. Perhaps, but it's not as simple as ABC. To do its job, let alone meet Coast Guard requirements, a foam must be durable enough not to break down from flexing and vibration, must not be affected by water, gasoline, oil or other liquids likely to be present in a boat, and so on. The common very light, soft styrofoam materials in white and light blue colors will be dissolved in a moment by polyester fiberglassing resin. We have seen some urethane-type foam board material from lumberyards used for flotation, but it was mounted well above the bilge area and thus away from water, gasoline, etc. Also, it was completely and securely sealed inside fiberglass materials for mechanical protection. Some lumberyards sell styrofoam logs made by Dow Chemical. These are orange in color and quite bulky. Their prime use is for flotation under docks and rafts. You can saw them up into blocks and strips to fit into available spaces in your boat. They can be covered with glass cloth and epoxy resin, which does not affect this material as does polyester resin.

Floating Power

Q. How much load will a given amount of flotation foam hold up?

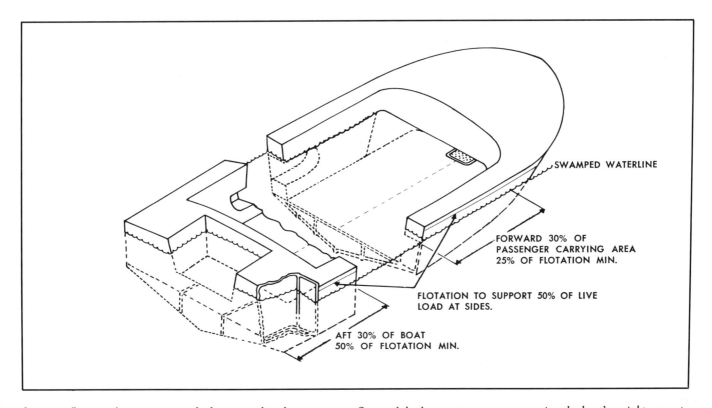

FORWARD 30% OF
PASSENGER CARRYING AREA
25% OF FLOTATION MIN.

SWAMPED WATERLINE

FLOTATION TO SUPPORT 50% OF LIVE
LOAD AT SIDES.

AFT 30% OF BOAT
50% OF FLOTATION MIN.

Locating flotation foam requires calculations and in-the-water tests. Some of the buoyancy goes to supporting the boat's weight, some to supporting passenger weight, and more to supporting the weight of the motor. Proper amount and distribution is arrived at by calculations and tests.

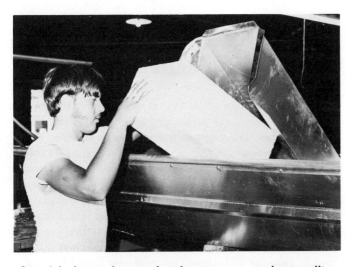

One of the factors that must be taken into account when installing foam is protecting it against mechanical damage and soaking up of gasoline, oil, etc. Here a workman places a precut block of foam under seat of an aluminum boat.

A. Fresh water weighs about 62 pounds per cubic foot. Foams are available in a wide range of densities to fit them to many uses. Weights typically run between five and ten pounds per cubic foot. You can get weight data from the seller from whom you buy foam, or you can measure a piece of it, calculate its volume, weigh it, and divide to get weight per cubic foot.

Will Foam Cause Rot?

Q. I am thinking of cementing pieces of foam to the inside of a plywood boat I am making, before putting in the floorboards and cockpit lining. Will it cause the wood to rot?

A. It could, but there is no pat answer. It depends on the particular boat. There is a good chance of rot if the foam is installed in such a way that it would hold dampness against the wood for an appreciable length of time. You could glue light battens on the inside of the plywood to separate the foam from the plywood and allow both drainage and air circulation. Or, you could brush epoxy resin on the plywood and on the foam, and press the foam firmly against the plywood until the resin has cured. This will seal out water. Read the chapter on wood rot and you will understand the problem better.

Foam-in-Place

Q. Where can I get some cans of the "foam-in-place" type of flotation material?

A. Many large marine supply stores have it. See your marine dealer and ask to look in his wholesalers' catalogs. Look in marine buying guides. If you live near a large city, look in the Yellow Pages for names of firms dealing in foam, flotation, insulation, etc., and contact them.

This material is expensive and you can use up a lot of it. How much the mix will expand depends very much on the temperature in the shop when the work is being done. It won't expand much in cold weather. At normal temperatures it may expand to more than twice its original volume. It can develop a fair amount of pressure when it expands inside a confined space, so it is necessary to bore pressure-relief holes at various likely places in a void being filled. It is possible for foam to push up the floorboards of a boat if holes are not drilled, or to bulge out the sides of the hull. Until you get the feel of this product, mix and pour small quantities at one time; you can always mix up more if needed to fill a given space.

Aerosol Foam

Q. Once I saw an ad for foam material sold in aerosol cans. Now I cannot remember where I saw that ad. I would like to get some of this material to add flotation to my boat; can you help me?

A. This product is available from most fiberglass supply companies. But we do not think it is what you need. You will not get much volume of foam out of one of those cans. They are made and sold for shop use, as a quick and easy way to fill comparatively small voids when doing fiberglass repair work or fixing up fiberglass blemishes to salvage parts in a production shop.

Altering Flotation

Q. My older fiberglass boat has foam flotation under the floorboards. I see now that all the new boats have this foam located higher up. Why the change? How much should I put up under the gunwales of my boat to make it conform to modern ideas?

A. When reading technical literature you will encounter the phrase, "state of the art." Every mechanical or technical innovation goes through various stages of development as time moves on. The cameras of 40 years ago differed from those of 20 years ago and those of 20 years ago are unlike the ones sold today. If you bought a quality camera 20 years ago, you got one that represented the best the state of the art could offer at that time.

The same with boats and flotation. The first all-aluminum and all-fiberglass boats were made of materials heavier than water, so they sank. A logical place to put flotation foam was below the cockpit floor, where it would not take up useful room. The original idea was to keep the boats themselves from sinking and being lost. As time went on it was realized

that foam under the flooring made boats want to roll over when a lot of water came into their cockpits—the foam below the cockpit water wanted to go up, the water wanted to hold it down, a slight roll of the boat to one side let the water slosh off-center, and the upward force on the foam took control so as to roll the boat.

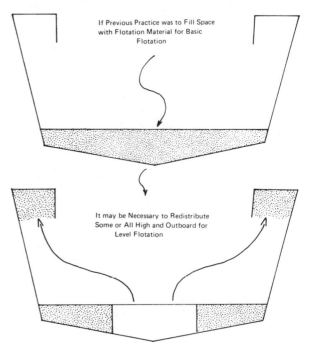

If Previous Practice was to Fill Space with Flotation Material for Basic Flotation

It may be Necessary to Redistribute Some or All High and Outboard for Level Flotation

Ways of doing things change. In the field of boat flotation, all the foam used to be put below the floorboards—it was out of the way, helped deaden wave noises, helped stiffen the hull and floor. Now some of the foam is put higher up in the boat to resist a tendency to roll upside down when swamped.

When small, fast boats suddenly capsize, people often have no chance to grab life preservers in lockers, and then when the boats end up floating inverted, they cannot get at the preservers. It is hard to hold onto the smooth, slippery bottom of a capsized boat; people can become exhausted and lose hold before help comes. Also, when buoyant seat cushions fly overboard during a capsize, they float high on the water and wind can blow them rapidly beyond reach. Upright flotation is supposed to ameliorate such problems.

To achieve it, the usual course is to take some of the foam out of the bilge area and relocate it higher up. Your problem is the foam already under your floor; it will be hard to remove just the right amount, which in most cases is that amount down the centerline of the bottom. If you have to leave it there, the only way to counter its propensity for rolling over is to put an above-average amount higher in the boat. Then there will be a space problem. Some fine boats have been taken off the market because their builders realized it would take too much space or cost too much to modify them to fit the altered flotation foam distribution needed to accomplish upright flotation. Your best bet is to brush up on your seamanship and keep your PFDs in good condition and stowed in an accessible place.

If capsized, a boat having upright flotation will tend to roll right side up again. One with old-style, below-the-cockpit floor flotation will tend to roll over.

Air Tank Flotation?

Q. My fiberglass sailboat has no foam in it that I can find. Will it sink if it should get swamped?

A. Some small boats get their flotation by means of sealed air chambers. For example, in the bows and sterns of some fiberglass canoes you will notice flat plates that seal off the spaces under the short bow and stern decks. That's one common example of air chamber flotation. Inspect the internal structure of your boat, looking for places that suggest they are air chambers. They could be of almost any shape, most likely fitted in under the side decks, or built into the seats. Safety officials generally frown on air chamber flotation, particularly in fast powerboats that take a lot of pounding and shaking in normal use. The possibility is everpresent that the seams of built-in air chambers can open up, so that flotation is impaired to an often unpredictable extent. The rationale for using air chambers in canoes, sailboats, etc. is that because they glide over the water so gently, fracturing of air chamber seams is much less likely. Also, such craft are used mostly on smaller bodies of water where help is quick to arrive after an upset.

Sprayed-on Foam

Q. My outboard boat has some foam-like material under the decks and behind the cockpit upholstery, which I assume

must be for flotation. It is a yellowish-brown color and has a rough surface, somewhat resembling an exaggerated case of poison ivy on one's skin—all lumpy! I had to pull some of it off to do some repair work. Now where can I get something to replace it?

A. You have a problem. That material is urethane foam of the type that is sprayed on with a special gun. It is much used for applying insulation quickly to the rough interior walls and ceilings of industrial buildings. You would have to find a firm that does contracting in this field and has the necessary equipment. They might laugh if asked to do a job as small as yours! Get a few one-quart cans of foam-in-place mixture from a marine or fiberglass supply house. Roll the boat over so the area to be treated is reasonably horizontal. Mix the two chemicals, pour onto the pertinent areas, and cover over with some well-waxed Masonite to make a "dam" to force the expanding foam to conform more or less to the level of the original foam.

Foaming a Surfboard

Q. I have a sailing surfboard which has a hollow fiberglass hull. I'd like to fill it with foam to assure it will never fill with water and sink when I'm out on rough seas. How should I do it?

A. It would be tricky. If you poured all the foam mixture in through one hole, it might or might not reach the far ends of the inside of the surfboard. You would have no sure way of knowing. If you put in too much mixture, or if the shape of the board was favorable, the mixture might expand so forcibly as to bulge out the surfaces of the fiberglass and give you a distorted hull. There are simpler ways to get flotation. If there is a cleanout or inspection plate, remove it and fill the hull with ping-pong balls. We are not being funny. In the early days of aviation, some trans-oceanic airmen put such balls inside the wings of their planes to provide flotation with minimum weight. Or find a few air pillows that will fit through the inspection hole, stuff them in, inflate them lightly and seal. You don't need much flotation in a craft like yours to assure safety.

Mysterious Rubber Plugs

Q. I bought an older fiberglass outboard boat that has not been used for several years. It's in beautiful condition, but one thing puzzles me. At the aft end of the cockpit floor, there is a drop-off and then a low place where the gas tank, etc. goes. On the vertical part of this drop-off there are four holes and each has a rubber plug in it. I am not sure just what they are for and what I should do about them. Do you know?

A. You have a boat that was built to sell for a low price. Air is free and foam-in-place mixture is quite expensive, so the boat's builder opted for air! The plugs are to close the holes to exclude water when the boat is in use. They should be in place when under way. When the boat is ashore or otherwise not in use, remove them to allow air to circulate. If you leave them in all the time, any wood used for reinforcing under the flooring could start to rot due to the humidity in that area.

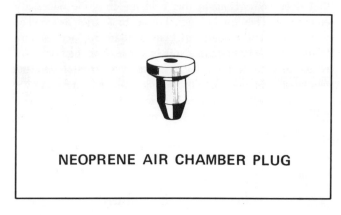

NEOPRENE AIR CHAMBER PLUG

Testing Flotation

Q. I have a 16-foot outboard boat that I use on open water. It has upright flotation. I often wonder what she might do if a big wave swamps her. How can I find out?

A. Remove the motor, seat cushions, instruments and anything else that could be damaged by water or which would be hard to dry out later. Borrow some lead pigs of a weight equal to that of the motor and C-clamp them to the transom where the motor goes. Anchor the boat in waist-deep water. Pull the transom drain plug and watch what happens. It will take a while for enough water to come aboard to start some action. Once it begins to roll or go under, leave it alone so as to see what it will ultimately do. If it rolls over it will probably trap some air under it, which will make it float rather high in the water. The air under it will be blown out the transom drain hole and the boat will gradually settle.

In actual service, of course, the plug will be in place and the air will remain under the overturned boat. This test will give you a fair idea of how much water the cockpit must take to reach a critical stability or flotation point. But just what will happen if you swamp in rough seas is anyone's guess. Ours is that, if it tends to trap air and float high, the seas will roll it over and over until much of the air has been spilled out and the boat will float low enough to stop this rolling over.

If your boat's battery and gas tank are located off-center in the boat, they will affect the boat's rolling-over characteristics when swamped. A typical outboard or small inboard storage battery weighs 50 lbs. ashore and about 25 to 30 lbs. when submerged. Mounted to one side of the stern, it will push that side down, even when immersed.

Full, partly full, or empty, a gasoline tank will have positive buoyancy because gasoline is lighter than water. When full, it will have a slight amount of lift. When empty, it will be very buoyant. If it is mounted on the side opposite to the battery, it will tend to lift that side of the boat. So, the battery and tank working together will tend to roll the boat, possibly with enough force to overcome the stability afforded by a marginal amount of upright flotation.

In Coast Guard upright flotation tests, all seat cushions, cockpit padding, etc., are slashed and the boat is allowed to soak for 18 hours before tests are made. Out on the sea, of course, your upholstery is not slashed and, as it has a lot of air in it, it will add to the flotation to some degree. Depending on its location in the boat, it could aid or enhance your flotation, and probably will further modify it from the standard calm-water testing as done to Coast Guard specifications.

You begin to get the idea—what an "upright flotation" boat will do when she swamps on rough seas is truly hard to predict. The best thing for you to do is to make up your mind that you're not going to panic if the boat does something entirely unexpected, and that you're going to stow those PFDs where you can get at them quickly in an emergency!

Controlling Foam Expansion

Q. If it's true that foam-in-place flotation material can develop pressure when it expands in a confined space, how do boat manufacturers keep it from distorting their boats during construction?

A. By means of clamps, pads, etc. designed to apply countering pressure to the boat's surfaces. These are too elaborate and too much work for a boat owner to attempt just for one-time use. If the shape of the boat is adaptable to it, of course, you can use sheets of plywood, particle board, etc., held snugly in place on the surfaces with wooden props, sand bags, etc.

Removing Wet Foam

Q. How can I remove all the waterlogged foam under the floors of my fiberglass boat?

A. There is no pat answer to this question. Boat structures vary so widely and use so many different foam formulations. Dig out a few small samples and see what common solvents do to them. With hole saws, make holes in the lower edge of the transom about two inches in diameter, and use a long metal rod with bent and/or flattened end to cut and pull out pieces of foam. Try air or water pressure—but don't lift the flooring off its support stringers by using too much!

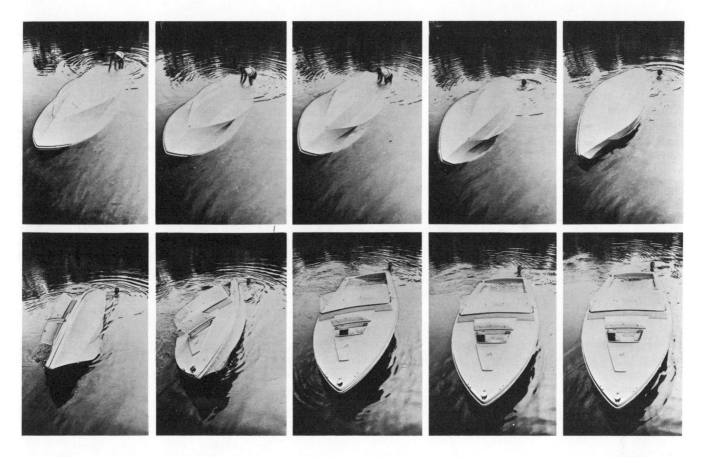

It is hard to hold onto the wet, smooth bottom of a capsized boat. This fellow was lucky—help came in time. There have been capsizings where help came too late. This led to the trend to "upright flotation."

Level flotation works well in calm water. What will happen if the boat swamps in rough water is unpredictable. This swamped boat's motor is still out of water; it could be started and by gunning the throttle much of the water could be made to surge out over the transom. The rest could be bailed out. Coast Guard level flotation requirements apply to boats up to 20 feet in length. (Mirro-Craft)

Air Bags

Q. Sometimes we use our big outboard boat for long trips on open water. At such times we'd like the peace of mind that comes from having more flotation aboard. Where can we get inflatable air bags?

A. Use of air bags for flotation is common practice in Europe, mostly in light, fast racing sailboats. A few companies in the U.S. that specialize in imported marine gear can supply them, or you can order them from England. Their manufacture and widespread use in the U.S. is discouraged because the Coast Guard will not approve inflatable buoyancy devices. By the time a Coast Guard officer reaches a rank that qualifies him for assignment to a tour of duty in Washington, D.C., his entire career has been in and around fairly large craft—from 42-foot utility boats up to 350-foot weather ships. For this reason, the Coast Guard has a "big ship" mentality. In their eyes, a flotation device is something that is stowed in a rack or container for an indefinite period before being grabbed for use in an emergency. They fear the materials used in inflatable emergency gear might dry out and become porous during long storage. They think of an emergency on the water as being a shipwreck or ship collision with jagged wreckage and flotsam all about, and fear an inflatable device might be punctured under such circumstances.

Your best bet is to get an inflatable life raft of the type used aboard aircraft, large ocean racing yachts, and commercial fishing craft. They inflate rapidly when a bottle of carbon dioxide gas is opened, unlike the increasingly popular inflatable boats which are blown up more slowly by hand or mechanical pumps.

If you wish to improvise extra flotation for occasional open-water trips, there's no law that says you can't. Inflated inner tubes have been used. Several 2-liter beverage bottles will displace a useful amount of water and offer some flotation. Ask pizza shops to save for you the 2½-gallon plastic jugs used for shipping cooking oil. One can easily think of other items that cost little and will add buoyancy.

If you ever fall overboard, slip your pants off, close the zipper and tie knots in the lower ends of the legs to close them. Flip the waist of the pants through the air above your head to fill the seat and leg portions with air. The water-soaked fabric will hold air fairly well. Your pants will form a sort of two-legged air bag that will retain air for quite a while and more air can be put in by flipping the pants again.

Chapter 16

Painting

Books on Boat Painting

Q. *Where can I get a good book on how to do boat painting?*

A. If you mean a hardcover book, there is none. Things change so fast in the modern marine paint scene that such a book would be hard to write and many parts of it would soon be out of date. But the several firms in the marine paint field put out excellent booklets that cover the subject well and are always up-to-date. First, visit local marine dealers and ask if they have copies. You may find that many of them don't— too many things are going on in a typical marine dealership for them to keep tabs on endless details like these. So, write to the marine paint firms and ask them for the prices of their "how-to-paint-a-boat" booklets—usually 50¢ or 75¢. As of the time of this writing, their names and addresses are:

Gloucester Paints, Inc., Box 860, Gloucester, Mass. 01930

International Paint Co. Inc., 17 Battery Point North, New York, N.Y. 10004

Jotun-Baltimore Copper Paint Co., 501 Key Highway, Baltimore, Md. 21230

Koppers Co. Inc., 1900 Koppers Bldg., Pittsburgh, Pa. 15219

Pettit Paint Co., 36 Pine St., Rockaway, N.J. 07866

U.S. Yacht Paint Co., Box 96, Roseland, N.J. 07066

Woolsey Marine Industries, Inc., 100 Saw Mill Rd., Danbury, Conn. 06810

Sav-Cote Chemical Labs, Inc., 1094 Rt. 9, Lakewood, N.J. 08701

There are others, but these are the most active in the retail marine paint field. You can always find up-to-date paint manufacturer listings in the annual marine trade directories, such as *Boat Owners Buyers Guide.*

Messy Paint Jobs

Q. *Why is it that some people make an utter mess of paint jobs while others turn out beautiful work?*

A. Alas, the world is full of duffers! They see someone else doing some painting and assume that moving a brush back and forth is all there is to it. But really, it's a form of art, and the ability to do it is acquired by much study and practice. When we worked at the famous Crosby yacht yard on Cape Cod years ago, we did a lot of boat painting and thought we were pretty good at it. Some years later, after we had gotten into the writing game, we visited a famous yacht building company in New Jersey for a plant tour. In the paint shop we saw some finished boats with hull paint so smooth we were sure it had been sprayed on. We asked one of the men how they managed to spray oil-base paint so smoothly —and we were both astonished and humbled when he assured me that the firm's master painters had done the mirror-smooth paint jobs with brushes! So you see, practice makes perfect! Our advice is, don't rush into it. Read as much literature as you can find. If in doubt about anything, practice or make tests on sample panels before rushing to paint a whole boat. Be a fanatic about cleanliness—clean workshop, dust-free air, clean paint brushes—and clean the sandpapered surfaces very thoroughly before starting to paint. Remove most dust with a clean brush, then get more of it off with a vacuum cleaner fitted with a brush tip, then take off as much imbedded dust as you can by wiping thoroughly with a clean cloth that is well dampened with painter's alcohol but is not soaking wet.

Paint Brush Quality

Q. Why do paint brushes vary so much in price?

A. The same reason that fishing reels, cameras, and oil paintings vary widely in price—quality! There are many kinds of paint on the market and all kinds of painting tasks to be done. There are jobs that can be done satisfactorily with cheap brushes, but boat painting is not one of them. Cheap brushes have coarse bristles with square-cut ends and no taper in them. Their blunt ends smear paint rather than spread it out well. A quality brush has its bristles well set in a durable base, and the bristles and brush tip both have taper so that the tip is thin and flexible and a good tool for flowing the paint out smoothly and uniformly. Don't look upon a brush as being a mop to slop paint on with—view it as a fine tool for applying paint uniformly and spreading it out well into a smooth coating. Your public library probably has home workshop and house maintenance books that contain good information on brushes.

Spray Painting

Q. I have a home workshop-type compressor and spray gun. How would it work when painting the hull of my 33-foot cruiser?

A. Probably not very well. Boat paints are formulated to have satisfactory brushing-out characteristics. You'd have to thin one out to make it spray well. Then it would be so thin that it would either be prone to running or would have poor covering qualities. You could spend more time fiddling with the gun and experimenting with viscosities than you'd save going right to work with a brush.

Foam Paint Brush

Q. Paint stores sell bristleless brushes made of a kind of grey plastic foam. How would these work on a boat job?

A. You can try one. We've had fine results with some paints on some jobs and poor results other times.

Using Paint Rollers

Q. To save time and get a more uniform coating, could I paint my boat's hull with a paint roller?

A. Rollers generally work best with latex and matte paints used for household jobs. You'd probably get a stippled or "orange peel" effect using gloss marine paint. Much depends on the kind of paint and the type of nap on the roller you use. Rollers have been widely used for applying anti-fouling paint to hull bottoms. The results are not quite as smooth as with a brush, but the job goes much easier and with less mess since you do get away from the tendency for paint to run down the handle of a brush used on an overhead surface.

Primer vs. Paint

Q. What's the difference between a primer and a paint? Why bother with primer? If you're going to apply a two-coat job, why not make both coats paint?

A. Paint is compounded to give good surface appearance and weather resistance. Primer is compounded to seal the wood, adhere to it well, and sandpaper readily. When paint is used as a first coat, some of the solvent in it soaks into the wood and when the paint dries it has thin spots and may cling poorly later on when it is really hard. It can remain soft so long that good sandpapering is difficult or impossible. When primer is used first, the succeeding coat or coats of paint can dry as the manufacturer intended them to and best results will be achieved. Primer dusts off, paint gums the sandpaper.

Primer vs. Undercoater

Q. At marine stores I see cans labelled "Primer" and "Undercoater." What's the difference, if any?

A. Plenty. A primer is compounded to seal the wood and cling to it well. It contains only a moderate amount of pigment. Undercoater is compounded to go over primer. It is heavily loaded with pigment and is made so it will dry hard in a reasonably short time. It is designed to sand down to a very smooth surface and thus provide an ideal base for the paint. The reason you see so many miserable paint jobs on homemade boats is that the builders didn't use available products properly, either because they were in such a hurry or through ignorance of simple principles.

Why So Many Paints?

Q. Why are there so many kinds of paints on the shelves in marine stores?

A. Fifty years ago all boats had wooden planking. Only linseed oil was available to paint makers to use as a base.

Now boats are made of many materials—conventional wood, plywood, aluminum, fiberglass, you name it. Chemists have created many new oils, resins, and other materials. Some customers want a low-priced paint for cheap or old boats, others want premium-grade paint for expensive yachts. It's like the situation you find in a fishing tackle shop—rods, reels, lines, and lures galore for different pocketbooks and different kinds of fishing. It helps to remember that an object on display in a store that adds to one man's confusion can prove to be the ideal solution to another man's special problem!

Why Not Ordinary Paint?

Q. My brother-in-law owns a paint store. I can get good quality house paint and trim enamel from him at wholesale. Why bother with special marine paints?

A. Trim enamels have been used successfully on small boats such as plywood prams and outboards. But people have also run into problems using common paints on boats! Some white paints that last well ashore turn yellow in a short time when used on boats, due to chemical reaction from gases rising from the muddy bottoms of mooring basins, and from various pollutants found in some waters. A high quality hull paint will have good abrasion resistance, but a house paint is compounded more for self-cleaning action than for abrasion resistance. Sunlight reflects from water much more intensely than it does from grass and shrubbery. A bright red paint that lasts and lasts on a lawn table may fade with surprising rapidity when used on a moored boat. You can get good results from hardware store paints—*sometimes!*

Hard and Soft Paints

Q. They say epoxy paint is wonderful. I was buying some for a kit boat I am making, but when the clerk learned what I wanted it for he switched me to something called "alkyd." The place was busy and I didn't get a very good explanation from him as to why. What can you tell me?

A. Epoxies and polyurethanes tend to form a hard skin. This is good over a hard base like fiberglass. But a paint that is to be used over wood or canvas cannot be hard; it will soon develop cracks because it can't flex and rebound with the material under it. Paint for wood and for canvas (on canoes, etc.) is compounded to remain tough and flexible so it will "follow" the material under it as the material flexes with bumps and swells and shrinks with weather changes. A soft paint put onto fiberglass won't last—gobs of it will be pushed off every time the boat grazes a dock.

Don't Mix Paint Brands

Q. I picked up a carton full of assorted boat paints at a flea market. I used the primer on a plywood rowboat I was reconditioning, then the enamel. The enamel took a number of weeks to set hard and not long after started to slough off. Do you suppose the enamel was "stale" from being in storage too long?

A. No. We can tell without even seeing the stuff what you did wrong. You used one brand of primer and another brand of enamel. Modern paint chemistry is full of complexities; long gone are the days when all paint was just linseed oil, dryer, and pigment. A cardinal rule in boat painting today is *never* use two or more brands of paint on one job! The chances of the formula used in one kind being incompatible with the ingredients used in another are high.

Gloss, Semi-Gloss, Flat

Q. Why do white and black marine paints come in gloss, semi-gloss, and flat types?

A. Various reasons. For interiors of cabins, some boat owners will prefer the soft appearance of a flat paint, perhaps not having had enough experience to realize a flat paint will show smudges and oil spots more and will attract mildew more readily. Some more particular builders of wooden boats prefer to follow the primer with three or four coats of flat white paint rather than one or two coats of undercoater, on the old theory that a number of thin coats makes for a sounder, more durable paint job than a few thick, leathery, or crumbly ones.

Gloss paint is favored by some for interior trim because it's easy to wipe clean, so fat droplets spattered from the galley stove won't spot it. It's used on cabin roofs and sides for a smart, shiny appearance. Used on cabin and hull sides, it has a fault—rainwater that has picked up dust on the topsides will make grey streaks down the hull sides. Semi-gloss is thus favored for hull and cabin trunk surfaces because it shows streaks less. Flat paint is sometimes used on "character boats"—reproductions of classic old time craft—for the sake of historic accuracy. Some long-distance cruising men also favor flat paint on their boats; it chalks more and surface pigment washes off, giving a self-cleaning action. Gloss, semi-gloss, and flat paints are made by varying the ratio of pigment to vehicle, a gloss paint having more oil or resin to make it shine.

"Runs" in Alkyd Paint

Q. I used some alkyd resin-type marine paint on my wooden boat and had a lot of "runs" and wrinkled spots

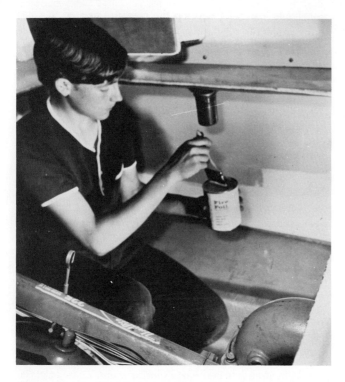

Gloss paint in cabins is easier to clean, shows fewer smudges and is less likely to attract mildew than is flat paint.

appear in it. It was very hard to brush it out smoothly in the first place. Was there something wrong with the gallon of it that I bought?

A. We don't think so. We have had the same problem many times ourselves. It seems to be a characteristic of the resin. Every time we use it, we remember the beautiful brushing-out properties of the old linseed-oil-based yacht paints we used in the past! The paint companies equivocate when one asks them about the poor brushing qualities of alkyd. Other types of synthetic paints have their own brushing quirks. We suspect that the paint people are stuck with alkyd resin for their lower-priced, general-purpose paints partly because each firm sees its competitors offering them, and partly because of a possible supply problem. Linseed oil is made from flax seed. Flax is grown to get fiber for making linen. Synthetic fabrics have made inroads on natural fibers such as cotton, wool, and linen. While the supply of flax seed has probably not increased, the demand for paint has boomed. Paintmakers may have been forced to use synthetic materials to keep up with demand.

To get the best possible results with alkyd paint, do the work when the temperature is 70° or higher and in dry weather. Use a quality brush and spread the paint as uniformly and thinly as you can.

Too Hot to Paint?

Q. I was very anxious to get my yacht into the water and the yard foreman knew it. But he pulled his paint crew off my boat when there was only half a day more of painting to do, claiming, "It's too hot to paint!" Sounds to me as if he employs a bunch of crybabies. Do you agree?

A. No. In very hot weather paint can start to dry or skin over so quickly that it is not possible to brush it out adequately. Painters say "The paint is beginning to pull on the brush!" They knew you wanted a good paint job so they were right in quitting before the heat resulted in a rough, stringy-looking surface due to the "pulling."

Too Late to Paint?

Q. I wanted to take part in sailing races one weekend, but just a couple of hours before quitting time the yard stopped work on my boat claiming, "It's too late to do any more painting!" And it was only three o'clock! I was furious. Have I grounds on which to sue them?

A. We doubt it. When working outdoors, experienced boat painters keep watch on the weather. The crew painting your boat probably realized that damp evening air was in the offing. If they had kept on painting, the last of the paint to be applied might have still been wet when dew settled on it. That would make it "blush," or dry with a milky cast to it. They felt that making you miss the races was the lesser of two evils.

Right or Left Handed?

Q. I was painting my boat's hull when an old coot came along and said, "Buddy, you're painting your boat in the wrong direction—shoulda started on the other side!" Then he walked off shaking his head before I could ask him what he meant! Do you know?

A. Sure—he knew what he was talking about! If one is right-handed, one starts at the stern on the left side, works forward to the bow, then down the other side to the stern. If left-handed, one starts at the stern on the right side and goes forward to the bow, then aft on the left side. Sounds crazy at first. One of the tricks of getting a smooth job is to lift the brush tip off the surface gradually. Proceeding as above, you lay the loaded brush onto unpainted surface in front of you, and sweep the brush to your right, spreading the fresh load of paint out and onto the already-painted surface, meanwhile lifting the brush gradually. Doing it the other way, the loaded brush plops down onto already-painted areas and makes a cowlick-shaped mark. Tack a big sheet of cardboard to a wall and try painting in both directions with some leftover paint. You will soon grasp the idea!

Follow Instructions

Q. *My wooden boat has been out of the water for three years. I wish to apply a well-known epoxy surfacing agent to its bottom. Should I put it onto the dry planking or soak the boat for a while and put it onto wet planking?*

A. Nobody knows all the answers when it comes to the wide range of special coatings on the market that are made by many firms. All we can say is, read the instructions that came with the product and follow them exactly. If you are in doubt about any point, contact the firm that made it for specific advice. Most firms are good about giving useful help, for after all, they want you to get good results and tell others that you are satisfied with their products. In many instances, the various marine trade directories we have mentioned earlier give company telephone numbers. If you're in a hurry, try calling them.

Spatter Paint

Q. *The cockpit of my big outboard boat is rather shabby. Where can I get spatter paint with which to spruce it up? How do I apply it?*

A. Spatter paint is a tough problem for the boat owner. It is done in various ways, practically all feasible only for professional use with appropriate equipment. The stringy-looking "cobweb" pattern is achieved by adjusting a spray-gun nozzle to squirt a fine stream of paint or surfacing gel coat without atomizing it, then waving the gun around to get the pattern. After a lot of experimenting, a few men in some boat factories have hit upon ways of jerking the trigger of a spray gun in such a way as to send vari-sized drops of paint or gel coat flying onto the surface being finished. Sherwin-Williams makes a commercial spatter paint used on store display shelves and cabinets, called "Multi-Color." They used to offer a score of colors, but now are limited to only a black-and-white mix, and we had to visit several Sherwin-Williams outlets to locate a few gallons of it. It smells like lacquer, so we presume it has a lacquer base. They do not recommend it for marine use, probably to protect themselves from complaints as it is manufactured for interior use. We've had excellent results with it in small fiberglass boats, using latex house paint as an undercoat to cover a shabby original finish before applying spatter. We use a "Fiber-Flo" spray gun designed for spraying stucco, flock, etc. and also widely used for spraying gel coat on fiberglass boat molds. Sherwin-Williams says "Multi-Color" can be used in a regular spray gun. Nozzle size and air pressure adjustment are critical to good results. Too little pressure produces a rough, gritty-looking surface; too much blows the color droplets apart and gives a muddy, vague look instead of distinct spots of color. In the past, auto and marine stores have sold spatter paint in aerosol cans, but it's been discontinued. We suspect aerosol

propellants just can't develop the pressure needed to spray heavy materials effectively.

Spatter paint is much used in mass-produced boats. Refurbishing it can be a problem for the boat owner since it is applied with industrial-type materials and equipment. (Sea Nymph Mfg. Div.)

Two-Part vs. One-Part Paints

Q. *Some epoxy and polyurethane paints come in two-part form; you mix the contents of two cans to activate the paint for use. Others come in one-part form, ready to use right out of the can without adding hardener. I'm confused. Why the difference?*

A. Progress in paint chemistry. The two-part types were the first to appear. Further research developed the one-part types. Would you believe they start their curing action by absorbing moisture from the atmosphere—that they are water-activated!

Epoxy Paint Bubbled

Q. *I used some expensive epoxy paint on my boat, following instructions to the letter, but the paint broke out in a rash of small bubbles. Why?*

A. We can't say exactly without knowing more about the circumstances. Perhaps the air was too damp or the temperature too high. Perhaps the epoxy was incompatible with whatever primer or old paint it was applied over. The more exotic the paint, the greater the chance that unanticipated variables can upset its behavior. Write to the manufacturer, giving as much information as possible about the circumstances under which the paint was used.

Epoxy Paint Faded

Q. I intended to use epoxy paint on my reconditioned sailboat but a friend tells me he used it and it soon faded. Why should a high quality paint do this?

A. Epoxy came into wide use because it will adhere well to fiberglass boats. Poor fade resistance was one of its shortcomings. Every product is basically a compromise between conflicting factors. Research goes on constantly to improve fade-resistance. Try some small samples of new-production epoxy paints on test samples and see how you like them.

Alkyd vs. Silicone-Alkyd

Q. Marine stores in my area stock both "alkyd" and "silicone-alkyd" marine paint. What's the difference?

A. Alkyd resin paints appeared in the marketplace first. Paint chemists found that adding silicone to them overcame their tendency to be a bit soft, and improved their water resistance. So silicone-alkyd paints were introduced. Paint firms employ chemists who are always coming up with new things.

Peeling Paint

Q. Every year I have the problem of paint peeling off the sides of the cabin of my wooden boat. It happens mostly around the windows. I sand the bad spots carefully, and use a good primer. But still the peeling.

Paint peeling from woodwork around windows, below railings, etc. shows that water has been leaking in through topside cracks and gaps and is keeping the wood damp. This is a warning that rot-breeding conditions are present. Take corrective action before it is too late!

A. Peeling paint is a sign that the underlying wood is getting wet and pushing the paint off. Check caulking, carpentry, and attaching hardware to find where and how the water is getting into the wood.

Priming Fiberglass

Q. I fiberglassed the cabin roof on my cruiser. Now I need advice. Should I use primer under the epoxy paint I plan to finish it with, or apply the paint directly to the fiberglass?

A. Do what the label on the paint container says. Some fiberglass paints require a primer, some don't. It all depends on their relative hardness when cured, adhesive characteristics, covering power, etc.

Maroon Paint

Q. When it was new, my fiberglass runabout was a nice, rich maroon. Now it has badly faded and I decided to paint it with epoxy paint. But after much searching I cannot find this color in any marine store. Why would this be?

A. The fiberglass factory that built your boat found maroon gel coat in the color chart of some gel coat manufacturer and decided to use it to be distinctive. Many things are made of fiberglass, such as furniture, equipment covers, etc. and maroon is a color that would often be used on such things. Hence the availability of maroon gel coat. But as you can see at any boat show or marina, maroon is rarely seen on boats—it just isn't fashionable. So the marine paint firms see no point to include this seldom-called-for color in their lines. Go to an auto-painting shop and ask the men there if they think they could use their skill at color matching to mix you some maroon paint by adding other colors to a can of red epoxy paint. Some paint firm might be willing to make up a gallon of maroon paint for you.

Fancy Paint Job

Q. I'd like to give my speedboat a flashy paint job patterned after the "flame" color schemes seen on racing cars and hot rods. Where can I get how-to-do-it information?

A. Simply because such paint jobs are uncommon in the boat field, the marine paint firms have no literature on the subject. Here's another case where one would have to look outside the marine field. We'd visit hot-rod supply houses and van and motorcycle customizing shops and ask where they get the know-how. We're told that the Ditzler automotive paint company has a manual on this kind of painting.

Sandblasting a Stern Drive

Q. Marine growths made a dreadful mess of the stern drive units on our twin-engined cruiser. We want to do a fast and thorough job of cleaning them by taking them to a sandblasting shop. A friend says we shouldn't, because the sandblasting will take the special chemical anti-corrosion treatment off the metal. What do you say?

A. We say it is a risky thing to do, but for a different reason. The units are made of die castings. Where strength is needed, the metal is quite thick, but in other areas, such as where the metal is shaped into streamline form for performance, it can be quite thin. The wrong sandblasting technique could eat holes in some very expensive castings! Don't take the parts to a place that uses heavy-duty equipment and a harsh abrasive for cleaning rust off of heavy machinery. Rather, go to an automotive machine shop and have them clean the lower units in their "glass blasting" tank. The abrasive is in the form of tiny glass beads. They will remove paint and dirt, but have less tendency to eat into soft metal and are not likely to eat into aluminum, provided the gun is kept moving. Caution the operator that the castings have thin spots and to go over them just enough to get the metal clean. All stern drive manufacturers sell refinishing kits containing appropriate primers and paint.

Barnacles have made such a mess of these twin stern drive lower units that sandblasting would seem the best way to clean them for repainting. But there is danger of the sand eating through thin parts of the aluminum castings. (International Paint Co., Inc.)

Black or White Hull?

Q. My big wooden cruiser is painted black. We've always wanted to cruise the Caribbean. A friend who has been there says we should repaint the hull white because black will absorb heat, cause the planking to dry out too much, and make the interior uncomfortably warm. Is he kidding me?

A. He's serious. Many boatmen believe as he does. Whether or not you should go to the expense of repainting would depend on conditions. For a few weeks in the tropics it would hardly be worthwhile. The hull sides are not going to get the full blast of the sun's rays constantly—at mid-day they'll be under the overhang of the gunwale, and when the boat happens to be going toward a rising or setting sun there won't be enough heat to really matter. Much would depend on the width and thickness of your planking and how much sunlight might make it come and go. We'd ask people who have had first-hand experience with Caribbean cruising to look at the boat and render an opinion.

Black paint on a wooden hull can cause problems in the tropics.

Wrong Paint Remover

Q. I got a good buy on paint remover at a surplus store, or so I thought! When I brush it on my boat's hull, it just runs down to the turn of the bilge and drips off. What's wrong?

A. Wrong kind of remover. You picked up some that was intended for use on floors, table tops, etc., where it won't run off. For vertical surfaces you need a creamy type that will stay in place. You can try salvaging your bargain remover by thoroughly mixing a modest amount of flour or starch into it to thicken it up. Experiment with small batches to find the right substance to mix with it.

Don't Slop Remover Around!

Q. While stripping paint from my boat's deck I was shocked to see that the remover was eating right into the red and green glass of the navigation light! If the stuff is that powerful, why doesn't it eat up wood, canvas, and brushes?

A. The lenses were not of glass, they were of molded plastic—which of course is readily attacked by the solvents in paint remover. Always remember that there's a lot of plastic on modern boats—lamp lenses, gunwale moldings, windshields, upholstery, and so on.

Sand vs. Skidproofing Compound

Q. *When painting a deck, should I use beach sand or the skidproofing compound sold by marine stores? I favor sand because it's free.*

A. And we favor skidproofing compound! It isn't so terribly expensive, and a little goes a long way. It is of more uniform size than sand so it gives a neater looking job. And the individual grains are well rounded whereas sand grains have many sharp points. The compound grains will give good non-slip qualities, yet they will not abrade skin or clothing if someone falls or slides on a deck.

Before or After?

Q. *Should non-skid compound be mixed into paint or be spread onto it after the paint has been brushed out?*

A. Mix it into the paint. You will get much more uniform, better looking coverage. Keep stirring the paint as you progress, for the compound will settle to the bottom of the can rather quickly.

Teflon

Q. *Do you think it is advantageous to apply Teflon paint to the bottom of a boat to improve its performance?*

A. Some low-friction bottom coatings have proven to be useful. It's a complex subject, though. On a smaller boat, such as an outboard, it's a question of whether you'll save

enough gas to cover the cost of a special paint. On big boats, the problem is the cost of hauling them out to apply it. Various types and brands of low-friction paint come and go from the marine market. The last we heard from DuPont, they were still evaluating the usefulness and adaptability of Teflon for boat hulls. We know that the outboard motor firms offer Teflon-coated propellers that seem to pay off in performance. The scene changes constantly. Write to DuPont for latest literature on Teflon in marine applications. Address it to E. I. DuPont de Nemours & Co., Teflon Div., 1007 Market St., Wilmington, Del., 19898.

"Sandpaper"

Q. *I am confused about the many kinds and colors of sandpaper on sale. What's what about them?*

A. Common "sandpaper," made with flint grains and having the familiar tan-yellow color, is too soft and short-lived to be of much use. Painters use it for smoothing of primer before applying succeeding coats; it's hard enough for this and, since it clogs fast on such jobs, little money is lost when it is soon discarded. Garnet paper, having a rather orange tint to it, costs more but is harder. It's an excellent general-purpose abrasive for woodwork, but won't last long when used with any but the smallest, least vigorous power sanders. "Production paper," either dark tan or white in color and made with aluminum oxide or silicon carbide synthetic abrasives, is the only kind that will stand up under the force of a medium- or high-power electric sanding machine.

Waterproof Sandpaper

Q. *What is the advantage of waterproof or so-called "wet-or-dry" sandpaper?*

A. For fine work, such as polishing fiberglass and doing auto body and outboard motor refinishing, the water used with it serves useful purposes. By keeping the working surface wet, it keeps down dust when doing finer sanding. It acts as a lubricant, producing a better, smoother cut. And it keeps fine dust from clogging the abrasive too soon. Leading abrasives manufacturing companies, like Norton and Behr-Manning, have good literature on abrasives of all kinds; get it from better hardware stores, wholesalers, mill supply houses or write to the abrasives firms.

Power Sanders

Q. *What's what about the various kinds of electric sanders?*

A. "Finishing sanders," with rectangular pads that vibrate or oscillate, are for light work. Cheap ones lack real power; good ones can smooth up large, flatter surfaces quite well. Don't use a too-coarse abrasive; it will make thousands of small circular scratches that will show through varnish or thin paint. Belt sanders are for large, flat surfaces and very vigorous cleaning-off and smoothing-down work. They are useful for cleaning up boat bottoms, but they are heavy and powerful and call for some muscle to control well. They will grind a flat spot if left too long at one spot on a curved surface. Disc sanders are good for rough work and rapid cleaning off of old bottom paint, rust, etc. They will quickly cut crescent-shaped scratches into a surface, so they are not good on the smooth topsides work on boats. They can do fine finishing work when fitted with soft foam rubber pads to which the abrasive discs are attached with an adhesive. Get literature from manufacturers of sanders to bone up on the subject.

Hand Sanding

Q. I see a lot of hand sanding being done at our boatyard. Is this another way in which they run up big bills?

A. No. The topsides of boats—especially wooden ones—are often broken up into many small surfaces with lots of angles, such as around windows and doors, at toe rails and trim strips, etc. A power sander can make a mess if used for such work. Hand sanding gives the most sensitive, accurate control of what the abrasive is doing. So it does the best job at many points on boats. It isn't all that tiring, for it can take time and effort to run extension cords to a boat and then keep an electric sander under control and held up against a surface.

Boot Top Paint

Q. What is the "boot top paint" I see on marine store shelves? How does it differ from other marine paints?

A. It's made so that it dries harder than bottom paint. This makes it better able to resist the occasional scrubbing to remove beginning accumulations of marine grass. It also contains enough chemical to give it a moderate amount of anti-fouling quality, so as to discourage such grass from attaching. It comes in various colors to suit boat owners' preferences on color schemes.

Waterline Tape

Q. The waterline stripe on my fiberglass outboard boat appears to be made of some kind of tape. It is torn at several places. How can I repair it?

A. You are right, it is tape. Marine supply stores sell it in a variety of widths and colors. It is made of a durable, water-resistant plastic such as mylar and has a pressure-sensitive adhesive on its back side that stands up to marine conditions. Usually, a strong, steady pull will get it off. If necessary a heat lamp or gun can be used to loosen stubborn adhesive—but keep it moving lest you scorch or spall the gel coat.

No Waterline Grooves?

Q. I hung around a boatyard when I was a kid and remember the wooden boats had lines cut in their planking to make guides for painting in the waterline and boot top. Now the fiberglass outboard boats we have lack such a useful feature. Why?

A. Various reasons. A large number of such boats are kept on trailers or in algae-free fresh water lakes, so they don't need anti-fouling bottom paint—hence no waterline stripes are needed. Some boatbuilders fear that molding such grooves into hulls might create starting points for cracks. If made deep enough to be really useful, they could interfere with lifting finished fiberglass hulls from the mold. But above all, the maker of an outboard boat has no way of knowing how heavily each of the boats he makes will be loaded by its owner. Outboard motor weight varies. Some boats will have electric batteries (about 40 lbs.) and others won't. Some will be loaded down with equipment and others will be moored almost empty. There is no way to know how deeply each boat they ship out will settle in the water.

Marking Waterline

Q. There is no waterline marking on my boat. I wish to apply one. How do I get a good, straight line, and how do I tell where to locate it?

A. When larger boats are being designed, naval architects calculate hull volume and figure where the water will come on the sides of the hull. The people and equipment added to a large boat are a much smaller proportion of its weight than with smaller craft, so larger boats will settle much less when equivalent items are put aboard. It's feasible to paint a waterline on before launching. The best way to do it with a smaller boat is to load it with such items as will normally be aboard when it is floating at its mooring, launch it in shallow water, wade in alongside it and mark the actual waterline with a soft pencil. Then haul the boat, let it dry, and apply masking tape an inch or so above the pencil line to allow for mooring basin waves lapping up on the sides.

There are various ways to get a true line. Don't put on masking tape a foot or two at a time—a wavy line is sure to result. Stick a few inches of the tape to the side of the boat at the stern, walk forward letting tape unroll for the full length of the hull, hold good tension on it, and "walk" the front end of the tape in toward the bow taking care to hold it at the same level. It will go on much straighter.

Tape at Spray Rails

Q. *The factory put waterline tape on my boat on the hull sides just above the spray rail. It runs the full length of the boat so the "waterline" curves up at the bow. I want to put paint on the bottom but don't want its color showing well above the water. How do I lower and straighten this tape?*

A. Sorry, no way. The tape is much less flexible than paint flowing off a brush, if you grasp what we mean. If you try to carry the tape over the angles formed by the spray rails, it won't want to conform to the shapes involved and will go on with wrinkles or warps. This quirk is exactly why factories put the tape on following the curve of the spray rails. The only thing you can do is float your boat, pencil on the water level, apply masking tape (which is made of puckered, and thus flexible, paper) and paint a line on.

Multiple Stripes

Q. *My boat is bare and colorless. I have seen boats with waterline stripes consisting of two and even three lines, sometimes of varying width. I bought one roll of wide waterline tape and one of narrower tape, to put such a line on my boat. Try as I did, I could not put the two tapes on at a uniform distance from one another and the slight wobbliness is only too visible. How do factories do it so accurately?*

A. They use a kind of waterline tape in which the two or three stripes are printed on a single strip of tape, with transparent spaces between the lines. It goes on just as any other single-piece tape—so the spacing between the lines is perfect. With a little looking around you can find this kind of tape in marine supply houses.

Molded-in Waterlines

Q. *Sailboats and cruisers often have their waterline stripes beautifully applied with gel coat in a contrasting color. It is perfectly smooth and blends into the background color flawlessly. How can I apply such a stripe to my boat?*

A. You cannot. It's done during manufacture in a way that cannot be duplicated in the field. Masking tape and paper are applied to the surface of the hull mold so as to mark off the waterline. Assuming they want a red stripe on a white hull, they will spray red gel coat on this masked area and after a suitable wait will pull off the masking tape and paper. Then the white gel coat is sprayed all over the mold, covering the red stripe. When the finished hull is lifted from the mold, there is the red waterline stripe smoothly and permanently incorporated into the hull's outer surface.

Varying Stripe Width

Q. *I own a trailerable fiberglass sailboat. I bought some two-inch waterline striping tape and put it on. It does not look right at all. It appears to be wide amidships and narrow at the ends when looking at the boat from some distance away. What do I do?*

A. The effect you have is caused by the curvature of the hull sides. Toward the bow and stern there is more vee in the hull sections than at the waterline level amidships. Your two-inch tape conforms to this shape; thus it has a twist in it that makes it appear to be narrower from any distance away. Look at the waterlines on some large sailboats. As you look up at them from under their bows and sterns you will see how the lines appreciably widen out. When viewed from some distance away, of course, this compensates for variations in hull shape and makes the lines appear to be of uniform width. Remove the tape and go to work with masking tape and paint.

Don't Paint Transducers!

Q. *We installed a depth sounder on our ocean-going boat. At launching time an argument ensued as to whether or not anti-fouling paint should be applied to the instrument's transducer mounted on the bottom of the hull. Some of the fellows said it should be done, others were completely against doing it. Who's right?*

A. Don't put regular anti-fouling bottom paint on a transducer. The copper or other metallic salts or powder in such paint will seriously affect the operation of the device. To keep marine growths off of transducers, some of the marine paint firms offer a special transducer paint that will not affect them electrically.

Chapter 17

Varnishing

Information on Varnishing

Q. People in my rural area don't know much about the fine points of boat work. I have to do a lot of varnish work to fix up the old boat I bought. How can I learn to do a good job?

A. The marine paint companies have literature on painting that includes coverages of varnishes—see Chapter 16 on Painting for their names and addresses. The various books on boat maintenance currently in print treat the varnishing matter rather superficially—one to three pages, mostly duplicating what's in the paint companies' literature. From time to time, the boating magazines have printed articles on varnishing. You can write to them asking if back copies or photocopies of more recent varnishing articles are available. Boat varnishing isn't so very different from other kinds of varnishing. Books on painting, home maintenance, craftsmanship, etc., at your public library probably contain varnishing information.

Varnished wood lent an air of warmth and richness to wooden boats that is sorely missing in today's fiberglass craft. If you were to find and restore such a boat today, you would have a treasure.

When to Revarnish?

Q. There's plenty in print on "how to varnish," but none of it that I've seen answers the big question—"when does one know it's time to revarnish?"

A. The right time is when you first notice a slight dulling on the surface of the original varnish. This is the precursor to more extensive deterioration, such as crazing, cracking, and peeling. *This* is the time to revarnish! Most boat owners put it off, thereby causing themselves a lot of unnecessary work and expense. The job will be agreeably quick and easy if done before the initial surface has begun to develop checking and flaking. A light but thorough sanding with medium-fine or fine abrasive paper will remove the dead surface varnish and leave a sound, well-dulled surface for the fresh varnish to cling to.

His Varnish Blistered

Q. Little over a month after I revarnished the mahogany seats in my outboard boat, the new varnish started to blister and peel off. It was a high-quality varnish, too. What would cause this?

A. There are various possible causes. The wood or the surface of the old varnish may have been damp. If you applied more than one coat, you might not have allowed adequate drying time between coats—solvent remaining in the first coat would have been trapped in it by the second coat. Later, under the sun's heat, solvent in the first coat would vaporize and raise bubbles in the top coat.

Or you may have used incompatible varnishes. The popular polyurethanes often give this trouble; they don't want to adhere to hard old varnish when applied as fresh coats. Varnishes are now marketed that are made with various natural and synthetic oils and resins. Molecular structures vary and some just do not want to cling to others. It is often difficult to tell what kind of varnish is already on a boat, so it's easy to blunder into the incompatibility trap. Whenever possible, try new varnish on an inconspicuous place and wait a week or two to see how it behaves.

Urethane or Polyurethane

Q. What's the difference between urethane and polyurethane varnish?

A. Same thing. "Polyurethane" is technically correct but it's such a mouthful to pronounce that people shorten it to urethane.

Varnish Sloughed Off

Q. When I started to varnish the mahogany on my boat, the top coat of varnish peeled right off the underlying coat and I ended up with a pile of peeled-off varnish flakes. Can you explain this?

A. Was the boat relatively new? Then we suspect we know the answer. In volume production work they just can't wait for several coats of varnish to dry hard so each can be sandpapered prior to application of the next coat. They use "production finishes," usually fast-drying and often thinned for spray application in a heated pot. Another coat is put on as soon as the preceding one has set firm enough to hold its shape, while still being soft enough to let the next coat adhere to it. You can usually tell this kind of varnish job by its leathery-looking surface, with numerous small depressions that were not filled by repeated sanding and varnishing. An expertly done brushed-on varnish job is as smooth as glass because all such depressions have been filled by the repeated sanding and recoating. In your case, possibly the last coat was put on after the men came back from lunch; the previous coat was a little on the hard side, so it held the last coat all right against weather but the pressure of sandpapering was enough to break it loose. Keep sanding until you get down to solid varnish or bare wood.

Varnishing Procedure

Q. Tell me how to do the best possible job of varnishing the spruce mast and mahogany trim on the nicely executed homemade sailboat I'm finishing up.

A. Woods such as oak and mahogany are first treated with "paste wood filler" to fill and seal the pits in their grain structure. These pits are where low spots in the varnish film get started. When the filler is so dry you can feel there is no more solvent left in it to cause trouble, apply the first coat of varnish after thinning it approximately 10% with whatever kind of thinner the label specifies. Expert varnishers disagree about thinning—some feel it helps the first coat penetrate and "lock" to the wood, others feel straight varnish will adhere well if brushed in carefully and that using it speeds up the "build."

When the first coat is hard enough to sand without gumming the paper, go over it lightly with medium-fine paper, just well enough to cut off any "fuzz." The second coat may be thinned slightly or put on full strength, depending on how you judge the first coat to have penetrated and filled the grain. A decent-looking varnish job requires at least four coats, more likely five or six, and for a really durable, supergloss job, anywhere from seven to nine. Each time you sandpaper a coat, you must keep at it gently but diligently until all traces of gloss have been removed.

Paste Wood Filler

Q. What is paste wood filler and how is it used?

A. It's a preparation that contains a solid material that will fill pores in wood to provide a level surface from which to start a varnishing job. It comes in clear, red, and brown colors. The coloring is imparted by a stain that shades the wood. It is possible to varnish mahogany without using this product, and it's often done in volume production work to avoid the time and labor involved. Wood not treated this way is easy to spot because it has a distinctive appearance. The grain is very easy to see in detail and the overall shading tends to be on the light, mild side.

Some woods, such as Philippine mahogany, show considerable variation in color in the raw state. The stain in paste wood filler brings the assorted colors in a structure made of several pieces of such wood closer to uniformity. When boatbuilders use this filler on mahogany, they generally choose the red color (actually more of a chestnut-brown). The brown tends to give an odd appearance to mahogany, with the brownness and darkness of walnut but without the pleasant grain pattern—rather a muddy appearance that just does not look right on a boat. Every can of paste wood filler has instructions on the label—do exactly what they say, even if it "goes against your grain." Depth of color can be varied by leaving the stain on the wood a shorter or longer time. Don't let it dry too much or it will be hard to wipe off.

Cleanliness is Vital

Q. I did what I thought was a fine job of revarnishing the woodwork on my boat. Next morning when I looked at it I was dismayed to find it had dried with a rough surface that had to be redone. What did I do wrong?

A. You were probably casual about the matter of cleanliness. Much more so than with paint, a fresh coat of varnish will show up dirt specks. The work place must be clean and free of drafts. Some experts won't varnish on a windy day, nor in a shop where people are walking around in an upstairs room. A little wind or vibration can start dust shaking off of overhead structures. Dust from sandpapering must be thoroughly cleaned from the work with a brush, then vacuum cleaned, then wiped with a cloth dipped in alcohol, and finally with a tack rag. A tack rag is a piece of cheesecloth impregnated with sticky varnish so it will pick up and hold specks of dust and grit. Hardware and paint stores sell them.

Never use a brush that has been in paint—some of the color is bound to remain in the heel of the bristles and will bleed out into the varnish. A varnish brush that was haphazardly cleaned the last time it was used will have bits of dried varnish in its heel that will work down and cause specks in the finish. Some experts keep their brushes in kerosene, diesel oil, or raw linseed oil when not in use, claiming that if one is kept in turpentine, remnants of the turpentine remaining in the heel of the brush will seep down and cause "mysterious" dull streaks in the varnish.

Handling Varnish

Q. I was at a boatyard. A kid working in their marine store put a can of varnish in the paint agitating machine. The boss came along, saw it, and blew up, claiming varnish must not be agitated. What's this all about?

A. We don't blame the boss for blowing up. There is no pigment at all in varnish, so—once you think it over—you will realize there's no need to stir it before use! Stirring fills it with bubbles that have a way of showing up later, causing a poor job.

No matter how carefully a surface to be varnished is cleaned, your brush will pick up dust as it works across the surface. Some of this dust will be carried back to the can when the brush is reloaded and the surplus load wiped off. As the contents of a can are used, dust accumulates in its bottom. The last inch or so of varnish in the can will give you a "mysteriously" rough tail-end to an otherwise good varnishing job. It's easy to keep brush dust out of the can. Pour an inch or so into a shallow tin can, such as one that cat food or tuna fish came in, and which has been very well cleaned. Dip your brush into this. If you need more, pour it from the big can. When the job is done, any small amount remaining in the smaller can should be discarded instead of being poured back into the main can, so its load of brush dust won't contaminate the remaining varnish.

Varnish Brushes

Q. I was buying supplies at a marine store, among which was a quart of varnish. The clerk asked me if I wanted a brush to go with it, so I said yes. When he was adding up the bill I was horrified to see he put down $12.95 for this little two-inch brush. You can get a brush at any hardware store for a tenth of that price! I would not take it. Seems to me there's a racket going on of printing the word "marine" on stuff and selling it for a lot more than the same things sold in hardware stores. Why don't consumer agencies get after the marine industry?

A. We can think of some things that are overpriced, but a good badger hair varnish brush isn't one of them. Go back and take a close look at that varnish brush. See how finely tapered it is? Look closely at the tips of one of the hairs and see how it is tapered, even subdivided into smaller ends at the tip. It is made to do a really good job of spreading out and smoothing down varnish. It is one of the keys to doing beautiful work. For occasional jobs you can do acceptable work with a $3.00 or $4.00 hardware store brush, but a real yachtsman or a professional boat painter will use a varnish brush—and take as good care of it as a test pilot does his parachute!

Pimples on Varnish

Q. When I finished, I thought I had done a good job of varnishing the brightwork on my cruiser. I went home. When I returned the next day I was dismayed to find the surface was covered with countless small bubbles. I did not stir the varnish. What might have happened?

A. Did the sun start shining on the varnish as it moved across the sky? Was it a very hot day? Varnish dries from the outside in; a slight skin forms on the surface exposed to air and has a slight tendency to trap solvent in the underlying varnish. A normal rate of drying will allow solvents to work their way out. Heat will accelerate formation of the skin, and at the same time make solvent under it vaporize more. The vaporized varnish can't get through the skin fast enough so it forms many small bubbles.

Handling a Weathered Boat

Q. I bought a used boat that had been neglected. It's basically sound but needs a going over. The old varnish is peeling, some of the wood has weathered—it's a mess. What do I do?

A. After all old varnish has been stripped and the bare wood sanded as smooth and clean as possible, take stock of its condition. Chances are it will exhibit a range of colors, from clean natural wood through water-stained and sun-bleached spots to scattered black stains. Try bleaching to restore it to uniform color. Paint stores sell wood bleaching products. The Forest Products Laboratory, U.S. Dept. of Agriculture, P.O. Box 5130, Madison, Wis. 53705 has a free booklet titled *Bleaching Wood*. There are many chemicals that can be used. If you achieve a reasonably uniform appearance but have inevitable scattered spots of varying color, try red paste wood filler, leaving it on as long as possible without running into difficulty in wiping it off. This should mask discolorations and give an acceptable appearance. From there on, varnish the work as you would any other job. If you cannot get the wood looking decent, it would be better to cover it with a good paint job.

Bleaching with Clorox?

Q. Is it possible and safe to use Clorox to bleach wood?

A. We've tried it on small samples and it works well. For some reason it is not standard practice; we don't know why. We would not expect it to harm wood or other boat parts any more than some of the strong chemicals used in bleaching preparations. After all, it is used for household jobs where it comes in contact with a lot of wooden items. Write to makers of household bleach and ask for any available pamphlets on the varied uses of their product.

Oiling Mahogany

Q. Instead of revarnishing the mahogany on my boat, could I use teak oil on it?

A. As far as looks are concerned, the results could be anything from good to poor, depending on the kind of oil you use and the coloring, etc., of the mahogany involved. We know that marine paint firms have made up bulk orders of a special mahogany oil for scattered boat manufacturers who wanted to oil their mahogany to save the expense of multi-coat varnish jobs. We have never seen it stocked in retail-size containers. The natural oil in teak keeps water out and makes this wood very stable against swelling and shrinking. Mahogany would not have this advantage and we suspect that just oiling the surface would leave it liable to expansion and contraction to the point of giving joint or fastenings trouble. Better stick to varnish.

Varnish Durability

Q. How much time can pass between revarnishing jobs?

A. How many inches of rain are going to fall on your town next month? There's no way to say for sure. Varnishes vary in durability, but this does not mean some are good and others defective—varnishes are made and used for many purposes. Of course, you will buy a recognized brand of varnish made by a marine paint firm for use on your boat. Many of these varnishes contain a chemical additive that helps them resist the sun's rays and thus retain their gloss longer. A boat used in the north for a few months in the summer may get by with a yearly revarnishing. But one that is used all the time in the deep south or tropics may need two, three, or four revarnishings per year. Covered docks are popular in southern waters because they keep rainwater and sunlight off of boats. These are the two biggest enemies of wooden boats. It comes down to the key point—if you revarnish when the first dullness shows on the surface, the work will go easily and quickly and the underlying bulk of the varnish will last and last. If you neglect to do this on even a superb varnishing job, as soon as crazing appears it will go bad with ever-accelerating rapidity!

Spar Varnish

Q. Just what is "spar varnish?" I see this term often on varnish containers.

A. It originally was used to differentiate weather-resistant outdoor varnishes from indoor types that were used on furniture and could not stand water without spotting. It has become a catchall phrase that generally means a good, durable varnish satisfactory for outdoor applications.

Prime with Shellac?

Q. My dad was a great furniture restorer. He always used white shellac for the first coat when varnishing a fine piece

Keeping varnish in good condition on a wooden boat is an endless chore, but when done well the results can be most satisfying.

of furniture, and got beautiful results. Any reason why I should not use his method on my boat?

A. Yes. Shellac has poor water resistance. Regardless of the quality of varnish you put over it, you won't get a job with good moisture resistance.

Steel and Bronze Wool

Q. I used fine steel wool to prepare the surface of old varnish on my boat for a fresh coat. A few days later I found thousands of little rust spots all over the deck. I've seen professionals use steel wool. How do they avoid the rust spots caused by bits of metal that drop from it?

A. You did not look closely enough. Those pros were using bronze wool. Fragments from it will not cause rust spots. Most marine stores in yachting centers carry it. The same firms that make steel wool also make bronze wool. You will find that there are a lot of backwoods and johnny-come-lately marinas and boat shops that don't carry it and never heard of it. You'll have to educate them. You can get it from marine mail-order firms. (*See* Chapter 1, Locating Parts and Information.) The main advantage of a metal wool over abrasive paper is that it will conform to round and concave section mouldings better than paper and minimize chances of cutting through the varnish at corners.

Varnish on Salt Water

Q. Our mahogany speedboat has always been used on a lake. Now we have a chance to spend a summer on the seacoast. Can you recommend a varnish that will withstand salt water?

A. Use any well-known brand of marine varnish. Salt water won't hurt it. After all, you never saw salt from perspiration take the varnish off a baseball bat or a piece of furniture. Because salt water is hard on metals, people seem to think it is hard on paint and varnish too. But there's nothing in a finish to corrode! Salt does hurt finishes in an indirect way, though. When salt spray dries and is allowed to remain on varnish, the flecks of crystal act like many small lenses to focus the sun's rays on the underlying varnish. Spotting results. Prevention is simple—rinse the boat with fresh water at the dock at the end of each day on the water. If this is not done, even a quality varnish will suffer.

Non-skid in Varnish

Q. Can the non-skid compound sold by marine paint firms be used in varnish as well as in paint?

A. It could be mixed in, and it would spread out. The trouble will come at refinishing time. It would be difficult to sandpaper such a rough surface well enough to assure that the fresh coat will adhere. You would do better to make use of the non-skid stripping with self-adhesive backing that comes in rolls and is sold by the foot in marine stores. Leave it on permanently and varnish around it.

Chilled Varnish

Q. What is "chilled varnish?"

A. Regular varnish will thicken, or at least not spread well, when too cold. An old-time yachtsman named H.A. Calahan found a way to mix varnish so it would spread well when cold. The container was set in a bucket of ice cubes when being used. The coldness kept an early surface skin from forming, giving solvent more time to evaporate early in the drying process. A richer, more durable finish was achieved and varnishing could be done in poor weather. The product has been on and off the market irregularly in recent years. Proliferation of aluminum masts and the popularity of oiled teak makes it hard for a small company to market a varnish.

Chapter 18

Anti-Fouling Bottom Paints

Why Paint the Bottom?

Q. I am new to boating, but already I have run into a lot of talk about the importance of putting an anti-fouling paint on the bottom of a boat. Just what is all the fuss about?

A. Hundreds of small marine organisms live in seawater. Some are small forms of shellfish, such as barnacles, which attach themselves to any available surfaces. As they grow in size and number, their roughness can increase hull drag appreciably. There are a variety of grass- or scum-like growths which also attach to surfaces and add their share to drag. There are some creatures, such as teredos ("ship-worms") and some buglike things called "gribbles" that eat into wood and riddle it with holes.

Anti-fouling paints keep such organisms from attaching themselves to boats that are left at moorings or docks for any length of time. While the kinds of creatures that bore into wood cannot harm fiberglass, anti-fouling paint is still needed on fiberglass boats to repel surface-attaching creatures, which can build up quite a thick layer of fouling in the course of a summer. In fresh water, boats sometimes collect an objectionably thick coating of algae. In addition to making the bottom rough and hurting performance, the stuff is quite a job to clean off.

Because there are so many types of boats operating under such a variety of conditions, there are many anti-fouling paints on the market. It is a very costly proposition to haul a 100-foot yacht out onto a marine railway and hire a crew of men to scrape and repaint the bottom. So an expensive paint

that retains its anti-fouling properties for many months can pay for itself by making haul-outs less frequent. On the other hand, there are rafts, floats, and workboats that move slowly or not at all and are hauled out at the end of each summer to save them from winter damage. For these, a low-cost paint is adequate.

How Does Bottom Paint Work?

Q. Someone told me that the copper dust which anti-fouling paint contains reacts with salt water to set up a galvanic electrical field that repels marine growths. Is this so?

A. Your informant was either confused or kidding you. The copper is poisonous to small marine creatures. This element can be used either in the form of finely powdered metal or in the form of some salt of copper. Anti-fouling paints have also been made using arsenic and mercury as the toxicants, but in many areas these have been banned as dangerous to humans, to the environment, or both. Anti-fouling paints made for use on aluminum boats contain one or another tin-based compound such as tributyltin oxide, commonly abbreviated as TBTO. It will not set up destructive galvanic corrosion reactions with the tin as will copper, mercury, etc.

To be technically accurate, these products made for boat bottoms are not paints but "coatings." They are not applied

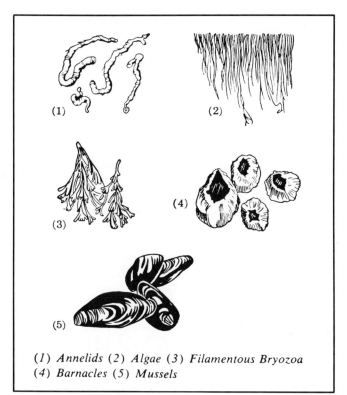

(1) Annelids (2) Algae (3) Filamentous Bryozoa
(4) Barnacles (5) Mussels

Some of the more common marine growths that attach to hull bottoms.

to beautify the surface and protect it from deterioration, but simply as a vehicle to hold the toxicant onto the boat. Putting copper on in the form of powder mixed into a vehicle is simply an easier and smoother way to do it than the old method of attaching copper sheets to ship hulls.

Some of these coatings are compounded to remain relatively soft, as paints go. They wash off gradually as a boat travels through the water, thus exposing fresh surface and toxicant. They can wash off too soon if used on fast boats, and can rub off of bottoms of small boats that often beach. They tend to be rougher than is desirable for speed, such as in racing or long-distance cruising. Others are compounded to set quite hard for the sake of staying on the boat and also of drying to an acceptable degree of smoothness. Their composition and the toxicant in them are compounded in such a way that the toxicant leaches out slowly, over a period of months, so as to present fresh growth-repellent material at the surface during the effective life of the coating. As a general rule, the soft paints have a creosote-like smell and the hard ones smell like lacquer.

Fresh Water Fouling

Q. I applied a good grade of anti-fouling paint to the bottom of my houseboat, which is moored in fresh water. But at season's end there was a lot of algae on the bottom.

Did I do something wrong or was I sold a gyp paint?

A. The paints made to keep saltwater creatures from attaching to boat bottoms are formulated to work as desired when exposed to salt water. Fresh water can neutralize their chemistry so they fail to work as intended, or the toxicants in them have no effect on fresh water algae. After all, farmers use a variety of insecticides to cope with various kinds of bugs. Most major marine paint firms make anti-fouling paints specially formulated to work in fresh water and discourage algae. We have found that a surprising number of people who live inland, far away from yachting centers, and operate on bodies of fresh water have never discovered these paints, and as a consequence suffer through season after season of speed-killing algae coatings on their boat bottoms.

Short Term Fouling

Q. I will trailer my boat to Florida for a couple of weeks this winter. Should I put anti-fouling paint on its bottom? I live in Indiana and have never had any experience on salt water.

A. If your boat just sat quietly at a mooring for two weeks while in Florida, you might get the beginnings of some growths, but not enough to worry about or to be hard to scrub off later. Since in all probability your boat will be used daily, the juvenile-stage marine growths that do manage to affix themselves to the bottom will have a hard time staying there due to the rush of water when the boat is under way. If you haul the boat out on its trailer at the end of each day of fun, exposure to air will kill any growths that just might have managed to hold on. As the intensity of fouling varies with the season, it would be best to ask local advice if you intend to moor your boat at a dock during your stay.

Mooring in Brackish Water

Q. I am going to moor my new cruiser a mile or so up a tidal creek where the ebb and flow of the water results in a mixture that is mostly brackish. Do I need anti-fouling bottom paint?

A. There is no pat answer. Your best course would be to ask owners of other boats moored in that particular spot. We have known barnacles to grow on the bottoms of boats moored in a lagoon that is separated from the sea by a dam and lock. You would consider it fresh water. It is possible that that particular colony of barnacles had adapted itself to life in brackish water, just as the popular striped bass native to the east coast has been successfully transplanted into fresh water lakes. It is also possible that the sewage pollution in that lagoon filled the water with nutrients that helped these barnacles to thrive in that lagoon. It is generally agreed that if a boat having a good crop of barnacles that grew on its bottom in a saltwater mooring area goes upriver to an area of truly fresh water, the shock will be too much for those barnacles and they will be killed off as the days go by. Of course, their shells will remain attached to the hull.

Erratic Paint Behavior

Q. *I used a certain kind of anti-fouling paint on the bottom of my sloop, with excellent results, for several years. Last summer I was late in launching my boat due to business pressures. It was in the water only a couple of months instead of four or five months, yet when I hauled it out there was more fouling than I ever saw before! Did the maker of that paint cheapen his product or weaken its potency to comply with some EPA regulation?*

A. People seem to expect uniform performance from a bottom paint, regardless of circumstances. But the performance of any bottom paint is affected by many things, just as you get some unusually wet summers and some unusually dry ones due to all the factors that govern the weather. Some paints are formulated so the boats they are applied to must be launched within a specified time, such as 12 or 24 hours, after being painted. If for any reason a boat is left out of the water for several days between painting and launching, the paint can dry too hard and then fail to release the toxicant after launching. Or you might have launched the boat while there was an oil film on the water around the boatyard. The paint would have picked up its own film of oil as the boat went into the water. This could have impaired the paint's effectiveness.

Barnacles Do It, Too!

Q. *I was short of cash and time so I launched my big outboard boat in April without giving its bottom a fresh coat of anti-fouling paint. By June the bottom was a mess of growths. At the same time I was hauling it out to take care of the mess, a friend launched his boat just as I had— without fresh paint. By September his bottom was very much cleaner than mine had been. Why did I get a big crop of barnacles while his boat didn't?*

A. Do you know what the birds and the bees do in the springtime? Well, little creatures of the sea, such as barnacles, do it too! You put your boat in the water just in time for its bottom to become a welcome home for freshly hatched barnacles. After hatching, they swim about in the water until they chance to find a good surface to attach themselves to. Your friend launched his boat after the height of the barnacle breeding season.

"Current" Events

Q. *My buddy and I painted the bottoms of our boats at the same time and with the same kind of anti-fouling paint. His boat's bottom remained very clear of fouling but I had quite a lot when I hauled mine. Mine was moored over in the cove while his was moored near the channel. Could this have had anything to do with it?*

A. Yes. The channel current moving past his boat with the coming and going of the tide made it harder for small creatures to get a grip on the surface as the current carried them along the boat's bottom. Your boat over in the cove was in more or less still water, so the creatures had more chance to affix themselves. Also, if the water in that cove was warm and the bottom was littered with sunken logs, ship timbers, etc., it could have been so full of nutrients as to further encourage marine growths.

Bottom Paint Durability

Q. *I bought the most expensive anti-fouling paint stocked by my marine dealer, but after only two seasons at her mooring the bottom was a mess. Was I gypped?*

A. No. You do not understand. The durability of a topside paint can indeed be judged by how many months or years it maintains good appearance. But that yardstick does not apply to bottom paints. It is taken for granted that a boat will be hauled out at intervals, either for winter storage or for annual checking of the condition of underwater parts. So there is going to be an opportunity to repaint the bottom before two or three years have passed. The potency of anti-fouling paints varies all the way from three or four months (a typical northern boating season's duration) up to about a year, the time that would likely elapse between inspection haul-outs in the south. The worth of a premium paint is not measured by its ability to maintain potency for two years or more, but for several more months than a lesser paint.

"Tropic" Bottom Paint

Q. *Some bottom paints have names that imply they are specially made for use in tropical waters. Just how do they differ from ordinary ones?*

A. You will find differences from make to make. Some will have more toxicants in them to give more potency at any particular time, others will retain potency for a longer time. They are all good, and worth their price where fouling is severe and/or the season is long, but it hardly makes sense to use such a paint in Maine, for example, where the boating season is short and the cold water keeps fouling problems to a minimum.

Bottom Fouled Irregularly

Q. *We had to haul my boat to repair a bent propeller after it had been in the water a few months. I was puzzled to find scattered patches of fouling on an otherwise clean bottom. Could you explain this?*

A. Did you apply just one coat of bottom paint? Then that's the trouble. You can't get real uniformity in coverage with a single brushed-on coat. The scattered patches of fouling are where the paint chanced to be a little thin. It lost its toxicant sooner and invited fouling organisms to attach to the boat. Always use two coats; then the thick and thin spots are averaged out into a much more uniform thickness.

More Irregular Fouling

Q. *There was no fouling on the lower parts of my boat's bottom when we hauled it out, but there was a fair amount in the area from the waterline to about a foot down. Do you suppose something floating on the water, such as oil, weakened the anti-fouling properties of the paint on the upper areas of the bottom?*

A. That could have happened, but we have a more likely explanation. Some marine growths, particularly the grass-like ones, thrive best when they are exposed to sunlight. There is less of that farther down on a boat's bottom.

Temporary Fouling Protection

Q. *We are taking our older wooden cruiser to Florida for a month or so this winter. It is normally used in northern rivers and lakes and has no anti-fouling paint on its bottom. Is there any kind of paint that could be put on temporarily to protect it from shipworms?*

A. There is no such thing, since every paint manufacturer strives for the longest possible protection. Some of the paint companies that make brightly colored TBTO bottom paints for aluminum boats also offer this type of paint in a clear form. It's normally used on bottoms of fiberglass boats when owners do not wish to change the color of their boats' bottoms. You could look into this. Young shipworms look for bare wood, since they are not equipped to attach to and then bore into a reasonably hard paint. Give your boat a fresh coat of the paint you normally use on its bottom, being careful to find and thoroughly cover any bare spots. Then navigate carefully so as not to strike any shallows or floating objects that would scratch the new paint and expose bare wood. For the short time the boat will be in Florida, we think that will give adequate protection. Any young shipworms that might get into the wood will die when you return to your fresh water river, and will not be in the wood long enough to grow and make holes of large enough size to matter.

What Is a "Worm Shoe"

Q. *I heard some boat owners talking down at the waterfront and one of them mentioned that his boat had a "worm shoe." What is that: some kind of a boot to cover the bottom as protection against worms?*

A. No. It is a strip of wood attached as a cap, or "shoe," to the bottom of the keel proper. It is made of some species of wood that is highly resistant to teredos, the proper name for shipworms. Greenheart and teak are often used. If the boat grounds and some anti-fouling paint is rubbed off the worm shoe, the wood's resistance acts as a useful deterrent to widespread entry into the wood of the keel by teredos. In a really well-made wooden boat, the worm shoe will be bedded in a special compound that contains toxicant, as further insurance against teredos getting into the ship's vital structural parts.

Copper vs. Tin Paints

Q. *Which type of anti-fouling paint has the best ability to repel bottom fouling?*

A. There's no real point in comparing them, since the TBTO types are made primarily to go onto aluminum boats. If you have a wooden or fiberglass boat, you will automatically choose a paint suited to those materials. Some early TBTO paints had indifferent ability to repel fouling organisms, but there has been much improvement since then.

Fouling "Colonies"

Q. *When we hauled our motorboat recently to change propellers, we found scattered patches of barnacles and other growth. The rest of the bottom was clean. Do you suppose inadequate stirring of the anti-fouling paint could have resulted in "weak spots" in the protective coating?*

A. That is possible. The copper dust or other toxicants in an anti-fouling paint are heavy and, after months on a store shelf, often settle to the bottom of the can and become so well-packed that a lot of stirring is needed to remix things thoroughly. The "colonies" of fouling could also be at places where the paint was scraped thin when the boat grounded on sand bars or rubbed past floating objects. Once a few organisms become established at any thin or weak spot in the coating, they thereupon cover over the coating. Then it is easy for more organisms to attach themselves to the first ones, piggyback-fashion, and there you have the beginning of one of these colonies.

Scrubbing Bottom

Q. I find that a few fouling organisms get a foothold on the bottom of my sloop about halfway through the season— we can see them when we are swimming and chance to dive under the boat. I have heard that in some ports young men who own scuba diving equipment will go under a boat and scrub early accumulations of growth off the bottom, so as to prolong the period in which one can enjoy the speed of a clean bottom. What do you think?

A. The paint companies in general are against this practice. While a good scrubbing will obviously remove early arrivals in the fouling program, it will also take off some of the anti-fouling paint. That can leave the boat's bottom with less protection, and you could end up with more growth by season's end! Check with the maker of the paint you are using before hiring scuba divers to scrub it.

Painting Without Hauling

Q. We moor our boat in a remote cove. It would take a lot of time and fuel to run it over to the nearest marine railway which is 80 miles away for periodic repaintings of the bottom. Is there any other way to get at the bottom? Does anyone make a paint that will work under water, like some of the emergency underwater patching compounds will?

A. Try the old method of "careening." Run the boat as close to shore as possible at high tide. When the tide goes out the boat will be high and dry. Some paints will go onto a bottom that has not thoroughly dried out. The boat will lean to one side as the tide goes out and you can do that side. On the next tide, load her so she will want to heel the other way. Sand may stick to the paint on the side finished first. As careening is rarely necessary in well-populated areas, yard men know little about it. Write to the maker or makers of the paint(s) you prefer for their advice on doing it.

Teredos Attack Plywood?

Q. Our boat is made of plywood and we wonder if shipworms (teredos) can attack this form of wood?

A. We have heard plywood people say it is unlikely or impossible, pointing to the fact that the diameters of shipworms are typically greater than the thickness of the veneers in a sheet of plywood, and that the waterproof glue

has a formaldehyde base which presumably would poison the worms. But we have seen samples of worm-riddled plywood, and have talked to marine biologists who doubt if the glue lines would discourage shipworms. Since you will want to apply anti-fouling paint to discourage barnacles and grasses from attaching, putting it on will also give you protection from shipworms. If the plywood boat is a small one which is regularly in and then out of the water, shipworms couldn't live in it.

Detecting Wormy Wood

Q. How can I tell if the planking of a wooden boat is infected with teredos?

A. It's hard to do visually. Probe suspected areas with an ice pick, moving it about perhaps half an inch at a time over an area some inches in diameter. If there are teredos in the wood, some of their tunnels will be near the surface and the point of the pick will break through. When you find such a spot, dig into the wood. If your digging leads to discovering tunnels roughly one-eighth to three-eighths of an inch in diameter and lined with a whitish, shell-like substance, the wood is worm-infested. If there is a living worm in the tunnel you discover, you will find the tunnel to be full of pulpy animal matter. The tunnel may be empty if the worm that occupied it died some time in the past. Teredos typically live one to three years. They have a facility for "navigating" in a piece of wood so their tunnels don't break out of the wood and so that the tunnel of one worm does not break into the tunnel made by another. They rarely go across the grain but may do so at times, such as when encountering a hard knot. The inside of a piece of badly-eaten wood is like a honeycomb, riddled with passages and easily broken.

Nature of Shipworm

Q. From the way some people talk, I visualize shipworms as being in the same league as the sea monsters of olden times that swallowed ships whole. What are they really like?

A. Pat statements about shipworms are risky. According to a leading encyclopedia, there are about 65 species in the family *teredidae*, from which comes the word "teredo" used by technical people in preference to shipworms. They are not worms but a type of clam adapted for life in wood rather than in sand or mud. Most will bore holes from one to two feet long in wood, but some species attain lengths between three and six feet. Some are distributed worldwide, others are common to certain regions. Some of the people who work at oceanographic laboratories make lifetime careers out of studying teredos. These and other wood boring and chewing

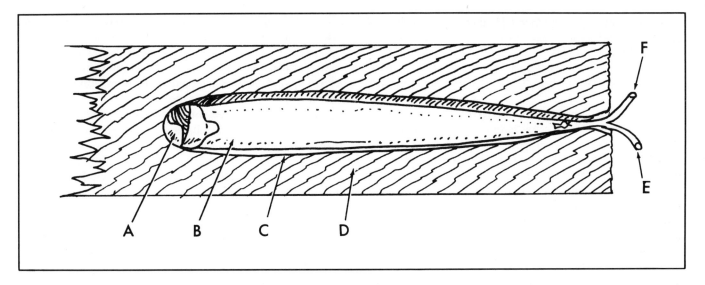

The shipworm, or teredo, is a strange and wonderful creature. Nature designed it to bore into wood and expand to fill the hole it makes. A, shell with boring serrations; B, body of teredo; C, tunnel eaten by teredo; D, wood; E, incurrent siphon; F, excurrent syphon.

creatures cause vast damage to dock and bridge piles, wooden barges, and other property.

In the embryo stage, the teredo is very small and swims freely in the water. It amounts to a tiny shell from which projects a "foot," two syphons or tubes for the intake and ejection of sea water, and a "byssus." A byssus is a long, thin, whip-like device by which the embryo grasps and attaches itself to any wood it chances to encounter. Entry is made into the wood by boring a pinhole-sized hole. Once in the wood, the shell is used as a boring tool. It has rasp-like ridges, or teeth, on it, and muscular action moves it so that it wears away slowly but steadily at the wood. As the wood wears away, the body of the teredo grows so as to fill the available space.

In time, the tunnels bored by several teredos can riddle a piece of wood. The only external indication of the presence of teredos is their siphons. These range from two tiny, translucent, feather-like projections, perhaps a quarter of an inch long, to two spaghetti-like tubes, perhaps half an inch long. One draws in water, the other discharges it along with waste and, at the right time of year, eggs. Teredos eat both microscopic forms of life in the seawater and the wood rendered into powder by their rasping shells. The siphons are very sensitive and will retract when the creature senses a disturbance in the water. Once retracted, a tiny flap-like valve closes the opening so it is practically invisible. Theoretically, a scuba diver who moved very slowly and quietly over the bottom of a boat might see the siphons. But in practice they are so small and shy that a typical cursory examination of the bottom of an infected boat would reveal no trace of teredo infestation.

Like other marine creatures, teredos have a breeding season. This is when a boat is most likely to become the home for a load of borers. In general, the milder months of the year pose the most risk. But it is not possible to say that there is little danger here and much danger there. Conditions vary so widely! One part of an inlet may have little wood in it, but another part may have many dock piles and a lot of waterlogged driftwood on its bottom. Naturally, a boat moored in the latter area is in more danger.

How fast teredos will move through wood depends on the type of wood and its hardness, the species of teredo, and general weather and water conditions. If a bad infestation is picked up because of an absence of anti-fouling paint or old paint in poor condition, there can be serious damage within a few months. Some infestations begin at places where there is no anti-fouling paint, such as at holes in the planking over which water intake screens are affixed. Good fittings are designed to cover all base wood that is exposed when intalling them. Generous use of bedding compound is an added precaution.

Gribbles

Q. What is a gribble? I have heard this word around boatyards.

A. It's a small creature that lives in seawater. It looks something like a lobster only one-eighth of an inch long and minus the lobster's long claws and antennae. It attacks the outer surface of wooden piles and any unprotected parts of wooden boats. Its jaws chew the wood away. The surface of the wood will be eaten away by numerous gribbles so it looks as though it had been subjected to concentrated attack by hundreds of tiny woodpeckers. Well-maintained anti-fouling bottom paint will save a wooden boat from their attention.

And Putty Bugs!

Q. Is there any such thing as a "putty bug?" I've heard the phrase and sometimes wonder if it refers to an imaginary creature.

A. There really are putty bugs! While they normally feed on other substances, for some reason they have an appetite for the putty-like compounds used in the seams of wooden boats to cover the cotton caulking compound neatly and smoothly, and for bedding compounds used between hardware, worm shoes, etc., and the main wooden members of a boat. Some marine paint firms make, or did make, a special compound that contained a toxicant to repel putty bugs.

Why the Spring Rush?

Q. Why do boatyards wait until springtime to start painting the bottoms of all the boats in their charge? This leads to a mad rush. Couldn't they spread the work out through the winter to avoid the stress and anxiety caused by the annual rush?

A. Most bottom paints will dry out too much if exposed to the air for any length of time. Many have to be put into the water within a day or two after being applied. Some new paints, such as the TBTO paint based on tin compounds, will retain their potency even when exposed to air for a long time. In some areas, these are being adopted for boats made of other materials so the bottom-painting work can be spread out over the off-season. But in other areas, local experience has shown that some other types of paint repel marine growths more effectively, so their use and the spring rush continues.

Using Different Paints

Q. I happen to have a lot of copper-type bottom paint on hand. If I put this on the bottom of my fiberglass stern drive boat, and use some TBTO-type, non-corrosive paint on the stern drive's lower unit so the aluminum won't be corroded, will things work out all right?

A. We'd be afraid to try it. Only laboratory or field tests would show what would actually happen. There is real possibility that the copper paint will upset and/or get through the TBTO paint so as to cause galvanic corrosion damage to the expensive aluminum parts of the outdrive. It would be wiser to sell the copper paint to someone who can use it safely and use only one kind of paint on both the hull and the stern drive of your boat.

Barnacles on Stern Drives

Q. I have seen some rather bad coatings of marine growths on stern drive lower units. How can I prevent this from happening to my new rig?

A. All manufacturers of stern drive engines sell antifouling paints containing safe tin-based toxicants in colors to match the paint regularly applied to their products' lower units. We are often surprised at how many people along the coast do not know of the availability of this useful coating, or don't bother to use it.

Barnacles Clog Water Passages

Q. Some people say that the lower units of outboard motors should be left down in the water, when used in coastal areas, to shut out air and hence oxygen from the motors' cooling passages and thus prevent internal corrosion. Others tell me this should not be done because freshly hatched barnacles floating in seawater can enter cooling system screens, affix themselves inside, and grow to block the flow of cooling water. Which group is right?

A. The latter one. We have seen motors overheat and seize up as a result of barnacles growing inside cooling water intakes and passageways. We have seen people have dreadful odor problems from barnacles growing inside the intake and discharge openings of sea closets. As there is usually no reliable way to get paint on these hidden surfaces, there is no pat solution. You can avoid the problem by tilting an outboard's lower unit out of the water. For those openings in a hull that are below the waterline, all you can do is be aware of the fact that young barnacles are small enough to pass through almost any common screen or strainer and think of this possibility when confronted by "mysterious" flow-stoppage or odor problems.

Fouling on Propellers

Q. Because of its position in the storage yard, my boat must be launched about a month before I can start using it. How do I keep barnacles from gathering on the propeller while the boat sits in the water awaiting my arrival?

A. Some yards just brush anti-fouling paint on propellers. It will come off as soon as the boat gets into service, but it will stay on well enough to discourage barnacles while the boat is idle. We have seen other yards solve the problem by smearing a thick, tenacious, water-resistant grease on propeller blades. It washes off as soon as the boat is used, but seems to discourage home-hunting barnacles while it is on the propeller blades. On the market are products with names like "Prop-Kote" and "Sea-Film," sold primarily to protect propellers from corrosion and erosion. But we have known a coating of one of these products to have discouraged barnacles for useful lengths of time. A coating of melted paraffin or beeswax brushed on will also work, and will later wash off.

Home Brew Bottom Paint

Q. Some time ago in a newspaper's "homecraft" pages I saw a formula for homemade anti-fouling paint. I neglected to clip it out. Now I wish I had done so. Do you have it, or do you know where I can locate it?

A. We too have seen such a formula in the past, but we didn't bother to file it away because it was obvious to us that it would produce a soft, rough paint of little value in today's boating scene, where smoothness for speed and an ability to stay on the boat when it goes fast are desirable qualities.

More on Home Brew Paint

Q. I have a large container of copper powder that I found when they were cleaning out the warehouse where I work. Can I mix it with regular, non-toxic hull paint to make my own anti-fouling coating?

A. Such a coating might keep growths off for a little while, as long as the copper that happens to be right on the surface retains its ability to repel. But after that, you can expect a sudden and rapid accumulation of growths, because the home-brewed paint won't wash off slowly so as to present fresh copper to the surface, and won't let the copper leach to its surface to present fresh toxicant.

Metal Primer Repels Fouling?

Q. On the spur of the moment I painted the bottom of my skiff with some leftover red oxide metal primer. In the fall I was surprised to find there was no accumulation of algae on the boat's bottom. So, would you consider this primer to be an effective anti-fouling paint for use in fresh water?

A. We can understand why that paint kept algae off. It is made with red lead and this metal of course has its toxic qualities. Using the primer on a skiff might be all right if you feel it works satisfactorily, but if you used it on a larger boat worth some money, you could in time have problems with smoothness, build-up followed by sloughing off, or other things that could cost a lot of money to correct.

Souping Up Anti-Fouling Paint

Q. I know an old fellow who always mixes a boxful of red pepper into the anti-fouling paint he uses on his launch. He says it really adds power to the paint and keeps all kinds of marine growths off much better than does undoctored paint. What do you think?

A. We have read and heard of people putting all kinds of things into bottom paint to "soup it up." Only laboratory tests run under controlled conditions would tell if it does any good. There are so many variables, as you must now realize after having read this far in this chapter! Such dosings might possibly work at some times, under some conditions, when added to one of the older type, simple, soft paints. But adding odd things to a more modern and sophisticated bottom paint might just run the risk of fouling up the paint's sophisticated chemistry, making its behavior much different from what it was intended to be. If you must tinker around, try your brainstorms out on test panels, not on boats. And use control panels alongside your experimental ones to see if there really is any improvement in anti-fouling capability.

Shelf Life of Paint

Q. I have some anti-fouling paint that has been in storage for several years. What is the shelf life of these paints? Is it possible the paint I have might have lost its potency?

A. As far as we know there is no shelf life limit. If the lid was on tight and there are no rust holes in the can, it's unlikely anything has evaporated away. We'd expect the cans to rust out before the toxicants in the paint deteriorated. Mix the paint well and try some of it on a small area. If it goes on all right, sets up normally for the type of paint it is, and otherwise shows no odd behavior, go ahead and use it. Keep stirring it as you work, to maintain uniform dispersion of the toxicant. Make sure you use the proper thinner for it if it is necessary to thin it out for satisfactory brushing characteristics.

New Paint Over Old

Q. Must all old anti-fouling paint be removed before applying a fresh coat?

A. If the old paint is basically sound and is adhering well to the hull, it is all right to put new paint over it. Scattered rough or chipped spots should of course be smoothed with a light sanding and "primed" with a dab of the new paint. This assumes the new paint is of a kind similar to the old. Of course, you would not put an expensive, sophisticated anti-fouling paint over some old, low-cost paint of the "soft" kind.

After several seasons, there can be so much old anti-fouling paint on the bottom of a boat that the coating will have become so thick and rough as to have an obviously deleterious effect on the boat's performance. It is then appropriate to remove old paint.

Removing Old Bottom Paint

Q. What's the best way to remove a thick coating of old bottom paint?

A. There's no one "best" way. You choose a method to suit the boat. Vibratory sanders are meant for smooth finishing work and can take forever to remove a lot of old paint. A belt sander has vigorous, rapid sanding action, but fills the air with paint dust. It can be extremely fatiguing to hold up its weight and guide it carefully. The sanding dust will of course contain whatever toxicants might be in the paint and can be bad to inhale. A disc sander will wipe old paint off rapidly but will make crescent-shaped cuts in the wood or fiberglass of the hull if your control of the tool is less than perfect—and we never saw anyone who had perfect touch with one of these heavy, powerful tools!

The best way, all things considered, is to use paint remover. When most of the heavy paint has been removed, the scattered spots remaining can be cleaned up with a commercial-grade vibratory or orbital sander having decent power, or with a disc sander of the flexible-pad type. This type has a pad of relatively soft sponge rubber and the sanding discs are held to it with adhesive. As the entire face of the disc is pressed onto the work, there is no danger of cutting crescents into its surface. Constant, gentle movement of the disc makes the abrasive grains take a criss-crossing path over the work. The result is a smooth, uniform, unmarred surface.

Sandblasting

Q. Can I use sandblasting to get old anti-fouling paint off the bottom of a fiberglass boat?

A. We would be afraid to try it. The gel coat is only about .015 inch thick. The abrasive power of the sand grains would almost surely eat right through it. A small, light-duty sandblasting gun of the type resembling a paint spray gun would take forever to do the job, as its main purpose is cleaning small metal parts. The only time sandblasting should be used is when refinishing the bottom of a steel boat, and then only when you are sure the steel is thick and sound enough not to present the danger of being eaten through.

We have heard that a sandblasting outfit can be loaded with some less-abrasive material than sand, such as medium-coarse sawdust, cracked corn, certain grains, etc., so as to take paint off without harming the underlying surface. But we have never heard any reports nor seen anything in the marine press about how well this might have worked out on actual boats. We would expect there would be a procurement and/or cost problem, and surely the use of any lightweight materials such as these would make a dreadful mess. The powerful stream of air from the hose nozzle would blow it all about the work area and beyond.

Primer Under Bottom Paint?

Q. What kind of primer is best under anti-fouling paint?

A. There's no pat answer. It depends on the hull material and on the particular paint being used. Many copper-type paints intended for wooden boats are applied directly to the bare wood. Some designed for use on metal boats require a primer, partly to seal the metal against corrosion and partly to make the anti-fouling paint stay in place. Some anti-fouling paints intended for use on fiberglass require a primer to make them stick; some don't. Read the label and do exactly what it says!

Amount of Sandpapering

Q. I sandpapered the bottom of my fiberglass boat before applying anti-fouling paint. But the paint sloughed off in large patches not long after launching. Why?

A. How do you interpret the word "sandpapering?" Sounds to us as if you swept the paper back and forth across the surface perfunctorily and thought that would do it. But it won't! Widespread sloughing off is just what we'd expect to happen as a result of doing it that way. What you have to do is sand every square inch so thoroughly that all trace of gel coat gloss is removed. Generally, the best job is done by a vibratory or orbital pad sander of sufficient power to give the abrasive vigorous action. It will dull the surface but pose no danger of chewing through the gel coat. Holding an electric tool of this weight up against a boat bottom can fatigue the arms of a champion weightlifter. It's such a hard job that boatyard men will skimp on it unless someone watches them constantly! Some yards make use of compressed air sanders, such as those used by auto body shops. They are smaller and lighter and, unlike electric tools, don't get uncomfortably hot after a long, hard session of sanding.

Paint Chipped Off

Q. Anti-fouling paint has chipped off at random places all over the bottom of my fiberglass boat. What might be wrong?

A. Could be any of a number of things, but it sounds to us like you failed to use primer under a paint that was supposed to go on over primer. Among other things, the right primer can act as a "cushion." The chipped spots on your bottom are probably where the bottom was struck glancing blows by driftwood, and the hard yet poorly adhering paint chipped off.

Sticky Spots in Paint

Q. We applied anti-fouling paint to the bottom of our fiberglass sailboat, and while most of it dried properly, scattered sticky spots remained and never set up hard. Why?

A. That's what happens when there are scattered wax spots on a surface. A new fiberglass hull is apt to have wax residue on its surface from the mold in which it was made. You did not adequately prepare the surface for painting. In addition to giving "tooth" to help paint cling to hard gel coat, a thorough sanding takes off all traces of wax.

The Easy Way to Sand

Q. Ours is a big boat. It sounds like a tremendous job to sand the hundreds of square feet on its bottom before applying anti-fouling paint. Is there any easier way to prepare a fiberglass hull to receive paint?

A. Some of the marine paint firms sell a solvent designed to clean and slightly etch a fiberglass surface so as to enable paint to adhere. Read the labels on both this cleaner and on the paint you are using to make sure the two will work together satisfactorily.

Paint Peels Off

Q. During winter storage periods the bottom paint on our old wooden launch dries out and develops cracks like those on an alligator's skin. Why?

A. It sounds as if you are using one of the "soft" types of paints made for slower boats. When exposed to air, it dries more than it can when in the water, and this alligatoring results. You have to live with it, or change to a more sophisticated bottom paint.

Painting Bottom in Fall

Q. We visited a boatyard last fall and were surprised to see workmen applying anti-fouling paint to the bottoms of some boats that had just been hauled out for storage. We thought paint was put on just before launching.

A. Those boats you saw were wooden ones, weren't they? Some yards think it is wise to apply this paint in the fall, on the theory that it will help keep water from drying out of the bottom planking so rapidly and so much as to allow the planks to shrink and open up the seams. When the seams open up, caulking dries out and then won't seal so well the following year.

Painting Centerboard Trunk

Q. How does one get anti-fouling paint spread on the inside of a centerboard trunk?

A. The usual method is to tie some soft cloth to the end of a stick and use it as a long-handled swab to smear paint around on the surface. The results may be messy and lacking in uniformity, but getting some anti-fouling protection there is better than nothing. The paint does not have to be put on all the way up inside the trunk; just up to the waterline or a few inches higher.

Removing a Mess

Q. We did not use anti-fouling paint on our boat before mooring it in salt water. Now we are sorry. There is a coating of fouling about an inch thick on it! How do we remove it easily?

A. Easily? No way! Tedious work with scrapers and brushes is the only way. The whole idea behind using anti-fouling paint is to avoid troubles like this.

Barnacle Feet

Q. We scrubbed a modest amount of grass and scum off the bottom of our fiberglass boat when we hauled it out in the fall, but several dozen barnacles were on the surface. We had to break them off. We got most of them off, but small, approximately circular spots remain where they were. We find these will not scrub off. What do we do?

A. Those are "barnacle feet," the parts of the creatures where they have cemented themselves to the boat's surface. The natural cement they make for this purpose is so tenacious that chemists have studied it, trying to learn how to make it in the laboratory to sell as a commercial adhesive. Get a rubber sanding block, put medium-fine aluminum oxide abrasive paper in it, and go to work on each spot. Sand it down carefully, trying to get it off without going into the gel coat. We have seen people do the job with a Dremel model-maker's rotary tool driving tiny sanding discs. When most of the "foot" has been taken off, finish the job with fine wet sandpaper to avoid scratching the gel coat.

Getting Dried Scum Off

Q. We hauled our fiberglass outboard from fresh water and found scum all over the bottom. As we were in a hurry to close the cottage for the summer, we left the boat on the porch with the scum still on it. Now we find the stuff has dried so hard it is most difficult to get off. Help!

A. Let that be a lesson to you! The time to remove both fresh water algae and salt water fouling from a boat's bottom is at haul-out time, when it is still wet and comparatively soft! Some of the companies that make lines of well-known boat cleaning and polishing compounds make products to help clean off messes like this. They are often hard to find in marine stores because demand for them is small and scattered. Try a mixture of Clorox or ammonia and water—it might help.

Very high-pressure water issuing from the wand of this Johnson cleaner will sluice most scum off the bottom of a boat at haul-out time. Most marinas have a device of this kind.

Anti-Fouling for Rope

Q. Each fall when I haul my mooring, I find the rope to be encrusted with barnacles, grass, etc. Is it possible to put anti-fouling paint or some special product on a rope that is going to be submerged in seawater?

A. You can soak manila rope in Cuprinol, Penta, or some other wood preservative and the chemicals in these products will usually repel marine growths for a useful amount of time. Various marine creatures can eat into manila rope and appreciably weaken it without your realizing what is happening. But most people use nylon rope for mooring lines today, partly because it stretches and absorbs shocks and partly because it is inedible to marine creatures and thus is not susceptible to attack by them.

There is no anti-foulant on the market made especially for nylon mooring lines that we know of. One rope expert said it is possible to soak the rope in household bleach before putting it into the water. It will soak into the rope by capillary attraction and seep out gradually, so as to possibly discourage growths from attaching. Presumably, you could also soak the rope in creosote, which is widely used to treat dock piles against shipworm infestations. The problem here is that creosote seeping slowly out of the rope could create an oil-like slick on the water, leading directly to your mooring line. If pollution authorities noticed and traced it, you might have some explaining to do. We agree. A coating of fouling on a mooring line is quite a messy thing. But remember that it is only a surface coating and that assorted creatures are not eating into the rope so as to weaken it.

Bagged Boats

Q. I have heard of a method used in Florida to protect boats from fouling. A big plastic bag is put in the water, the boat is floated into it, and some chemical is poured into the water that's inside the bag to kill any growths that might be in it so they can't attach to the hull. This way, the hull is shielded from seawater and does not foul. What do you know about it?

A. We saw advertisements for it in boating magazines some years back but have not seen anything about it in print for the last several years. We've also seen sonic devices at boat shows that are fitted inside a hull. They make ultrasonic vibrations that are said to discourage marine growths from attaching to the hull. But we have seen nothing of them in recent years. A characteristic of the pleasure boating business is that its rapid growth has attracted a great number of entrepreneurs offering a wide range of products and devices. Many have merit. But there are so many things for a boat owner to do with his boating dollar that competition for it is ferocious. Many useful products fall by the wayside, not so much because there is something wrong with them but because of the time and expense needed to get a firm foot in the door of this tough marketplace. Also, the managements of many small companies know nothing at all about publicity, promotion, and public relations and so do not do a good job of keeping their products in front of boat owners.

Why Hoists?

Q. *Recently I visited Florida for the first time. My hosts live in one of those developments made by filling in fingers of land with material dredged from lagoon bottoms. Every house there had a channel behind it. Some houses had boats moored to the retaining walls, but I was struck by how many boats were held out of water on hoists and davits. Was this to keep them safe during storms? I can't see how storm waves could get at them in those well-protected channels.*

A. Those boats are kept out of water to solve two problems at once. A boat that's out of water does not collect a lot of marine growths on its bottom, and the metal parts of its drive system do not suffer the effects of galvanic corrosion. The water in those channels is both warm and stagnant, which encourages rapid growth of fouling organisms. A hoist can pay for itself in reduced hull maintenance and deterioration. Boats that are kept on trailers when not in use also benefit, as do those stored in racks in "dry land marinas."

Bottom Paint Colors

Q. *Does the color of the paint on a boat's bottom affect the fouling rate?*

A. Some people think it does but no firm evidence has been offered. Copper-containing paints tend to be brown and dark red because that's the color of the copper. Other antifouling paints are offered in many colors for the sake of attractive boat appearance.

Chapter 19

Decks and Roofs

Teak Deck Leaks

Q. *Do you consider it normal and reasonable that a teak deck only two years old should leak badly?*

A. This brings up the old saying, "It doesn't matter so much what a boat is built of as who built it!" Some teak decks are very good; others are very poor. On a fine custom-built yacht, the individual planks are narrow and quite thick so they resist cracking, and each one expands and contracts rather little with weather changes. Then there are boats built to sell for a price; their teak decks are made of rather wide, thin planks to keep labor and material costs down. Naturally, they expand and contract and crack more.

There's more to it. Teak comes in various grades, and you will of course find the best grades in quality boats. Like other woods, it has to be well seasoned, and in today's mass-production shops there is a temptation to use inadequately seasoned wood. There are even other species of woods that look like teak and are used in its place, either to save money or due to shortages of good teak.

Teak's Advantages

Q. *Today one can see boats with teak all over them. What's so good about it, really? My impression is that it requires endless care.*

A. It's in style, so the boatbuilders rush to use it. You can't blame the boatbuilders for producing what the public has shown itself eager to buy! Teak was used on fine old-time seagoing yachts for reasons that were valid then. It was

available in large, knot-free planks. Exposed to sunlight and clean salt spray, it bleached to a silver-grey surface just rough enough to offer excellent footing, yet its oiliness made it very durable without the bother of keeping paint in good condition. On large yachts its original rich, light brown color could be maintained by putting the paid crew to work scrubbing it with a kind of soft sandstone called "holystone."

Modern builders of mass-produced boats began using a little of it and found it helped to sell boats. Presto, it became a status symbol! Boatbuilders used more of it and found it had advantages for them. Where mahogany needs several coats of varnish, with drying time and hand sanding between coats, teak can be installed bare and "finished" with a wipe-on coat of teak oil. There is little waste, because scraps can be made into small trim pieces.

Now people are complaining that it weathers to an unsightly grey unless they apply teak oil regularly. These same people will exclaim in delight when they visit Cape Cod and see cottages with unpainted, weathered, silvery-grey cedar shingles on them! People are funny animals, eh?

Teak Deck Turns Black

Q. *We are distressed about the teak decking on our yacht. It has a persistent tendency to turn a dirty grey, even black in places. What causes this?*

A. Are you using a teak oil with a lot of linseed oil in it? That would tend to darken under the hot sun. Also, as it is a vegetable product, it often becomes a feeding and therefore a breeding ground for mildew fungus. Do you moor the boat downwind of an airline terminal where the soot and kerosene-laden exhaust from big jetliners drifts onto your teak decks? Is a diesel-engine generator running constantly in the neighborhood of the marina? Is there a chemical factory nearby? Under such conditions the paint on your car would get dirty and dark too! You cannot expect your teak to look just like that on a yacht that spends most of its time at sea.

To Oil or Not to Oil?

Q. My dreamship is being finished off and will soon be delivered. Some people tell me to leave the teak decks bare and let them weather. Others insist I should oil them to preserve the like-new look. I'm confused and would like your opinion.

A. Is your boat a sailing craft? You might prefer the good non-skid qualities of a bare teak deck that has weathered to a slightly rough surface. Is it a cabin cruiser aboard which you will do much entertaining? Then oiling the decks will minimize spotting from dropped bits of greasy food. If you elect to oil your decks, expect to have to repeat the oiling at intervals. How often? Depends on whether the boat is in a cool, damp place like Maine, or a sunny place like Florida, whether it is stored indoors or outdoors, and other factors involving exposure to sunlight, wind, and rain. Remember that teak oil is a liquid and that liquids evaporate. You just have to watch the wood and re-oil when your eyes tell you the wood needs it.

Many teak care products are on the market. Available are cleaners, bleaches, oils and sealers. If you have much teak on your boat it would pay to study the literature put out by various firms active in the field. (Rule Industries, Inc.)

Oil to Prevent Cracking?

Q. Will regular application of teak oil keep deck planks from cracking?

A. Maybe, and maybe not. A lot depends on the relative thickness and width of the individual planks. We have found that in spite of its reputation as a durable wood, teak will split with surprising ease when the screws that hold it are snugged tight in their holes. The underside of a flat-head screw acts just like a wedge!

Homemade Teak Oil

Q. Can you give me a formula for making my own teak oil? The stuff in marine stores is rather expensive.

A. We've been on the lookout for such a formula for years but thus far have not encountered one. Many people use linseed oil from hardware and paint stores but often end up regretting it. Some don't know the vital difference between raw and boiled linseed oil. The former soaks in well and then takes a very long time to dry; the latter will dry fairly rapidly but forms a glossy, leathery skin. Both kinds eventually blacken under the hot summer sun and encourage mildew. Some commercial teak oils contain ingredients that reduce the tendency of the sun's rays to darken the oil and fungicides to discourage mildew. So you get assorted benefits when you buy a quality teak oil that you could not get in a homemade oil brewed from non-professional ingredients.

What's Teak Oil Made Of?

Q. What is commercial teak oil made of?

A. The companies in the business tend to be secretive about the ingredients in their products. Trade secrets, you know. We have heard various people say they think the following things are used: mineral oil, tung oil, linseed oil, safflower oil, soy bean oil, kerosene, naptha, Stoddard solvent, varnish, silicone, pentacholorphenol, factory floor oil, distillate, fish oil, and a dozen other things we can't remember. How much of this is fact and how much hearsay is anyone's guess.

Teak Deck Spits Its Caulking

Q. The black material used in the seams between teak planks on my boat tends to lift out. It's a rubber-like substance and does not appear to be hard and dry. Can you suggest what makes it lift out?

A. It is being repelled by the oiliness of the teak. The builder of your boat either cut corners or didn't know his business. Some of the major marine paint firms make a special primer for teak seams. It seals in the oil and enables most synthetic seam compounds to adhere dependably.

Fiberglassing a Teak Deck

Q. Deck planking on my fiberglass boat is made of teak planks that are obviously rather thin. Every time I go to sea the deck flexes and more leaks appear. Is it possible to cover this leaking deck with fiberglass?

A. Yes, but it can be a bit uncertain. A well-weathered deck may be rough enough and have lost enough of its oiliness to give fiberglass a good chance of staying on. It would be best to use the more expensive epoxy resin, as this will adhere to the wood much better than the more common polyester resin.

Varnishing Teak

Q. Instead of having to apply oil at intervals, wouldn't I be better off varnishing my teak deck?

A. Probably not. It would be quite slippery when wet, and varnish needs sanding and refinishing at regular intervals lest it go to pieces.

Cracks in Fiberglassed Deck

Q. Within a few months after fiberglassing the deck of my boat, several cracks appeared in the fiberglass. I am disappointed; I thought fiberglassing the deck would stop the leaks once and for all.

A. This is another example of fiberglass being oversold and of people believing all they hear about fiberglass being everlasting! You probably used a single layer of fiberglass cloth. Such a covering has little resistance to cracking. It cannot stand the stress applied to it in the areas over seams when the boat flexes and the deck planking "works." Reputable boatyards always use at least two layers of glass cloth on deck and cabin roof jobs. The extra cost pays off over and over again in durability. Fiberglass is brittle; wax a piece of glass, brush activated resin onto it, lay a specimen of glass cloth in it, brush more resin on and allow it to cure for several days to make sure its "rubbery" stage is past. Then lift the specimen off the glass and bend it. You will be surprised. Then make up samples having two and three layers of cloth and you will be amazed!

Fiberglass vendors belittle "old fashioned" canvas covering for decks and roofs. They overlook the fact that it remains flexible for a long time, which is an advantage on a boat.

Deck Too Flexible

Q. When people gather in one spot in the cockpit of my cruiser, the floor sags. It is made of half-inch plywood covered with fiberglass. How would you stiffen it?

A. Although plywood is basically strong material, it is of course flexible, and half-inch material seems marginal to us for a large boat's cockpit floor. One would have to go underneath and look at the support timbers. One might be loose or cracked. If all are sound, and it appears that an excessive amount of awkward work would be necessary to install additional supports, you could try the following. With a hole saw run by an electric drill, cut a circular sample of the fiberglass covering off the floor. Burn away the fiberglass resin, taking care not to disturb the specimen while it is burning. When it has cooled you can count the number of layers of glass cloth. If you find only one, try the following. With paint remover and/or a heavy-duty rotary sander, remove paint down to clean fiberglass. Then put on two or perhaps three layers of fiberglass mat, using rollers from a fiberglass supply house to roll it down. When cured, this extra thickness could add materially to the floor's stiffness. The pattern of the mat will be visible through the paint you use to finish it off and will give a fair non-skid surface. Or you can mix non-skid compound into the paint for extra surefootedness.

Deck Vibrations

Q. This season I noticed a vibration in my fiberglass boat's deck that was not there before. It shows up only at intermediate speeds and, even more puzzling, only when a passenger is sitting in one of the stern seats. If he moves across to the other stern seat, it goes away. What would cause this weird behavior?

A. With the passage of time, the fiberglass could be getting harder and that would change its vibration characteristics compared to what they were when the boat was new. A person jumping onto the deck could have broken a support or loosened a seam, so as to allow the vibration to show up. Since it occurs when a person sits in one seat but not the other and therefore local strain is unequal, the hull will twist differently and either encourage the vibration or stop it. The occurrence of the vibration at intermediate speed shows the deck is vibrating in harmony with some other vibration, so check the propeller for nicks, a bent blade, or bad balance. And check engine hold-down bolts. When the boat is under way and the deck is vibrating, look under the deck (and in other places) to try to spot what is going on. There has to be a logical explanation for the vibration and there is a good chance it is something simple but heretofore overlooked.

Fiberglass Non-skid Pattern

Q. I note that fiberglass boat floors, decks, and cabin roofs have all kinds of non-skid and decorative patterns molded into them. Can you tell me how boatbuilders achieve these effects? It seems like a lot af painstaking labor would be involved.

A. It's really very simple—once you know how! The first step in making a fiberglass boat is to build a "plug." This is a mockup of the actual boat. It's made of rough plywood, pine, hemlock, scrap wood, wood putty, auto body putty—just about anything that the plug maker's resourcefulness suggests would do the job and keep the cost moderate.

When the wood and putty work is finished, the whole is given a covering of one or sometimes two layers of fiberglass cloth to firm it up and provide a good sanding surface. Once this is sanded smooth, it is given many coats of primer, with careful sanding and spot-puttying of small blemishes between each coat. Finally, wet sandpaper is used to get it extremely smooth, after which it is given many coats of wax to impart a high polish. The mold is then made by spraying and brushing fiberglass over this plug, which is really just a kind of pattern.

Now that you know how the boat mold itself is made, we'll tell you how the patterns you mention are achieved. The boatbuilder shops around in vinyl warehouses to find patterns he likes. He buys several samples and takes them back to the shop to make tests from them with fiberglass. When he finds a pattern that looks good and poses no problems in fiberglassing, he buys more, cements it to the sections of the plug where a non-skid or decorative-texture pattern is wanted, waxes the vinyl along with the rest of the plug, and when the mold is made the desired pattern is imprinted in the surface of the mold and then in the surface of all boats made in the molds!

Undoing a Mistake

Q. To get a contrasting color, some previous owner of my boat brushed pigmented gel coat over the non-skid areas molded into my boat's deck. The brushmarks show badly, it obscures the non-skid pattern, and is chipping off in places. It would be a tedious job to pick it all off with the point of a knife. How can I get it off easier?

A. Try pressing many strips of masking tape onto the areas, with a fraction of an inch between the strips. Let it stay in place for several days—the longer it stays on the tighter it will stick. Then jerk it off. With luck the unwanted gel coat will come off with it, leaving the original pattern unharmed. Or, try a small, powerful air jet from a workshop-type air jet gun. The air jet could literally balloon the gel coat off.

Painting Fir Plywood Deck

Q. I have seen examples of weather checking in Douglas fir plywood and it looks very unsightly. Now I find myself fixing up an older boat and using this material for a new cockpit floor. How can I paint it so it won't check?

A. Various primers are on the market, supposedly for use on fir plywood, that claim to minimize checking. Our own observation is that they work better on vertical than on horizontal surfaces like decks. So there is really no simple painting procedure that will positively stop checking. Ask your lumberyard to contact their plywood wholesaler and see if they can supply "overlaid plywood." It has a plastic material firmly glued to its surface in the factory; the appearance is somewhat like Masonite. This covering binds the surface in such a way as to quite effectively cope with checking. Ask for "MDO,"—Medium Density Overlay. It is hard enough to be durable but soft enough to hold paint well. The epoxy resins used for cold-molded boat constructions will also stop checking. (See Chapter 7, Wooden Boats.)

Painting Canvas Deck

Q. I bought a boat that has a canvas-covered deck. People tell me I must use special canvas paint when I refinish it. Who makes such paint?

A. There is really no special paint, unless you mean "canoe enamel." This is an ordinary-enough paint but it's formulated to remain somewhat on the tough and flexible side for a long time. It is glossy, as befits the way we like canoes to look. A glossy paint can be very slippery when wet if used on a deck. A good choice would be a semigloss marine paint designed for use on the topsides of wooden boats. It, too, is formulated to remain tough and flexible, so it will do the job. From time to time one hears of firms offering some type of rubber-like or plastic paint claimed to be ideal for canvas decks, but lack of widespread experience with them makes evaluation a matter of try-it-if-you-want-to-and-see-how-it-works. We have heard of people stripping cracked old paint off of canvas and then successfully "rebuilding" the surface with two or more coats of the type of epoxy resins used for cold-molded boat construction.

About Leaking Decks

Q. Having rainwater drip on one while trying to sleep in a bunk located under a leaking foredeck is an experience comparable to the Chinese water torture. And they call it "pleasure boating!" Why can't boatbuilders make watertight planked decks?

A. Many a planked deck is good and watertight when the boat is launched. But planks in a deck will expand and contract with changes in weather and climate, just as planks on the hull's bottom will swell upon launching and shrink after a long period out of the water. If it rains often and a boat is used a lot so its decks are frequently drenched with spray, that boat will have fewer deck leaks than will an identical one that spends most of the time sitting at a dock in a locality where the climate is dry. Maybe your boat just doesn't get her deck wet often enough. Try hosing it down more often, preferably at sunset so the water won't dry off quickly. If you live in a very dry climate, re-caulk the deck to fill the seams better.

Removing Paint from Canvas

Q. The paint on my canvas deck is worn thin in some areas, while in other areas it is so thick it has become brittle and is cracking. I ought to even things up before repainting. The obvious way is to go over the high spots with a sander—but there is a risk of going too deep and cutting the canvas. Your advice, please?

A. There's no pat answer. Obviously a fast-cutting disc or belt sander will pose the risk of cutting into the underlying canvas. A professional-grade vibratory or oscillatory sander with a powerful motor and good cutting action would take old paint off at a useful rate, yet slowly and gently enough so you can see what's happening and ease off before it's too late.

Paint remover can be used on a canvased deck, but it is slow and messy going. It shouldn't hurt the canvas since canvas is a vegetable fiber; a remover that won't hurt wood shouldn't hurt canvas. The problems can be in scraping the mess off neatly and uniformly, and the possibility of wax in the remover penetrating and remaining in the cracks, only to later come to the surface and interfere with the drying of the paint. So using a remover that contains no wax would be a good precaution, as would using a water-wash type. There is the chance that once you get the paint off you will find the cracks in the canvas are so bad that the fresh paint won't hold it from breaking up. Any way you look at it, a badly worn, cracked canvas deck is a problem.

Paper Under Canvas

Q. When we pulled the old canvas off the deck of my boat, we found underneath it what seems to be a heavy brown paper, possibly house builder's paper. What would this be doing there?

A. Probably some boatbuilder's way of trying to make the canvas last as long as possible. Over the years, people came up with a variety of ideas on how a deck should be canvased.

A common way was to brush thickened old paint onto the wood and lay the canvas into it, on the assumption that the paint that went on top of the canvas would seep through, bond to the underlying paint, and then bond the whole skin to the wood, yet remain flexible enough to resist cracking under the flexing of deck planks. But eventually the paint will harden and transmit plank flexing to the canvas, which will crack. The heavy paper might act as a separator and cushion. We guess that your deck has some crown to it, and this arc would encourage canvas to lie snug to the deck even when fastened only around the edges.

Undercoating a Deck

Q. Instead of attacking the problem of leaking decks from the topside, wouldn't it be better to apply one of the transparent epoxy leak-sealing products now on the market to the underside?

A. We're skeptical. While on one hand the deck planks should receive enough rain and spray to keep from drying out enough to open the seams badly, putting a coating like that on the underside would tend to hold water in the wood so long as to encourage rot. If there is already paint on the underside of the deck it will have to be tediously removed before the epoxy can be successfully applied. If there are beams under the deck you can't get the epoxy on the planking over them, so water would go down into the beams and almost surely rot them.

Carpeting a Wooden Deck

Q. The cockpit deck in my cruiser is planked with spruce boards. Maintenance is a constant job. I'm considering putting outdoor carpeting over it. Will this pose a rot hazard?

A. We think it would. Bilge dampness going up into the wood would encounter the more or less nonporous carpet and would condense under it. This would give you a combination of heat, dampness, and a rot-prone species of wood that could easily spell trouble in a short time. Sure, you see outdoor carpeting often in modern boats—but you will find fiberglass flooring under the carpeting!

Reconditioning Vinyl Roofs

Q. My cruiser is several years old and the vinyl sheeting on the cabin roof has become brittle. There are many cracks and it is chipping off in places. What should I do?

A. Visit vinyl sheeting supply stores, auto body shops, upholstery shops, and specialty paint stores. Ask them what they have in the way of vinyl paints. A number are on the market and not all are to be found in marine stores. Vinyl is used for many things besides boats. You'll have to try samples of the paints you find on small areas and see how well they cover, what the resulting appearance is, how many coats are needed to get good coverage, and what the cost might be. You may find that it would cost no more to replace the vinyl, and doing so will give better appearance.

The reason why boatbuilders have been using vinyl for roof coverings is that it goes on fast and thus saves much labor cost. Once it's stapled on, the job is done. Once canvas is on, more time has to be spent to prime and paint it. And since the ladies love the smart appearance of a vinyl-covered roof, it helps to sell boats. Marine Development & Research Corp., 116 Church St., Freeport, N.Y. 11520 sells a vinyl paint called "Recoatit" in a few primary colors. It's meant for use on cushions, upholstery, etc., but you can look into it for other purposes.

No Cement Under Roof Vinyl

Q. I was rather surprised when we removed the old vinyl from my boat's roof. The material had no cement under it and only the trim strips around the edge held it down. I can't decide whether or not to use cement when installing new vinyl. What do you think?

A. Our guess is that your boat's roof has enough crown so that the tension applied by the staples under the trim strips will hold it down snugly enough.

Used Wrong Cement

Q. We laid a well-known brand of deck covering material on the cockpit floor in our motorboat, using the cement provided by the manufacturer. Now, weeks later, the cement is still soft and lumpy under the sheeting. What's wrong?

A. You used a cement intended for wooden decks. Applied to nonporous fiberglass, the solvents in it cannot evaporate and let the cement settle down. The manufacturer's literature does not make this small but vital point clear. You would be amazed at how many people in the marine supply business turn out to have never worked on boats, so they, too, overlook just these small but vital points! Use Pliobond #2011, manufactured by Goodyear Tire & Rubber Co., Akron, Ohio 44316.

Deck Material Instructions

Q. Is there a book that tells how to lay vinyl decking on boats?

A. Go to any marine dealer who sells "Nautolex" material and ask him for a copy of the manufacturer's pamphlet, Nautolex Application Instructions. You can also get it from the company—Nautolex Division, General Tire & Rubber Co., Box 875, Toledo, Ohio 43601.

Self-Adhering Deck Materials

Q. Does anyone make a vinyl deck covering that has self-sticking properties? Seems it would save messing around with cement.

A. Some firms make it but it seems to be sold mainly for use in manufacturing shops. If used on an old wood deck it would show every imperfection in the wood and would adhere poorly over seams. It seems to work best when laid

It is important to use recommended adhesives when working with various flooring and upholstery materials. (Farber Bros.)

onto smooth, uniform fiberglass surfaces. It has to be used with great care. If wrinkles or folds appear when it is being laid down, it's hard to "shift" compared to a material with still-soft cement under it. Great care has to be taken to remove all traces of grit, drill chips, sawdust, etc. from the surface, and to keep the back side of the material from touching any other surfaces after the backing paper is off. It will pick up foreign matter like a magnet and this will show through in the finished job in the form of small bumps and pimples.

Other Covering Materials

Q. Are there any other materials besides canvas, fiberglass, and vinyl that one could consider using on decks and roofs?

A. Get a copy of the book, *How to Fiberglass Boats*, from Glen-L Marine Designs, 9152 Rosecrans, Bellflower, Cal. 90706. It tells about some other products such as Vectra, Polypropylene, Arabol, and Cascover.

Chapter 20

Moldings, Upholstery, and Fabrics

Gunwale Molding

Q. *The rubber molding on the gunwale of my fiberglass boat is in sorry condition. Now that I want to buy some, I realize I have never seen it on sale at marine stores. Where can I get it?*

A. You'll have to hunt! The reason marine stores rarely carry it is because there are so many sizes and shapes; it isn't economical to stock a lot of them. Demand is spotty, too. The material is rarely rubber; in a majority of cases it is extruded vinyl made by companies that specialize in this material. There are many such firms, scattered about the country. Some sell at wholesale to major boat manufacturing corporations and specialize in marine shapes. These companies won't sell small quantities to boat shops or individuals. Others produce a wide range of moldings for all manner of applications, and sell marine shapes to smaller boatbuilders in their home territories as something of a sideline.

Some marine stores sell general-purpose moldings made by W.H. Salisbury & Co., 7520 N. Long Ave., Skokie, Ill. 60076. Two firms that sell by mail order are Wefco Rubber Mfg. Corp., 1655 Euclid St., Santa Monica, Cal. 90400 and Rupco Industries, 4722 Spring Rd., Cleveland, Ohio 44131. You might find a workable replacement among the offerings of these firms.

Many fiberglass boats use an aluminum gunwale molding which is held on with pop rivets, with the rivet heads being covered with a strip of molding that presses into grooves formed in the aluminum for this purpose. Where vinyl molding can be rolled up for shipment, straight pieces of aluminum extrusion have to be put into long, sturdy boxes or be taped to lengths of wood. It is too time consuming to handle individual orders for such molding. Your best course is to see what local marine dealers can do for you. If your boat is an "orphan," the molding used on some other make of boat of the same general type might fit acceptably. This aluminum molding with a pressed-in, rivet-covering stripping was originally used for aluminum door weather seals and adapted to marine use. If there is a company near you that specializes in aluminum moldings, a visit or call might be worthwhile.

Installing "Rubber" Molding

Q. *I bought some new rubber molding for the gunwale of my boat. A friend says he did the same kind of job a while ago and had a very bad time getting the stuff on. Can you offer any tips?*

A. Yep! The material is in all probability vinyl. Just like a vinyl garden hose, it becomes stiff in cold weather and softens under the summer sun. Don't try to put it on in a cold room. Coil it in a tub and soak it in hot water before use. Move the tub along as you progress, keeping it filled with hot water. At sharp corners, it can help to use a heat gun or heat lamp. Keep any source of heat moving constantly and do not let the vinyl get so hot that it is uncomfortable to touch.

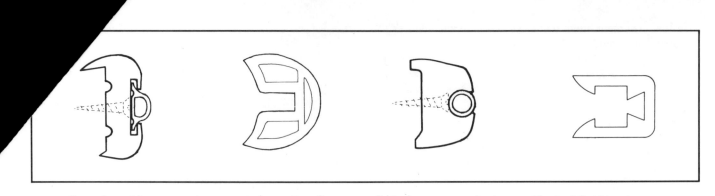

Gunwale moldings come in many cross sections. Some are all-vinyl, some are aluminum with vinyl finishing inserts.

When it gets a little too hot it can char, blister, or stretch too much. When putting the half-round finishing strip in over rivet heads, have a helper pull on it as you work it into the groove with a rounded-off screwdriver blade.

White vinyl molding used to hold glass in wooden windshield frames is often hard to get. Many firms make it, problem is to find out where the builder of a particular boat got his.

Cleaning Gunwale Molding

Q. The nice white vinyl gunwale molding on my sailboat is a mess from rubbing against tarred dock piles. Detergent is useless, gasoline just spreads the smearing. How do I clean it?

A. Try a cloth moderately wet with acetone. Wipe in one direction only; it seems to work better than constant back-and-forth rubbing. Boat and hardware stores sell acetone under the label of "fiberglass cleaner-solvent."

Window Channel

Q. The white plastic molding that holds the windshield glass into the wooden frame on my older boat is in bad

shape. The boat manufacturer is out of business. What can I do?

A. You may have a problem. It's the same situation as with gunwale molding, described earlier in this chapter. Boatbuilders buy the material in wholesale lots from a variety of pastics and extruding firms. So many cross-sections, made by different companies, have been used that there's no way the marine supply stores can stock it. Some do stock quarter-round rubber molding that can be held to a wooden frame with small brass nails. Slice thin sections from your old molding and mail them to plastics companies, asking for clues. Look up vinyl extruding firms in the Yellow Pages for the nearest industrial cities. Take samples of your molding to boatyards and ask mechanics if they have seen anything like it. As a last resort, experiment with a rubber-like marine seam compound, such as "Boat Life," and see if you can bed the glass in it; then mold more of this product into a retaining fillet, much as you'd use putty to install glass in a house window.

Cementing Vinyl Stripping

Q. The U-shaped vinyl molding around the lower edges of the cockpit in my fiberglass boat keeps dropping off the fiberglass. I have tried several hardware store glues and cements and none will adhere to the vinyl, or to the fiberglass, or both. Help!

A. Jobs like this often call for special cements, usually not available at retail outlets. Look up manufacturers and suppliers of industrial adhesives in the Yellow Pages. They make suitable products. You may be able to buy, beg, or wheedle a small can of it for your job. The reason marine and hardware stores don't stock this kind of cement is that it tends to have a short shelf life.

Vinyl Became Sticky

Q. The vinyl upholstery in the cabin of my boat has become rather sticky to the touch. I've tried cleaning it with

Clorox, detergent, and white gasoline to no end. What should I do now?

A. The material could have been put on with an unsuitable cement, solvents from which have softened the vinyl. Or someone could have been using an improper cleaning product on it. If such has happened, it's possible nothing can be done to remove the stickiness. Try automotive or marine vinyl cleaning compound. If that fails, start thinking about reupholstering. By the way, never use household cleaning powders on vinyl—they will scratch and dull the surface. Stick to approved vinyl cleaners.

Use only products made and sold for the purpose for cleaning vinyl upholstery, folding tops, etc. Use of improper cleaning products can result in a variety of problems such as dulling, scratching, staining, stickiness, etc. (Rule Industries, Inc.)

Vinyl Coated Hardware

Q. I have a "silent" fishing anchor. It's coated with vinyl so it won't make noises when moved about in an aluminum boat. The plastic has been cut in some spots and rust is spreading under the vinyl. The dealer won't send it back to the manufacturer for recoating; he wants to sell me a new one at wholesale to settle the matter. Why is he opposed to sending it back?

A. Because of the economics of it. It will cost something to send the anchor back and forth by parcel post. The factory is not set up to strip old vinyl and shepherd your particular anchor through its production system. There is just too much overhead and paperwork involved. Take the new anchor or contact specialists in industrial paints and see if you can get some neoprene paint with which to refinish the anchor yourself. You could probably patch the cuts with the liquid sold in hardware stores for brushing safety grips onto tool handles.

Inflatable Boat Repairs

Q. Where can I get a paint to put on my old inflatable boat to stop hundreds of tiny air leaks?

A. We often get requests for such a paint. We know of none. One problem is that by the time an inflatable boat develops that many small leaks, the material from which it is made is already far gone. A paint manufacturer would be concerned about lawsuits arising from helping people get afloat once more in an unseaworthy craft. Another problem is that air pressure inside would tend to bubble off a paint that was flexible enough for a boat that will be deflated and rolled up. Yet another problem is that inflatable boats are made from a variety of fabrics and synthetics, not just "rubberized fabric." A paint that would adhere to one might not adhere to another. When repairs are needed, go to a place that specializes in inflatable boats, not to a marine store.

Book on Inflatable Boats

Q. Where can I get a book on inflatable boats?

A. *The Complete Book of Inflatable Boats* by Commander Don Hubbard, U.S.N. (Ret.), is available from Western Marine Enterprises, Inc., P.O. Box Q, Ventura, Cal. 93002. The price is $7.95 plus $1.25 for shipping, it's 256 pages, and has data on inflatable boat care.

Cleaning Tops

Q. A diesel-powered dredge working in our mooring basin spattered oil and soot all over the bimini top on my sportfisherman. What cleaner should I use on it?

A. It depends on what the top is made of. It could be any of several synthetics. The best thing to do is take it to a sailmaker and let him decide. If there is none in your area, it would be safe to try general-purpose detergent in warm water. You might also ask the local dry-cleaning establishment for advice.

Needle Holes in Vinyl Tops

Q. Water trickles through needle holes in our vinyl folding top. Is there any way to stop it? Vinyl tape would probably work, but would look bad.

A. Try "Liquid Vinyl Top Leak Sealer" by Marine Development and Research Corp., 116 Church St., Freeport, N.Y. 11520. Your marine dealer can probably get it from one of his distributors.

Foam for Boat Cushions

Q. *The seat cushions in my boat soak up water like sponges; those in my friend's boat never do. Why?*

A. There are many kinds of foam on the market. Some have an "open cell" structure and act like sponges. Others have "closed cell" structures and will not absorb water. Some foams come in various degrees of firmness. Prices vary widely. A good foam that won't soak up water is apt to be somewhat more expensive. A well-made seat cushion will have a zipper on its back side so the foam can be removed to dry it out. Try enclosing your foam in plastic waste disposal bags.

Chapter 21

Windshields and Windows

Replacing Curved Windshield

Q. *My runabout's curved plastic windshield is in poor condition and I wish to replace it. The boat is no longer being manufactured and the dealer I bought it from cannot supply a replacement. What can I do?*

A. Such windshields were once very popular, but the advent of the more rugged aluminum-framed type caused designers to turn away from them. It is hard to find replacements at the local level; marine supply stores do not like to stock things like this because the shipping cartons are bulky to warehouse and demand is low.

Write to the N. A. Taylor Co., Gloversville, N.Y. 12078 for their catalog. Currently, they still offer "SportShield" and "SpeedSport" curved plastic windshields. Look under "Plastics, Sheet" in the Yellow Pages for your area. Most cities have at least one or two firms that specialize in sheet plastic materials, as there is much demand for it in the building, automotive, decorative, and aircraft fields. Some have ovens that heat popular windshield plastics to around 340° F., at which temperature they are easy to bend. If the fragments of your cracked or broken windshield can be tied together with fiberglass, duct tape, wood strips, etc. well enough to hold it fairly rigid, it might be used as a bending form. Edges can readily be cut with a bandsaw or sabre saw fitted with fine-tooth blade to fit your deck. Sharp edges are easy to smooth with abrasive paper.

Companies that make windshield plastic have shop manuals that explain how to work with this material. Write to Plastics Department, E.I. Du Pont de Nemours & Co., (Inc.), Wilmington, Del. 19898 and ask for a copy of their "Lucite" shop manual. Write also to Rohm and Haas Co., Independence Mall West, Philadelphia, Pa. 19105 for their shop manual on "Plexiglas."

Curved plastic windshields are a vanishing breed.

Curved Glass Windshield

Q. My older fiberglass boat has a curved windshield made of safety glass, just like you see on automobiles. It got broken. The builder of my boat went out of business years ago. How could I find a replacement?

A. In most cases, rather than go to the expense of having a relatively small number of special windshields made to order, boatbuilders simply looked at various makes and models of automobiles, found one that had a windshield they felt could be fitted into their new boat, and went ahead and designed the fiberglass curves in the windshield area so the auto glass would fit right in. Take your boat or the broken windshield to an auto glass shop and ask them if they can tell by looking at it what make and year of car it came from. If they can identify it, they could order a replacement for you, or you could tour auto junkyards to find a serviceable replacement at lower cost. If you can't find anything, make a replacement from sheet plastic, as in the preceding question.

Spilled Paint on Plastic Windshield

Q. When someone painted their boat next to mine in the boatyard, the wind carried drops of paint onto my boat's plastic windshield. By the time I discovered what had happened, the paint had dried. I dare not use paint remover for fear of marring the plastic. How can I get the paint off?

A. There are chemicals that will remove the paint without harming the plastic, but they are chiefly for professional use and not easy for most people to locate. And they must be used with some knowledge. Rohm and Haas has a pamphlet, *Painting Plexiglas Cast Acrylic Sheet*, that has a section on this.

For small, scattered paint drops the best thing for you to do is get some 400- and 600-grit waterproof sandpaper. Cut and fold a small piece so that with fingertip pressure you can carefully sand off each drop. The abrasive will dull the plastic slightly but will be so fine that it won't really scratch it. Then get a plastic windshield scratch-removing kit and use its polishing compound to buff away the dull spots. Some marine supply stores sell such kits. If stores in your area can't help, contact a sheet plastics supply firm via the Yellow Pages, or ask mechanics at local airports where they get such kits.

By the way—if you spill paint on plastic windshields or windows while working on your boat, wipe off as much as you can with a clean, soft cloth. Then get some trisodium phosphate, a powerful cleaning agent, at a hardware or paint supply store. Use this mixed with warm water to wipe off as much paint residue as possible. Whatever smudging may remain, let it thoroughly dry and clean up the windshield with the buffing and cleaning compounds contained in a plastic windshield cleaning kit.

Stopping Windshield Cracks

Q. When installing a plastic windshield, we got one bolt too tight and it started a small crack in the plastic. Can we do anything to keep it from spreading?

A. While this will be a trifle unsightly, it will be better than a badly cracked windshield. Drill a hole of perhaps one-eighth inch diameter right at the end of the crack. This will spread the stress and probably halt the progress of the crack.

A neater-looking, more permanent patch can be made by cementing a suitably shaped piece of repair plastic to the windshield. Special cements and techniques are needed. Shop manuals available from Du Pont and Rohm and Haas tell how it's done. A skilled sheet-plastics worker can perform minor miracles. A good military aircraft mechanic, for example, can repair a bullet hole so it scarcely shows. He'd cut out the damaged section so as to make a nice round hole. He would bevel the edges slightly. Then he'd make a plug to fit the hole from a scrap of identical plastic, set it into the hole, and bond it with suitable plastic cement. When hard, he would wet-sand the edges flush and smooth and then polish with suitable compounds. Talk to a good plastics shop about your damaged windshield—it just could be saved to serve for many more seasons!

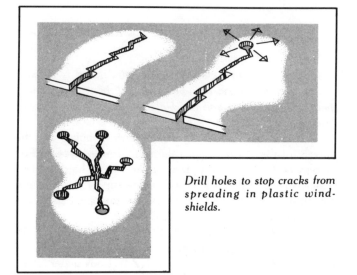

Drill holes to stop cracks from spreading in plastic windshields.

Scratched Plastic Windshield

Q. I dropped a screwdriver onto the plastic windshield of my boat and made quite a scratch on it. Can this be fixed?

A. Yes, provided the scratch isn't extremely deep. Starting with moderately coarse waterproof sandpaper, such as No. 320, and using plenty of water to lubricate the work, sand in circles around the scratch. Use a felt or soft rubber block to back up the sandpaper. The reason for the rotary motion is to avoid sanding a localized flat spot on a curved surface, as would happen if you used back-and-forth strokes, which would create an area of optical distortion. It will take a lot of patient sanding to take down the surface of the plastic enough to remove a deep scratch. Do not use a power sander because it will generate enough friction heat to pose a danger of softening and distorting the plastic. Once the scratch has been removed, use 360, 400, and finally 600 waterproof sandpaper to get the sanded area progressively smoother and free of visible scratches. Then use plastic buffing compound to polish the surface. Do not bear long and hard with the buffing wheel in an electric drill, lest overheating occur.

Cause of Windshield Crazing

Q. *My boat has been outdoors for several years and now the plastic windshield is beginning to show numerous little cracks. They look rather like scattered fish scales in the plastic when the light happens to strike it just so. What causes these marks and how can I remove them?*

A. "Crazing" is caused by use of unsuitable cleaning agents, or by the plastic having been given too sharp a bend, or a combination of both. People use household and automotive glass cleaners on plastic boat windows and windshields without stopping to think that such products are intended for glass. The solvents in them are often harmful to plastic. You can get a windshield looking clean with one of these products and think, "Well, that's that!" But the solvent will have started to work on the plastic's surface and the ill effects will show up later. Once crazing has started, there's no way to stop it—it is inside the plastic, below its surface, where nothing you might apply to the surface can reach it. When crazing gets so bad you can't stand the sight of it, you'll have to get a new windshield.

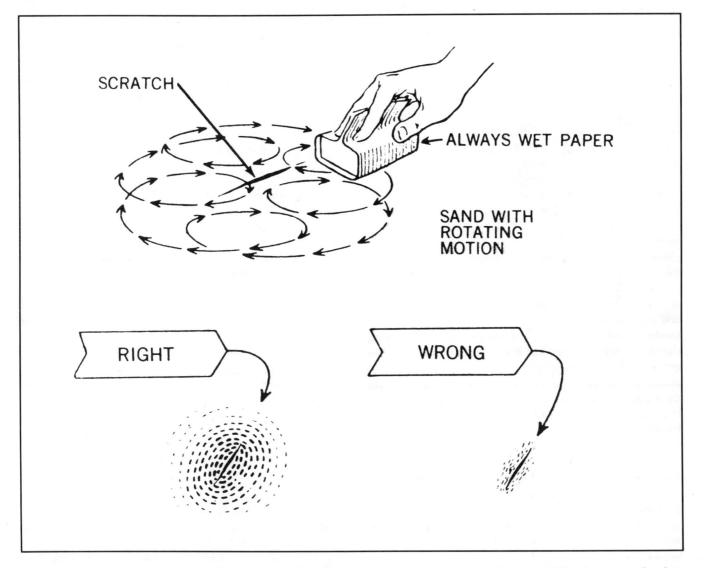

Use fine grades of wet sandpaper to work out deep scratches. Circular motion shown takes down the surface of the plastic as uniformly as possible so as not to make flat spots that would cause optical distortion.

Cleaning Plastic Windshields

Q. Please explain the proper way to clean a very dirty plastic windshield.

A. If there is mud, thick dust, or dried salt spray on it, first wash it gently with warm water, mild bar soap, and a soft cloth. After wetting them, use your fingernail to gently break up stubborn mud deposits. Avoid rubbing mud and dust across the surface.

When all gritty spots have been rinsed off, wipe dry with a clean, soft cloth or dab water off with paper toweling. Then remove water spots and brighten the surface by using a liquid-type plastic window cleaner. If your marine store does not have it, you can probably get some at a small airport catering to private airplanes, as they use a lot of it on airplane windows, which are made from similiar plastics.

Use a cleaner intended for plastic on your boat's plastic windows and windshields. Types intended for glass can harm plastic. (Mirror Bright Polish Co.)

Plastic Windshield Turned White

Q. My plastic windshield has turned a milky white and is now quite hard to see through. What went wrong and what shall I do?

A. The plastic is beginning to show its age. After all, there comes a time when the paint on a car becomes too dull to respond to polishing! Use of cleaning fluids meant for glass could have accelerated the appearance of this milkiness. There is no product that will restore the original clarity. The windshield will have to be replaced.

Curvy Windshield Frame

Q. I loved the graceful curves in the wood-framed windshields of older boats. The aluminum-framed ones on today's boats have stark straight lines and sharp corners. Where could I get an aluminum-framed one with nice curves?

A. Probably nowhere, unless you care to spend a lot of money on a custom job. It was simple to make patterns and then use power tools to saw and rout wood to any desired curve. But the aluminum channel material used in modern windshield frames comes in long, straight lengths from the aluminum mills. It can't be easily or economically bent. So, all things considered, windshield styling has changed to make the best use of the available material—cost included. Because wood needs several coats of varnish, it can be expensive, due to the time and labor involved in finishing it.

Where to Get Side Curtains

Q. Where can I buy a set of side curtains to fit my inboard runabout?

A. Although some companies sell "universal" folding tops, they don't make side curtains to go with them. The reason is that the shapes of the windshield side wings and the cockpit side coaming vary so widely among the many different makes and models of boats that trying to design, manufacture, and stock sets to fit all popular models would be a no-win proposition. Look up a sailmaker. Contrary to what most people think, sailmakers don't confine themselves to sails alone. Most of them also do folding tops, cockpit covers, spray dodgers, and so on, and if you take your boat to a good one (or arrange for him to go to the boat) he can tailor up some side curtains that will fit well and look nice.

Drilling Holes in Plastic

Q. How do I make holes for installation bolts in sheet plastic? Someone told me there is great danger of cracking the plastic if drilling is done improperly.

A. Use common high-speed twist drills for holes up to about three-sixteenths of an inch in diameter. Use a new or freshly sharpened drill. Feed the drill into the plastic carefully,

Side curtains have to be tailored to fit the boat.

Wooden windshield frames, top, gave way to aluminum ones, bottom, to overcome production problems posed by varnishing time. Made from extruded strips, aluminum frames tend to have straight lines to avoid expensive bending.

watching for any tendency for it to "burn" (overheat) the plastic and to grab too much material and jam, so as to start a crack.

Holes for windshield installation bolts should be larger than the bolts. The sheet plastics commonly used will expand and contract with changes in air temperature. Thus, when bolts are a tight fit in the holes, there is no provision for the plastic to shift slightly as its dimensions change. The localized stresses can start cracks. It is also common for boats to flex when going over rough water, so again there has to be some play in the installation bolts. Good practice is to make the holes large enough so they will accept rubber grommets or bushings to separate the bolts from the plastic. Also, rubber or fiber washers can be used to distribute bolt hole pressure gently into the plastic.

If you must make holes larger than about three-sixteenths of an inch, you can get twist drills ground for use in plastics at a machine shop or plastics supply house. To regrind regular drills for plastics use, use these specifications:

Rake or helical angle 17°
Drill point angle 110° to 140°
Lip relief angle 8° to 15°
Cutting edge angle dubbed off to 0°

For holes of half an inch or more, common round "hole saws" for use in electric drills can be bought at hardware stores. You must feed the saw into the plastic slowly and carefully, as their teeth are fairly large and can "grab." Lift the saw free often to let chips drop out of the tooth gullets.

Making Holes in Glass

Q. The only way I can fit a windshield wiper onto my boat's windshield is by drilling a hole for the wiper shaft in the safety glass windshield. Can this be done?

A. If the windshield uses the type of tempered safety glass common in auto windows, any attempt to cut or drill it is likely to cause it to shatter into countless tiny fragments. If it is laminated safety glass, you can make holes. It would be wise to talk to people at a local auto glass shop before starting work to get their opinions.

To drill glass, select a piece of copper tubing having an outside diameter the same as the desired hole. Cut a piece perhaps two to four inches long, depending on its diameter and the size of electric drill being used. Put it in the drill chuck. Set the electric drill or drill press for slow speed. Smear automotive valve grinding compound on the lower end of the tubing and press gently against the glass. The cutting action will be slow; you will have to watch things closely and replenish the compound often, but you will eventually get a clean, true hole. It would be wise to practice on some scrap glass before going to work on the windshield.

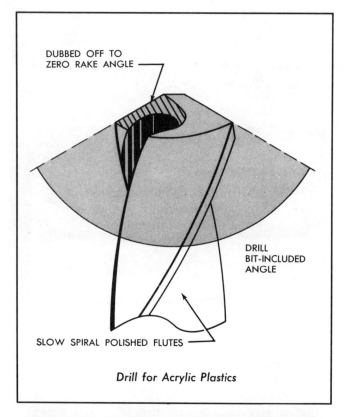

DUBBED OFF TO
ZERO RAKE ANGLE

DRILL
BIT-INCLUDED
ANGLE

SLOW SPIRAL POLISHED FLUTES

Drill for Acrylic Plastics

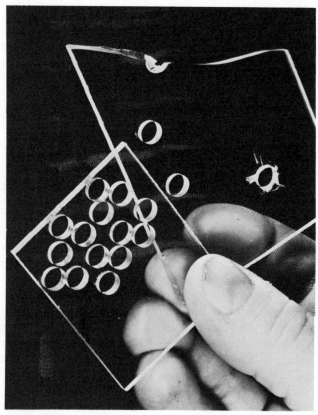

A drill with the wrong grind can make sheet plastic split. Man is holding shattered piece drilled with improper bit, and sound piece with clean holes made by suitable drill. Sketch shows how to grind drill point for plastic.

Screens for Portlights

Q. *How does one make insect screens to fit round or oval portlights in a yacht?*

A. Most companies that make portlights make screens to fit them. As these are well made and easy to install, inspect your portlights for some trademark. If you can determine who made them, look in the catalogs at your nearest marine stores to see if you can order ready-made screens.

If you can't do this, well, there is no standardized way of making your own. Inspect screens in other people's boats. The metal frame will be the biggest problem. If you're a good mechanic you could make some up of brass rod or strap, and solder the bronze screening to the brass. It will be slow, fussy work. Most marine stores sell "Velcro," a type of tape that sticks to itself yet pulls apart readily. A sailmaker or canvas shop could sew nylon mosquito netting to suitable strips of Velcro to make up a set of easy-on, easy-off screens that can be attached to the surfaces around the portlights.

Portlight manufacturers supply mosquito screening to fit their products.

Replacements for Aluminum Windshield Frames

Q. *Salt water has corroded the aluminum frame of my boat's windshield. Local marine stores don't know where to* get the special aluminum channel stock from which it is made. What should I do?

A. Due to the limited demand in any particular locality, and the many cross sections used in various windshields, retail establishments find it impractical to stock this material. And some of the companies that make it sell only at wholesale. N. A. Taylor Co., Gloversville, N.Y. 12078 markets at retail a "universal" walk-through aluminum-framed windshield. Your best bet may be to get the catalog of Imperial Marine Equipment, 7601 N.W. 66th St., Miami, Fla. 33166. If these leads don't produce solutions to your problem, go to your marine dealer and ask to see his marine trade directories that are put out by boating trade magazines. Look for names such as Bonnell, Campbell, and Young Windows.

Seeks Deck Prism

Q. I noticed small windows on a fine yacht set flush into the surface of the deck. The glass in them was made in the form of a prism. They had the effect of gathering outside light and spreading it nicely in the cabin below the deck. Who makes them?

A. Try Jay Stuart Haft Co., 8925 N. Tennyson Drive, Milwaukee, Wis. 53217. They specialize in importing fine

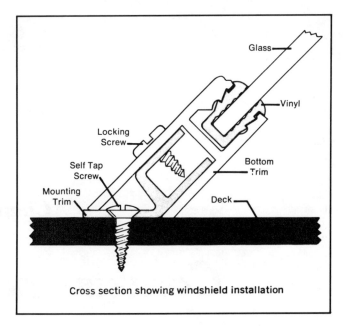

Cross section showing windshield installation

Aluminum windshield frames make use of a variety of special extrusions. Finding a replacement that will fit can call for much searching. (N. A. Taylor Co.)

yacht hardware from England and as of this writing their catalog lists "prismatic deck lights." Some American marine hardware firms make round deck lights.

Chapter 22

Canvas and Canvasing

Merits of Canvasing

Q. *Every time one meets a boat owner who has badly deteriorated canvas on the deck or cabin roof of his wooden boat, all he talks about is replacing the canvas with fiberglass. What are the pros and cons of each material?*

A. Fiberglass cloth is too loosely woven to be stapled down snug and true—it will exasperatingly twist and open its weave. So one must depend on the resin to hold it down. One layer may be durable on a relatively flat, seamless plywood deck or roof, but on a cabin trunk or roof having much curvature and several corners the inevitable flexing of the structure will make the fiberglass crack. Polyester resin isn't a particularly tenacious glue and if a surface warps or pants much, separation can occur sooner than you'd expect.

Two layers of cloth resist cracking—but then weight and cost go up. Resin does not brush out and flow like paint, and it tends to run easily on sloping surfaces, so on other than horizontal surfaces you get runs and sags, and because cured resin is surprisingly hard, sanding is tedious work. You will work and work and work to get a good-looking finish. Done right, though, a fiberglassing job can be very durable.

Canvas and the associated bedding compounds, tighteners, and paints can turn out to be cheaper than fiberglassing materials for the same surface—a little cheaper or a lot cheaper, all depending on the individual job. You do not need to get involved with the figuring of air temperature, amount of hardener to add, the pot life of the ingredients involved with fiberglassing, etc. You can take your time while canvasing. Put on well, canvas is flexible and will remain so for some years, so cracking and lifting-off won't be immediate problems. You can shrink it by brushing water onto it and get a nice, tight, smooth job—put it on dry, wet it, let it dry, and all the little wrinkles will be gone! A few coats of "canvas tightener and sealer" will fill its weave, make it fairly water resistant, and thus quite rot- and mildew-resistant. Finished off with suitable paint, it is durable, nice looking, has a yachty air to it, feels nice underfoot, and will last quite a while. We recently had a letter from a man who bought a boat we had built 25 long years previously and he remarked on how the canvas job on the deck was still in perfect condition.

A canvas cabin roof that is as badly cracked as this one cannot be fixed with simple, easy methods. Recanvasing calls for removal and replacement of all wood trim strips. If the canvas under the paint is reasonably sound, some modern products might be used. Good results have been had from pulling off all old canvas and giving the wood a coating of suitable tough epoxy resin.

Books on Canvasing

Q. *Is there a book that tells how to do a good job of canvasing a deck?*

A. Not that we know of, and we've had our eyes open for one for years. Boatbuilding books, such as *Boatbuilding* by Chapelle, *Amateur Boat Building* by Crosby, and *Small Boat Construction* by Steward, have two or three pages on canvasing but nothing detailed or profound. The latter two may be hard to find today. *The Woodenboat* magazine, P.O. Box 78, Brooklin, Maine 04616 has in recent years printed some good material on canvasing decks and might oblige with photocopies. Send a business-sized, stamped, return addressed envelope to Old Town Canoe Co., Old Town, Maine 04468 and ask them to send you a copy of their folder on recanvasing canoes. The number of boatyards who have men who really know how to lay canvas is getting smaller and smaller. You will get a bewildering mixture of horse sense and baloney if you talk to people in a number of places!

There is a book called *Boat Canvas from Cover to Cover* by Bob and Karen Lipe. It deals with making bags, buckets, awnings, sail covers, and similar things, not with covering decks and roofs. It may be obtained from International Marine Publishers, 21 Elm St., Camden, Maine 04843.

Canvas Durability Varies

Q. *I've heard of some deck canvasing jobs lasting for years, and others going to pieces quickly. Why this variation?*

A. Simple—lots of variables are involved. Some jobs call for a light, thin canvas that will conform to boat shapes readily. Others call for a heavy canvas that will stand much foot traffic. On various jobs, people use 8-, 10-, or 12-oz. canvas. Naturally, a thin canvas used where there's a lot of foot traffic won't last as long as thicker, tougher stuff. On some boats, deck planks are flexible and yield under the canvas when people walk about; on others, there's negligible flexing. When deck planking is going to be hidden under canvas (the canvas is to provide watertightness) it isn't necessary to lay the planks in a handsome pattern of bent, tapering pieces. So the deck can be planked with straight strips running parallel to the centerline of the hull, and these strips can have tongue-and-groove joints. This will materially reduce the amount each plank will flex when a heavy person's heel comes down on it, so of course cracking of canvas above deck plank seams is reduced.

There is no agreement among old-timers as to whether canvas should be laid onto the wood with nothing spread over the wood first, or if it should be laid into a coat of wet, thick paint to bond and cushion it. Along toward the time when wood was fading from the scene and fiberglass was appearing, marine paint firms started offering "canvas bedding compound" and "canvas tightener and sealer." The first mentioned was a cream-colored product that smelled much like linseed oil paint but was about as thick as a stiff molasses—it couldn't be brushed but it could be spread with a linoleum cement spreader. It was sticky enough to adhere well to wood and canvas, yet it did not harden as quickly as would paint. So it acted as a cushion for the canvas. The sealer was basically butyrate-type airplane fabric dope, and as it was of fairly thin consistency it would soak into canvas well and more or less seal it into a durable plastic, which is what the dried dope amounts to. These products can still be found with some inquiring.

Some old-timers preferred to brush thinned-out flat white paint liberally into the freshly laid canvas, feeling it would lock the fabric to the underlying heavy paint and also fill the weave so as to waterproof it. Others felt the way to do it was to wet the canvas with water to shrink it tight and smooth, and then apply the first coat of paint when the top surface was just beginning to feel dry. They reasoned the paint would cling well to the surface but not penetrate into the weave so as to make it rigid and encourage cracking.

High-gloss paint is shiny because of a high oil content. Many coats of it create a thick skin that will eventually dry hard and brittle under the sun's rays. It can readily crack. Flat paint is dull because it has less oil, and for this reason it has less buildup with repeated coats. Many landlubbers will automatically choose gloss paint over flat for appearance sake, not realizing there can be a difference in canvas longevity. In the last score of years we have seen less and less use of linseed oil and more use of alkyd, urethane, latex, epoxy, and other bases. How this variety of resins will behave when used on canvas is hard to say. One man will apply his paint in one very thick coat, which dries into a leathery skin that will start cracking when it gets really dry. Another will take the time and care to apply his paint in two thin but uniform coats. It's well known that two thin coats produce better results than will one thick coat on any job. Predicting how long a canvas job will last is like guessing what will happen next in the World Series!

Buying Canvas

Q. *My local marine stores don't have any canvas in stock. Where can it be bought?*

A. In this age of fiberglass boats, there isn't enough demand for it to justify stocking it in marine stores. Go to awning and tent shops in your area. You may find canvas specialists in the Yellow Pages in some areas. About the best assortment of canvas materials in the mail order marine trade is offered in the catalog of Defender Industries, Inc., 255 Main St., P.O. Box 820, New Rochelle, N.Y. 10801. No. 6 weight is suitable for heavy duty applications. Nos. 8 and 10 are suitable for decks. No. 12 is adequate for cabin roofs and other places that will not receive foot traffic. Canvas comes in both "treated" and "untreated" form, referring to rot- and mildew-proofing treatment.

Canvas Products Association International, 350 Endicott Bldg., St. Paul, Minn. 55101, puts out an annual canvas products *Buyers Guide*. If you want to look into canvas use on boats in a serious way, get a copy. The price for the 1980 issue is $7.50 post paid.

Special tools and materials are needed for canvas repair work. Most marine supply houses catering to the sailing fraternity have them in stock. (Crook & Crook)

Lay Canvas in Wood Glue?

Q. What do you think of laying deck canvas into Weldwood glue?

A. We're skeptical. That's a glue intended for wood. It depends on a well-fitted joint with close wood-to-wood contact to produce strong joints in woodwork. Any of this glue that fills gaps between poorly mated pieces of wood will simply be a rather brittle filler, with no strength. While it would adhere to the wood of the deck, it would also soak up into the canvas and more or less saturate it—possibly unevenly. One would have to make test specimens to see how well it would bond to the canvas. We suspect that if the canvas was saturated with it, you'd have a hard and brittle covering that would crack with every heavy footstep or dropped object. Remember, one of the advantages of a canvased deck is the flexibility of the fabric and hence its ability to give with stress and strain. Before we canvased a deck with Weldwood we'd make test specimens to evaluate the results.

Fiberglass Over Canvas?

Q. What do you think of stripping old paint off a canvas deck, then covering the canvas with fiberglass to seal all the cracks better than paint would?

A. It would cover the cracks and give watertightness. How well it will work in other respects is anyone's guess. Much depends on how well the underlying canvas is adhering to the wood. If it's soundly and firmly bedded, it might work. But if it's loose and lifting, we'd expect the whole works to lift itself loose because the fiberglass will be hard and unyielding and will take charge over the loosely adhering canvas. We'd try a small spot, say 12 inches by 12 inches, and see how it worked.

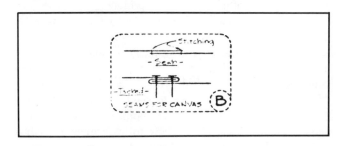

How to sew seams in canvas when one piece is too small to cover a deck area. An advantage of fiberglassing decks is that cloth can be overlapped and fastened with resin instead of doing any fussy stitching.

Removing Old Canvas

Q. Are there any tricks to removing old canvas from a deck?

A. If you mean very clever expedients, there are none. So much depends on how the old canvas is put on. It will just lift off of one boat but will have to be pried and disc-sanded off another. The big problem is coping with the edges and items of hardware. A good recanvasing job—that is, one which duplicates the old one—will require removal of all deck hardware and whatever is used around the edges.

Often the inner edges are attached to the bottom of the cabin in ways designed to shed water and minimize rot. (See sketches.) Obviously, a considerable amount of removal and careful replacement of woodwork is involved. This is why boat owners often search for alternatives, such as a miracle coating that will cover up bad canvas. You could read the literature from companies such as Travaco, Sav-Cote Chemical Labs., Clark Craft, Gougeon Bros., and Chem Tech, Inc. for ideas in this field.

Some folks resort to leaving the hardware and wood on, cut the canvas around its edges with a sharp-pointed knife, trim the new canvas to fit around hardware and up against wood strips, cement and staple it down, and then cover the edges with supplementary strips of wood shaped to fit. It works, but it looks bad, and doing a good job can be almost as tedious as taking off and replacing the original parts.

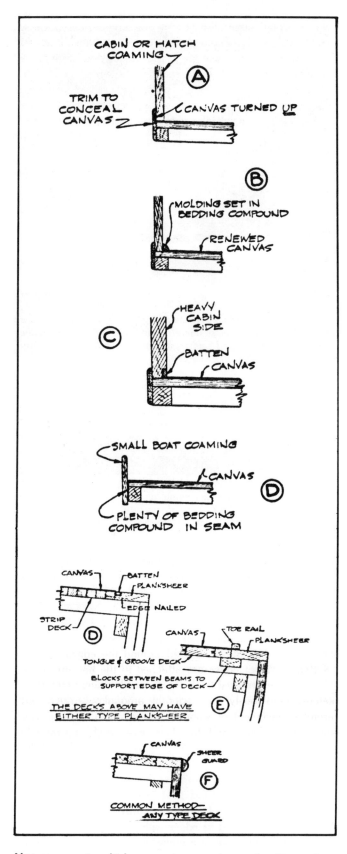

Canvasing a Fir Plywood Deck

Q. I'm building a plywood boat. Some kibitzers tell me I should put canvas onto the fir plywood deck and cabin roof to keep the plywood from weather-checking. Others say it will be a waste of time, and that I should use this-or-that miracle coating that's easy to brush on. What's your opinion?

A. Planked decks are canvased to keep the many seams from leaking. This problem does not exist with plywood. Canvasing the plywood will be a nice-looking, seaman-like and durable method of covering the decks against weather-checking. After you have laid the canvas in "canvas bedding compound" or "canvas cement" and wet it with water to pull it tight, you can go over it with an electric flatiron set to "warm" as soon as the water has largely dried off. This will smooth down the cement under the canvas, bond the cement and canvas well, and result in a very neat and durable job.

Canvasing a Kayak

Q. We're building a kayak. We're arguing whether to have the covering canvas wet or dry when we stretch and tack it onto the frame. What would you advise?

A. Wetting the canvas might make it more pliable and facilitate pulling and stretching the canvas to shape. But if you put it on wet, you can't wet it more to pull out any wrinkles that might have shown up despite your care. If it's put on dry, its natural flexibility will enable most wrinkles to be pulled out as you go along. Nine times out of ten, if any small ones remain, wetting the canvas will pull them out. An experienced person probably could do it either way with good results. But for a first try, common sense suggests that putting it on dry would be best.

Kayak Frame Distorted

Q. A few years ago we built a canvas-covered kayak and, following instructions with the plans, applied airplane fabric dope to it to tighten and waterproof it. Now the frame has been pulled in and warped so the craft looks like the hip bones and ribs of a starved cow. Did we do something wrong?

A. Possibly. There are various kinds of airplane fabric dopes. Some have strong tightening action, some have little or no tightening action, some stop tightening as soon as they're dry, others continue to pull the fabric tighter and tighter. Seems that you chanced to use the latter. While most modern small planes are all-metal, many fabric-covered ones are still around. People think they are covered with canvas.

This simply is not so! Various fabrics are used, including a high quality cotton type called "Grade A," an aircraft grade of Irish linen, a special light, tough fiberglass cloth called "Razorback," and a Dacron (polyester) type variously labelled "Poly-Fiber," "Eonnex," and "Ceconite" by vendors. Talk to mechanics at small airports about these dopes and fabrics. Some are lighter, stronger, and smoother than canvas, and the synthetic ones are rot-proof. They could make a superior kayak covering.

Recanvasing a Canoe

Q. Can you give any advice on recanvasing a canoe?

A. Many people have botched this job, and the sorry-looking results that most of us have seen have spread the notion that it is a very difficult job. But we've done it and have found it to be simple enough. The mistake many make is to start tacking canvas to the gunwale at some random point, putting tacks in a few inches apart. As the work progresses, a few big and unmanageable puckers result. The right way is to start amidships with a few tacks or staples spaced about a foot apart and work toward the ends, alternating from side to side and end to end, putting in a few more fastenings at a time. Large puckers are left between these widely spaced fastenings; therefore, by the time the ends of the canoe are reached there are no oversize puckers that can't be gotten rid of.

One then gets a pair of pliers with broad jaws. Some experts braze steel plates to the jaws to get a "hammerhead shark" effect with even wider jaws to grip the canvas. Using this tool and starting again at the amidships point, the canvas is gripped at the mid-points of the large puckers and pulled to reduce them into two puckers, a staple or tack being driven in adjacent to the jaws. This divides all the large puckers into smaller ones. The process is repeated until all that is left is a large number of rather small puckers. The canvas is then thoroughly soaked with water. This will shrink it and pull out the remaining puckers.

The American Red Cross book, *Canoeing*, ISBN 0-385-08313, available through local Red Cross offices, has several pages on canvasing canoes and also goes into detail

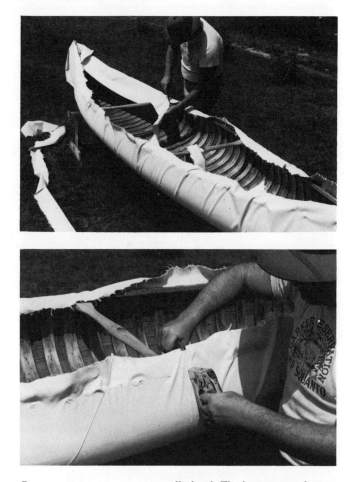

Recanvasing a canoe is not really hard. The basic principle is to get the canvas shaped to the hull roughly, as in the top picture, with large puckers between widely-spaced tacks or staples. This avoids getting a few huge and unmanageable puckers at a few places. Then one goes around the gunwale with wide-nosed pliers and pulls on the middle of a large pucker to divide it into smaller ones. This process is repeated, working around the gunwale several times, each time pulling the puckers into smaller ones. The very small puckers remaining will come out when the canvas is shrunk and tightened with a water soaking.

on repairing wooden ones. Or, send a self addressed stamped envelope to Old Town Canoe Co., Old Town, Maine 04468 for a copy of their pamphlet, *Maintenance and Care of Fabric Covered Wood Canoes.*

Chapter 23

Sails

Broken Stitches

Q. At season's end I was dismayed to find many broken stitches in the Dacron sails of my boat, which were new this spring. Did I get a set of "gyp" sails with this boat?

A. We do not think so. Dacron sailcloth is much harder than the old cotton material which is now obsolete. The stitching does not bury itself in the weave but stands out on the surface. It is thus much more susceptible to chafing. One must always keep this in mind. Watch for places where the sails—especially the seams—rub against parts of the mast and rigging, and do whatever can be done to alleviate the situation. Don't leave a sailboat at the dock with sail raised and slatting in the wind. This kind of whipcracking can quickly loosen up stitching.

Finding Sails

Q. I bought a used sailboat of an old and famous class type which is not common on my waters. Local boatyards know nothing about it and can't help me locate a set of good used sails and some needed deck fittings. Can you help me?

A. The various yachting and sailing magazines have annual issues that contain directories of known active sailboat classes. Such lists also appear from time to time in both soft and hard cover sailing books. There is such a list in the 1980 issue of *Boat Owners Buyers Guide,* for example. There are "sail brokers," companies that specialize in buying and selling used sails. Some are straight brokers, and others combine brokerage and sailmaking. A prominent brokerage

firm is Bacon & Associates, Inc., 112 West St., Annapolis, Md. 21403. Typically, a boat owner who has sails he does not need sends them to a broker; the broker inspects, cleans, and repairs them, puts them on his list, and collects a commission when they are sold. You may have trouble finding good used sails for a less popular class of sailboat, though. Contact the class association; if they don't know where to get used sails they will probably know of a source for good new ones that will fit well.

Storing Sails

Q. I live on a lonely lake and do all my sailing alone. There's nobody here to compare notes with. I have been storing my sails by folding them up. Now I see pictures of "sail bags" in magazines and wonder if my method of storage is wrong?

A. Gentle folding usually will do no harm. Sail bags are for temporary storage aboard boats, usually for larger sails that cannot be spread out for folding aboard a boat when it is out on the water. The bags identify various sails aboard a racing boat, for example, and keep them from becoming mixed up in the excitement of a race. Cramming them into a bag for a day or two does not put permanent creases in them, but if a sail is left rumpled up in a bag for a long time, it will come out with crease lines all over it. If you fold yours one way one winter and another way the next winter, fold lines should even out and not show. The ideal way to store sails is to get a long cardboard tube, such as are used for rolling rugs for shipment, roll the sail onto it, and wrap with clean paper.

A sail is basically a wing that works in a vertical rather than a horizontal plane. Its shape is carefully made to coax maximum drive out of the wind. Sailcloths are made to resist stretching so as to hold the shape worked into sails by sailmakers. (Hobie Cat)

Fixing Small Holes

Q. There are several small holes and tears in my Dacron sails. How can I repair them?

A. Use sail repair tape that is available in marine supply stores. Cut small pieces to fit the sizes and shapes of the holes, remove the backing paper, and press on. It has an adhesive on it that will tenaciously cling to sailcloth. It has a translucent off-white color that renders the repairs fairly inconspicuous, and can be used to fix other things made of canvas, vinyl, etc. Keep some handy!

Ironing Sails

Q. Would it be safe to try to take a lot of creases and wrinkles out of my Dacron sails with a flatiron?

A. Don't try it. There are numerous types and grades of sailcloth to suit various sailmaking and sailing purposes. Some of it is coated with a plastic surfacing material that controls the stretching characteristics. This could be hurt by the heat of ironing. If the iron is very hot it could melt the cloth. The best way to get wrinkles out is to find someplace where you can hang the sail horizontally by its three corners for a week or two. Its own weight will pull out most of the wrinkling—if not perfectly, at least acceptably. All sails have some wrinkling; don't expect perfection in this matter.

Stiff Sail

Q. The synthetic cloth sail on our Sunfish has become stiff after only a few summers of use. Please tell us how to soften it up.

A. The material from which the sail is made has been affected by sunlight and has begun to suffer molecular change. There is no way to soften it. The same thing happens to synthetic rope. Too many uninformed boat owners leave sails laying on the dock or beach all summer, confident that mildew won't hurt them. Then the sun damages them! Keep sails in the shade as much as possible when not in use.

Washing Synthetic Sails

Q. Please tell me how to wash synthetic sails.

A. If a truly smooth and clean surface that is large enough to spread the sails out on is available, you can do the job with bucket and brush. Otherwise, fill a bathtub and turn the folds of the sail over and over to get at all parts of it. Use water as hot as your hands can stand, and a mild bar soap—not a detergent. Mildew does not attack synthetic sailcloth but does discolor it. Remove as much as possible with a brush having only moderately stiff bristles, working the water in well. If any staining remains after rinsing, soak the sail for a few hours in a one percent solution of household bleach and water, then rinse thoroughly. Some greases and oils may contain metallic compounds which can cause stains, and leaving a sail in contact with a piece of rusty metal will cause reddish stains. Soak the stained areas with a two percent solution of hydrochloric acid in water, and rinse very thoroughly.

By the time a sail is dirty enough to really need a cleaning, it will probably have collected some small tears and may have some broken stitches. The easy way to get everything fixed as well as possible is to let a sailmaker do the job. Many boatyards have arrangements under which one can leave sails with them; a sailmaker will come around, pick up a pile of sails, take them to his shop, and bring them back to the yard when done.

Aluminum Stains

Q. There are grey streaks on my synthetic sails from rubbing against the aluminum mast. How can they be removed?

A. Try gentle scrubbing with a moderately stiff brush and warm water to which a little liquid detergent has been added. If this fails, better let a professional sailmaker see what he can do.

Sail Cleaning Kits

Q. Where can I get a kit of approved materials for cleaning synthetic sails?

A. Many marine supply stores have them. As different firms come and go in this specialized field, get on the trail of current makers by looking in marine trade directories. You can make do with household bar soap and mild detergents, plus a little hydrochloric acid from drug or hardware stores.

Buying Sailcloth

Q. Where does one get sailcloth? None of the marine stores in my area can find it in their marine hardware catalogs.

A. Few such places stock it as there is little demand at the retail level. Go to sailmakers. Defender Industries, Inc., 255 Main St., P.O. Box 820, New Rochelle, N.Y. 10801 sells it

by mail order; their catalog lists a wide range of cloths, vinyls, fiberglass and general boat maintenance items. Some firms sell kits of materials for making sails for various popular class and homemade sailboats. A prominent company in this field is Sailrite Enterprises, Rte. 1, Columbia City, In. 46725.

There are problems in making one's own sails. Home type sewing machine needles have trouble penetrating hard, dense, synthetic sailcloth; broken needles are common. The cloth is both stiff and slippery and is apt to give trouble to a person accustomed to handling and feeding soft household fabrics into a machine.

Sailmaking Books

Q. Is there a book on sailmaking?

A. Yes. *Modern Sailmaking* by Percy W. Blandford, and *Sails* by Jeremy Howard-Williams, are available from International Marine Publishers, Inc., 21 Elm St., Camden Maine 04843.

Use Sail Covers

Q. I get tired of putting the sails on and taking them off every time we use our 20-foot sloop. But if I leave them on all the time, sun and dirt will ruin them. What should I do?

A. Wise up! Get a set of sail covers—long fabric boots cut and sewed so they fit over furled sails. Their use is standard practice on larger sailboats; you can do it on yours, too. Sailmakers and awning shops can make them up to size from canvas or one of the synthetic fabrics.

A sail cover will protect your sail when it is not in use. (Evinrude Motors)

Sail Repair Tools

Q. Where can I get a set of sail repair tools to take with us on long cruises?

A. Marine supply stores catering to yachtsmen carry them. Mail order marine supply companies list them in catalogs—see *Boat Owners Buyers Guide*. They are made for the marine trade by Moody Tools, Inc., 52 Crompton Ave., East Greenwich, R.I. 02818.

Duplicating Old-Time Sails

Q. I am making a replica of a type of small sailboat that was common in my region a century ago. Dacron sails would look out of place on it. What kind of common canvas or other sheet material could I use to make good reproductions of old-time cotton sails?

A. Watch your step! Sail cloths are designed and made to resist stretching under wind pressure. If you make sails from an unsuitable material, they may stretch out of shape after a short breaking-in period. Better get in touch with others who have made reproductions of old sailboats and get the benefit of their experience.

Nylon Sails

Q. Why are some sails made of nylon when most are made of Dacron?

A. Dacron is used for sails that are to be used when sailing on various points of the wind; they resist stretching so they hold their shape. Nylon is not good for such general-purpose use because sails made of it will not hold shape. Nylon is used for sails such as spinnakers, which are used when sailing with the wind. Such sails are rather bag-shaped, and a little distortion does not affect their performance. Because nylon cloth is very strong, very thin, light sailcloth can be made of it. Very light weight is an advantage when going with light winds, since it does not take much air to hold such sails well up and filled with what little wind there may be.

Dacron and nylon cloths are used for different kinds of sails to make the most of the special characteristics of each fabric. Working sails are normally of Dacron, which does not stretch. Spinnakers are usually of nylon, which is very light in weight and lets such sails fill well in gentle breezes.

Sailmaking has changed with time. Anyone making a reproduction of some old craft, whether large or small, must consult experts on old-time marine matters to find a way to make authentic-looking sails from available modern materials. This is the Mayflower II as she looked when arriving at Plymouth, Mass. from England. (Plimoth Plantation)

Chapter 24

Masts and Rigging

Straight vs. Tapered Masts

Q. Why are the aluminum masts used on modern sailboats straight? I liked the looks of the tapered wooden ones better. Does anyone make tapered aluminum masts?

A. Aluminum mast blanks are made by the extruding process. Heated metal is loaded in a large hydraulic cylinder that has a die fitted into one end. The die is of the same shape as the desired cross section of the finished extrusion. The hot metal is squeezed and flows out through the die. Since the extruding is done through a die, the cross section must remain constant. Some aluminum masts are given a taper in the upper several feet by sawing out deep V-shaped pieces, pressing the sides together, and welding together along the cut. Of course, they cost more due to the extra labor involved.

Use "Slugs!"

Q. The sail on my small sailboat has a boltrope sewn into it along the luff. This fits into a groove molded in the aft edge of the aluminum mast. Friction makes it hard to raise and lower the sail, and the aluminum makes black marks on the sailcloth. Can anything be done?

A. Have a sailmaker sew "slugs" to the luff of the sail. These are small plastic objects available from sailmakers' supply houses. They will slide up and down in the mast groove much easier and keep the sail separated from the mast.

Aluminum Mast Cleaner

Q. How does one clean aluminum masts after they become dulled from weathering? Is there anything to get grey discoloration from masts off of synthetic sails?

A. Products have been marketed for these purposes but we have not seen them in marine stores or catalogs for some time. Our guess is that the increasingly popular practice of anodizing aluminum masts for corrosion protection has cut the demand for these things. The anodizing would reduce aluminum's tendency to soil sailcloth. If you have an unanodized mast and the problem exists, try applying a number of coats of wax. Auto or fiberglass wax should work.

Rapeseed Oil

Q. I saw some small containers in a marine store labelled "Rapeseed Oil." What on earth would this oddly named stuff be used for on boats?

A. It's used for lubricating sheaves, sail tracks, etc. on sailboats. It lubricates the metal but resists washing off in rain and spray, and does not stain sails as would a mineral oil. Made from seeds of an herb called rape, it dries slowly or not at all.

Sail "slugs."

Fastening Items to Aluminum Masts

Q. Is there any other way than using stainless steel self-tapping screws to attach hardware items to aluminum masts?

A. Yes. Most professional mastmakers and rigging shops use "drive rivets." As you can see in the sketch below, a metal nib projects from the rivet's head as it comes from the rivet maker. The rivet is inserted in the hole and this nib is struck smartly with a hammer. This drives the nib in and it expands the inside portion of the rivet, as shown in the second sketch. It works rather like a pop rivet in reverse, the mandrel being pushed in rather than pulled out.

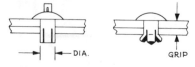

Cutting Steel Cable

Q. I had a terrible time cutting some steel rigging cable with a pair of diagonal cutters. Is there an easier way to do it?

A. You found out how tough steel cable is! Marine stores catering to sailing people sell wire cutters like those in the sketch. They will bite tough cable apart with surprising ease. It's all in the cutting edge angles and leverage built into this special tool. In an emergency, quick work can be done with a sharp cold chisel and a small anvil or other block of steel.

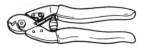

Types of Wire Rope

Q. Why are there so many kinds of wire rope? I am all confused by such figures in catalogs as 1 x 19, 7 x 7 and 7 x 19. Can you explain?

A. A 1 x 19 cable means a single cable made of 19 solid wires. It stretches little but bends hard. It's used for braces and stays that do not pass through pulleys. A 7 x 7 cable describes a cable made of seven strands, each composed of seven wires; 7 x 19 means the cable is made of seven strands, each of which is composed of 19 fine wires. Naturally, such a cable will stretch more but will also bend through a pulley sheave better. Boat riggers choose from among these various wire ropes as best fits a particular function aboard a boat.

STAINLESS STEEL WIRE ROPE

1 x 19 (Standing rigging)

7 x 7 and 7 x 19
(Running rigging)

Dents in Mast

Q. An accident put an appreciable dent in the aluminum mast of my cruising sailboat. It is roughly the size of a potato and is about an inch deep. We want to ferry the boat some distance to a place where it is going to be overhauled. Do you think it's safe to do so with this dent?

A. You'd have to watch the weather and plot a course with plenty of harbors of refuge along it. When wind presses on sails, the top of the mast is held in place by the stays. Tension on the stays puts a download on the mast. Some designers claim that in severe conditions this download can be equal to the weight of the boat. Such a download could encourage the mast to buckle in heavy weather. If that happened, your insurance could be declared void by reason of your having put to sea with a mast in unseaworthy condition. Make the trip if you feel sure you can complete it without running into strong winds. If you get caught out at sea, lower the sails and use power until the blow has passed. A lot depends on where the dent is. If it is near the mid-point of a space between step and stays, it would weaken the mast the most, for it would be located at the point of maximum bending stress. Be careful, mate!

Masts and booms transform the wind's energy into "horsepower" to drive sailboats at delightful speeds without noise or vibration. To work well and be dependable they have to be made with care. (Cape Cod Shipbuilding Co.)

Attaching Hardware to Aluminum Masts

Q. I attached some pieces of hardware to the aluminum mast of my sailboat with stainless steel screws. A friend says I did the wrong thing and that galvanic corrosion will result. What do you think?

A. You did it the accepted way. Your friend is misinformed. (*See* Chapter 3 on Corrosion and Chapter 5 on Fastenings.) Although you have two dissimilar metals, the very small areas of the screws compared to the large area of the mast renders the galvanic situation acceptably safe.

Straightening a Bent Aluminum Mast

Q. My big aluminum mast got bent. My brother is an expert welder. We have tried to get a five-foot section of aluminum mast extrusion so he can repair the bend. But marine dealers say no such thing is available, we'll have to buy a whole new mast blank. What's your opinion?

A. We'd bypass the dealers and go to the mastmakers. Bent masts often can be straightened by people who understand them and the metal they are made of. If the bend has not exceeded certain limits, straightening is possible. Mastmakers have short pieces of waste left over when long mast blanks are cut down to the desired length for a particular boat. We do not know enough about welding aluminum to say if the kind of repair you propose is feasible. We have never chanced to hear of it or read of it being done. The company that made your boat in all probability bought their masts all made up and ready to install from a mast specialist, which means they themselves are not the ultimate authority on masts. So we say find out who made the mast and get their advice on repairing. We were at a mastmaking shop once when a customer drove in with a bent mast lashed atop his car. The mast men there looked at it and said, sure, they could fix the bend. Whereupon they stuck one end of it between two handy trees and pressed on the free end. In a few minutes, their "feel" for the metal enabled them to straighten it as good as new—to the amazement and delight of the owner!

Painting Aluminum Masts

Q. The aluminum mast on our older fiberglass sailboat is rather shabby. Can it be spruced up with a paint job?

A. In general, yes. The aluminum is hard and when rigging cables, spinnaker poles, etc. happen to bang against the mast, the paint can chip and in time will be unsightly itself. But you can try painting to see how it works on your craft. Some of the companies that make fiberglass copies of Cape Cod catboats paint their masts a buff color to imitate old wooden masts. They have developed various ways. We would contact the company that made your mast and see if they have any ideas. Paint companies have literature on priming and painting aluminum boats; the information could be applied to masts.

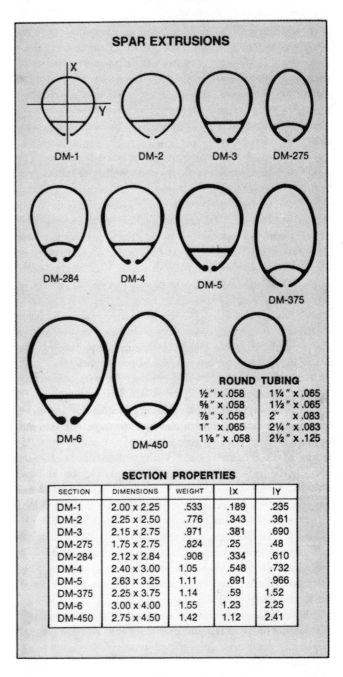

SPAR EXTRUSIONS

DM-1 DM-2 DM-3 DM-275

DM-284 DM-4 DM-5

DM-375

DM-6 DM-450

ROUND TUBING

½" x .058	1¼" x .065
⅝" x .058	1½" x .065
⅞" x .058	2" x .083
1" x .065	2¼" x .083
1⅛" x .058	2½" x .125

SECTION PROPERTIES

SECTION	DIMENSIONS	WEIGHT	IX	IY
DM-1	2.00 x 2.25	.533	.189	.235
DM-2	2.25 x 2.50	.776	.343	.361
DM-3	2.15 x 2.75	.971	.381	.690
DM-275	1.75 x 2.75	.824	.25	.48
DM-284	2.12 x 2.84	.908	.334	.610
DM-4	2.40 x 3.00	1.05	.548	.732
DM-5	2.63 x 3.25	1.11	.691	.966
DM-375	2.25 x 3.75	1.14	.59	1.52
DM-6	3.00 x 4.00	1.55	1.23	2.25
DM-450	2.75 x 4.50	1.42	1.12	2.41

Several firms offer "mast blanks" of extruded aluminum in a variety of cross sections, for both new boats and replacements on old ones. These sections are typical. Made by Dwyer Aluminum Mast Co.

Silencing Slatting Wires

Q. We can't sleep at night in our cruising sailboat, which has wires running up inside its hollow aluminum mast. When there is a swell or when passing motorboats send wakes our way, the wires slat noisily and the mast telegraphs the noise down into the cabin. What can be done?

A. It's a common problem. When complete mast assemblies, including wiring, are made up by conscientious mast manufacturers, the wires are clipped to the inside surface of the mast in one way or another. When wind indicators, electronic equipment, etc., are installed on mast tops later by boatyards, the men may not secure the wires—either because they do not know how or because it would cost too much to do.

Filling a mast with foam-in-place foam has been tried. The mast must be upended to do this, which puts its butt high in the air and hard to get to. If water ever leaks in, it will stay there, held by the foam. If there are halyards inside the mast, this method is out. One can cut oval pieces from some kind of stiff foam perhaps an inch or two thick, notch the pieces where necessary to clear wires, etc., and push each piece up into the mast true and square with a long stick having a pad affixed to its end. If the fit is snug they will stay in place, or a bit of epoxy will hold them.

We have heard of people upending their masts and filling them with ping-pong balls. The balls keep the wires from slatting, add negligible weight, and permit air to circulate and water to dry out. We have heard of people punching many holes in toy rubber balls and shoving them up inside their masts; the holes allow for circulation and drainage.

You can buy some plastic water tubing in coil form, run the wires inside it and push it up inside the mast. It will be stiff enough to stop much of the slatting and will muffle the sound from any that remains. Usually one or two clips holding the wires to the inside of the mast will be enough to stop slatting. One has to use ingenuity to get them up inside the mast and fastened to the inside of the mast walls. Tie them to a long stick with thread, coax them up inside, align them with holes drilled for the purpose, and affix them with pop rivets. We have seen people prop mast butts up at a moderate angle so the wires fell to the lowest parts of the mast interiors. They then poured catalyzed epoxy resin into the masts. It flowed along the low part of the mast interiors and stuck the wires firmly in place. All these suggestions should fire your imagination so you can think of a suitable solution for your particular mast and slatting problem.

Lightning Protection

Q. We have a lot of thunderstorms in our area and we worry about lightning striking the aluminum mast of our sailboat. What should we do?

A. Sailboats made by reputable manufacturers have their masts grounded to some kind of underwater metal part or plate. This makes the mast act like a giant lightning rod. By steadily carrying electrical potential from the atmosphere down into the water, the grounding avoids the buildup of electrical pressure that culminates in a lightning strike. To ascertain if your boat is grounded, look for copper wires leading from the mast, stays, etc., down to some metal object that is in direct contact with the water. This should be at least one square foot in area.

Since strong currents can jump from one metallic object to another, metal parts that are fairly near the mast or stays should be connected to the grounding system. During a storm, people should remain inside the cabin or as low as possible in the cockpit and clear of these pieces of metal.

Small sailboats that do not have grounding can be given protection from lightning strikes by carrying aboard a piece of sheet copper one foot square, to which is attached a length of heavy copper wire terminating in a strong alligator clip. When a storm is seen approaching, hang the copper overside and clip the wire to the mast.

Wooden masts usually have metal sail tracks on them, and of course their stays are of steel cable. So all these metal parts must be bonded together and connected to the ground plate. When larger boats are fitted with radios, it is common to use one of the mast stays for an antenna. For radio purposes, such a stay will have insulators of suitable electrical and mechanical strength inserted in them. To do a good job of grounding a larger and more complex boat, one needs a detailed knowledge of how to cope with various grounding problems. There are several pages on the subject in the American Boat and Yacht Council's standards manual for small craft safety.

As an aside, we must note there have been several recorded electrocutions resulting from aluminum-masted sailboats contacting low-hanging high tension electric utility wires. In some cases, contact has been made while sailing along rivers, and in others it was made while moving small boats about in boatyards on trailers or dollies. So one must be ever on the alert for overhead wires that hang low enough to contact the mast on your boat.

Replacing a Wooden Mast with Aluminum

Q. The built-up wooden mast on our fine old sloop is too far gone to recondition. Could we replace it with an aluminum one?

A. Yes, but the conversion will have to be done with due attention to various problems. Your sails will have to be reworked in some way, probably by replacing the track slides with slugs chosen to fit the mast's boltrope groove. A capable aluminum mast designer will have to be consulted to choose a suitable mast blank and plan the location of spreaders and stays on the new one so it will equal the old one in strength. The vertical center of gravity of the new mast would probably have to be calculated and compared to that of the old wooden one, to make sure the boat's stability will not be affected. It may be necessary to modify the terminals on the stays to mate with aluminum mast hardware. The aluminum mast men might ask you for an accurate drawing of your wooden mast. If you live far from the mastmaker, shipment of a longer mast may have to be

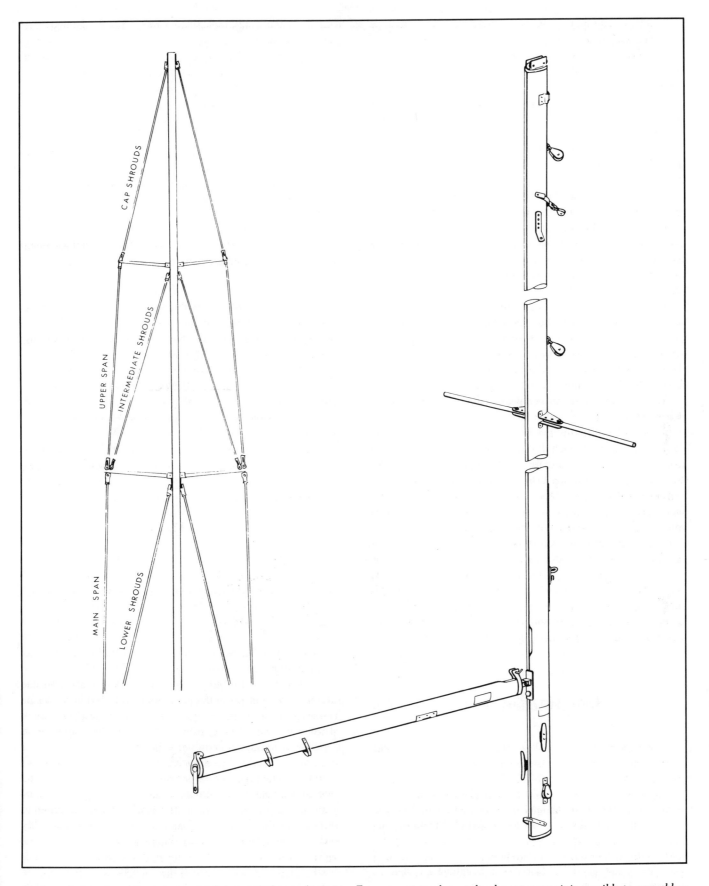

Modern aluminum masts are marvels of design and manufacturing. From a variety of specialized components it is possible to assemble a mast for any boat.

decided upon and the cost determined. It could be a shocker for a big mast!

Fiberglass Masts

Q. The solid spruce mast of my old sailboat is full of rot spots and cracks. Can I make a new hollow one of fiberglass?

A. Fiberglass masts have been made by men who are skilled with the material. Some have been successful, others have failed. One has to figure how to do it so the mast will be strong enough on one hand, yet not too heavy. There are various ways to do it. This is where knowledge of fiberglass work is needed, as some ingenuity may have to be used to solve design or fabrication problems. Hollow fiberglass masts have been made of right and left halves made up in separate molds. Suitable flanges have been incorporated in the two molds so there are overlaps for bonding the halves securely together. Masts have been made by winding strips of cloth around and around a suitably shaped mandrel and then sliding the mandrel out. The problem is to give the mandrel enough taper to enable the fiberglass form to be pulled off it.

Long blocks of foam have been slipped onto pipes or rods shish-kebab fashion, then the rods rotated to allow the foam to be turned and sanded to the desired dimensions and taper. Sometimes the foam has been left inside the finished mast, sometimes it has been dissolved out with an appropriate fluid. Built-up hollow cores for rectangular cross-section masts have been made of long strips of wood and thin plywood, then covered with enough layers of glass fabric for the needed strength. People have even used space-age carbon fiber techniques to make masts. The book *Fibreglass Boats* by Hugo du Plessis has a chapter on the subject. It is now several years old, so some newer ideas have probably come along in the meantime. You will have to contact fiberglass experts and study up on the subject.

Solid Wooden Masts

Q. Our fine old schooner has solid spruce masts of round cross section. The time is coming when they must be replaced. Where can I learn how to make a new mast?

A. *Boatbuilding* by Howard I. Chapelle has a chapter on mast- and spar-making. *Dinghy Building* by Richard Creagh-Osborne has a chapter on making small-boat masts; the techniques can be applied to larger ones. Other boatbuilding books have a few pages on masts. Supposing you can find trees tall enough for your needs, your first problem will be to find one with suitable taper. You will look at many that are thick enough at the base, but their trunks taper so much that they will be too thin up where your spreaders and shrouds will be attached. You may have to start with a tree that's much thicker than necessary at the bottom and do a lot of cutting down. It will have to season for a long time before you can work it down without risk of longitudinal splits forming. Instead of trying to use a tree felled on your property, you may find it faster, more dependable, and easier to laminate up a blank of suitable dimensions using lumber-yard spruce and epoxy. Here and there about the country are makers of wooden flagpoles; if you can find one, his knowledge of big sticks and his special oversize lathe might solve some of your problems.

Wooden Mast Builders

Q. My big sailboat's wooden mast is shot. It's a pretty big piece of woodwork. I do not have a place to make one myself nor all the clamps needed for the glue work. Does anyone still make wooden masts?

A. Here and there about the country are obscure boat-yards that can make built-up masts. There is just one firm that we know of that still specializes in wooden masts. It is the Pigeon Hollow Spar Co., Box 626, Plaistow, N.H. 03857; their shop is at 13 Water St., Newmarket, N.H. They have been in the business since 1830! They know how to ship long spars and masts to distant places.

Repairing a Broken Mast

Q. The solid spruce mast on my catboat broke off at the deck when one of the kids let the boat slide under a highway bridge while in the grip of a strong tide flow. After pricing a new one, I'm interested in trying to repair it. Can this be done?

A. Probably, but with some care. Your main concern is to retain strength in bending at the point where it is broken. A likely way to do the job is as follows. Apply glue to the broken ends and press the broken-off stub firmly in place. You might want to jig up the mast so you can apply pressure to the stub with a jack, in order to press the jagged ends together as tightly as possible. When the glue has set, go to work on the mast with a draw knife, whittling away the wood to get an hourglass shape extending perhaps a few feet to each side of the break. Bandsaw and plane lengths of wood to fit into this thinned place—they will amount to "splints" and will encircle the mast. A modern epoxy glue will be a big help here as its strength does not depend on perfect and close wood-to-wood contact. When hard, the outside of the splints can be planed down to match the roundness of the mast. If you want to, you can "bandage" the repaired area with perhaps three or more layers of glass cloth and epoxy resin for added reinforcement. Neatly done, a repair like this should do. Some kids in our town sawed down the flagpole in front of the high school on Halloween night several years ago, and the local boatyard repaired it this way. It is still standing proud and sturdy.

Glue for Masts

Q. What would be the best glue to use for making a built-up wooden mast?

A. A glue rated "water-resistant," such as the "Weldwood" found in all hardware stores, is of adequate durability. Its light tan color blends inconspicuously with wood. Some two-part glues rated "waterproof" are strong and durable but can show dark-colored glue lines that many would consider unattractive under a varnish finish. We would look beyond hardware stores today, though, and consider various epoxy type glues. Hardware stores don't sell them. Go to resin supply houses, aircraft and wooden boat suppliers, etc. Look in the Yellow Pages for adhesives specialists. Read advertisements in magazines such as *The Woodenboat*.

Paint or Varnish?

Q. What are the pros and cons of paint vs. varnish on wooden masts?

A. Varnish is preferred on pleasure craft masts. Because it is transparent, it allows continuous visual inspection of the mast for beginning cracks, separation of glue lines, and the black spots around fittings that indicate water is seeping in and starting rot. It also allows the pleasant-appearing wood grain to be seen, adding character and warmth to the boat.

Paint contains pigment, which tends to shut out the sun's rays more than varnish. Thus a coating of paint is likely to retain good appearance longer than varnish. Paint was often used on old-time working sailboats whose solid wood masts were made from smoothed-up tree trunks. As these took a long time to season, it was common to use them in semi-seasoned condition. The paint would slow down the rate of drying and minimize the appearance of seasoning cracks.

Modern varnishes usually contain a chemical that tends to filter out harmful rays in sunlight and improve durability. Sitka spruce rates fairly low in rot resistance, so the transparency of varnish is useful in detecting rot spots early. Commercial boats often used (and still use) masts of Douglas fir, which has good rot resistance, so paint can be used on them without compromising the rot situation. Any mast will get its share of bumps and chafing from normal use and will need to be refinished periodically for the sake of appearance. So it comes down to this—varnish will be the choice in most cases, with paint being used on a "character boat" mast for the sake of authentic appearance.

Fiberglassing a Mast

Q. Would it be feasible to cover an entire mast with fiberglass cloth and resin to eliminate the need for periodic revarnishing?

A. We have never heard of it being done. Common sense makes us skeptical of the idea. A single layer of cloth and resin would be brittle and would crack every time it got a respectable whack from a flying block or spinnaker pole. It is not very scratch-resistant and we'd expect halyards, etc., to leave marks on it. Two layers would add considerable weight to the mast, probably more than would be good for the boat's stability. Resin cannot be brushed out smooth like varnish; you'd either have to settle for a somewhat dull and rippled-looking surface, or spend countless hours sanding very hard resin smooth. And even then to get it to have a bright, glossy glow, you'd have to finish it off with varnish, so you'd be right back where you started. After all that work, the fiberglass might develop local cracks when the mast flexes. Masts have been wrapped with fiberglass tape, each turn of the tape overlapping the preceding one 50% to get a double thickness—strong, but odd-looking. On the whole, we wouldn't try it.

Redwood for Mast?

Q. I have a copy of the Forest Products Laboratory's book, Wood Handbook. *In it I find tables of wood properties and notice that redwood matches Sitka spruce in strength and weight. Since redwood is available in most lumberyards, could it be used for making a mast?*

A. It has been done for smaller sailboats where breakage of such a mast could be laughed off. The problem is that redwood does not hold metal fastenings well. Wood screws pull out easily and bolts quickly enlarge their holes. Also, fiberglassing jobs done with polyester resin won't stay in place on it; epoxy has to be used and that costs more. We have seen dinghy masts of redwood in which the problem of fastenings was solved by boring oversize holes and filling them with oak or mahogany deck plugs, which were then drilled to the proper size to take the fastenings. You can do almost anything if you are willing to use your head to overcome the problems posed by unusual methods. The Eskimos learned how to make very able seagoing kayaks from driftwood, bones, and sealskin, and the Indians made canoes from birch bark!

New Set of Stays

Q. I bought a used sailboat that's in good condition except most of the stranded cable stays are in bad condition.

The manufacturer of the boat is out of business. Is there any company that makes up sets of stays for "orphan" sailboats?

A. You can have new ones made up without trouble. Go to a boatyard that does a lot of sailboat work and ask them where they go in your area to have cable swaging work done. There are rigging specialists in or near most popular sailing areas and many marine hardware distributors are also equipped to do swaging. Mast and rigging manufacturers can also do the work. Send such a firm your old cables and they can use them as patterns for a new set. There are both power- and hand-operated swaging machines. The cable is inserted in the end of the fitting, the fitting is placed in the machine's die, and either rotary or hammering action compresses it very tightly onto the cable.

Shortening Stays

Q. I have used up all the adjustment distance available in the turnbuckles of my sailboat's stays, and can't get the stays adequately tight. Where can I get a new set of shorter stays?

A. You don't need a whole new set. Any place that has equipment for swaging terminals onto cables can cut off the old ones and install new ones, shortening the cables by whatever length you specify.

Corrosion in Terminals

Q. I have been told that stranded stainless steel cable mast stays can develop crevice corrosion where they enter the swaged terminals. Is this true? Can anything be done about it?

A. It can happen. Water—especially salt water—can get into the lay of the cable by capillary action. It tends to collect at the bottom end of the cable where the cable enters the terminal. The pressure caused by corrosion can expand the end of the swaged part of the terminal and cause the metal to crack open. Inspect the last quarter to half inch of the terminals regularly for such cracking. Some claim that a drop of rapeseed oil put on the cable an inch or so above the terminal is helpful; do it after a period of several days of dry weather. It will seep in between the cable strands and tend to repel water. Near major yachting centers there are a few companies that will make X-ray inspections of the terminals on a set of stays for a flat rate; this is usually done on the stays for expensive boats about to enter races or sail across the ocean.

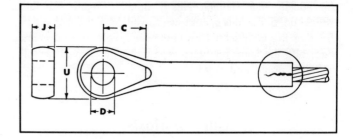

Inspect at circle for corrosion cracks.

Splicing Wire and Synthetic Ropes

Q. I have seen steel cable halyards that have been spliced to synthetic ropes; the steel part up on the mast has low windage and the rope part below is much easier on the hands. How is this done?

A. There isn't room to describe the method in step-by-step manner here. It can be a fussy job. The companies manufacturing yacht rope have how-to-do-it pamphlets that you can get for the asking. Look them up in marine trade directories and write.

Winch Literature

Q. Where can I get literature on overhauling sailboat winches?

A. Clymer Publications, 222 North Virgil Ave., Los Angeles, Cal. 90004 puts out a book called *Sailboat Maintenance*. It has a chapter with detailed information, including exploded drawings, of Barient, Barlow, and Lewmar winches. You may be able to get a copy at marine stores that have good book departments, or order direct from Clymer.

Mooring a Sailboat

Q. I'd love to own a sailboat but there are no marinas in my area. I'd have to moor it in a bay that is exposed to wind. I worry that the constant pitching on wind-driven waves might subject the mast and rigging to undue strain and wear. How do you feel about this?

A. It would depend on the particular sailboat. A hull having a deep, short keel under the amidships area and a lot of "rocker" in its bottom can tend to "hobbyhorse" on waves. But a sailboat with a long hull having comparatively little rocker and no overhang, such as a Chesapeake sharpie or some schooners, would have higher longitudinal stability and would only pitch moderately. A racer with a towering mast would whip the mast around more than a catboat would its comparatively short, stiff mast. A boat built for speed might have lightweight rigging, one built for cruising would have heavier rigging. Consider these things, choose your boat accordingly, and it should withstand the pitching all right. Make it a practice to adjust and leave various lines, stays, booms, etc., so they won't slat around while at the mooring.

Chapter 25

Rope Problems

Stiff Rope

Q. Some of the nylon rope aboard my boat has turned stiff and grey. How can I treat it to restore its whiteness and softness?

A. There is nothing you can do. Like all plastics (and nylon rope is made from plastic) it will eventually deteriorate when exposed to sunlight. Some of the rays in sunlight cause a slow change in the molecular structure. There's no way to reverse it. Relegate those ropes to unimportant jobs. Keep your new ones under cover as much as possible.

Kerosene in Rope

Q. A can of kerosene was spilled on some of my boat's ropes. Now they smell terrible, even after being washed with soap and water. Can you suggest a way to get the smell out?

A. Kerosene is famous for its long-lasting odor. On old-time fishing boats all the lamps burned kerosene; it was stored and handled constantly, and much of the food aboard picked up its taste and odor. The crew got used to it but it often made visitors ill. We do not think there is any way you can get it out other than by passage of time.

Washing Synthetic Rope

Q. I was washing some of my synthetic rope in a washing machine, using regular clothing detergent, when one of the boatyard workers came along and saw what I was doing. He said it would ruin the rope but was too busy to elaborate. I've seen a lot of people doing it and it does a fine job. What's so wrong with having clean rope?

A. Nothing wrong with clean rope, but vigorous threshing in a washing machine with detergent will in time remove the special lubricant put onto the synthetic fibers to reduce internal friction. Without it the hard, smooth filaments inside the rope have a way of grinding against themselves when the rope is under load and is bent sharply, such as at a sheave or mooring bitt. The rope can break down internally and break unexpectedly even though it looks sound on the outside. Different synthetics vary in this quirk, but why take chances?

The approved way to clean synthetic rope is to wipe the surface with a cloth that has been dipped in water containing a mild general-purpose detergent, then wrung out lightly so there isn't enough water and detergent to soak into the rope. Forget about trying to impress the Joneses with a linen-white set of lines. After all, back in the days of manila rope it came off the coils with a nice straw color to it—but it soon turned grey and nobody tried to wash or bleach it!

White vs. Gold Dacron

Q. Why is some Dacron synthetic rope white and some a golden color? Does it indicate a difference in composition or strength?

A. It's just a matter of looks. Some people prefer the golden color; it looks more like fresh new manila rope on a smart old-time yacht. However, some rope companies do make use of colors to identify certain ropes. For example, one firm we know of uses a pale blue to identify an extra-strong Dacron formulation. Some polyethylene ropes are black to give this type of plastic better resistance to sunlight. One has to get the color codes from rope manufacturers to figure out what is what. Most firms in the business turn out hundreds of different ropes, counting different diameters, twists, and weaves. They have to do it in order to supply ropes for a staggering variety of general and special uses. Sailboats often use ropes with strands of various colors incorporated in them to help crewmen identify ropes that do various things aboard a sailing craft.

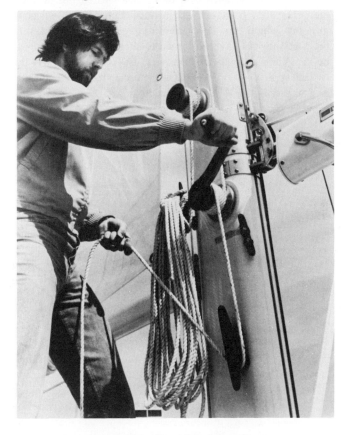

Color coded ropes are often used aboard sailboats to make it easy to tell which line does what job in a large boat's complex rigging.

Thinning "Whip-End-Dip"

Q. I have several cans of "Whip-End-Dip," a red coating sold in small cans in marine stores for coating the ends of synthetic ropes to keep them from unlaying. It has become too stiff to spread. As it is rather expensive I hate to throw it away. What solvent can I use to thin it out?

A. Loosen the screw cap to relieve internal pressure and set the container in a pan of hot water (keep it away from open flame, of course). In a short time you will find it has thinned out enough to readily brush out.

Splicing Braided Rope

Q. The seamanship books show how to splice an eye in the end of conventional three-strand twisted rope, but they are silent on how to do the same with braided rope—and this type is much used on sailboats. Where do I get how-to information?

A. The books probably shy off from it because to show how to do it takes a good number of step-by-step illustrations, and they don't care to devote this much space to it. Also, a simple but special tool is used in the job. The companies that make braided rope for yacht use have instructional pamphlets and learn-how-to-do-it kits.

Dacron is used for sailboat lines because it does not stretch; once a sail is adjusted it will remain in that position. Yacht ropes are often specially made to bend easily around sheaves and to have a good feel and grip. (Johnson Motors)

Choosing Synthetic Rope

Q.   I am going to completely re-outfit a sailboat I bought. I am as confused as a dog in a fire plug factory about the proper uses of the various synthetic ropes. Help!

A. The following comments are generalizations; use them as a guide but remember there are many facets to the subject.

Three-stranded twisted rope is satisfactory for many uses. Double braided rope having a herringbone-weave cover over a stout inner core bends easily and has a firm yet comfortable grip in the hands, so it is favored for sailboat lines that pass through sheaves and call for much hand-hauling.

Nylon tends to stretch under load—up to 30%. This gives it good shock-absorbing qualities, so it makes fine anchor and mooring lines. But because it will stretch under load, it is not used for the lines in sailboats that set and hold sails in position.

Dacron does not stretch much, so it is used in sailboats where nylon's stretching would make it difficult to keep sails properly adjusted.

Polypropylene and polyethylene are not as strong as nylon and Dacron, but are still stronger and more durable than manila. When single braided of continuous filaments, they can be very slippery, so they are poor for lines that must be handled a lot. When made of strands twisted out of short filaments, they have a rough surface that is much easier to grip but which has an uncomfortable feel. These plastics float, so they are favored for water-ski tow lines, which must be kept clear of towboat propellers. The rough surface of the twisted type is not objectionable for use as trailer winch rope, and the roughness helps it to hold knots. The smooth, braided type will hold knots very poorly, so it is spliced.

Chapter 26

Keels and Ballast

Painting a Cast Iron Keel

Q. What is the best way to paint the external cast iron ballast keel of a large sailboat?

A. There is no one best way because there are so many variables. It might be safe to say there is a best way for a particular situation. Without doubt the best way to prepare a keel to receive and hold new primer and paint is to thoroughly sandblast it. If the boatyard has a large-capacity air compressor able to make a sandblasting gun do an able job, fine. If it lacks one, then you have to look into the availability and cost of renting and bringing in a portable compressor. The cost then depends on how far it is necessary to travel. Perhaps several keels can be sandblasted on one visit of the compressor and the cost divided among the owners. If no way can be found to sandblast, then the best solution—for this situation—will be to use a powerful disc sander to clean the casting down to bright metal. Wire brushing tends more to burnish an iron surface than to scour off rust and roughen it.

If there is rust in the gap between hull and iron keel, the only way to get it all off is to drop the keel—and that is a major task. If some rust remains there after sandblasting or grinding, rusting will continue and it will push out the paint around the top edge of the iron keel. So you see, it's a matter of evaluating each keel job and deciding the most logical way to cope with its particular set of circumstances.

Many primers and paints are on the market. All major marine paint firms have lines of primers and paints for use on metal surfaces, and literature on how to use them. There are excellent anti-rust finishes in the steelworking trade but only expert advice from their makers could tell whether or not one

of them would be suitable for a marine environment. Will the anti-fouling paint you use adhere to it, or react to it? It is best to use paints and primers made by one firm, to assure compatibility. Sometimes a very good paint of one brand will be incompatible with a quality primer of some other brand and will not adhere well. Epoxy paints, and special-purpose resins such as "Gluvit" by Travaco, have excellent adhesive qualities—but merely using something labelled "epoxy" does not guarantee top performance. The surface still has to be properly prepared and the paint applied according to instructions.

Painting Iron Ballast Weights

Q. Paint keeps chipping off the blocks of iron used for ballast in my sailboat, and the rust that comes off them makes a mess of the bilge. How can I paint them to minimize this problem?

A. When a relatively soft substance like paint is applied to a hard substance like iron, it's the softer material that is bound to yield when the blocks bump and chafe. Sandblasting followed by several coats of primer and paint is about all anyone can do. You could look into and experiment with plastic- and rubber-based finishes that might produce a tough, non-chipping surface. After sandblasting, it would be easy to fiberglass the weights. Two layers of mat would give excellent chip and crack resistance, and seal out water very effectively. Or scout around for scrap lead, borrow a plumber's lead melting pot and torch, find some pie or cake tins, and cast up a set of lead ballast weights to replace the iron ones. They'll never corrode and will be smaller; one cubic foot of cast iron weighs 450 lbs. and one cubic foot of lead weighs 706 lbs. We have seen people have good results from fiberglassed iron ballast weights coated with tough epoxy resins.

Galvanizing a Centerboard

Q. The sheet-steel centerboard of my small sloop is rusting and needs regalvanizing. Where can I have this done?

A. Look under "Galvanizing" in the Yellow Pages of phone directories for the nearest sizeable communities. Or call metalworking firms in your area and ask where they send completed units for galvanizing. For boat use, you want "hot dip" galvanizing in a tank of molten zinc. Galvanizing done by the electroplating method won't last long in seawater. You could clean the metal with a disc sander and coat it with epoxy as an alternative to galvanizing.

Inspecting Keel Bolts

Q. I bought a used sailboat that has an external lead keel. There is some doubt about the condition of the keel bolts. How does one check them?

A. If the paint around the nuts and washers on their upper ends seems sound and uncracked, that's one indication they are sound and tight—but no guarantee. The usual method is to twist them forcibly with a large and sturdy wrench. If they turn appreciably or break off, that's the bad news rather plainly. If you want to be really sure, they have to be taken out for inspection. Doing this can be a job. If they come out from underneath, the boat will have to be hoisted high enough to let these long bolts—they are actually rods—be pulled down and out. If they have to be pulled from above, you may need to clear out a lot of cabin flooring, etc., to make room for the pulling rig. One man's ingenuity is as good as another's. Some yacht yards have hydraulic pullers. You can rig up a couple of hydraulic auto jacks with a piece of U- or I-beam between them and a rod with pipe coupler on the lower end to connect to the threads on the bolts. Or weld straps to a nut of the same size as those on the bolts.

Some keel bolts are made of wrought iron, some of bronze, some of stainless steel and even Monel. Monel is the best metal but costly. There are many alloys of bronze, some good and some poor, for keel bolt use. Used for keel bolts, stainless steel will be shut off from the oxygen it must have to retain its self-insulating qualities, and some stainless steel keel bolts have shocked boat owners by promptly corroding away.

A few large yacht yards now have arrangements with inspection firms to have portable X-ray machines brought to their yards. With this machine, the keel bolts on several craft can quickly be inspected without resorting to any mechanical work. Keel bolt durability is greatly affected by the galvanic corrosion setup of the particular combination of metals present in an individual keel installation. One has to trust the designer and boatbuilder to use a combination with good durability.

The usual procedure by yards and marine surveyors is to remove one or two keel bolts and inspect them. If they are quite sound, the others are probably also good. Sometimes when it's obvious that keel bolts are in dubious condition, instead of battling to remove them—or their broken-off ends—it is possible to drill and tap new holes between them and install supplementary keel bolts as a precaution against the original ones failing at sea.

Work on the keel and keel bolts can call for expensive hauling and hoisting of a boat.

Lead Ballast in Fiberglass Boats

Q. How are lead keels installed on fiberglass sailboats?

A. There are various ways. The book *Fibreglass Boats* by Hugo du Plessis, (published in England by Adlard Coles and handled by U.S. boat booksellers) contains a whole chapter on the subject. Each way has its pros and cons. An external keel will serve as a protective shoe if the boat grounds. Scratches and dents can be filed or sanded smooth. We have seen them filled with auto body solder and with epoxy putty. If the mold exists, a battered lead keel can be recast. Several layers of resin-soaked mat between hull and keel usually serve to join the two with no gaps between them. To carry the weight of a heavy lead keel, the lower regions of a fiberglass hull must have many laminations for strength. When the ballast is carried inside, grounding on a rocky bottom can chafe through the fiberglass, admit water between lead and laminate, and pose a repair problem. Keels are an involved story and unfortunately all the books on boat design, construction, and maintenance treat the subject superficially.

Iron Ballast and Wood Rot

Q. My sailboat uses iron pigs for ballast. There is a lot of rust in the bilgewater from them. I wonder, will the rust hurt the wooden plank and frame members?

A. It could. Rust seems to affect the chemical composition of wood so as to make it more susceptible to rot. You often see indications of this in the rotted spots surrounding iron and steel fasteners in old boards and posts. It's hard to say for sure if iron oxide (rust) in the bilgewater would do the same. It certainly wouldn't hurt to keep the bilge clean.

White Powder on Fiberglass Keel

Q. My fiberglass sailboat has lead ballast inside the keel. There are several spots where a whitish powder appears to be leaching out through the fiberglass. Have you any idea what is causing this?

A. Detective work is in order. If the whitish powder is showing on the more or less vertical surfaces of the keel, it is possible that the fiberglass laminate there is porous due to "resin-starved" laminate. Before it begins to cure, resin tends to respond to the pull of gravity and can flow down and out of a newly laid laminate. Good shops control this by adding a feather-like, powdery filler material to the resin to make it more flow-resistant, and by watching the progress of the curing closely. The deep place in the mold that forms the keel would be an awkward place to watch. Also, vapors from the evaporating solvents in the resin would collect in such a low spot and slow down the rate of curing, thus encouraging resin-starved spots. A good shop would use an air fan or suction hose to draw vapor out of such a place.

That explains the porous spots. Expert inspection of the boat would be necessary to pinpoint the source of the white powder. If the lead is completely encased in fiberglass, one could be a little suspicious that it might be some contaminated lead from a junkyard—or it might even be much cheaper "white metal" from melted-down die castings from the same source. An old saying once again comes to mind: "It doesn't matter so much what a boat is built of as who built it!"

Centerboard Trunk Leaks

Q. My wooden sailboat slowly but surely fills with water while at the mooring and I feel sure it's coming in around the centerboard trunk. How do I find and fix it?

A. Trunks are fitted together in many ways. One thus has to inspect a particular boat thoroughly and try to figure out how the parts are put together. Then one begins to get an idea of where it's leaking and why. Put the boat on horses, run some water into it, and watch the bottom to see where the water starts to come out. That's probably where it is going in. As we write this we have several boatbuilding and maintenance books in front of us, and they all carefully steer away from the subject of centerboard trunk leaks! About the best coverage (two or three pages) is in *Boatbuilding* by Howard I. Chapelle, W. W. Norton & Company. It's an old book but considered a classic. Your public library might have it or any bookseller can order a copy.

If your boat was built before World War II, the trunk was probably set into some outdated type of bedding compound. It was common to use strips of canvas set into white lead or putty, or even thickened paint. Such materials will by now be dry and brittle. It could be worthwhile to remove the trunk and rebed it into a flexible but tough modern sealing compound.

While your boat is up on horses to check for leaks, lower the centerboard and push from side to side on it while someone watches inside for signs of looseness. There is a lot of side pressure on a centerboard when a boat is sailing and this in time can loosen the trunk's hold-down fastenings. The gradual "working" can make screw threads chew the wood surrounding them. Better-built boats have the trunk held down with bolts, but wood under the washers can become wet and soft, letting the bolts work and causing leakage.

Marine stores sell a caulking compound called "Sealer 900." It is a thick liquid that will flow into crevices better

In a well-made small boat, the centerboard trunk will be braced against flexing as water pressure works on the centerboard. In this dory, the fore-and-aft member ties the centerboard top to both of the thwarts.

than compounds of butter-like consistency. It comes in plastic squeeze cans and it's worth trying.

Centerboard trunks can be fiberglassed on the inside surfaces. The boat has to be inverted and the wood must be completely dry for this to have a chance of working. All old paint must be removed from the inner surfaces, usually by scrubbing it off with very coarse sandpaper glued to a flat stick. Resin and glass cloth is spread and worked down by using long-handled brushes and small rollers. Or, cut two sheets of Formica to the same shape as the inside of the trunk. Apply several coats of wax to their surfaces. After the cloth is in place, fit them down inside the trunk and press a board between them to apply uniform pressure to the fiberglass and get it to smooth out nicely before it cures. That's what boat maintenance is all about—a mixture of common sense and ingenuity.

Cracks in Fiberglass Trunk

Q. When I turned my fiberglass sailing dinghy over I found several cracks in the surface right around the centerboard slot. Is this bad? What should I do?

A. Side pressure on the centerboard while underway flexed the centerboard trunk enough for cracks to appear in the gel coat. Many small sailboats built to a price are not stiff enough. Well-designed ones make use of the amidships thwart, which is affixed to the trunk one way or another and serves to brace the top of the trunk against the sidewise forces. If you can't incorporate a fix like this into your boat, sand the finish off the inside around the trunk and put on two or three layers of glass mat and resin. That should appreciably stiffen the trunk. If the gel coat cracks are no deeper than the gel coat itself, they probably don't penetrate into the strength-giving laminate and won't hurt.

Crack in Deep Keel

Q. My big sailboat ran aground. On hauling it out for inspection we found a crack going up and down the leading edge of the deep keel. As the keel is filled with ballast, we can't see if this crack is visible on the inside. What should we do?

A. Without seeing the boat we can't be positive, but we think we can deduce what happened. The boat was made in a so-called "split mold." That is, port and starboard sides of the hull were made in separate molds and then joined together along the centerline. This is often done on large keel boats for various reasons—easier for men to get at some surfaces, better ventilation of fumes, no problems in withdrawing from the mold a boat having tumble-home in her sides, etc. The two sides are well bonded together from the inside with many layers of laminate, and the parting line on the centerline outside is puttied, sanded, sprayed with gel coat, and polished. It's likely the keel flexed on impact and spit out some of this cosmeticizing. If inspection shows this is what has happened, a reputtying and painting will fix things; the hull is almost surely undamaged.

Chapter 27

Steering Systems

Cable Tension

Q. How much tension should there be in a cable-and-pulley type steering system?

A. Enough to prevent any chance of the cables slacking off where they wrap around the drum to make sure they won't jump off of it. If they should do so, boat control would be lost. A well-planned system of this kind has a lot of thought put into it, and may even be subject to geometrical analysis before being finalized and installed. The point to remember is that as a rudder's tiller arm moves from side to side, it is possible for one of the cables to slack off while the other tightens up. This is why a quadrant is used when a motorboat's rudder is controlled by cables. A quadrant is basically a segment of a circle, and of course a circle has a constant radius. It is a mistake to use a tiller arm on a rudder controlled by cable. As the arm moves from side to side, the cable angularity and distance of travel will change such that the cables will slack off. A tiller arm would properly be used with a gear-type steerer which transmits its action to the rudder by means of push-pull tubes. Coil springs can be used to compensate for cable tension variation in a cable steerer used on an outboard boat. Since they will be in plain view all the time, it is safe to use them since serious rusting can be seen long before there is danger of the springs breaking. It would be a mistake to use springs in an inboard system that is out of sight down in the bilge area.

Outboard Steering Layout

Q. Can you tell me how to lay out a good cable control system in my small outboard runabout?

A. The accompanying drawings will enable you to visualize cable routings. The reason for the pulleys at the stern, which are arranged to give a two-to-one reduction in motor travel, is to keep steering from being too "quick" and therefore too sensitive.

It is important to only use pulleys designed for steerer systems. Their diameter and sheave grooves are such as to place a minimum of bending and chafing stress on the cable. Never install pulleys with short wood screws. Whenever possible, use through bolts, washers, and nuts. If wood screws must be used, have them as large and long as possible. Do not make them subject to loads that tend to pull them out, only to loads from the side. Do not put any more tension on the cables than is necessary for secure control; too much tension places excessive loads on all parts of the system. High tension in a system using plastic-coated tiller cable makes the cable crush the plastic against the surface of the pulleys, and soon cuts through it.

A very important feature of a cable-type outboard motor steerer is that the cables must not slack off when the motor tilts up. Outboards often tilt up; for example, when beaching or when striking a floating object. If the cables slack off, they can jump the drum and result in loss of control at high speed. It takes a lot more time to install a good cable-and-pulley steering system than it does to put in a modern push-pull sealed cable system, because location and angles of the pulleys and their eye straps have to be carefully determined to be sure the cables will feed into and out of them without chafing on the edges of sheave grooves.

Racing Steerers

Q. We built a racing hydroplane from magazine plans.

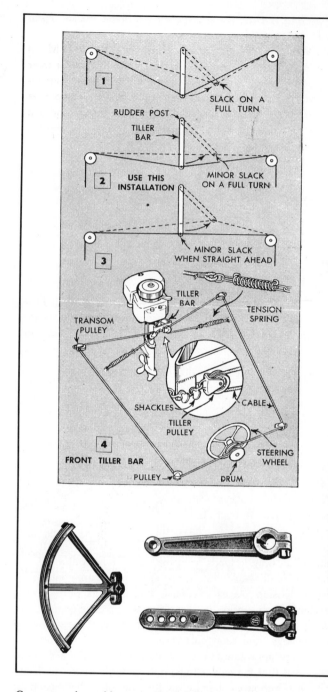

Geometry of a cable steerer (top) has to be planned to minimize slacking and tightening of cable. Quadrant for cable steering of a rudder (lower left) has constant radius to avoid changes in cable tension. Rudder arms (lower right) are used to connect push-pull steering rods to rudder. One with several holes allows steering sensitivity to be altered to suit boat or operator's preference.

The plans showed an old-fashioned cable-and-pulley steering system. We bought a modern mechanical steerer and were just about to install it when a kibitzer came around. He said he had attended a recent outboard race and noticed all the boats had cable-and-pulley steerers. We can't figure out why. Can you?

A. Yes. There is always a little slack motion in a mechanical steerer having a push-pull cable moving in a protective sheath, and it is too much for sensitive control at racing speeds. One must be able to sit in a wildly bouncing boat, grasping the wheel firmly while crouched in the cockpit, and still be able to feed very small corrective motions into the motor. The lack of play in a fairly tight cable-and-pulley system is the first step. The second is to affix a long steering arm to the motor that translates a large motion of the cables into a very slight angular change in the motor's heading. This tiller bar is carefully positioned in relation to the motor's steering pivot to avoid tightening or slacking of the cables, within the normal range of steering movement at high speed. Do not play around with high-speed boats if you do not know anything about their design and handling peculiarities!

Steering Action Reversed

Q. I did a lot of reconditioning on my big outboard boat. This included taking the mechanical steerer off the dashboard to apply wood-grain vinyl to the dash. Later, when the boat was finished and tried out, we almost crashed because when the steering wheel was turned one way, the boat turned the other way! I don't think we changed anything in the way the steering cable was hooked up to the motor. What's wrong?

A. You pulled a very common goof! You fed the forward end of the push-pull cable into the wrong boss in the mechanical steering head, thereby reversing the direction of steering motion.

Inspecting Push-Pull Cables

Q. How long should a modern push-pull steering cable last? Ours is several years old and although it is sealed and has lifetime lubrication, sometimes when the going gets rough we begin to wonder how reliable it might be.

A. Service life is not unlimited. At the same time, no specific life expectancy can be quoted. So much depends on how much use a cable gets in a given period of time, and the conditions under which it is used. A cable on a constantly used workboat might well be replaced after a few seasons of use. Salt water can be hard on cables—it normally can't get inside the housing, but cuts or chafed spots on the outer sheathing can admit salt to the steel-wire housing inside. An accompanying sketch shows what to look for when judging a cable's condition. (See page 203)

Move the wheel through the full range of its travel. If there is binding or roughness at any point of the movement, first see if it is caused by something on or around the motor—lack of grease in the steering pivot, interference between two moving parts, etc. If you can't find anything like that, disconnect the cable from the motor. If the binding can still be felt, it is certain that there's something seriously wrong inside the cable. Worn or defective ones cannot be repaired; a new one must be installed. About an inch or so of free play in the rim of the steering wheel is normal. Much more than that indicates there may be something wrong with the way the cable is engaging with the mechanism within the steering head. Get advice from the manufacturer or a competent boat mechanic.

Worm Gear Steerer

Q. My old powerboat had an automotive worm-gear type steerer. When it wore out we could not find parts for it, so replaced it with a modern push-pull cable type of mechanical steerer. Ever since, the boat has wanted to veer off to the right and we have to hold pressure on the wheel constantly to keep on course. What's wrong?

A. The old steerer doubtless had irreversible or semi-irreversible gearing, a standard feature in automotive design. When you move the steering wheel, the worm gear at the lower end of the shaft transmits rotary motion into the sector, which makes the steering arm move. But when a wheel strikes a bump or obstruction in the road, the sector—due to gear tooth angles—cannot transmit the pressure back to the wheel through the worm. This keeps road irregularities from pulling the wheel out of a driver's hands.

In a boat, it can keep irregular pressures on the rudder from feeding back to the control wheel. With this built-in feature, we would guess your boat probably has an unbalanced rudder. But a push-pull mechanism is not irreversible. The spiraling wash from the propeller strikes the rudder blade with more pressure on one side than on the other, and the pressure feeds back to the steering wheel. The ideal solution would be to install a rudder that is balanced so as to compensate for the turning force created by the spiraling prop wash. A cheap interim solution would be to affix a sheet brass or stainless steel trim tab to the trailing edge of the rudder. Something about the size of a business card would be suitable as a starter. Make trial runs to determine which way and how much to bend this tab to take the pressure off the steering wheel. Ask a Mercury outboard motor mechanic to show you the adjustable trim tab on a large Merc outboard. It will help you grasp the idea.

Connecting an Auxiliary Motor

Q. I want to use a small outboard alongside my big one,

for trolling and as an emergency get-home motor. How would I steer it?

A. Write to West Wind Products Div., Western Metal Products Co., 150 Tejon St., Denver, Colo. 80223 for their descriptive folder. They make a range of links and connectors for this purpose. Some of the outboard motor companies offer brackets of use in this application; see dealers and ask to look in accessory catalogs. Also, see your OMC dealer; they have a link of their own design.

Crowell Steerers

Q. My cruiser is equipped with a "Crowell" steerer. This company and its products were often seen at boat shows not so many years ago. Now I can't find a trace of them in any of many marine supply catalogs and trade directories. Do you know how to contact them?

A. No. Several other people have also asked us about this firm. It seems to have just vanished. As boating grew into a big business, many companies rushed to get into it. Inevitably, some didn't make the grade and went bankrupt. Others became parts of conglomerates and sometimes, in such cases, top management decided to have one of the branch plants stop making one kind of product and switch to some other, and hopefully more profitable, type. It's tough for those who need spare parts. But then, airmen can't get parts for Waco airplanes and motorists can't get parts for Hupmobiles! Go to a marine supply house and look into the Morse and Teleflex control catalogs. Take time to get a good idea of the range of items offered. You may find you can update your system using currently available items.

Owens Controls

Q. I own an Owens cabin cruiser. Owens went out of business some years ago. The word "Panish" appears on parts of the steering control system. Where could I get parts for it?

A. The company that made those controls is still in business; Panish Controls, 191–203 Bennett St., Bridgeport, Conn. 06605. Some former dealers for the Owens line of boats have stocks of parts, or make replacement parts, such as exhaust manifolds. Look around in boatyards and marinas for other Owens boats, talk to their owners, and compare notes.

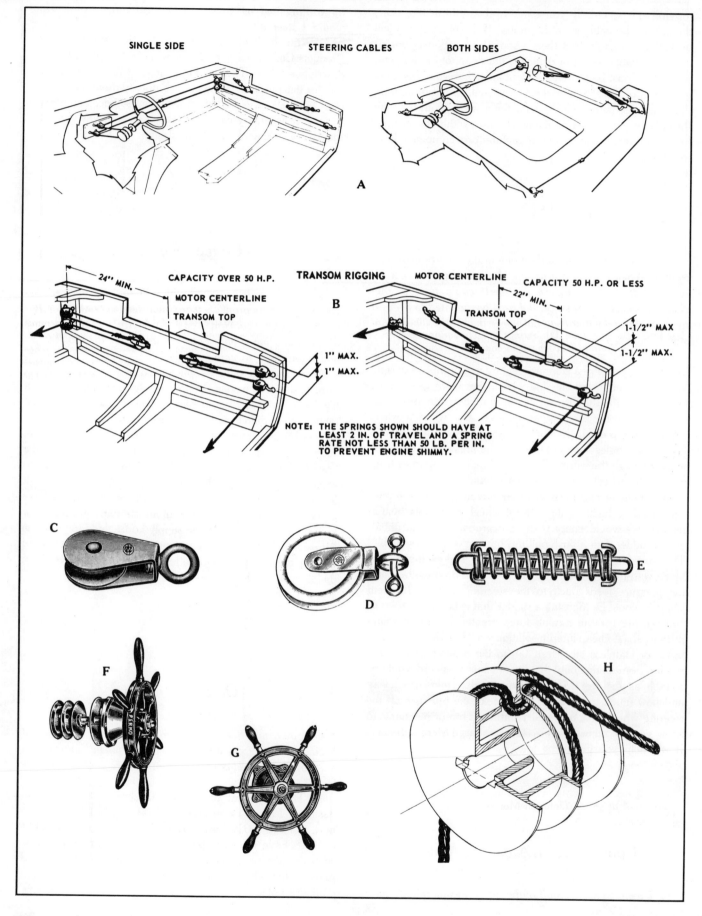

SINGLE SIDE   STEERING CABLES   BOTH SIDES

A

24" MIN.   CAPACITY OVER 50 H.P.   TRANSOM RIGGING   MOTOR CENTERLINE   CAPACITY 50 H.P. OR LESS

MOTOR CENTERLINE   22" MIN.

TRANSOM TOP   TRANSOM TOP

B

1" MAX.   1-1/2" MAX.
1" MAX.   1-1/2" MAX.

NOTE: THE SPRINGS SHOWN SHOULD HAVE AT LEAST 2 IN. OF TRAVEL AND A SPRING RATE NOT LESS THAN 50 LB. PER IN. TO PREVENT ENGINE SHIMMY.

C   D   E

F   G   H

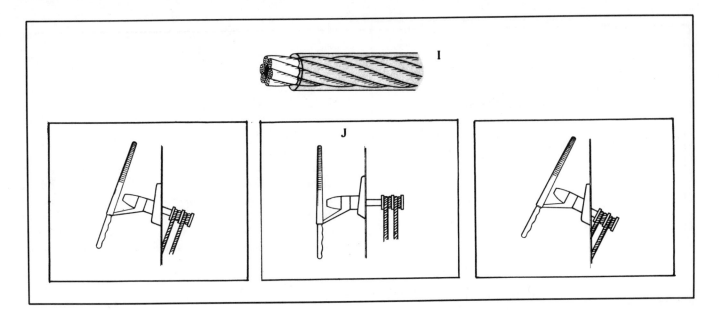

Cable layout at top left (A) is for boat with side console. One at top right is for boat having a bridge deck. Cable system at middle left (B) is for larger outboard motors, one at middle right for smaller ones. Don't use small-diameter pulleys like this (C); they bend the cable too much. Use larger-diameter type (D). Springs come in varying lengths and tensions (E). When drum is behind the dash (F), cable can jump off if it slacks. When drum is between wheel and dash (G), jumping-off is unlikely. Cable has to have enough turns around drum (H) to allow wheel full port-to-starboard movement. Feeding it through center hole prevents slipping. Plastic covered steering cable (I) must be watched. Tension makes cable press plastic onto sheave and can cut through. Most modern wheels (J) have either an adjustable or a two-piece bezel (the part that goes against the dashboard). It can be positioned so as to hold wheel at various angles for comfort, leg room, etc.

"Old-fashioned" cable-and-pulley steering is still used on racing boats. Tight cables give slack-free steering. Tiller bar on motor "slows down" reaction of motor to wheel movements, gives precise control at speed. (Johnson Motors)

Things to look for when inspecting push-pull steering cables. (Morse Controls)

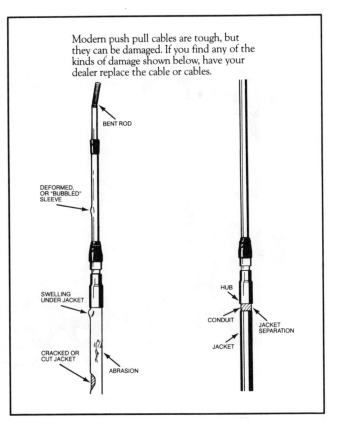

Modern push pull cables are tough, but they can be damaged. If you find any of the kinds of damage shown below, have your dealer replace the cable or cables.

BENT ROD

DEFORMED, OR "BUBBLED" SLEEVE

SWELLING UNDER JACKET

CRACKED OR CUT JACKET

ABRASION

HUB

CONDUIT

JACKET SEPARATION

JACKET

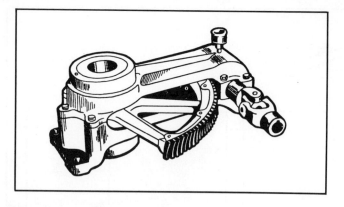

Worm gear steerer has "irreversible" action; it won't feed rudder feel back into wheel.

Sailboat Steerer

Q. Our grand old catboat has a long wooden tiller. Holding onto it on long sails gets tiring. We asked the boatyard about installing a heavy-duty mechanical steerer like those used in powerboats. They said no—said we should consider an Edson if we wanted some kind of mechanical steerer. Those cost more than we can see paying. What do you think?

A. You found a local expert who knew what he was talking about! Special sailboat steerers such as the Edson have their gearing and leverage systems worked out so as to keep steering effort low on one hand, and yet to "feed back" enough of the rudder pressure to avoid deadening its feel, without which handling the boat well would be compromised.

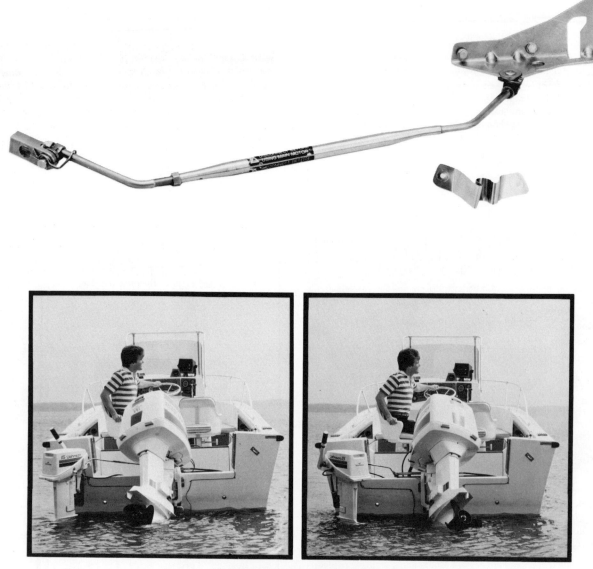

◀ ENGINES TURN TOGETHER ▶

Special connecting rods are available to enable a small trolling or auxiliary outboard to be steered from the main outboard or stern drive's lower unit. (Outboard Marine Corp.)

Hydraulic Controls

Q. *What's your opinion of hydraulic steering controls?*
A. In the past, they have occasionally had fluid leakage and pressure-maintaining problems. But they have been much improved. They lack the friction characteristic of longer push-pull cables used in larger boats. They make two-station controls easy to install and keep their operating friction low. They are becoming increasingly popular for the big outboard motors in the 150–300 h.p. range. By all means give such a system serious consideration for your larger outboard or stern drive boat, or for your flying-bridge cruiser.

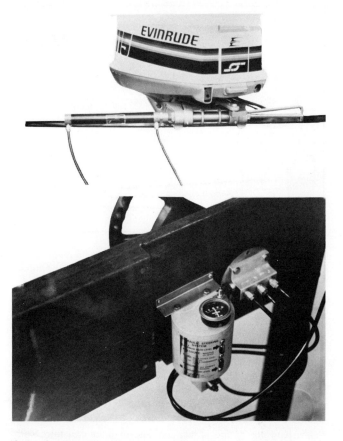

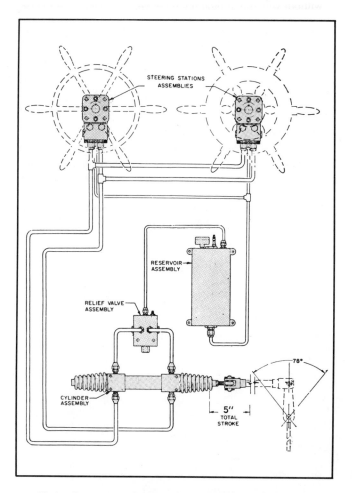

Hydraulic steering features low friction, smooth action.

Hydraulic steering systems are coming into favor for use with larger outboard motors. Less friction than with a long push-pull cable, easy to route the lines, dependable. (Hynautic, Inc.)

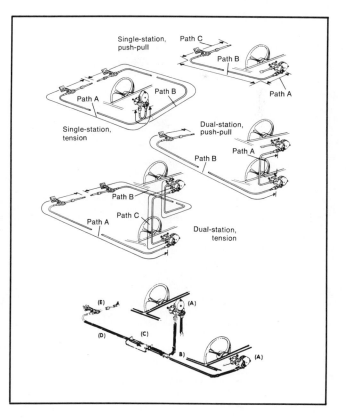

Push-pull cable control systems are versatile. Top right, simple single-cable layout for average outboard. Top left, dual cable layout provides added cable durability and reliability for a larger outboard. Center right, a dual-station layout using a single cable to motor. Center left, dual steering with twin cables to a larger motor or to twin outboards. Bottom, object (C) is a clutch to disengage one of the two steering systems; eliminates drag and heavy feel resulting from having to move the idle wheel and cable when steering from the other position. (Teleflex, Inc.)

205

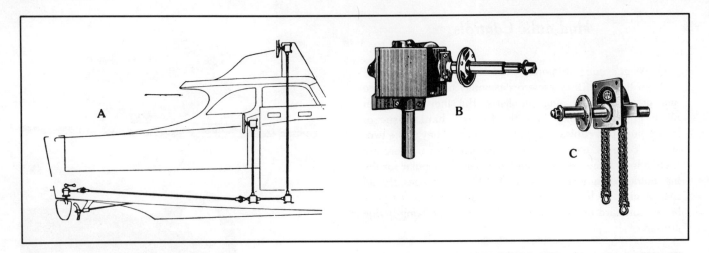

A system of gearboxes and shafts (A) is one way of creating a dual-station steering layout. Bevel-gear steerer (B) will feed rudder pressures back into wheel, unlike worm gear steerer (page 204). Sprocket steerer (C) is used with cables; no cables to slip on or jump off a drum.

Dual Control Stations

Q. *What's involved in installing a two-station control system?*

A. Routing of the shafts, cables, or lines can take some thought. Design should be such that when you're using one wheel, it does not feel dead and heavy due to drag imposed on the system by the other wheel and its connections. There are various ways of doing it. The accompanying drawing will give you an idea of how various layouts have been contrived.

Obtain steerer manufacturers' catalogs and study them carefully.

Chapter 28

Propellers

Trimming Prop Blades

Q. There is a slight but noticeable amount of roughness on the leading edge of the blades of my boat's propeller. Is it permissible to smooth them up by careful filing, or will this upset balance too much?

A. Common sense must be your guide. If the roughness can be taken off with no more than several strokes of the file, it will usually do more good than harm. Of course, you must count the strokes and give each blade the same attention in order to keep from disturbing balance too much. If this treatment has to be repeated perhaps three or four times, obviously enough metal can be taken off to affect balance. Then a propeller shop should do the next smoothing-up job, during which they will restore balance.

A lot depends on circumstances. If it's a small aluminum prop from a fishing outboard, worth ten dollars, one need not be so concerned about taking a little metal off now and then with a file. But if it's a prop from a big cruiser and worth a three-figure sum, more caution is in order. The bigger the prop or the faster it turns, the more one can upset balance by being too easygoing with a file.

Repairing Propellers

Q. The bronze propeller on my sportfisherman whacked the top of a coral head. All four blades got badly bent and two of them have tears in the blade metal. We had a spare, which we installed. We live in a remote area. A person passing through saw the bent prop on our scrap pile and said

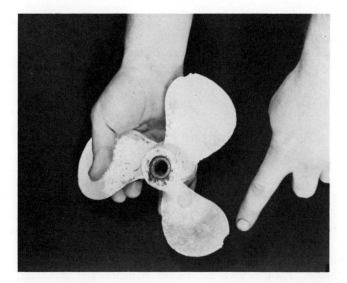

It is permissible to remove nicks from smaller, less expensive propellers like this one by filing. Take an equal amount of metal off each blade. Finish by smoothing up with abrasive paper for best results.

we should send it to a mainland repair shop for fixing. Can I believe him or was he kidding me?

A. A good repair shop can work wonders in straightening rather badly bent bronze props. The metal is malleable, and can be hammered back to shape. Cracks and tears can be repaired by a skilled man with welding torch and brazing rod. A good shop will have tools and equipment to restore accuracy, balance, and appearance. Give it a try. Die cast aluminum propellers commonly used as stock equipment on outboard motors can be fixed when blades are only slightly bent, but when they are cracked it is not feasible to try to

207

make repairs—a new one will not cost too much and at today's labor rates it can cost more to try to do a fussy repair job.

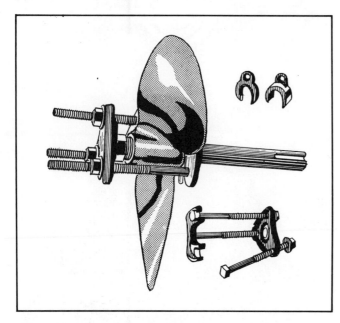

Boatyards use propeller pullers like these to get props off of shafts. It is safer for both the prop and the person doing the work. Hydraulic pullers are available for the bigger wheels. Turning the nuts on the "Safe-Way" puller does the job on average-size pleasure craft props.

Changing Prop Size

Q. When I had nearly completed a homemade cabin cruiser, someone gave me a bronze prop he had in his garage. It is just a bit too large, and the pitch is off a bit for my boat. Is there a propeller exchange shop anywhere?

A. Not that we know of. But there's no need to get a different prop. Any good propeller repair shop can trim the blades down to give the desired diameter, and they can increase or decrease the pitch with their bending and measuring equipment.

Pitch Blocks

Q. In a book on boat work I encountered the term "pitch blocks" in a discussion of propellers. What are these?

A. It's a set of iron blocks curved to different angles of pitch. The repairman chooses a block corresponding to the pitch he wants to give a blade that he is straightening. This block is installed on a heavy metal working base, which has a vertical shaft on which to mount the block and the propeller. Each blade in turn is put up against the pitch block

It takes special skills and equipment to do quality propeller work. Here a workman trims a stainless steel prop for a large outboard. (Mercury Marine)

to check its pitch. If need be, pitch can be corrected by carefully hammering the blade to fit onto the face of the pitch block.

Books on Propellers

Q. Where can I get a book on repairing propellers, shafts, stern bearings, and related items?

A. We have never seen anything like this in our years of writing about boats and boating. We suspect the market potential is too small to encourage anyone to publish it because one can't do much professional work without a well-equipped shop having a lot of expensive equipment. Those who are in the business learned by on-the-job training.

Can't Locate Stern Bearing

Q. The propeller on our cruiser has begun to vibrate. A scuba diver went under and says the bearing in the strut is worn so the shaft literally bounces around in it. The local marina does not know where to get a new one to fit. What do I do?

A. We never cease to be amazed at how little some people in the boating business know about boats! Shops specializing in propeller and shaft repairs stock them. Many major marine distributors stock them. Companies like Stokes, Barr, Osco, Lehman, and Marine Engine Center that specialize in marine conversion kits for auto engines and rebuilt marine engines also stock them. Prominent names in the stern-bearing manufacturing field are Arguto, Lucian Q. Moffitt,

Propellers come in an amazing range of sizes and types. Top left (A), a folding propeller for auxiliary sailboats—it reduces drag when under sail. Black spots are magnets that hold blades together when folded. When engine starts, centrifugal force and then water thrust holds blades open. (Michigan Wheel) Top right (B), a very high speed racing outboard propeller. Blade shape was found by experimenting, lets prop bite into water to best advantage at speed. (Mercury Marine) Bottom right (C), the girl is holding two molded plastic propellers—low in cost, abrasion-resistant, good for use in shallow water areas. (Mercury Marine)

Buck Algonquin, Johnson and Morse Chain Division of Borg-Warner—look them up in the marine trade directories.

Propeller Repair Tools

Q. I would like to equip my marine engine repair shop to handle propeller work. Who makes the needed special tools and equipment?

A. Rundquist Propeller Tools, 7730 Water St., St. Louis, Mo. 63111 (pitch blocks, gauges, etc.), Mindermann Marine Div., Port Clinton Mfg. Co., P.O. Box 269, Port Clinton, Ohio 43542 (pullers), Buck Algonquin Marine Hardware Div., Algonquin Co., Second & Columbia, Philadelphia, Pa. 19122 (pullers), and the major propeller companies like Michigan Wheel and Columbian Bronze.

Installing Inboard Engines

Q. We are rebuilding an old cruiser and part of the job is installing a whole new engine and shaft system. Where can we get helpful information on doing a good and safe job of installing and aligning an engine?

A. Get a copy of the book *Inboard Motor Installations in Small Boats* from Glen-L Marine Designs, 9152 Rosecrans, Bellflower, Cal. 90706. If much rewiring is to be done, get a copy of *Your Boat's Electrical System* by Conrad Miller, from Motor Boating & Sailing Books, 224 West 57th St., New York, N.Y. 10019. Look under "U.S. Government" in the Yellow Pages for the address of the U.S. Coast Guard District Office nearest you, or get it from your local post office. Write to them, explaining what you are doing, and ask them to send you pertinent booklets on safety and equipment requirements. Get the propeller catalogs from Columbian Bronze Corp., 216 N. Main St., Freeport, New York 11520 and from Michigan Wheel Div., Dana Corp., 1501 Buchanan Ave., S.W., Grand Rapids, Mich. 49705. If you provide them with data on your boat and engine, they will give advice on a suitable propeller.

Eroded Blades

Q. When we hauled out my big cruiser we found that the faces of the propeller blades had a number of shallow,

209

smooth grooves worn in them, as if someone had gone back and forth across the blades with a disc sander with the exception that the surface of the metal was not bright—it was the same dull color as the rest of the blade surfaces. We can only assume that the prop was made of defective bronze. What is your opinion?

A. The grooves are typical of "cavitation erosion." It is more common with large propellers than small ones. As the leading edges of the blades slice through the water at very high speed, pressure-change effects break down some water into a steady flow of small bubbles, often at points where the leading edges are slightly nicked. Believe it or not, these streams of bubbles flowing back over the blades for a long time can erode the metal. Consult an experienced propeller repair shop or the manufacturer of your prop for advice. A prop of a different size or shape may be the best way to get rid of the cavitation.

Blade Broke Off

Q. One day we were coming up the channel in our yawl, using auxiliary power. All of a sudden a terrific vibration set in. We had to stop the engine, anchor, and wait for a tow. When the boat was hauled, we found one blade had broken off the prop at its root, and what was left of the prop was a weak, almost granular metal. Did the boat's manufacturer use a cheapie prop?

A. We don't think so. Your prop finally succumbed to "internal galvanic corrosion." Long immersion in seawater caused the copper and tin molecules to "fight," and the substance of the bronze was gradually weakened. If the boat was only a few years old, the rapidity with which this corrosion acted could very well mean there is something wrong with the boat's electrical system, so as to send stray current into the propeller and literally make it "sizzle" in the brine. Have a good marine mechanic check it over.

Chapter 29

Oars and Oarlocks

Oarlock Socket Location

Q. I am modifying an outboard boat for fishing. It had no oarlock sockets on it when I bought it. How do I determine the correct location for them?

A. Stand beside the boat. Place your elbow on the gunwale at a point directly above the middle of the seat, with your forearm pointing aft. Where the palm of your hand comes on the gunwale is the place to install the sockets. Since the lengths of peoples' arms vary, this is a compromise location; it will work all right for adults of average stature. You may want to locate the sockets an inch or two farther aft if you come from a family of tall people, or a few inches forward if the boat is for children. The average distance works out to about 15 to 16 inches.

There are others things to consider. If the seat is mounted too high in the boat, your knees will get in the way of your hands as you pull on the oars. If the sides of the boat are too low, the oars will operate so close to the water that you will often catch or drag the blades on the water during the recovery strokes. Go to the nearest Red Cross office and purchase a copy of their booklet, *Basic Rowing*. Ask a Boy Scout what store in your area sells official BSA equipment; go there and get a copy of the Merit Badge Manual on *Rowing*. These booklets will help you to learn to row well. Magazines such as *The Small Boat Journal* and *The Woodenboat* contain much material about rowboat design and construction. Also, see *The Ash Breeze* under "Magazine Plans" in Chapter 8. If you want to get serious about rowing, read *Boats, Oars and Rowing* by R. D. Culler, available from International Marine Publishers, 21 Elm St., Camden, Maine 04843.

In a really good rowboat, distance between seat and oarlocks, height of seat above floor and distance of oarlocks above seat level are carefully worked out to position oars well and enable them to be manipulated most effectively. If something is wrong, oar handles will foul user's knees, blades will drag on water, etc. (Squadron Yachts)

Unvarnished Grips

Q. I bought some new oars and am puzzled by something. They are nicely varnished all over but the hand grips are bare wood. Why?

A. A varnished surface can be quite slippery when it gets wet, either from rain, spray, or perspiration. Then it can easily raise blisters on one's hands. Bare wood makes a comfortable, secure gripping surface.

Making Oars

Q. We need a pair of very long oars for a big old skiff we are restoring for use in historical pageants. Local marine stores stock oars only up to 8 feet; we need 12-footers. Could we make our own? How is it done?

A. Oar manufacturers such as Foster Oar Co., P.O. Box 1185, Conway, Ark. 72032 and Smoker Craft, Inc., Box 65, New Paris, Ind. 46553 can probably make oars long enough for you. What the stores stock are just the lengths they find are most in demand; it's no problem to select wood a few feet longer and turn out a special pair to order. Various oar makers have developed their own methods and equipment. An oar shop we once visited did it as follows. A plywood pattern of the outline of an oar was laid onto a 2-inch-thick plank and positioned so as to avoid knotholes and splits. The outline of the oar was marked on the wood and sawn out on a bandsaw. This blank was then mounted in a lathe that turned the handle and loom sections to round shape, stopping close to where the blank widened out for the blade section. Then the blade portion was repeatedly dragged across a rather large sanding drum running on a horizontal shaft. This "wiped" wood off and gradually took this part of the blank down to the finished blade thickness.

You can make your own by using appropriate tools such as a spokeshave, plane, belt sander, etc. If you can't find single pieces of wood large enough, you can make up blanks by laminating several smaller pieces together with a strong, waterproof glue. Spruce makes lightweight oars that are

handy to manage, but this wood is not very good for hard use. Ash makes heavier oars that last well, won't break under hard pulling, and tend to stay down in the oarlocks on windy days.

Oar Protection

Q. When used bare, wood oars soon become chewed up at the area where they fit into the oarlocks. Could I fiberglass this area to improve abrasion resistance?

A. The hard metal of the oarlock horns would wear away the fiberglass covering rather quickly, because the resin is brittle and thus not well suited to withstanding abrasion. Marine supply catalogs show rubber sleeves intended to be slipped onto oars; we have tried them and find there are problems. If the oar is of a slightly smaller diameter, these sleeves fit loosely and soon get chewed up. If the oar is of a slightly greater diameter, it can be almost impossible to pull the sleeves on to the desired position due to the rubber's great sliding friction. Some supply catalogs still list "oar leather" kits, which contain pieces of tough leather of suitable size. It is easy to wrap the leather on snugly at the desired location and the row of small brass nails does not seem to weaken the wood. Locate the row of nails so their heads will not rub against the oarlocks and wear. The leather wears well.

Pop Riveted Oarlock Sockets

Q. I bought a low-priced fiberglass pram. The oarlock sockets were held in place with pop rivets. They came loose

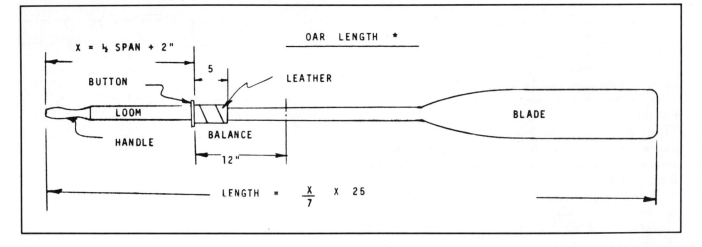

Length and balance are of primary importance in choosing a pair of oars for any given boat. The distance between the rowlocks is the basis for determining the proper length of oars. A leverage ratio of 7 to 18 is preferred by most oarsmen, but individual preferences and also the height of freeboard may be reasons for slightly altering the ratio. If an overlap grip is used for increased leverage, the inboard length of the loom should be one-half the distance between the rowlocks plus 2 inches. The total length of the oar equals one-seventh of the inboard length multiplied by 25. Oars are generally purchased too short for comfortable and easy rowing. Try a pair of oars the proper length and you will be surprised how much your rowing ability improves. (Grumman Boats)

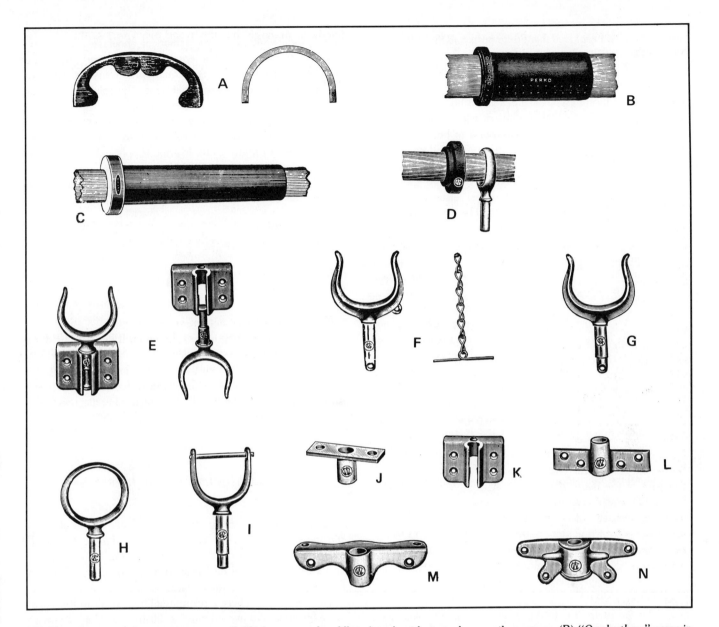

(A) Shaped copper protective tips are available for oars and paddles. Attach with rivets, brass nails or epoxy. (B) "Oar leathers" come in packages; each package will do a pair of oars. Rows of nails are on top of oar, away from oarlocks. Attach with small brass nails, trim leather to fit. (C) Rubber oar sleeves are neat but fit only if oar is close to same size. (D) Rubber stops slip on easily, keep round oarlocks from being lost. (E) "Davis" oarlocks are common on livery and summer camp boats, can't get lost. (F) Horn-type locks have eyes cast in them for a safety string or chain. Chain goes down thru oarlock socket. (G) Oar can be set down into or lifted out of horn oarlock quickly, without disturbing lock. Good on dinghies used around docks and other boats. (H) Round oarlock good for rental or fishing boats; can't get lost if oars have stops on them. Lock comes out of socket every time oar is lifted out, as when coming alongside dock. (I) "North River" oarlock has pin thru oar. Won't get lost, but oar can't be feathered in windy weather. Good for duck boats, etc.; can let go of oar quickly, grasp it again fast. (J) Common socket goes on top of gunwale, fits in hole bored for snug fit. Rowing force all goes onto the rear bolt; tends to crack at bolt hole, or loosen bolt. (K) Davis type sockets must be installed on inboard side of gunwale; otherwise stowed oarlocks will hang outside boat, foul dock, mar other boats, etc. (L) Side plate can go inboard or out. If installed outboard, dinghy gunwale padding will be in way. Can scrape larger boats. Handy way to raise level of oars to fit a tall person better. (M) Angle plate socket looks neat; strain is well distributed. Same remarks for side plate sockets apply. (N) "Moline" pattern also distributes strain well. Can be the answer for some fiberglass installations. Same remarks for side plate apply.

within a week! I replaced them with bolts and those loosened too. What now?

A. Using pop rivets in such a place is typical of what you find today, with a lot of fly-by-nighters in the business for a quick buck. They think "If it looks like a boat, it is a boat." And they manage to find customers who think the same way! Such people have no background in boats, have no idea of the forces boats experience in service, and don't know how to put things together to stay. In regard to oarlock sockets, there is a hardware problem. We have spoken of inertia in the marine hardware business elsewhere in this book. It shows up in oarlock sockets. The ones now on the market are all hangovers from the days of wooden boats. There are none specially designed for easy and durable attachment to fiberglass. So we have to make do by improvising attachment methods. Some are neat and durable but there are also many miserable jobs to be seen.

It's the repeated and quite heavy loads applied to the fastenings that cause loosening. An oar is a long lever and the lock is its fulcrum. Wood screws press hard on the wood around them and gradually soften the fibers so they break down and let the threads loose. With machine screws, the high parts of the threads are what contact the wood and that's not much bearing surface for the loads involved. A modern trick is to bed the oarlock sockets in epoxy glue; the epoxy takes much of the load off the fastenings. In your case, the best thing would be to build up the laminate thickness with more layers of glass cloth and resin, and perhaps imbed hardwood strips in this patching to distribute the forces.

Split Oar Blades

Q. How should I repair a split oar blade?

A. An old method is to drill a series of small holes along each side of the split and lace things together with copper wire, somewhat after the fashion of shoelaces. You could modernize this by using epoxy glue to bond the lacing together more durably. You could spread any strong wood glue onto the wood at the split, close the split with clamps, and, when the glue has hardened, cover the whole blade with fiberglass cloth. But go easy on larding on the resin, for you can add enough weight to the blades to make them heavy and clumsy to manipulate. Marine supply catalogs list copper tips to fit over the ends of blades and prevent splitting in the first place. Originally they were riveted or screwed on; today one could bed them into epoxy for greater durability.

Oar Length

Q. How does one determine oar length?

A. Here's a drawing and explanation. It can also be done by "feel." Oars that are too short give short, quick strokes having little power. When they are too long for a boat, it's hard to lift their blades clear of the water on the recovery stroke and things are generally awkward to handle. (*See* page 212)

Oarlocks and Sockets

Q. There are so many styles of oarlocks and sockets in marine catalogs that I'm all confused! And the catalogs all seem to be written on the assumption that everyone who reads them will have had at least 50 years of experience in boating and know what's what!

A. We agree. There's no imagination at all in the hardware business. An accompanying illustration will give you an idea of what's what. (*See* page 213)

Chapter 30

Compasses

Compass Fluid

Q. My boat's compass is only three years old but there is an air bubble in its bowl. I have been to several marine stores asking for compass fluid and the kids behind the counters look at me as if I were asking for hornbeam belaying pins! They never heard of it and can't find it in their suppliers' catalogs. One of my friends tells me to use kerosene, claiming that that is what compass fluid really is. Another says to top the compass up with a mixture of alcohol and water, but he does not know what proportions to mix. Can you tell me just what to do?

A. Send the compass back to its manufacturer or to one of the manufacturer's approved service shops in your area. The compass-fluid scene today is vastly different from what it was when some local waterfront characters were kids. Kerosene and a water/alcohol mix were used in the long-ago. But today, compass manufacturers have access to a much wider range of materials. They make much use of plastics, synthetic sealants and gaskets, modern bearing alloys, etc. Most compass makers now use a fluid made to order to fill their individual requirements.

Use of an improper fluid in any particular make of compass can have a variety of unfortunate effects. Plastic parts may soften or swell and affect operation. Use of a fluid with the incorrect buoyancy may affect the accuracy and durability of the compass; a fluid that does not buoy the card up enough can cause the pivot bearing to be overloaded, and a fluid that buoys it up too much can make its action erratic and unreliable. An improper fluid may cause the markings on the card to discolor or even dissolve.

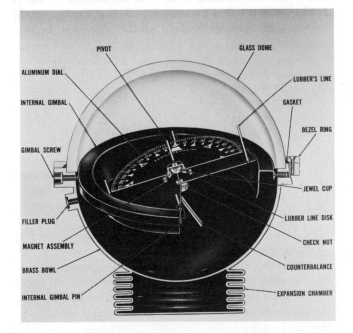

Modern pleasure boat compasses are very sophisticated. Ham-fisted tinkering is definitely not recommended! (E. S. Ritchie & Sons, Inc.)

The reason why common kerosene is not a suitable substitute for approved fluid is that it is not very pure. It may contain bacteria that will discolor the kerosene in time, or cover the card with scum so it is hard to read. When a petroleum-base fluid is used as a compass liquid by a manufacturer, it will be something that has been specially refined and otherwise made suitable for the purpose at hand.

Compass Globe Discolored

Q. The glass globe on my compass has become a discolored milky white and is almost impossible to see through. Is there any way to clean it without taking the instrument apart?

A. The globe is not glass. It is a high grade of cast plastic such as Plexiglas or Lucite. Somebody probably put kerosene into your compass instead of an approved fluid, and the kerosene discolored the plastic. Better send the compass to a competent repair agency, and if you know that kerosene was used in it, tell them so they will know what caused the trouble.

Can't Get Bubble Out

Q. No matter how I twist and turn my compass when putting kerosene into it, I cannot get a small air bubble out completely. Am I doing something wrong?

A. Yes, but we cannot say just what other than that kerosene will be bad for it. Some makes and models of compasses must be filled in the factory with special equipment or techniques to get all their air out.

Purpose of Bellows

Q. My compass has a part on it that looks like some kind of a bellows. My guess is that it is part of the compensating system. Do you know what it is and can you tell me how to adjust it?

A. That bellows has nothing to do with compensation. It is an expansion chamber to cope with expansion and contraction of the compass fluid with changes in temperature. If you filled an older compass with water/alcohol mixture on a cold day, at some later time it will get hot under the summer sun, the liquid will expand and create pressure, and will force its way out past the gaskets and seals. That is one way bubbles get into compasses. Using a bellows avoids variation of pressure with temperature changes and eliminates the forcing out of fluid and drawing in of air. The reason why some old compasses used a water/alcohol mixture was so they would not freeze in wintertime. The reason why other old ones used a refined type of kerosene is because this liquid afforded suitable lubrication to some kinds of pivot bearings. The design of compasses is not static; new ideas come along all the time. These days, for example, digital compasses are coming into use. Imagine what a sea captain of 1850 would think of that!

Parts for Surplus Compass

Q. I bought a high quality Navy compass at a surplus store. It worked well for a while but now needs attention. I wrote to its maker, using the name and address given on the identification plate, and my letter came back stamped "Addressee Unknown." What do you advise me to do to get a service manual and parts?

A. We get inquiries all the time from people searching for parts for military surplus equipment. Unfortunately, we can't offer much help. When the armed services buy a quantity of some kind of equipment they buy a stock of spare parts at the same time. The equipment is installed in their boats, aircraft, tanks, etc., and travels to many widely-scattered places. The spare parts go to supply depots and maintenance bases. When the forces decide to get rid of old equipment, it is put up for sale by bidding on an as-is, where-is basis. It is not often that the successful bidder on a quantity of compasses at, say, the Brooklyn (N.Y.) Navy Yard is also successful in bidding on a quantity of spare parts being sold off in San Diego. The low price you pay for a piece of military gear takes into account the fact that the seller is not going to be able to help you with parts and service.

Contact compass repair services listed in *Boat Owners Buyers Guide*. Contact compass adjusters in your area through the Yellow Pages. Write to the City Clerk or Chamber of Commerce in the city named on the identification plate on your compass, and ask if they have any information on what became of the company that made your compass.

Crazy Compass

Q. My outboard boat's compass card often starts spinning around and around when I am operating on choppy water. Why does it act crazy like this and how can I stop it?

A. At certain speeds and under certain wave conditions, the dashboard of your boat begins to vibrate at a speed that causes the card to start vibrating in harmony. This sets up eddies in the fluid such that the card is set to spinning. The fluid chosen for a good compass tends to be on the thin, watery side to offer minimum resistance to the card's normal turning as the boat turns. But it is also too thin to snub out the vibration caused by speeding over choppy water. Try relocating the compass on a more rigid place, or try stiffening up the dashboard. You can temporarily attach pieces of wood to it with C-clamps to see if stiffening will help.

Magnets You Can't See

Q. My driveway just happens to lie straight east-west. I learned this by chance when studying real estate maps. It's handy to have such a reference line at times, such as when I want to make sure my boat's compass is true. Recently I installed a new outboard motor and an electric tachometer. As soon as I got this instrument into place, I was startled to see the compass card had swung almost 30 degrees off true! I can understand how electric current in the wires could cause this when the motor is running, but darned if I can figure out how the tachometer affects the compass when the engine is not running. So okay, Sherlock Holmes, can you solve this mystery?

A. Elementary, my dear Watson! One part of an electric tachometer's innards is a rather powerful permanent magnet. Next mystery, please?

A New Twist?

Q. I was in a boatyard when one of the men was wiring a windshield wiper. I noticed he was twisting the wires leading to it around and around to make them look like a loosely-laid rope. Is this one of the ways yards use to make simple jobs take a lot of time and thus build up whopping bills?

A. That workman was a good one and he was doing the right thing. When several wires are twisted like that, the twisting makes the electrical field emanating from one wire cancel out that coming from another wire, thus tending to neutralize the overall field and minimize its effect on a nearby compass.

The Core of the Problem

Q. The compass in my stern drive boat worked fine. Then this year I took out the old, shabby steering wheel and replaced it with a new one—same manufacturer, same style. All of a sudden the compass decided north was east and west was south. What could have happened?

A. Even though the wheel was made by the same company and looked like the old one, it may be an improved model with a steel reinforcing core, where the old one was just solid plastic. Get a magnetic "stud finder" at the hardware store (or use your kid's Boy Scout compass) and hold it close to both the old and new wheels. The needle will swing smartly toward the new wheel if it has the steel core we think it has.

Chapter 31

Marine Stoves

Cantankerous Alcoholic Stoves

Q. My small cruiser has an alcohol stove in its galley. The thing has my wife terrified—getting it to burn steadily is like getting the IRS to approve listing your dog, Edgar, as a dependant. Why are these cantankerous things so common on boats?

A. Safety. Alcohol is a safe shipmate; it won't fill the bilges with explosive vapor as will gasoline and propane stoves. Spilled alcohol will readily mix with water and can be bailed or pumped out without fire or explosion risk. An alcohol fire in a galley can be doused quickly with Coke, milk, soup or any other water-based liquid that might be handy at the moment.

One has to understand the nature of these stoves to make them behave. An alcohol flame is not as hot as some other stove flames. If the cook does not realize this, he or she is apt to think there's something mechanically or functionally wrong with the stove. There are many kinds of alcohols on the market. Using an unsuitable one in an alcohol stove just because it says "Alcohol" on the can in the hardware store is asking for trouble. Use only alcohol from marine stores that is specifically made for this purpose.

It's important to understand that these stoves do not burn alcohol in its liquid form—they vaporize it and then burn the vapor. Inadequate pre-heating of the "generator," the part that converts liquid alcohol into vapor, can cause everything from a sputtering flame to terrifying flare-ups. Failure to keep the working parts clean can cause erratic functioning. Failure to keep air pressure up affects fuel feed. The best thing to do about a cook who would rather sit down on a cobra than use an alcohol stove is to take him or her and the stove out into

the backyard. There they can practice with the stove and get accustomed to its quirks, without the claustrophobia that comes from trying to get acquainted with it in a cramped cabin.

Camp Stoves on Boats

Q. I've had it with the infernal alcohol stove in my boat. Would it be OK to junk it and use a propane-burning camping stove?

A. No. Such stoves are not designed or approved for marine use. They can leak gas, which will tend to collect in the bilge area. They do not have suitable provisions for holding down utensils and preventing them from sliding off into the cook's lap when the boat rolls. They will quickly rust in a salt atmosphere and become even less safe. Use of such a stove will probably void your boat's insurance. There are gas stoves designed for boat use but they differ as much from camp stoves as a yacht compass does from a pocket compass.

Alcohol Stove Won't Burn

Q. At a yacht club flea market I bought a yacht stove that is a real beauty—all stainless steel and polished up. I took it home, filled the tank with alcohol, and could not get it to burn worth a damn. Can you give me a trouble-shooting list?

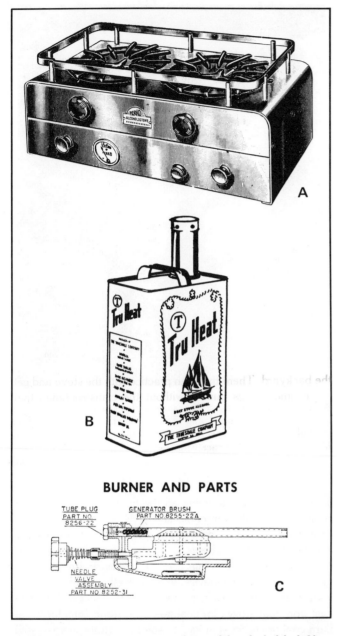

BURNER AND PARTS

TUBE PLUG
PART NO.
8256-22

GENERATOR BRUSH
PART NO.8255-22A

NEEDLE
VALVE
ASSEMBLY
PART NO 8252-31

C

(A) *Here's a typical marine stove designed for alcohol fuel. Note guard rail that keeps utensils from sliding off. Some stoves even have clamps to hold the utensils firmly in place over the burners. (Perko Corp.) (B) Use only alcohol specifically refined and sold for marine stoves if you want trouble-free operation. (C) An alcohol stove's burner is designed to vaporize the fuel for burning. Lack of understanding about how such a stove works is the basic reason some people have trouble with them.*

A. No need for a list. We think we can hit the bullseye on the first shot—that stove has jets designed to handle kerosene, not alcohol. Some stoves can be converted to burn either fuel by changing the jets. Some yachtsmen prefer kerosene for such reasons as it gives a hotter flame and it may be easier to buy than stove alcohol in the out-of-the-way places a cruising boat can go to. Try kerosene in it ashore, in

Modern marine stoves come in a wide range of types and styles, to fit everything from a day-sailer up to a luxury houseboat. This Optimus-Princess burns clean, hot propane. If the flame is extinguished in any way, an automatic shutoff stops gas from flowing to avoid explosion danger. If you want a stove in your boat, its design and installation must comply with safety standards. Consult reputable marine stores and yacht yards. (Optimus-Princess, Inc.)

a safe outdoor spot, and with a dry-powder fire extinguisher handy. If you find it burns well on kerosene, that's your answer. You will probably find the kerosene smell will get into everything unless you are very careful not to let it spill or leak.

Stove Makes Soot

Q. My kerosene galley stove produces a lot of soot. Do you suppose modern kerosene is different from that available years ago?

A. Make sure your stovepipe is of the diameter recommended by the stove's maker. Too small a pipe will keep things from venting adequately and cause sooting.

Installing an Alcohol Stove

Q. We are converting an old lifeboat into a small cruiser.

What do I do to make a safe installation of the alcohol stove in the galley?

A. There should be a metal splash shield on the galley walls in the area of the stove. It could be aluminum sheet in a simple boat, or stainless steel in a more pretentious one. There should be a drip pan under the stove with a rim high enough to retain any alcohol that might spill or leak from cold burners. Half an inch will be enough in most cases. The stove must be fastened down so it won't shift as the boat rolls. Unless the stove is very close to a hatch or window you can open, there should be a ventilator in the roof above it to allow heat to escape. Locate a fire extinguisher between the stove and the cabin hatch or door, so that a fire in the stove will not cut off access to the extinguisher when leaving or entering the cabin. Give some thought to how persons in the cabin could or should make an escape in case of a stove fire. Buy or make a folding splash shield to set up around three sides of the utensil when frying bacon and other meats that could flare up. Keep a pot cover handy that will fit the frying pan to quickly snuff out flaming meat or grease.

A basic feature of any marine stove is that it must not allow hot utensils to slide around and dump contents onto people. This gimbal-mounted Sterno stove by Bremer is for small sailboats used for short cruises. (Bremer Mfg. Co.)

Catalytic Heater

Q. Is it all right to use a camping-type portable catalytic heater in a boat cabin?

A. It would depend. Generally no, but it might be all right in something of the sort of an aluminum johnboat with aluminum shelter cabin having a curtain across its after side. Such heaters burn a prepared fuel supplied by their manufacturers. It is essentially naphtha, which is a close relative of gasoline. Since gasoline stoves are illegal in boats, some officials would be inclined to rule that this would include naphtha stoves. Use of such a stove would probably void your insurance. If you choose to use one in a semi-enclosed small craft, make sure that stale air can get out readily and that fresh, oxygen-bearing air can get in to replace it. People have been asphyxiated using portable heaters in confined places.

time, and having one going all the time in the summer for cooking can make the cabin into a sweatbox. But a warm coal fire in a boat used for early spring and late fall fishing and hunting can be cheering. We have never encountered examples of wood being used in pleasure boat stoves; probably its bulk, messiness, and the likelihood of harboring insects all weigh against it. Specialty firms still make small cast iron boat stoves for coal, and soapstone "fireplaces" to burn coal or charcoal in yacht cabins for atmosphere as well as heat. See *Boat Owners Buyers Guide*.

Coal and Wood Stoves

Q. Coal and wood stoves are coming back in style for home heating. What about boats?

A. Coal was once quite popular in yachts. It is explosion-proof, spill-proof, and has no bad odor. It's heavy. Poorly handled, it can be messy. Getting a coal fire going takes

Homestrand Parts

Q. Where can I get parts for a "Homestrand" galley stove? Letters addressed to the maker in Larchmont, N.Y. come back stamped "Addressee Unknown."

A. Homestrand sold out to Kenyon Marine, P.O. Box 308, Guilford, Conn. 06437. The last we knew, this firm was supplying parts.

Imported Stoves

Q. I have a "Punker" stove in my boat's galley. I think it was made in Sweden. Where can I get parts?

A. We often get requests for sources of parts for Punker, Optimus, Primus, and other Scandinavian stoves. Here are a few addresses:

Punker AB, Strandgatan 12, S-633 43 Eskilstuna, Sweden.

Optimus, Box 16, S-194 01 Upplands-Vasby, Sweden.

Primus is represented in the U.S. by Primus-Sievert Division of Sievert, Inc., 354 Sackett Point Rd., North Haven, Conn. 06473.

See Chapter 1 for ways of locating the things you need.

Chapter 32

Sea Closets

Locating Maker of Sea Closet

Q. We bought a used boat that has a sea closet bearing no trademark at all. It needs overhaul and we do not know where to get parts. Can you help?

A. The best thing to do is take it apart during the off-season and clean up all the bits and pieces. Lay them out on a board and get a good photo of them. Look up sea closet manufacturers currently in business in the various marine trade directories. Write to each, enclosing a print of the picture, and ask if they recognize the thing. If one of them does, that's it. Or, one might recognize a few standard parts as being identical to those he uses. If you live near a city, visit marine hardware distributing companies, show the desk man your box of small parts, and see if one such place might have a universal sea closet repair kit. Such kits are also shown in some of the mail order marine supply catalogs. But remember, you might have an imported sea closet; the nuts and bolts on it would in that case have metric threads which won't accept any American nuts and bolts. If you thus determine it is imported, your chances of finding parts are small, as your closet could have come from any of a dozen countries.

Parts for a "Carlson"

Q. My boat is equipped with a "Carlson" sea closet. Where can I get repair parts?

A. We have had many people ask this question, and we have kept our eyes open for a source for several years without luck. Possibly a universal repair parts kit would have

the items you need. We have also had people ask us about parts for "Dahmer" sea closets. We remember seeing that name in the boating press many years ago but have seen no trace of it in the last several years. Another name that crops up fairly often is "E. J. Willis." When we looked under "Sea Closets" in the marine trade directories we could not find it. Later, while looking up marine stoves for another job, we found this name listed among other firms presently making stoves. So that's a point to remember—as time passes, it is common to find that companies drop some products and start making others. If you can't find the item you want under its proper name, be it hardware or equipment, see if the directory has a section in which manufacturers are listed alphabetically. You may spot the name you're looking for there.

Books on Sea Closets

Q. Does anyone sell a book on servicing sea closets?

A. As far as we know, there is no book devoted entirely to this subject. But *Powerboat Maintenance*, published by Clymer Publications, 222 North Virgil Ave., Los Angeles, Cal. 90004, has a section containing information and exploded drawings of Thetford, Craft-Toilet, Monogram, Mansfield, Jensen, Ball-Head, and Raritan sea closets.

Special Toilet Tissue

Q. A friend says he was visiting on board somebody's

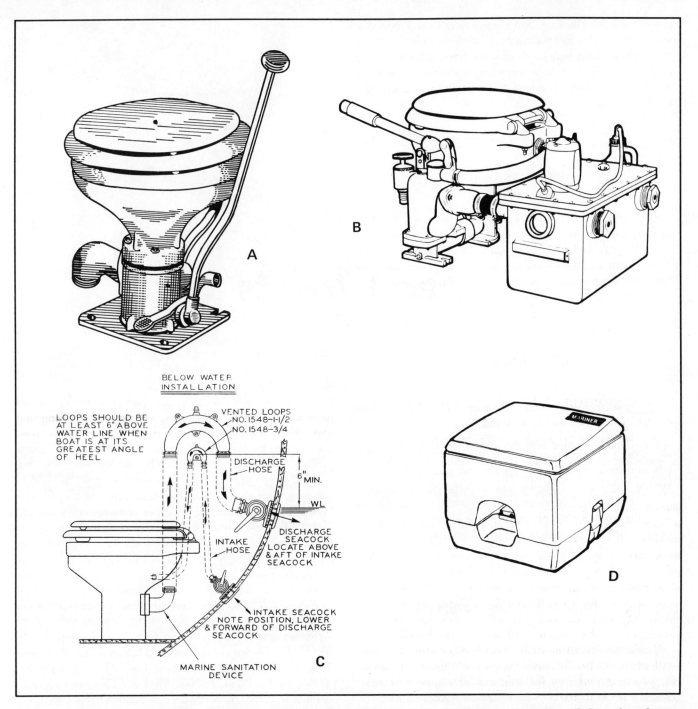

Sea closets come in many types. Their basic parts tend to last a very long time, being made of porcelain and installed in safe enclosures. Getting parts can be a problem. Top left (A), a typical old-style hand-operated unit. Top right (B), before MSD regulations came along, sea closets discharged overboard. The inlet and discharge lines sometimes became restricted due to marine growths and "mysteriously" affected operation. Bottom left (C), a modern chlorinator-type that treats waste before discharge. Lower right (D), portable units sometimes are the answer when changing government MSD regulations make other recourses too confusing, complicated or costly.

yacht and claimed they had a roll of self-disintegrating toilet tissue in their boat's head. Was he kidding me?

A. No. There really is such paper. Many marine stores in areas where there are cruising boats stock it. It helps the macerator, chlorinator, and holding tank problems by disintegrating and thus not forming clumps that could block mechanisms.

Sluggish Sea Closet

Q. Only a couple of months after we launched our new boat, the sea closet started working very sluggishly. We took it apart and could find nothing wrong. What now?

A. Remove the water intake and discharge lines and

check them for blocking. Some guest may have dropped a washcloth or other indigestible item into the sea closet. Algae or marine growths may be choking the lines. If it's a holding tank system, there could be something in the tank or perhaps inadequate venting. The only thing to do is to check the whole system.

Vent Line Odors

Q. Since the holding tanks now required by law must be vented, doesn't the vent line discharge bad odors?

A. Yes. A variety of chemicals are on the market for coping with it. Some work all right, some create odors or other problems of their own. New developments come along regularly.

MSD Literature

Q. I'm all confused about marine sanitation devices! How do I decide which model to install?

A. The several firms active in the field have explanatory booklets. You can get some at local marine dealers. Look for ads and announcements in the boating publications. New literature comes out all the time to keep abreast of both technical and legal developments. Contact the Coast Guard district office or station nearest to you and ask for a copy of *Federal Marine Sanitation Device Regulations.*

Rubber Holding Tanks

Q. My small cruising sailboat is already pretty well filled with appointments and equipment. I can't figure out how to fit a holding tank into the only available spaces because they are so inaccessible and irregular in shape.

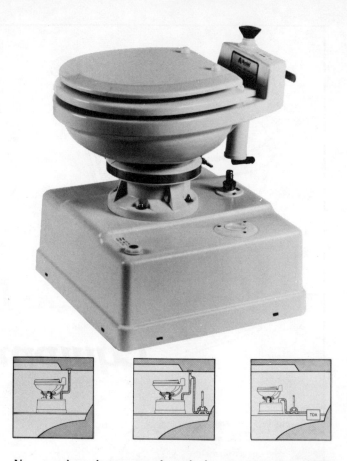

New sea closet designs comply with changing government MSD regulations. This Mansfield can handle waste in various ways. In three bottom panels, it is installed for 1) pumping out where pumpout facilities are available; 2) equipped with a "Y" valve to permit pumping out when in port or discharge overboard when beyond the three-mile limit at sea; and 3) fitted with a treatment device to render waste non-objectionable prior to discharge overboard. Boat owners know what regulations apply to their cruising areas. (Mansfield Sanitary, Inc.)

A. Look into a rubber holding tank. When collapsed, it will fit through a rather small opening, then expand to fit the available space. At this writing such tanks are imported by W. H. DenOuden (USA) Inc., P.O. Box 8712, Baltimore, Md. 21240 and Inland Marine Co., 79 E. Jackson St., Wilkes-Barre, Penn. 18701. They are also available from leading U.S. marine hardware and sea closet manufacturers.

Chapter 33

Docks, Handling Equipment, and Storage

Boat Hoists

Q. Our boat club wants to install a boat hoist. Where could we get plans for one?

A. It has been a very long time since we saw anything like this in a boating publication. Years ago, when the sport was small, the magazines did publish how-to-make-it articles. But

Several firms sell prefabricated small-boat docks. (Mercury Marine)

in the last 20 to 30 years there has been such a growing need for boat-handling equipment that numerous companies have designed and marketed such gear. They are well designed and regular production keeps the prices reasonable. You can spend a lot of time and money cobbling up your own equipment, and if you make mistakes you're stuck with the results. The various marine directories, such as *Boat Owners Buyers Guide* and those published by the marine trade magazines, have listings of makers of boat handling equipment. They offer dollies, large and small docks, a variety of hoists, portable boathouses, small marine railways, motor lifts, and so on. Write to these companies for their literature; you may get some extremely useful ideas.

Ramps and Docks

Q. We are going to establish a hunting and fishing camp on a large lake. Where can we get good information on designing and building a launching ramp and boat docks?

A. Write to the Outboard Boating Club of America, c/o National Marine Manufacturers Association, 401 North Michigan Ave., Chicago, Ill. 60611 and ask for a copy of their free booklet, *Launching Ramps and Piers.* If you need advice on designing a facility, ask for their booklet *Directory* of *Architects and Engineers;* it lists persons and companies with professional experience in designing waterfront facilities. Before going too far with planning even a modest dock or ramp, check with the government agencies that in one way or another have some jurisdiction over waterfront development. They will include the town or city clerk's office, the local conservation commission, the Army Corps of Engineers, EPA, etc. You may have to go through certain procedures to obtain necessary construction permits. If you build without proper permits, you may be ordered to dismantle your structure.

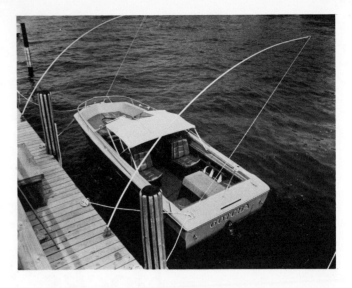

Flexible "whips" keep tension on lines, keep boat from banging against dock with wind and waves. (Monarch Tool & Mfg. Co.)

Boat Bangs on Dock

Q. I find it necessary to tie my stern-drive boat to the dock with its bow facing out toward the channel; otherwise, waves from passing boats will dash against the transom and keep the stern quarters soaked. But in this position the raised lower unit of the stern drive is in constant danger of banging into the retaining wall. What's your advice?

A. Look in books on seamanship. In the sections on docking you will find information on rigging "spring lines" to keep a boat from moving fore and aft alongside a dock. But there are some docking situations where lines won't adequately secure a boat. Look in *Boat Owners Buyers Guide* and the marine trade directories in your marine dealer's office. A number of firms make varieties of boat positioning devices that will let a boat pitch with the waves but not bang against the dock—positioning arms, "whips" that keep constant tension on the lines, rubber shock absorbers, etc. There are also various kinds of fenders and bumpers made of white rubber or vinyl that will prevent damage when a boat does contact its dock. If you can afford one, a boat hoist or davits would best solve the problem by raising the boat above the water and its waves.

Waterfront Retaining Wall

Q. We bought some undeveloped waterfront property. In order to landscape it and provide a good place to erect a boat dock, it will be necessary to put in a retaining wall or bulkhead along the shoreline. Any advice would be appreciated.

A. Making a good retaining wall calls for specialized knowledge about local soils, tide and ice conditions, the scouring action of waves and currents, metal corrosion, marine growths, and local, state, and federal regulations covering waterfront structures. Because these things vary so widely, it hasn't been feasible to establish large, nationwide companies specializing in such work. The best thing to do is gather information on waterfront structures as previously mentioned in this chapter, read it to get an idea of what's available and what you'd like to have, and then seek out a local contractor who specializes in waterfront construction. Steel and aluminum companies make interlocking metal strips that can be driven into the earth to make strong retaining walls with a minimum of labor.

Make a Work List

Q. It happens every year—my boat goes into the water in the spring with too many needed things left undone. I admit I'm a procrastinator and not a good organizer. But I love my boat! Can you help?

A. At haul-out time in the fall, go over the boat thoroughly and make a written list of the things that need attention. Then sit down and go over this list, rewriting it in a more orderly way. Use headings such as "Engine," "Hull," "Cleaning," "Equipment," and so on. Listing the jobs under appropriate headings really does make things less confusing and formidable. Set the launching date, and work back from there to schedule the various jobs. Do things in logical order. Take care of the dirty jobs before getting to the cleanup jobs, do engine work with its attendant climbing in and out of the boat before doing the varnishing work, and so on. Everything that needs professional attention, including instruments, electronics, galley equipment, sails, etc., should be taken to appropriate shops in the fall to be sure it will all be ready at fitting-out time. Another good thing about having a work list is that as each task is crossed off, the amount of work remaining will look progressively smaller and less discouraging.

Dirt-Floored Storage Sheds

Q. We bought a fine old wooden boat and restored it to top condition. One local boatyard has modern concrete-floored buildings on high ground. Another has old dirt-floored buildings on low-lying ground. Each says theirs is the best place for us to store our boat. What do you say?

A. We'd want to see it first, but from this distance our choice would be one of the old dirt-floored buildings. Concrete-floored buildings have come into vogue in our fiberglass age because it's easy for forklift trucks to move around in them and for men to push boats around on castered dollies. In the old days of wooden boats, storage sheds tended to have dirt floors so that water vapor could come up from the earth and keep planking from drying out too much.

Second Hand Canvas

Q. A friend who owns a store gave me his old canvas awning to use as a winter cover for my boat. I was getting ready to waterproof it using a method I found in an old outdoorsman's manual—soaking it in a mixture of paraffin and naphtha. Then another friend came along and said I should not do it because paraffin-impregnated canvas would be a bad fire hazard. Is he right? What should I do?

A. It would burn fiercely once it got going. In cold weather it might be so brittle as to crack when shaken by wind. Canvas does not have to be 100% waterproof to shed rain. Even though you can see daylight through the weave, when rain starts falling the canvas gets wet and the threads swell somewhat, tending to close the gaps. Surface tension makes water form tiny "lenses" in the square gaps between the weave. Then the canvas will shed rain well. Water will come in only where something chances to touch the inner surface so as to encourage it to bleed through.

Tour marine and hardware stores, reading labels on commercial waterproofing products. They work through a chemical action that makes the fabric repel water before it can penetrate the weave, much like waterproofed jackets and coats. A homemade waterproofing can be made by mixing soybean oil and turpentine in the ratio of two parts of the former to one part of the latter.

Fireproofing Canvas

Q. My boat is now in a shed where workmen are doing a lot of painting and welding on a nearby boat. I'd like to fireproof some canvas to cover my boat with. How?

A. Canvas supply houses may be able to supply you with commercial fire retardant products. Note we say "fire

Interlocking corrugated aluminum panels make a simple, durable retaining wall. (Kaiser Aluminum)

retardant," not "fireproofing." Nothing will keep canvas from burning once the flame gets hot enough. A homemade treatment can be prepared by mixing half a cup of ammonium phosphate and one cup of ammonium chloride in a quart of water and brushing it on thoroughly. This will offer some protection indoors, but it's a treatment that will rinse out with the first rainstorm if used outdoors.

Boat Covers

Q. Where can I get a canvas cover to fit over my outboard boat when it is not in use?

A. Visit marine stores and ask to look in their wholesaler's catalogs. N. A. Taylor Co., 10 West 9th Ave., Gloversville, N.Y. 12078 makes universal covers. Go to the mail order counter at the nearest Sears, Roebuck & Co. store and ask for their current *Boating & Fishing Catalog*. There is a list of canvas and plastic supply houses in *Boat Owners Buyers Guide*. (See "Buying Canvas" in Chapter 22.)

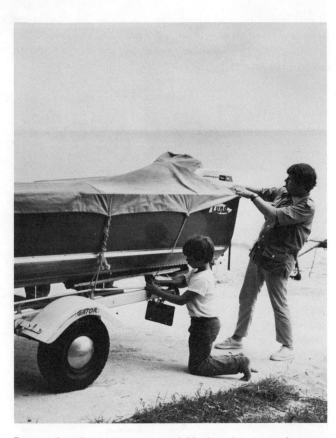

Boat and cockpit covers are available from boat manufacturers, marine supply houses and mail order companies. (Johnson Motors)

Plastic Winter Cover

Q. Where can I get tear-resistant plastic covering material to use over my boat in the winter?

A. Go to contractors' supply houses in your area. Look under "Plastics—Film and Sheet" in the Yellow Pages. Sears, Roebuck & Co.'s Farm Catalog lists tough sheeting of various kinds. Stamford Packaging Co., Box 3091, Stamford, Conn. 06905 sells a boat cover material called "Weave-Cote" to the marine field.

Canvas vs. Plastic

Q. How does canvas compare to sheet plastic for a winter cover?

A. A large tarpaulin will not be cheap. But then, a tough plastic that is able to withstand wind for a number of seasons may not be cheap, either. When canvas dries out after a storm, it becomes porous and helps to ventilate the boat. Yet, any good cover should be open at bow and stern to allow air to circulate freely. Clear plastic will let more sunlight get through onto varnished surfaces and upholstery, with gradual

fading the result. A tightly sealed plastic cover is bad because it will sweat and lead to a rot- and mildew-producing atmosphere inside the boat during mild weather in late fall and early spring.

A plastic winter cover that has no ventilation at all amounts to a hothouse that will breed rot and mildew.

Seagulls on Canvas

Q. I have to replace my canvas cockpit cover every few years because seagull droppings rot it quickly. Is there anything on the market with which to treat canvas and give it more resistance to this vile substance?

A. We have never seen anything like this on sale in marine stores or listed in marine supply catalogs. A regular waterproofer might help to minimize penetration of the droppings, but you'd have to learn from experience if it was worthwhile. Many sailmakers and boat upholstery shops now use vinyl materials rather than cotton duck for covers, an advantage being that it is easier to hose off and the fluids in droppings don't penetrate its solid surface. Your best bet is to keep the gulls off. (See Chapter 2, Boat Owner's Common Problems.)

Storing a Battery

Q. Should my boat's storage battery be drained of electrolyte for winter storage?

A. No! That would play hob with the electro-chemical setup in the plates. Do not put a battery into storage in a state of low charge. In that condition the electrolyte has a higher percentage of acid in it and this will be harder on the plates. Also, a discharged battery will be susceptible to freezing of the electrolyte, with resultant mechanical damage. A fully charged battery will not freeze in any winter temperatures likely to be experienced. Ideally, store it in as cool a place as you can find, such as in a basement and well away from the furnace. If the outside is constantly damp, such as from rain or sweating, the moisture will mix with traces of acid on the top of the battery and a self-discharging current will leak from one terminal to the other. That is why batteries are often washed with baking soda and water—to neutralize the acid.

A battery that is allowed to stand for long periods in semi-discharged condition will suffer a shortening of its life due to sulphation—accumulation in the bottom of its case of a chemical by-product from the plates. When the sulphation becomes deep enough it will reach the bottom edges of the plates and short them out. Keep your battery fully charged by periodic use of a "trickle charger," available in any auto store. You can also keep a boat battery alive by using it in your car intermittently, if it will fit.

Wet vs. Dry Storage

Q. Can you please give the pros and cons of wet vs. dry storage for a boat of cruiser size?

A. Dry storage becomes necessary when there is no place to leave a boat in the water where it will be safe from storms and moving ice. Large chunks of floating ice drifting past a boat with the current can scar a hull badly. Thick, solid ice forming around a hull can crush it. Wet storage is thus feasible only in protected inlets and coves where storm waves do not enter and where there are people around all the time to keep an eye on things.

To protect boats left in the water from being crushed by ice, methods of agitating the water have become popular. One system consists of a loop of tubing set on the bottom of the lake or cove directly below the boat. It has small holes in it. A compressor located on shore delivers air to the loop. Bubbles rising to the surface around the boat keep the water from freezing. Another method makes use of sealed electric motors with small water propellers mounted at the upper ends of their vertical shafts. A steady upward flow of water under the hull keeps ice from forming. How many such units are needed depends on the length of the boat, severity of weather, etc.

The weak point in these methods is that if there is mechanical breakdown or electrical failure, flow of bubbles or water will stop. That is why wet storage is safe only at a place that is frequented by responsible persons who will keep watch. A good point about wet storage is that a hull is supported gently and uniformly by the water, rather than having pressure concentrated at the points where blocking contacts it. It is very common to see large boats stored on land with far too few supports—which causes hull sagging. Wet storage is often preferred for larger wooden boats having heavy planking—it keeps the planking from drying out and shrinking. The heavier a boat's planks are, the more

it may suffer from severe drying-out. More can be said, but you now have an idea of what the pros and cons are. Make your decision after considering your particular boat and local circumstances.

Why Cover a Boat?

Q. Boats are built to live outdoors. Why bother to cover them for winter storage?

A. For many reasons. Sunlight slowly but surely fades paint and gel coat, takes the life out of upholstery, plastics, and deck seam materials. During thaws, snow melts and water seeps into the many small gaps and spaces between topside parts. When this water freezes at night, it can exert a powerful pushing-apart force. A cover will keep dirt and leaves from collecting in a stored boat. It all makes good sense.

Why Wax Fiberglass?

Q. If a good grade of fiberglass wax will protect a boat's surface as well as claimed, why bother to cover a fiberglass boat with canvas or black plastic for the winter?

A. Wax will slow down the rate at which the surface will turn chalky, but it won't keep sunlight from penetrating through the translucent gel coat. It will thus slowly but surely fade all the pigment in the gel coat, after which no amount of polishing will restore original color.

A prefab shelter like this will keep your boat clean and bright despite the hot sun and driving rain.

Bilge Odors

Q. We live in the middle Atlantic area and don't have enough ice in the creeks to make damage to a boat likely, so we leave it at the dock all winter. Bilge water keeps developing a foul odor and none of the bilge cleaning chemicals we have tried do much good. Have you any suggestions?

A. Here's an example of where it would pay to go outside the marine field for help. Get a sample of the bilge water and give it to a bacteriologist, perhaps at a local high school or college, or maybe the county board of health. He or she can look at it under a microscope and might come up with some ideas about using an appropriate type of chemical in the bilge water to stop the algae or other growth that causes the odors.

Winterizing Water System

Q. In marine stores I see jugs of special marine water system antifreeze. Wouldn't automotive antifreeze do the job just as well?

A. No. The marine types are compounded to be nontoxic and to leave the tank and lines with an agreeable taste and odor. Automotive antifreeze would poison you if some of it remained in the system after spring cleanout, and even if you escaped that fate, you might find the water to have a disagreeable taste for a long time.

Working in Winter

Q. I want to do a lot of reconditioning on my boat while it is stored in the backyard for the winter. Any suggestions?

A. Working outdoors in the winter is the ultimate misery. Metal tools are so cold they will make your hands ache. You can't do fussy work with gloves on. Glues won't cure properly. Primers and paints take forever to harden. Rain and snow stop progress often. If you have much work to do, it would pay to make an A-frame over the boat and cover it with tough plastic sheeting to make a tent of sorts. Or make a similar lean-to on one side of your garage. Sunlight coming through the plastic will make the shelter bright and cheerful, and will help warm the air in it. If you don't have the time or money to make a shelter for the whole boat, at least make one over the cockpit to keep rain, snow, and wind out. Spend the colder months working inside the boat and do the outside work later when the weather improves.

A sheet-metal wood stove can heat a shelter enough to sweat you out. It will heat the shelter up rapidly if you light a quick, hot, kindling-wood fire in it. It can get red hot, so must be well shielded from the shelter walls. Its heat can dry out parts of a wooden boat close to it, so erect a sheetrock or corrugated tin heat barricade between the stove and boat. Kerosene-burning space heaters can heat a shelter rapidly but can be noisy and smelly. Coleman-type camping stoves are nice for smaller shelters or boat interiors. Any fuel-burning stove can consume the oxygen in the air of a confined space, or fill it with noxious fumes, so be very careful about providing a way for fresh air to come in and fumes to exit. For work inside a boat, a portable quartz-type electric heater would be safe and can cast a most comforting glow of heat toward the area where you are working.

Finally, buy as large a dry-chemical fire extinguisher as you can afford and keep it close by where you are working. When you close the shelter to go to bed or to work, leave it just inside the door so it can be seen and grabbed by anyone in an emergency.

One more pointer. If you're working barehanded in a cold place in order to do fussy detail work, spread Vaseline over the backs of your hands and fingers. It will help to keep the chill out, just like a coating of grease helps long-distance swimmers stand the cold water.

Chapter 34

Water Tanks

Fiberglass Tank Taste

Q. *Our cruiser was new last year. It has a fiberglass water tank. All summer long, the water coming from it had such a bad fiberglass taste that we could use it only for washing purposes and had to carry a separate supply of drinking water in jugs. Is there any way we can avoid the taste in the future?*

A. There is hope. Fiberglass taste in water is common. Resin sets hard in half a day or so when being used to make fiberglass parts, but its final curing tapers off at a gradually diminishing rate. How long it will take to get a tank completely cured is hard to say. A lot depends on how much exposure it gets to direct sunlight, the prevailing temperatures, the nature of the resin used and the build of the laminate, etc. A tank that has been installed in the bilge of a boat as soon as it is out of the mold will get no sunlight (which accelerates the final cure). A tank that is filled with water soon after manufacture will have no chance to fully cure and will give water a bad taste for a long time. You get the idea. One month of curing at room temperature and with reasonable ventilation would be a likely minimum. If your tank is allowed to stand empty and with all filler and withdrawal lines opened for ventilation, that might fix things.

A common quickie cure is to empty the tank and steam it out for, say, half a day. Rig a kettle or other suitable container on an electric plate, or perhaps on the galley stove, and lead a hose to the tank. The hose should go to the bottom of the tank. Let steam go into the tank steadily—it isn't the pressure, it's the heat that does the job. It's worth a try.

Another method is to fill the tank with water containing Clorox in the ratio of three-fourths of a cup of Clorox to a gallon of water. Let it stand for a day, then drain and rinse the tank until the Clorox odor and/or taste has gone. This won't fix a poorly-cured tank, but it can get lingering odor out of a well-cured one.

Yet another trick is to mix some baking soda with water to form a light paste, pour it into the tank, then fill the tank and allow to stand for a day or two. No specific proportions are specified—probably a tumbler-full of soda to every five or ten gallons would do. If the tank is not quite filled, a day out on choppy water will keep the water and soda mix sloshing around to advantage. Drain, rinse well, and refill.

Glass Filaments in Water

Q. *Is it possible for glass filaments to be ingested by drinking water from a fiberglass water tank?*

A. It's possible, if the tank was badly made by an incompetent outfit. A resin-starved laminate would let sloshing water dislodge glass filaments. If there's plenty of resin and all the glass is well-encapsulated, the danger is nil. We have seen custom boat shops finish off fiberglass water tanks by pouring in a pint or so of resin and turning the tanks over and over to coat the interior with a glossy layer of resin. We've seen the same thing done using surfacing-type gel coat, which can give an even more thorough surface sealing. Another source of filaments in the water is from drilling, sawing, and sanding operations when installing fittings and a

Water tanks can be made of fiberglass. They have to be properly made and fully cured to be satisfactory. One advantage is that they don't become rusty.

cleanout plate. There are boobs who will not think to clean that debris out as a final step in their work. Our personal belief is that while fiberglass dust will remain in one's lungs if breathed in, it would pass through one's digestive system without being absorbed.

Is Resin Toxic?

Q. If I made a water tank of fiberglass, would the resin poison or otherwise contaminate the water?

A. There's nothing toxic about resin, provided it is allowed to cure thoroughly. It is one of the most inert of chemical products in common use—food trays, food-processing tanks, and similar objects are made of fiberglass.

Plywood Water Tanks?

Q. I have heard talk at marinas of water tanks being made of plywood. Is this another tall story?

A. No. It has been done. The plywood simply serves as a form over which to laminate mat and cloth. Typically, a simple box is put together, but left open at the top. There will be strips of wood around the top to form flanges. The inside is covered with perhaps three layers of mat. A cover is made of plywood, also with that many layers on its inner surface.

The flange is wetted with resin and a couple layers of mat in narrow strips laid on and wetted with resin, or a fiberglass putty is mixed up and buttered onto the flange. Then the top is lowered in place, a couple brads driven in to keep it from slipping to one side, and weights laid on. When the resin "kicks," the lid will be on securely and the exterior can then be covered with fiberglass, perhaps two layers of mat on a small tank or three on a large one. The plywood is encapsulated in fiberglass and will not rot.

Our own preference would be to do it as follows. Wax some sheet glass or Melamine-coated Masonite with several coats. Brush on resin, lay mat into it, brush on more resin and roll out, lay another piece of mat on and repeat. When cured, lift off. Make up as many sheets of "fiberglass plywood" in this way as needed to make the tank. Saw pieces to shape, prop up to form an open-topped box, fasten together on the inside with strips of mat or tape two or three inches wide, and let cure. When hard, you will have a fiberglass box. Make a lid the same way, position it, and affix it carefully using small tabs of resin-soaked tape or mat. Let these cure to secure the lid, then tape all around. Cover this box with as many layers of mat and roving as seems needed to get a tank that will withstand the water's weight and sloshing. Slosh resin around inside the finished tank to smooth and seal the inside of the cover joint. Gas tanks can be made in the same way, but should have baffles. Make them of three or four layers of glass mat on the Masonite, cut to fit, and tape in place before the cover goes on. Cut off corners of the baffle to let gas flow from one compartment in the tank to another when filling and withdrawing. There's no plywood at all when this method is used, so there are no worries about delamination.

Consider Water's Weight

Q. Could we make up a bulkhead of fiberglass and fix it into place in the bow of my cruiser with resin and tape to make a big water tank in the bow using the hull itself for the sides? I calculate there'd be enough volume to hold 100 gallons for long cruises.

A. Mechanically, it would be possible, with proper attention to workmanship, strength, and cleanliness. But don't overlook weight! That much water will weigh over 900 pounds. That weight so far forward could put your boat out of trim, and probably strain the hull when the bow lifts over large waves. On this basis, we wouldn't do it.

Rusty Galvanized Tank

Q. The galvanized water tank in our older cruiser is getting rusty and of course this discolors the water in it. Is there any product with which to coat the interior and seal it?

A. If you mean some kind of sealant or coating, we know of none. The problem is that no coating will stay in place on a surface that has loose rust or scales on it. Unless there's a cleanout plate on the tank and you can reach all rusted areas through it, there's no way to prepare the surface for a sealant material. A boat mechanic who knows what he's doing might cut access holes, clean off rust, brighten the metal with abrasive paper, apply epoxy resin, and seal the holes with epoxied patches. A lubber might only botch things. Write to Sudbury Laboratory, Inc., 572 Dutton Rd., Sudbury, Mass. 01776 for a copy of their advertising folder. One of their products is "Liquid Aqua-Clear." As we understand them, it conditions the inside of a rusty tank so the water will be reasonably potable. It can help extend the useful life of a rusting tank.

Gasoline in Water Tank

Q. A dock attendant who was daydreaming inserted a gas line nozzle into the water tank filler cap on my boat, and before anyone realized what he was doing several gallons of gas went into the tank. We pumped the gas out and rinsed the tank for a long time. But the smell and odor of gas remain in the water supply. The tank is built in. What can we do?

A. If it was unleaded gas, that's one thing. If it was leaded, there could be a toxicity problem. If you were lucky and it was unleaded gas, try the old baking soda trick as described earlier in this chapter. Steaming might also work. If it was leaded gas, there is a question whether the tank can ever be safe again for drinking water. If the tank is metal, the above cleaning will probably suffice, but if it's fiberglass, the resin can be just porous enough to absorb and retain some of the tetraethyl lead antiknock compound. We asked a petroleum man about it. His feeling is that only a thorough scrubbing of the interior with a stiff brush and strong ammonia and water solution could be depended on to get the lead off the fiberglass. A good fiberglass man may be able to open up the tank so this cleaning can be done, then patch it without having to remove it. Show the bill to the kid whose daydreaming caused all the trouble. It might add to his education!

Water Tank Leaks

Q. My boat has a water tank that cannot be removed without tearing up some of the cockpit floor. There is a small leak in it somewhere. I can see the water from it trickling slowly down the hull surfaces to the bilge. The leak might be where I can reach it and stop it with epoxy glue, if I could find its exact location. Any ideas?

A. Boatyards have various tricks. When the tank is, say, one-quarter full, add some kitchen-type vegetable dye to it and watch the bottom of the tank for the first telltale appearance of color. Rig up a cap for the water-fill opening with a tire valve stem in it. Using a hand tire pump, put a little air pressure in the tank. A few pounds is ample. Watch for some increase in water flow out of a pinpoint leak, or listen for the hiss of escaping air. A soap-and-water mixture lathered over the tank surface with a dishmop will cause bubbles to form over a tiny leak.

Before resorting to these methods, make sure the water you see is not just condensation. Fresh water put into a tank tends to be cold and will make warm, damp bilge air condense on the tank's surface. It can fool you into assuming there is a tiny leak!

Plastic Water Tanks

Q. New stainless steel water tanks custom built to fit my boat would cost too much. What other materials might I consider? I'd rather not have fiberglass.

A. "Vetus" and "Talamex" collapsible rubberized-fabric water tanks are one possibility. The former is distributed in

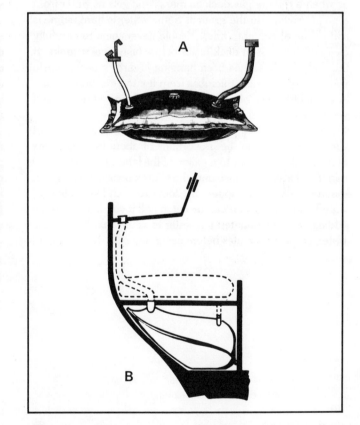

Tanks made of flexible material are becoming more popular. A big advantage is that they're easy to install in the odd-shaped spaces likely to be found on completed boats. (Inland Marine)

the U.S. by W. H. DenOuden (USA) Inc., P.O. Box 8712, Baltimore, Md. 21240 and the latter by Inland Marine, 79 E. Jackson St., Wilkes-Barre, Penn. 18701. Tempo Products Company, 6200 Cochran Rd., Cleveland, Ohio 44139 is one firm that offers molded polyethylene water tanks. The Wilcox-Crittenden and Raritan firms in the U.S. also supply this type of tank. This material imparts no taste to water and does not rust. When installing any water tank, bear in mind the weight of water—62 pounds per cubic foot and 8.34 lbs. per gallon. Make sure the tank is built and supported so as to withstand the weight and sloshing forces that will be imposed.

Water Tastes Stale

Q. Have you ever ridden in an old railroad coach and gagged at the vile taste of the water from its gravity-feed drinking-water tank? Well, the water from my tank tastes like that. Is there any cure?

A. People are so accustomed to getting potable water from kitchen faucets that they forget water stored in a tank is a different matter. A cruising boat takes aboard water at a variety of docks. Some of it is chlorinated, some is not, such as when a remote gas dock on marshland gets its water from a point driven into the ground. Some water is hard, some is soft. Mineral content varies. People never think to carefully clean off the ends of dock hoses before filling water tanks. If the end of a hose has been hanging in dirty mooring-basin water, you can wash microbes from it into your boat's tank. A potable supply of water begins with being careful about what goes into the tank!

If you have a foul tank, start by filling it with a mixture of Clorox and water in the proportions of about three-quarters of a cup of the former to a gallon of the latter. Let it stand 30 minutes. Drain and rinse until the Clorox taste is gone. From then on, add one teaspoon of Clorox to each five gallons of water. This proportion can be cut in half if you know you are adding pure, chlorinated tap water to your tank. Let treated water sit for 30 minutes before using any of it. If you cannot

Sometimes the best answer to the problem of potable drinking water is to carry it aboard in a separate container that can be kept clean and sweet with normal washing and rinsing. (Mercury Marine)

taste any chlorine, you do not have enough Clorox in the water for effective disinfection. Marine stores sell water tank sweetening products, as do mobile home and travel trailer dealers.

The nontoxic antifreezes used in boat water systems during winter storage can also help. They contain antioxidants that help prevent rust and corrosion in tanks, another cause of poor taste, and usually have some bacteriocidal properties to keep algae from breeding during mild autumn and spring weather.

If you keep your tank full but use very little water, you will have more taste problems than if you use each fresh tankful promptly. Learn to control your water supply so that you don't run out of it on one hand, yet don't leave any quantity in the tank for so long that it has time to sour. Rather than fight a tank and its bacterial inhabitants, some boat owners settle for keeping bottled spring water aboard for drinking and cooking, and use the tank water for washing.

Chapter 35

Fuel Tanks

Gas Spits Back

Q. I installed an extra-capacity gas tank in my big outboard boat, following instructions that came with it. Now I find that every time I fill it, gasoline keeps spitting and bubbling back out of the filler neck. I have to meter gas into the filler slowly in order to avoid this. What could be wrong?

A. Our first thought is that there are too many bends in the filler line. Gas comes out of pump hose nozzles at a rather rapid rate, usually faster than it can flow under the force of gravity through a twisting or constricted filler pipe. Our second guess is that there is a kink or obstruction somewhere in the vent line, such as to cause air pressure to build up in the tank.

Locating Extra Tank

Q. In your opinion, what is the best location in a large outboard boat to install a big extra-range gas tank?

A. There is no one best location. It's a matter of studying the boat in question and evaluating the problems involved. The first thing to think of is the total weight that will be added to the boat. At an average of six pounds per gallon, the weight of gasoline adds up rapidly; the contents of a 50-gallon tank will total 300 lbs. That much weight too far forward, too far aft, or too far to one side of the centerline will have an adverse affect on the boat's trim and riding qualities.

In general, tanks far forward in a hull are to be avoided if at all possible. When they try to follow the up-and-down movements of the forward part of a fast boat, they can put great strain on their supports and hold-downs. A heavy one will hold the bow of a boat down and impair its ability to rise to steep seas. Added to the weight of the motor and its battery in the stern, a big tank too far aft can impair a boat's ability to get up onto plane and will make it want to run along in bow-high attitude at intermediate speeds.

Deep-vee boats naturally have more space below their floorboards for big tanks running fore-and-aft above their keels. The large fuel capacity of these boats often fools owners of shallow-vee boats into thinking they can easily install tankage for similar capacity in their boats. Alas, it is often far from easy! The usual solution is to fit a number of tanks into the boat, wherever they will go, and figure things so their total capacity will be what is wanted. Tank manufacturers offer a variety of tank sizes and shapes for this very reason. They also offer assorted selector valves so that fuel may be drawn from one tank or the other as desired.

Fuel tank leakage is a serious matter. Study catalogs and installation instructions carefully before plunging into the job.

Temporary Tankage

Q. We have to ferry our cruiser a long distance over open water. We have discussed a number of ways to provide extra fuel capacity, such as using aluminum beer kegs, 55-gallon oil drums, plastic chemical drums, fuel tanks salvaged from old trucks, tanks from old hot water heaters and other brainstorms. What's your advice?

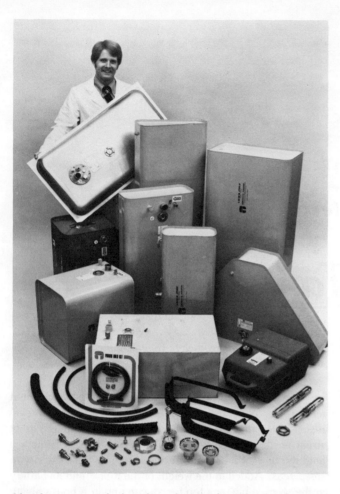

Most boat owners don't realize what a wide range of replacement gas tank sizes and shapes are available. These are but a few of the many in the Tempo firm's line.

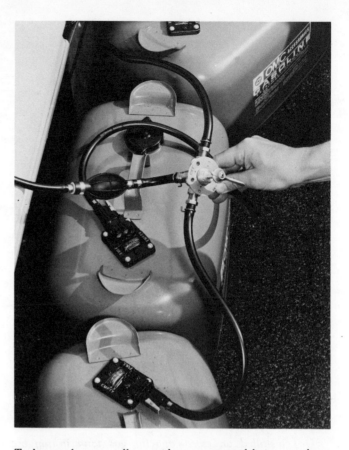

Tank manufacturers offer a wide assortment of fittings so that a number of tanks can be used when needed to increase range. With a setup like this, one can make cruising-range and miles-per-gallon test runs without risking running out of gas on the water. (Outboard Marine Corp.)

A. We assume your boat is of such a size that it is insured with a company that regularly writes marine insurance. Talk to the local representative of this company. We feel sure your insurance people will be very much interested in how you rig the boat for extra fuel capacity!

Steel oil drums will rust quickly in a salt water environment. Non-marine tanks probably will not have internal baffles to keep fuel from sloshing. Remember, many gallons of fuel rushing from one end of a tank to the other on rough seas can act like a battering ram to break a tank loose. If beer kegs or oil drums break loose from lashings in a storm, they can roll about and wreck a boat. Many tanks stowed on deck can make a boat dangerously top-heavy. Makeshift methods of transferring fuel from temporary to permanent tanks could be liable to spillage, the gasoline vapors from which could be drawn into quite the wrong ventilators. If you go ahead and cobble up makeshift tankage, you could find out after the mishap that in so doing you have voided your boat's insurance! See the man and do as he says in regard to temporary tanks.

Convert Water Tank to Gasoline?

Q. My boat has a large water tank that we never use. Could we convert it to a gasoline tank? The extra range would be very useful to us on long one-day fishing trips.

A. Don't do it! Tanks designed and built to hold water would not pass design and safety requirements for gasoline tanks. You would void your insurance and quite possibly suffer even worse misfortune than that.

Built-In Gas Tanks

Q. Some years ago I saw a fiberglass boat that had built-in gasoline tanks. The hull formed the outer parts of these tanks. It seemed like a good way to save weight and cost. Why don't I see the idea used on more boats?

A. It's one of those good ideas that turn out to have serious flaws. If the boat's hull is punctured in the area of the tanks, gasoline will spill out. If flexing of the hull or imperfect workmanship causes the inboard part of the tank to separate even slightly where it bonds to the hull, gasoline will leak out into the boat's bilge. The dangers are too great.

Tank Stops Feeding

Q. I bought a boat that has a strange quirk in its fuel system. Fuel stops flowing and the engine quits when the tank is still one-quarter full. I know the gas gauge is not lying because I know the tank's capacity and it only takes three-quarters of that amount to top it up again. What might be wrong?

A. The pickup tube that projects down into the tank might be too short, or might be bent, so its lower end is some distance above the bottom of the tank. It would thus stop drawing gasoline while there is still one-fourth the tank capacity left. If the tank is a long one and is located fore-and-aft in the hull, some bonehead might have installed it with the pickup tube at the forward end. When the boat is under way in the bow-up attitude typical of a modern planing hull, gas will flow to the aft end of the tank and leave the pickup tube high and dry. With these clues in mind, check over the installation and you'll probably find something like this is the answer to the mystery.

White Sludge in Tank

Q. While overhauling an older boat, we removed the galvanized steel gas tank. This gave us a chance to clean it out thoroughly. We got quite a bit of a greyish-white sludge out of it. What might have caused it to collect in the tank? We thought gas dock pumps had good filters to keep foreign matter out of boat tanks.

A. The sludge formed inside the tank as a result of interaction between chemicals present in the gasoline and the zinc which constitutes the galvanized coating. It is characteristic of galvanized tanks. Gasoline blends change with time and the trouble varies.

Homemade Galvanized Tank?

Q. The original galvanized gas tank in my older boat has rusted out. A friend owns a sheet metal shop and works with galvanized iron all the time. He offered to make up a new tank for me. Should I let him go ahead?

A. No. The sheet material he uses for heating ductwork, etc., is galvanized by the electroplating method. You can tell by the appearance of the zinc coating; it has a mottled effect remindful of frost on a windowpane in very cold weather.

When this metal is cut into pieces to make up a tank, bare iron edges will be exposed and tools will make small scratches in the plating. Such a tank will have substandard rust resistance for boat use. Safe and durable boat tanks are made using bare metal, and when completed the entire tank is dipped in a vat of molten zinc to galvanize it by the "hot dip" process. All of the surface, including edges at seams, is thus completely covered with a thicker coating of zinc.

Replacement for Galvanized Tank

Q. The maker of my boat is out of business. Where can I get a replacement for its original galvanized steel gasoline tank?

A. Some of the major marine hardware suppliers carried replacement tanks of this type in popular sizes as a regular item. But due to dwindling demand, most have dropped them. You might locate a dusty tank up in the storage loft of such a firm, if you're lucky. (See Chapter 1 on locating parts.) In seaport cities, especially those that have a local commercial fishing industry, there are shops that make all kinds of tanks for this activity and one of them can make up a gasoline tank. See if one of the modern, mass-produced tanks of aluminum or aluminized steel made by one of the major marine tank firms like Tempo, Mirax, and Skyline could be made to fit the available space in your boat. Good, safe tanks can be made of fiberglass by any person having reasonable skill at working with this material. There are endless clever ways in which it can be done. The books *Fibreglass Boats—Fitting Out, Maintenance and Repair* by Hugo du Plessis and *Fiberglass Boats* by Boughton Cobb have sections on tanks. Check the ABYC standards book for latest safety specs for fiberglass tanks. They are legal—some very well-known, mass-produced powerboats use them.

Fiberglass Tank "Flaked"

Q. My boat had a fiberglass gas tank put into it. Soon we began to get flakes or scales of fiberglass-like material in the fuel strainer. We removed the tank and on flushing it out found more and larger flakes. Did gasoline eat into the resin?

A. Your problem is not a common one. The most likely cause is that the tank was put into service before the resin was thoroughly cured. A new fiberglass gas tank should be allowed to "age" for a while—a month or so—to make sure the resin is really hard. It would help to put the tank out in the sunlight to aid the curing. There are many types of polyester resin, formulated for all kinds of uses. There is an outside chance an unsuitable type was used in your tank. Regular boat hull laminating resin made by one of the several companies prominent in the field should work well.

Foam-Filled Gas Tanks

Q. I have read of a new type of foam material with very open, bubble-like cells that is used to stuff airplane gas tanks. It does not reduce capacity significantly and is said to prevent explosions. Could it be used in boat gas tanks?

A. There would be no point to it. When an airplane crashes and its tanks burst open, fuel is scattered all over and any spark or hot metal will ignite it. Boats don't go fast enough to crash and break up as airplanes do. The foam material keeps gas from flying about when a plane's tank bursts. It just would not have a chance to "do its thing" in a boat. The danger in boats is not the gas in the tanks but the gas that leaks undetected into the bilge area and forms an explosive mixture with the air.

Gum in Gas Tank

Q. I bought an old boat that had been in a farm shed for several years. It's in surprisingly good condition, but I find on looking inside the gas tank that there is a mess of gummy material all over its bottom. What is this? What can I do?

A. You have a typical case of gas tank gum. As time passes, gasoline gets stale and gradually decomposes. This is especially true of modern gasolines made by the "cracking" process of distillation. They are less stable and tend to decompose more readily than the early-day gasolines distilled by simpler methods.

The cure is simple. Pour enough acetone into the tank to cover the gum with a layer an inch or so deep. Let it stand. Slosh it around from time to time and drain the resulting mixture. Repeat the treatment until all gum has been dissolved.

If gum is found in the tank of a boat that is in service and you do not wish to remove the tank, add approximately 5% acetone to the gas in the tank. Boat motion will mix acetone and gum together. Acetone will dissolve in the gasoline and the gum will be carried through the fuel system and be burned away in the engine without harm. Handle acetone with care as regards fire and explosion hazards, since it is even more volatile than gasoline. Automotive gas line antifreeze consists mostly of the type of alcohol called methanol; it will also dissolve gum in gas tanks, although not as quickly as will acetone.

Fiberglass Tanks for Diesel Fuel

Q. Can diesel fuel tanks be made of fiberglass?
A. From the mechanical and chemical standpoints, yes. But there is no practical reason for doing it. Diesel tanks are normally made of plain steel. The oiliness of diesel fuel

protects tanks from internal rusting and a good paint job on the outside takes care of external rusting. Any metalworking shop can make and finish them, as no special skills or equipment are needed. Some small shops specializing in custom-built boats make their own diesel fuel tanks of fiberglass material simply to save the time and cost involved in having a metal shop do the work.

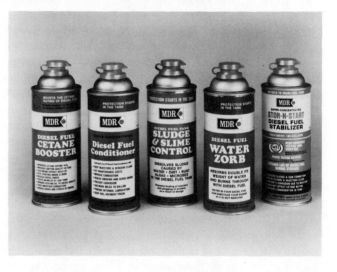

Diesel fuel tanks have their own special problems. Products like these Marine Development & Research specialties are available to cope with them.

Custom Made Tanks

Q. We are building a high-quality world cruising motorsailer. Where can we have Monel and/or stainless steel tanks made to order?

A. See "Tanks" in the marine trade directories mentioned in Chapter 1. Look for such companies as Allcraft and Aquamaid. They specialize in these materials.

Stainless Steel's Achilles Heel

Q. My boat has a stainless steel gasoline tank. Some other boat owners have told me their insurance companies made them take out their boats' stainless steel tanks and replace them with tanks of some other material. They say the insurance men claim stainless steel—of all materials— is subject to corrosion. Sounds crazy to me. How about you?

A. Stainless steel is not on the list of approved materials for gas tanks that appears in pleasure boat safety standards manuals. Some boats do use it. Some insurance companies will accept it, others won't. The problem is "crevice corrosion." The metallurgy of stainless steel is simple but few laymen understand it. When stainless steel gets scratched, air gets at the exposed fresh metal. The oxygen in the air reacts at once with the metal in such a way as to form a thin and invisible oxide coating. This in turn shuts out the air and further corrosion does not occur. The seam overlaps and weld-puddle ripples on a stainless steel gas tank create minute valleys or crevices into which air does not reach. So, tiny spots of "crevice corrosion" start. These can lead to pinhole leaks. Such leaks are dangerous not only because they can fill a boat's bilge area with gasoline vapor, but also because people who don't understand stainless steel don't realize this can happen. The first they know about a leak is when, to their astonishment, the boat blows up! Crevice corrosion can also occur underneath stainless steel tank supports and padding materials. If your boat has a stainless steel tank, inspect it periodically for reddish streaks coming out of such places, and for gasoline dye stains coming out of weld lines.

Terne Plate Gas Tanks

Q. I have heard the term "terne plate" used when boatyard men were talking about gasoline tanks. What does it mean?

A. Terne plate is sheet steel having a thin coating of lead. "Terne" is the French word for "dull," referring to the material's surface appearance. It is widely used for automobile and portable outboard motor gas tanks. For the latter use, it holds paint acceptably well on the outside, and oil mixed with gasoline, combined with the lead coating, gives the inside acceptable resistance to rusting from water that collects on tank bottoms. In the past, gas tank manufacturers quite naturally used it for the early large-capacity, semi-portable outboard tanks. These in time came to be used as permanent tanks in stern-drive boats. They worked reasonably well in fresh water areas, but in salt water use spray that soaked into the padding on tank hold-down straps quickly rusted the outsides. At the same time, the lack of an oil film on the interior, when used for four-cycle fuel, lets water cause rust sooner. Terne plate is no longer approved for permanent tanks. Aluminized steel and all-aluminum tanks are taking over.

Beer Keg for Gas Tank?

Q. Can I convert a used aluminum beer keg for use as a gasoline tank in my boat?

A. We would not advise trying it. Aluminum alloys vary. It took a long time to get approval for aluminum as a gas tank material, and it was granted only when suitable alloys

and fabrication techniques became available. Why spend a lot of time fooling around trying to convert a keg when you can buy and install an approved aluminum or aluminized steel tank in less time, at a reasonable cost, and without voiding your insurance? Remember, if there is a fire or explosion in your boat as a result of your having installed unapproved tanks, lawyers representing victims can find it easy to prove your negligence!

Fiberglassing an Old Steel Gas Tank

Q. Can you give advice on how to fiberglass an old steel gas tank to stop it from leaking at scattered rust spots?

A. This is a ticklish subject. The slightest mention of it will set safety experts to hollering "Don't do it!" But we know, from what we see in boat shops, that people do do it. We have even seen information on the subject in an English book on fiberglass work. We don't approve of it ourselves—but because people will do it, we will pass along some useful advice. If you're going to do it, better you should do it as well as possible!

If the interior of the old tank is badly rusted, fiberglassing the outside will not stop rust from continuing on the inside. As rust continues, fragments of it will show up in the gasoline strainer in steadily increasing quantities, finally reaching the point where frequent engine stoppages result. If only one or two layers of cloth are put on the bottom, the thin fiberglass will have to carry more and more of the gasoline's weight as internal rusting continues and the metal becomes weaker. The bottom can fall out some day when rough water is encountered. If the tank is made of galvanized steel, polyester resin will not adhere well to the zinc. One must either sandblast the tank well to remove all zinc and roughen the steel so resin will adhere, or use epoxy resin. Either way, the job can become complicated and expensive.

If a tank has external rust spots but is clean and sound on the inside (so that there is no risk of rust sediment in the strainer), it can be feasible to glass the outside to strengthen any small thin spots and afford an overall sheathing against further external rusting. A patch affixed only to the bottom of the tank can gradually work loose from the metal and may one day drop off. It may be better to wrap the whole tank in cloth. If it's a big tank, a layer of roving (which has high tensile strength) could very well be used along with two or three layers of mat. Again, cost goes up. So much work and expense can be involved in doing a good, safe job that it might make more sense to make a whole new gas tank of fiberglass.

If you must fiberglass a gas tank, do it like a porcupine makes love—very, very carefully! And realize that you are doing it entirely on your own responsibility.

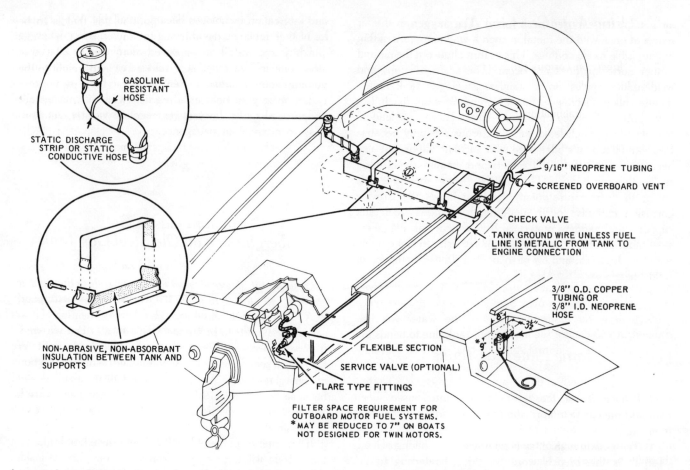

GASOLINE RESISTANT HOSE

STATIC DISCHARGE STRIP OR STATIC CONDUCTIVE HOSE

9/16" NEOPRENE TUBING

SCREENED OVERBOARD VENT

CHECK VALVE

TANK GROUND WIRE UNLESS FUEL LINE IS METALIC FROM TANK TO ENGINE CONNECTION

3/8" O.D. COPPER TUBING OR 3/8" I.D. NEOPRENE HOSE

NON-ABRASIVE, NON-ABSORBANT INSULATION BETWEEN TANK AND SUPPORTS

FLEXIBLE SECTION

SERVICE VALVE (OPTIONAL)

FLARE TYPE FITTINGS

FILTER SPACE REQUIREMENT FOR OUTBOARD MOTOR FUEL SYSTEMS.
*MAY BE REDUCED TO 7" ON BOATS NOT DESIGNED FOR TWIN MOTORS.

A gas tank installation must comply with safety specifications. This is recommended practice for a stern drive or large outboard boat. Static discharge strip on filler hose is to ground filler cap against static electricity sparks. Note inverted "U" bend in gas tank vent line, to minimize entry of spray. Filter must be designed and installed so it can be cleaned without danger of gas spilling into boat.

Water in Gas Tanks

Q. I know that they are very careful about keeping water out of the storage tanks and pumps at the marina where I buy gasoline for my boat. But I repeatedly find water in my fuel strainer. Where does it come from?

A. For the most part, it comes from atmospheric moisture that has condensed on the inner surfaces of the tank. This is why it is standard practice to keep tanks filled when boats are idle. There's no damp air in a full tank. If you have been leaving your boat at the dock with the tank only partly full, try topping up after each day's use and see if that helps the water situation. Also, take a look at the through-hull fitting where the gas tank's vent line terminates. Once in a while one gets turned or is improperly installed so that the air holes in it face forward enough for spray to enter. These vent holes have fine-mesh bronze screening in them. The purpose is to act as a flame arrester. (It works just like the backfire trap on a marine engine's carburetor—the screen absorbs the heat of the flame and snuffs it out.) Sometimes previous owners or

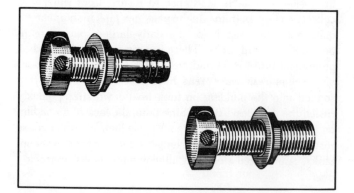

Typical hull fittings for gas tank vents. One is for tubing, the other for pipe. Note fine-mesh screen in openings. Serves as miniature flame trap.

poorly trained mechanics think the mesh is to keep insects out. When it becomes corroded, they just pull it out on the assumption that it is useless, and that leaves the openings more likely to admit water. A good vent tube installation has an inverted "U" bend in it just inside the hull. If water does enter the vent holes from spray, the inverted "U" will keep it from trickling down the vent line to the tank.

Using Auto Gas Line Antifreeze

Q. The labels on various products sold to keep auto gas lines from freezing say these chemicals will remove water from gas tanks in cars. Will they work in a boat's gas tank?

A. Yes—with qualifications. They are all just methanol, the trade name for wood alcohol, a very common industrial chemical. Alcohol readily mixes with water. When put into a gas tank, it goes to the bottom and mixes with the water. This mixture, as it sloshes about on the bottom of the tank, is picked up bit by bit by the pickup tube. It passes through most fuel filters and burns harmlessly in the engine. When put into an auto tank, by mixing with the water it prevents the water from freezing and blocking the flow of gas to the engine. This benefit is of small value in boats that are normally used in warm weather. While a dosing of it will get some water out of a boat's tank, one can of it will dissolve only a small amount of water. So pouring a canful into your boat's tank is no assurance that all the water will be removed. If you cannot see inside your tank due to bends in the filler pipe, there is no way to know how many cans of the stuff to pour in to get rid of water. About all you can do is keep watch over the fuel filter and stop the dosings when it appears that abnormal amounts of water are no longer coming through. The water/methanol mix will settle to the bottom of a glass strainer bowl but if your filter is all metal only repeated cleanings of the bowl will let you check on this. About the best use of gas line antifreeze in a boat would be to keep on top of a water-accumulating problem until you have time to check into the source of the water.

Getting Water From a Tank

Q. The gas tanks of my boat are located below the cockpit floor. A lot of pulling-up of the flooring and framing would be necessary to remove the tanks. We are going on a long cruise. How can I make sure there is no water in the tanks?

A. If the boat is on its cradle ashore, you can use a siphon. If it's afloat, you'll have to use a pump. Never put a siphon line to your mouth to suck on it to start gasoline flowing. Gasoline in the stomach and lungs is a serious matter!

One way to start a siphon is to hold both ends of the tubing together in one hand and pour gas into one end of the tubing from a can held in the other hand. When gas rises and comes out of the other end of the tubing, you know the tubing is filled. Keep thumbs over both ends, lower one end into the tank, drop the other end to ground level, and remove your thumb. This trick may require two people, one in the boat and one outside. Or, scout local auto supply and hardware stores for low-cost, all plastic pumps and siphons. *Do not use any kind of electrically driven pump for gasoline.* Have

plenty of clean, safe containers for the gas that is to be removed. Heel or tilt the boat so that any water in the tanks will flow to one end or corner, the one closest to the inlet pipe. It may be necessary to affix some kind of lead weight to the end of the tube that goes into the filler pipe. If the pipe has no bends, wire the end of the tube to a length of brazing rod. Then it can be manipulated into puddles of water, yet there will be no danger of creating a spark. Transparent plastic tubing is excellent for gas tank siphoning as you can see what is happening to the flow.

Outboard Gas in Cars

Q. Some people dump out unused outboard motor gasoline mix, claiming it would harm the engine if they put it into their car's gas tank. I say it's a waste of perfectly good gas to dump it out. Who is right?

A. You are. Most modern outboard motors run on 50-to-1 gas/oil mixture. If you pour a few gallons of left-over outboard mix into a car's tank that already has several gallons of straight gas in it, the percentage of oil in the resulting fuel fed to the car's engine is negligible. Funny thing—many people who won't use outboard mix in their cars will willingly dump container after container of "Doctor Quack's Engine Elixir" into their boat's gas tank!

Grounding a Tank

Q. While working in my boat I noticed a length of copper wire running alongside the synthetic rubber fuel tank filler line. What's it for?

A. It is part of the boat's electrical grounding system. It connects the filler cap on the boat's deck to the metal of the gas tank. The tank in turn is connected by a wire to the boat's overall grounding system. If that wire were to be removed or become broken, the filler cap would not be grounded and a static electricity spark could jump to it from a gas can or nozzle.

Fuel Tank Cartridges

Q. I have seen something in marine stores called "Sav-a-Tank Cartridges." What are they for?

A. When placed into iron or copper gas tanks (the latter are obsolete), they keep water in tank bottoms from turning to acid by picking up sulphur from the gasoline. For the period of time in which a cartridge is effective, tank corrosion is inhibited.

Bags that Absorb Water

Q. I have been told there is a kind of small, narrow bag with a string attached to it and some kind of chemical in it. When lowered into a boat's gas tank it is supposed to absorb water. Then the bag can be pulled out and set in the sun to dry. What can you tell me about this item?

A. We have seen them. These bags were developed to get small quantities of water out of chemical and industrial tanks. Entrepreneurs selling gadgets to the pleasure boating trade saw them and offered them to pleasure boat owners. From what we could see, the devices look as if they would not soak up much water on each immersion, and we'd expect to have trouble making one negotiate the bends in many filler lines. We have not seen these devices on the market lately.

Bugs in Diesel Tanks?

Q. Someone told me that there are some kinds of bacteria that can grow in diesel fuel and that they can clog fuel filters. This sounds crazy! Was he kidding me?

A. No. It's a fact. Some microorganisms can subsist on the hydrocarbons in diesel and also in jet aircraft fuel. When some water chances to collect in the bottom of an infected tank, they breed at an accelerated rate. Rusting of steel tanks and corrosion of aluminum ones is aggravated. Fuel filter clogging is common. The problem is not encountered so much in commercial boats where one tankful after another is promptly burned. But it can become a serious problem in pleasure boat tanks. Often weeks pass before an owner has time to take his boat out. That's when bacteria growth can proliferate. There are chemicals on the market with which to dose diesel fuel that is going to stand in a tank for a while. It's a fungicide compounded to satisfactorily mix with the fuel. The most widely available is called "Biobor JF," made by Bull & Roberts, Inc., 785 Central Ave., Murray Hill, N.J. 07974. You can locate it in your area at marinas selling diesel fuel and at local petroleum wholesalers who carry this fuel. Marine Development & Research Corp. has a whole line of diesel fuel-treating products.

Stopping Tiny Leaks

Q. A friend is an airplane mechanic. He told me about a product called "gas tank slushing compound." He says it is used to seal pinhole leaks in airplane gas tanks. Could I use it for the same purpose in my boat's tank?

A. We would not care to try it. Airplane tanks are made of materials such as aluminum and stainless steel and tend to have a lot of rivets and spot welds in their construction. Tiny, weeping leaks are common there. Vapor from leaks passes outside through the many small openings in a plane, such as drain holes, control cable openings, etc., and also the tanks are located in the fuselage and wings where they are separated from the engine compartment by the firewall. In a boat's tank, internal corrosion is the most common cause of leaks. If there is rust inside a tank, a slushing compound won't adhere well. No finish will adhere well to the zinc used for galvanizing. In short, a boat tank is a much different proposition from an airplane tank. If you tried this slushing compound, you'd probably get poor adhesion, little or no stoppage of the leaks, no strengthening of weak spots, and probable sloughing-off of the compound, which could lead to fuel line blockage.

Copper Gas Tanks

Q. I work in a sheet metal shop. Making things with sheet copper is easy for me. Can you give me some tips on making a good copper gas tank for the sloop I am building?

A. Sorry, the only tip we can give you is this—don't do it! Copper was used a lot a very long time ago, before the oil companies started making "cracked" gasoline in the 1920s. When cracked gas became common, it was found that the copper in those early tanks acted as a catalyst to accelerate the breaking-down of the gas. Gumming problems were common. So boatbuilders stopped using copper tanks. Today, there is another objection to copper tanks. The solder used to make the seams leak-tight will melt at so low a temperature that a copper tank would not pass modern fire resistance tests.

Acetone for Winterization?

Q. If acetone will get gum out of gas tanks, wouldn't it be a good idea to put some into a boat's gas tank when preparing the boat for winter storage?

A. No. Acetone will loosen up gum that has already formed, but it will not stop the gasoline from oxidizing and breaking down during months of storage. To prepare a tankful of gas for storage, dose it with one of the gasoline winterization products now on the market, such as "Sta-Bil" by Knox Laboratories of Chicago and "Stor-N-Start" by Marine Development & Research Corp. of Freeport, N.Y. OMC has a similar product, "2 + 4 Fuel Conditioner." These stabilize the gasoline chemically and delay its breakdown for several months.

Products such as Stor-N-Start, by Marine Development & Research, and Sta-Bil, by Knox Laboratories, stabilize gasoline against decomposition during the months of storage.

Tanks Full or Empty?

Q. Some people put their boats into winter storage with the gas tanks full, others with the tanks empty. I'm confused! How should I do it?

A. The rationale behind storing with full tanks is that since there can be no air in a full tank, there can be no condensation of water inside it. As atmospheric pressure changes with weather patterns, an empty tank "inhales" and "exhales" through the vent line. Naturally, some damp air is inhaled. If the boat catches fire, it will take a long time for a substantial volume of gasoline in a tank to heat up to the combustion point. If a boat is stored with an empty tank, it is usually impossible to drain a built-in tank of gasoline completely. The small amount that remains will keep the tank full of vapor. If a fire happens, the empty tank will heat up rapidly and vapor in the tank can violently explode. If a full tank finally gets hot enough for the gasoline to burn, it is assumed that by that time the rest of the boat would be so engulfed in flames as to be beyond saving.

The best thing for you to do is find out how the yard where you store your boat prefers to do it. Rather than worry about what might happen in case of fire, it is better to look around and pick a yard that is fussy about fire prevention. Which way a particular yard will prefer to store boat tanks usually is decided upon after conferences with their insurance people and the local fire department. The decision is made for you by those people, so you just go along, as it can be fruitless to argue with them.

Outboard motor gas tanks are normally stored empty for various reasons. Usually they are emptied and put away in garages and basements where it would be against local ordinances to store the amount of gasoline such tanks can hold. As they normally have air vents in their filler caps which can be closed to prevent sloshing out while trailering, leaving these caps closed tight keeps air and moisture from being inhaled during storage. Since these tanks are easily removed from a boat and inverted for draining, all gasoline can be removed from them. Any small amount of gasoline (along with water and dirt) that remains after emptying such a tank can be swabbed out with a cloth tied to the end of a stick. If left upside down for several days after draining and cleaning, gasoline vapors will dissipate and then there will be no explosion hazard during storage.

Chapter 36

Trailers

Parts For Orphan Trailers

Q. Where can I get replacement parts for an "Elf" boat trailer? The maker has been out of business for several years.

A. We often get requests like this. There are a lot of "orphan" boat trailers around. Some were made by large companies and sold on a nationwide basis, others were made by obscure metalworking shops for local or regional sale. People seem to think that every part on a trailer was made by the trailer manufacturer, and that only parts obtained from that company will fit. The good news is that practically all trailer manufacturing companies use certain components that they buy ready-made from specialty firms. This includes hitches, rollers, winches, tires, wheels, hubs, bearings, springs, and tail lights. Many of these parts are readily interchangeable from one make to another, and some can be made to fit with a little modification.

Visit your local marine dealers and ask to look in their distributors' catalogs. In these books you will find name-brand winches, hitches, rollers, and tail lights. Many dealers stock bearing kits in blister packs. Half a dozen different stock-size bearings will take care of a majority of replacement needs. You can often get these standard bearings at bearing supply houses in cities. Look for a number—usually five digits—stamped on the races of your bearings. There is also usually the bearing maker's name. Suppose you find that your hubs have bearings marked "Timken" and carry a five-digit number. Call a bearing supply company and read off this name and number to them. If they don't carry that brand of bearing, they can look it up in a cross-reference list and usually come up with an identically sized bearing made by some other firm.

Also remember that many stock parts like hitches, wheels, hubs, bearings, and lights can be bought from camping trailer dealers. Don't waste time and gas chasing all over trying everyplace for "Elf" trailer parts—instead, look in likely places for interchangeable stock parts.

Boat trailer manufacturers buy their axles, springs, hubs, wheels and other parts from specialty firms. There is a lot of interchangeability of parts like these between one make of trailer and another.

Cleaning a Rusty Trailer

Q. My boat trailer is rather badly rusted. What's the best way to get the old paint off—with a disc sander, with a power-driven wire brush, or with paint remover?

A. None of those methods is really satisfactory. You can't get at many areas with a sanding disc or rotary brush. Paint remover doesn't leave the metal cleaned of rust and well-roughened to hold the fresh primer well. The one really best way is sandblasting. It knocks old paint off, eats through rust spots to sound metal, gives good "tooth" for the primer, and is far faster.

A variety of establishments regularly use sandblasting in their work—steelworking shops, equipment maintenance shops, boatyards specializing in steel workboats, granite and tombstone shops, building-cleaning contractors, and so on. Look under "Sandblasting" in the Yellow Pages. Or phone places such as those just mentioned to see if any of them have or know of sandblasting equipment. If you take your trailer to such a place with rollers, winch, fenders, lights, and other parts removed, they can sandblast a small trailer in about an hour, a medium-sized one in a couple of hours, and a large one in under half a day.

Plan to go on a clear, dry day, and to put the primer on just as soon as you possibly can—preferably the same day. Water vapor in the air can start to oxidize the bare metal very quickly. Any oxidation or small, fresh rust spots under the new paint will be starting points for rust blisters. Use a metal primer with rust-inhibiting properties. We have had good results with the widely sold "Rust-Oleum" primers and metal paints.

You can rent a powerful contractors'-type air compressor and sandblasting outfit at many tool rental agencies and you and your friends can sandblast two or three trailers in the usual 24-hour rental period. Do the job on a tennis court or other paved area so the special sand can be swept up and reused. It keeps your consumption of sand down to a financially comfortable level. The agency that rents the outfit will supply you with as many bags as you want and give a refund on ones not used.

With a rented contractor's-type air compressor and sandblasting outfit, a fast and thorough job can be done of cleaning old paint and rust from a boat trailer.

Paint Job Faded

Q. I use my boat and trailer in salt water, so when I sandblasted and repainted the trailer, I used high quality epoxy paint. Only a year later, the paint had badly faded. Have you any idea what might have gone wrong?

A. Fading has been a characteristic of epoxy paints. Their resistance to sunlight is being improved as research work continues.

About Original Paint Jobs

Q. I regularly sandpaper and touch up rust spots on my painted trailer, but new rust spots regularly appear. Is there something wrong with the trailer's paint job?

A. Yes and no. It is obviously a quickie job. Some painted trailers come with good paint jobs having a primer and a nice enamel finish coat. Others have just one coat of quick-dry, production-type lacquer. It's a matter of keeping costs down. After people have bought new boats and motors and all the wanted and needed equipment, they begin to feel stabs of pain in the area of their wallets. So when they get to selecting a trailer, they are inclined to look for the lowest possible price. Trailer manufacturers and boat dealers thus tend to offer the public "economy" and "deluxe" models, to cater to various customers' wants.

When shopping for trailers, if you are interested in a painted one use the point of a pen knife blade to make a small scratch in its paint job at some inconspicuous place. You will be able to tell by the contrasting colors if there is a primer under the finish paint. If there is none, you're being offered a finish that may have little durability. But if the price is in line and the trailer fills your needs in other respects, buy it. You will want to refinish a painted trailer in a few years anyway, at which time you can have it sandblasted and then give it a good finish that will last for several years.

Trailer Brakes

Q. Is there a book on trailer brake servicing?

A. *Powerboat Maintenance* by Clymer Publications, 222 North Virgil Ave., Los Angeles, Cal. 90004 has a chapter on the subject. You can get a service manual from the manufacturer of the make of brakes on your trailer.

Plans for a Trailer

Q. Where can I get plans for a homemade boat trailer?

A. There is a book titled *How to Build Boat Trailers* available from Glen-L Marine Designs, 9152 Rosecrans,

Bellflower, Cal. 90706. Remember that as the size of cars continues to shrink and engine power diminishes as a result of government gasoline mileage and emissions standards, the trailer-towing capability of cars is going to diminish drastically. In fact, many models will not be able to tow trailers at all because there is no way to install hitches on them so as to satisfy government rear-end collision resistance requirements. Don't buy or build a heavy trailer and/or boat without making sure your car can manage it!

Tail Lights Won't Work

Q. I installed new tail lights on my boat trailer. Now they won't work. I am sure I got the wires on the trailer connected to those on the car correctly.

A. Are you doing your testing with the trailer hitch disconnected from the car? Then hook things up and watch the lights come on! The trailer amounts to an extension of the car's frame and is thus the electrical ground for the trailer's wiring system. Unless the trailer is connected to the car's hitch, you have no ground, hence the lights get no current. Hitching up the trailer in effect connects the trailer's lights to the negative terminal of the car's battery—assuming your car has the negative-ground system common in American cars.

Incidentally, too much grease on the hitch ball (often put there to stop squeaking) can give a bad electrical connection and cause the trailer lights to dim or flicker. Travel trailer dealers sell a grease that will stop squeaks but won't also stop current. Or, you can run a ground wire from car to trailer if you wish to grease the hitch ball. The white wire seen dangling from many boat trailer wiring sets is a ground wire

The trailer forms an extension of the car's frame and thus serves as the ground for the trailer wiring system. Lights will not work unless trailer is hitched to car. If you grease the ball, make use of the white ground wire to maintain positive ground. A good padlock serves two purposes—it keeps hitch from opening accidentally while on the highway, and keeps thieves from making off with your boat while you are in a restaurant or motel. (Master Lock Co.)

intended to be used when the wires are installed on a homemade wooden trailer; you can use these as a good ground when the hitch ball is greased.

Trailering With Imported Cars

Q. I have a new small Japanese car and want to start towing a small boat trailer. People tell me that I will have trouble connecting the wires on my American-built trailer to the lighting system on the Japanese car. What do you think?

A. You've been correctly informed. Wiring systems do vary. Now on the market are "converters," little black boxes that go between the car and the trailer wiring systems to make the American style lights on the trailer work properly. One such device is the "Tail Light Converter Unit" by Valley Tow-Rite, 1313 S. Stockton St., Lodi, Cal. 95240.

A "Tail Light Converter Unit" makes connecting American trailers' wiring systems to the different ones on imported cars an easy matter.

Three Hitches, Three Trailers?

Q. I saw a boatyard's truck. It had three trailer hitch balls mounted side-by-side on the rear bumper. Do they tow three trailers at once, or do they run some kind of a nautical hock shop?

A. Neither. Each of the balls is a different size. The truck is thus able to hook up to trailers having any size hitch without taking time to remove one ball and install another. One of the balls is on the truck's centerline, the other two are perhaps five or six inches off center. This amount of off center has no appreciable effect on trailering capabilities, at least for the kind of short local trips a dealer's truck is likely to make.

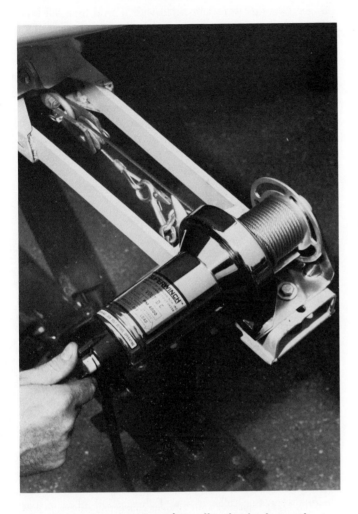

Installing a longer cable with a pulley that hooks onto boat doubles the mechanical advantage. (Superwinch)

How to Make Haul-Out Easier

Q. I have a bad heart. The doctor says that winching a large outboard boat onto a trailer could be too much for me. What can I do to remain active in boating?

A. Various things. Install a longer cable on your winch. Fit it with a pulley of good strength that has a hook that will fit the boat's bow eye. The cable will go from the winch to the pulley (which is hooked to the boat) and then back to any convenient attaching point on the winch or winch stand. This will double the mechanical advantage of the winch. Less effort will be needed to turn the crank, although the crank will

have to be turned twice the number of times. A better answer is to install one of the electric winches now on the market. These really save a great amount of effort.

Anyone with a physical handicap should get a copy of a soft-cover book called *Boating for the Handicapped*. It gives ideas on how to make boating feasible for persons with assorted disabilities. You can get a copy for $5.95 from the Human Resources Center, Albertson, N.Y. 11507.

Speeding Up a Winch

Q. My big boat trailer winch is geared low for power. It takes endless turns of the crank to haul the boat all the way onto it. Is there any way to speed things up?

A. Some manufacturers of hand-operated winches offer bolt-on electric power conversion kits. Another trick—we suspect your winch has a steel cable on it. Replace this with a length of synthetic rope of adequate strength. Due to its small size, cable fills the winch up slowly. Rope will fill up a winch drum faster. When the diameter of the drum is small at the beginning of haul-out, you will have the power needed to pull the boat onto the trailer. As the boat comes out of the water and the trailer's bed tilts down, the rope will then have filled the drum so its diameter is larger and more rope will be taken onto it on each turn of the drum, thus speeding up the last phase of the haul-out.

The Trailer Sways

Q. I trailer a sailboat and when we hit about 45 m.p.h. on the open road, the trailer and its load begin to sway from side to side, making the trailer "fishtail." What might be wrong?

A. That behavior is characteristic of a trailer that has its load too far back and thus not enough download on the hitch. Rearrange the load or shift the axle on the frame so that from about 5% to 6% of the total weight of the trailer and its load is on the hitch. This should stabilize things.

The Trailer Yaws

Q. When we cross an unevenness in the road, such as a railroad track, I can feel a sidewise twitching at the back of the car as if the trailer tongue were pushing sideways on the hitch. The same thing happens sometimes when one wheel of the trailer strikes a pothole. What might be causing this?

A. It sounds like unequal tire pressure. When one tire is softer, that side of the trailer will bounce differently than the other side. That will send a sideways twitch into the trailer's tongue and thus into the rear end of the car.

Cleaning Wheel Bearings

Q. A neighbor who is an old-time mechanic came over one day when I happened to be cleaning the bearings from my boat trailer in a can of gasoline. He said I should not use gasoline because it will leave a film on the clean bearing metal that will keep new grease from spreading onto the metal for a while. What do you think?

A. We have encountered that story too. We asked bearing and petroleum people about it. They cannot think of any way in which the negligible residue left by drying gasoline could prevent grease from spreading, and they do not know how this story got started—it has been going around for a very long time. When you think of it, all two-cycle motors run on a mixture of gasoline and oil, and nobody ever tells you that the gasoline will impair the ability of oil to spread on the motor's bearings! The only objection to using gasoline is the fire hazard, and even then, when you clean trailer bearings outdoors in a small can the fire hazard has got to be much less than when you refuel a hot lawn mower. Kerosene or range oil can of course be used, but they remain on the bearing metal much longer and really could repel grease for a while. Whatever you use, make sure the bearings are really dry before applying grease. Do not "spin" a dry bearing with a jet of compressed air; that can really scar dry bearing surfaces.

Trailer Bearing Grease

Q. My son works at a gas station. He offered to take my trailer wheel bearings there to clean them off and refill them with the station's special bearing-greasing device. I let him. Later an acquaintance said I might have done the wrong thing. What do you say?

A. It might or might not lead to trouble—it will depend on circumstances. There are various kinds of grease. If your trailer bearings were lubricated with a kind that will break down when water mixes into it, and then if you get water in your wheel hubs during a launch, a subsequent long trip with a water-and-grease emulsion for lubricant could lead to bearing failure. A long period of idleness after a short trip could lead to overall fuzz-rusting of the bearing surfaces. The safe thing to do is always use a grease from a marine store or a reliable gas station that is clearly marked as being made for use in boat trailer bearings.

Rusted Rims

Q. My trailer wheels have tubeless tires. Lately I have been plagued with a rash of slow leaks. When I dunk the wheels in a tank of water, I can see tiny bubbles of air coming out at many places where the rim and tire bead come together. What caused this to appear all of a sudden?

A. Rust has been building up in the vee-shaped space where tire and rim meet. The paint there was probably scraped off by tire-mounting tools. When a car goes through a puddle, centrifugal force throws water away from that area. After a boat has been launched, a trailer is slowly rolled a short distance to a parking place, so water remains in those vee-shaped spaces long enough to start rust.

As rust progresses, it pushes the bead slowly away from the rim. Eventually there is a crust of rust there. It pushes the tire away from the rim until slow leaks begin. The cure begins when the trailer is new. Either install tubes so there won't be slow leaks later or have a tire shop deflate the tires, force the beads off the rims, and spread onto the rims the compound they have which they use to stop slow leaks at the rim with tubeless tires. When the tires are reinflated, the compound will create a seal. Wipe oozing surplus off with a rag or finger, to form it into a small fillet where tire and rim meet. This will seal out water from this critical area.

Index